Roadside History of
IDAHO

Betty Derig

Mountain Press Publishing Company
Missoula, Montana
1996

Fourth Printing, April 2010

Roadside History® is a registered trademark
of Mountain Press Publishing Company

Maps by Jennifer Hamelman

Cover art: Idaho Statehouse Historic Murals
"A Legend of Dreams," by Dana Boussard

Library of Congress Cataloging-in-Publication Data

Derig, Betty B.
    Roadside history of Idaho   /   Betty Derig.
        p.   cm. — (Roadside history)
    Includes bibliographical references and index.
    ISBN 0-87842-327-3 (cloth : alk. paper). — ISBN 978-0-87842-328-6
(pbk. : alk. paper)
    1. Idaho—History, Local.   2. Historic sites—Idaho—Guidebooks.
3. Idaho—Guidebooks.   4. Automobile travel—Idaho—Guidebooks.
I. Title.   II. Series.
F746.D44   1995
979.6—dc20
                                                                                        95—42565
                                                                                        CIP

PRINTED IN THE UNITED STATES

Mountain Press
PUBLISHING COMPANY
P.O. Box 2399 · Missoula, MT 59806 · 406-728-1900
800-234-5308 · info@mtnpress.com
www.mountain-press.com

For Melissa, Andrew, Laura, Adam,
Kate, Joel, Jake, Dan, and Connor

Contents

Acknowledgments

My thanks go to the many people who provided information, pictures, and encouragement during the preparation of this book. I am especially grateful to Dr. Merle Wells, who gave generously of his time and his knowledge of Idaho history. Many local museums across the state supplied valuable photos, and I owe special thanks to Guila Ford and Elizabeth Jacox, who led me through the photo archives at the Idaho State Historical Society. The Idaho State Library helped by supplying dozens of books.

Many individuals who no doubt had other important things to do spent considerable time enlightening me in one way or another. Boyd Cook organized a field trip to introduce me to the techniques of phosphate mining. Poof Wagner whisked me off on a historical tour of the backcountry near Elk City and Dixie. Suzanne Miller sent me reams of material on Idaho archaeology. Mary Reed took time to write a long letter describing the work of the Latah County Historical Society. And Chuck Skilling wrote me a wonderful letter delineating life in Clarkia.

Other individuals I am indebted to include Clarence Stark, for his work in the photo lab, and the patient, helpful staff of the Dark Room. Thanks also to Mary Ann Davis, Rick Just, Larry Sandvol, Doug Sterrett, Larry Kingsbury, Keith Peterson, Fred Schley, Bonnie Curtis, Ruth Ann Olson, Mike and Chris O'Brien, Stephanie Kukay, Steve Wherry, Lavina Palmer, Bea Hennings, and others whose names have regrettably slipped into the recesses of my computer.

Several private companies such as the Port of Lewiston, the Potlatch Corporation, the Idaho Power Company, and the Appaloosa Horse Club contributed information and/or pictures that proved useful. And the fine folks who work in the state departments of Agriculture, Transportation, and Parks and Recreation were all helpful and congenial, as were those at the Wheat and Potato commissions and the U.S. Forest Service.

Finally, special thanks to all those historians and writers who have preceded me and whom I have quoted or relied upon for countless details; to Margaret Fuller for connecting me with Mountain Press; to editor Dan Greer for his patience and for bringing me into the computer age; and to my husband and family for giving me moral support and long stretches of uninterrupted time.

About the Cover Art

The murals pictured on the front and back cover of this book are on permanent display in the state capitol building in Boise. They were created by the acclaimed western artist Dana Boussard to capture and memorialize Idaho's heritage. They were photographed by Kurt Wilson.

The six panels are paired to compose three murals that depict history in Idaho's three primary geographic regions—the north, the southwest, and the southeast—as recognized by the Idaho Community Foundation. (In this book a fourth region, "Central Idaho," has been carved from the indistinct border zone between the southeast and the southwest.)

The murals are designed to be read horizontally. The top, middle, and bottom sections each tell Idaho's story from a different perspective. The top band is a continuous timeline that portrays a symbolic narrative of Idaho's past from the time of its original inhabitants to the present. It begins with ancient pictographs that represent Idaho's first inhabitants and then proceeds to symbolize events that culminate in statehood, television, and ethnic diversity. The middle band, largest of the three, features the dominant landscape of each region—lakes and forests in the north, rivers and canyons in the southwest, and mountains and deserts in the southeast—and shows how the land influenced human activity. The bottom band chronicles the natural and environmental events that affected development in each of the three regions. Plants, animals, and fish as well as fire, mining, and religion figure into these symbols.

For a detailed account of the artist's interpretations—or to see and develop your own interpretations of these intriguing, enormous murals—visit the exhibit at the statehouse in Boise or contact the Idaho Commission on the Arts.

About the Author

Betty Derig, a native-born Idahoan, has resided in the small town of Weiser all her life. *Roadside History of Idaho* is her third book on Idaho history, following *Weiser, the Way It Was* (1987) and *The Idaho Rambler* (1982), which she co-authored with Florence Sharp. In addition, Derig has written numerous columns and feature articles for such publications as *Idaho Yesterdays*, *Idaho Heritage*, *Incredible Idaho*, and *Northwest Edition*.

Derig received a master's degree in American history from the University of Montana in 1955. She served for six years (1988–94) on the Idaho State Historical Society's board of trustees and taught history for ten years (1966–76) at Treasure Valley Community College in Ontario, Oregon, just across the Idaho state line. In 1987 the Idaho Writers League named her Writer of the Year.

Derig is an avid gardener and a member of the Garden Writers Association of America. Her love of Idaho's changing terrain, from its deserts to its lush farm country to its evergreen forests, may lead her to her next book project: a guide to Idaho's plants.

Idaho Chronology

1803   The United States buys (Louisiana Territory extending west of the Mississippi River to Idaho) from France for $15 million.

1805   August 12—Capts. Meriwether Lewis and William Clark are the first white men known to enter Idaho.

1806   Lewis and Clark spend more than six weeks with the Nez Perce Indians near Kamiah before returning eastward across the Lolo Trail.

1809   David Thompson of the British North West Fur Company builds Kullyspell House by Lake Pend Oreille.

1810   Andrew Henry of the Missouri Fur Company establishes Fort Henry near St. Anthony, the first American post west of the Continental Divide.

1811   Wilson Price Hunt leads an overland party of Astorians (John Jacob Astor's Pacific Fur Company) to the Columbia River. In Idaho they meet disaster after trying to navigate the Snake River.

1812   Donald McKenzie establishes a winter fur trading post at Lewiston for the Astorians.

1813   Astorian-turned-Nor'wester John Reid builds a trading post at the mouth of the Boise River.

1814   Bannock Indians kill John Reid and his men and destroy his post.

1818   First British fur trapping brigade enters the Snake River Valley.

        Donald McKenzie explores southern Idaho after the British-American joint occupancy treaty leaves the Oregon Country (including Idaho) open to citizens of both nations.

1819   Adams-Onis Treaty establishes the southern boundary of the Oregon Country (including Idaho) at the forty-second parallel.

1824   American fur trappers cross the Continental Divide and enter Bear Valley.

1827   Fur traders and Indians rendezvous at Bear Lake.

1829   Fur traders and Indians rendezvous at Pierre's Hole in the Teton Basin.

1830   Fur traders and Indians rendezvous on the Blackfoot River.

1832   July 18—Fur trade rendezvous in the Teton Valley near Driggs culminates in a battle between trappers and a party of Gros Ventres.

1834   Nathaniel Wyeth builds Fort Hall and Thomas McKay builds Fort Boise, a Hudson's Bay Company post. Both forts falter with the dwindling fur trade but serve Oregon Trail pioneers in the decades to come.

1836   Whitman-Spalding party visits Fort Hall en route to the mission field. Henry Harmon Spalding establishes a Nez Perce mission at Lapwai.

1837   The first school in Idaho opens for Indian children at Lapwai. Eliza Spalding, daughter of Henry and Eliza, is the first white child born in Idaho, at Lapwai.

1839   Henry Spalding publishes a Bible in the language of the Nez Perce on the first printing press in the Pacific Northwest.

1840   Father Pierre Jean De Smet begins Catholic missionary work in Idaho.

1843   Father Nicholas Point establishes the Jesuit Coeur d'Alene Mission of the Sacred Heart near Saint Maries.

        Year of the Great Migration over the Oregon Trail.

1846   Father Point moves his mission to Cataldo on the Coeur d'Alene River. It is transferred in 1877 to De Smet, where it stands today. The United States acquires all land south of 49 degrees north latitude by a treaty with Great Britain.

1849   Over 20,000 emigrants cross southeastern Idaho en route to the gold rush via the California Trail. The U.S. Army establishes a post near Fort Hall.

1852   French Canadians discover gold on the Pend Oreille River.

1853   Father Anthony Ravalli and a building crew of 320 Indians finish construction of the Cataldo Mission.

        Washington Territory is established with the land that later becomes Idaho divided between Washington Territory and Oregon Territory.

1854 Snake River Indians massacre twenty-one emigrants led by Alexander Ward near the present-day town of Middleton. This leads to the closings of Fort Boise the next summer and Fort Hall in 1856.

1855 Mormon missionaries establish Fort Lemhi and are the first to reclaim Idaho land by irrigation.

1857 The Oregon constitutional convention establishes Oregon's eastern (Idaho's western) boundary.

Bannock Indians attack the Mormons at Fort Lemhi.

1859 Oregon becomes a state, placing all of present-day Idaho in Washington Territory.

1860 Mormon leader Brigham Young founds Idaho's oldest town, Franklin.

Hannah Cornish starts the first school for white children in Idaho.

Discovery of gold on Orofino Creek in August leads to the establishment of Idaho's oldest mining town, Pierce.

1861 Lewiston becomes a service community for Idaho mines.

1862 A. S. Gould starts Idaho's first newspaper, the *Golden Age*, in Lewiston.

George Grimes and a party of prospectors discover gold at the Boise Basin mines, leading to the creation of Idaho City.

Packer John builds his cabin between present-day New Meadows and McCall.

1863 President Lincoln signs an act establishing Idaho Territory with its capital at Lewiston.

Soda Springs is founded.

September 29—*Boise News* of Idaho City publishes its first issue.

Gold mining begins in the Owyhee Mountains.

Merchants under the lead of Cyrus Jacobs lay out the townsite of Boise.

1864 Ben Holladay establishes Idaho's first stagecoach line.

The *Idaho Statesman* begins triweekly publication in Boise.

December 7—A resolution to make Boise the territorial capital passes the legislature.

1865 Boise becomes the capital of Idaho.

J. M. Taylor and Robert Anderson erect a bridge across the Snake River near present-day Idaho Falls.

1866   Gold is discovered at Leesburg in Lemhi County.

1867   March 25—Gutzon Borglum, the sculptor of Mount Rushmore, is born in Bear Lake County.

1869   A statue of George Washington, carved from native wood by Charles Leopold Ostner, is unveiled on the capitol grounds at Boise.

President Grant sets aside the Fort Hall Indian Reservation for the Shoshones and Bannocks of southern Idaho.

First telegraph office comes to Franklin.

1870   Idaho's population: 14,999. A later census figure reveals 17,804, after the Utah-Idaho border is clearly established.

Caribou gold rush begins in southeastern Idaho.

1874   Idaho's first railroad, the Utah & Northern, comes to Franklin.

Silver City publishes Idaho's first daily newspaper, the *Owyhee Avalanche*.

1877   June–October—The Nez Perce Indians, forced to relocate from their homelands onto the reservation at Lapwai, engage troops and volunteers led by Gen. O. O. Howard in a running battle from White Bird to Yellowstone to the Bear Paw Mountains in Montana.

1878   Bannock Indians led by Chief Buffalo Horn and Paiutes led by Chief Egan terrorize settlers after the government opens Camas Prairie. General Howard brings a swift end to the Bannock War.

1880   Idaho's population: 32,619.

Lead-silver lodes are discovered in the Wood River area. The rush to Bellevue, Hailey, and Ketchum transforms south central Idaho.

1882   The Northern Pacific Railroad completes its route across northern Idaho.

1883   Coeur d'Alene gold rush begins.

First telephone service in Idaho begins at Hailey.

The Oregon Short Line Railroad reaches Weiser, connecting Idaho to the Pacific Coast.

1885   The legislature approves $80,000 to construct a territorial capitol and locates the insane asylum at Blackfoot.

October 30—Famous poet Ezra Pound is born at Hailey.

Noah Kellogg discovers the silver-lead ore mines Bunker Hill and Sullivan near the future site of Kellogg.

1887   An electric light plant illuminates Hailey.

The Wardner miner's union grows from wage reductions at the Bunker Hill and Sullivan mines.

1888   Rexburg establishes Ricks Academy, now known as Ricks College.

1889   Willis Sweet introduces a bill to establish the University of Idaho at Moscow.

1890   July 3—Idaho becomes the 43rd state with a population of 88,548.

1891   October 9—College of Idaho opens in Caldwell.

1892   Gov. Norman B. Willey declares martial law on Silver Valley following the dynamiting of the Frisco Mill near Burke.

October 3—University of Idaho opens.

1893   Union officer George Pettibone and colleagues form the Western Federation of Miners.

1894   Coxey's Army brings a national protest movement to Idaho.

1896   August 13—Butch Cassidy robs the Montpelier bank.

1898   Idaho volunteers are called to military service for the Philippine insurrection during the Spanish-American War.

1899   Gov. Frank Steunenberg calls in federal troops to suppress a riot in the Coeur d'Alene mining district following the dynamiting of the Bunker Hill and Sullivan concentrator.

1900   Idaho's population: 161,772.

1901   The Academy of Idaho (now Idaho State University) opens in Pocatello.

Col. William Dewey finances the building of the Swan Falls Dam hydroelectric plant on the Snake River near Kuna.

1903   Miller Dam on the Snake River opens the Twin Falls area to irrigated farming.

1904   City of Twin Falls is platted.

September 21—Chief Joseph dies.

1906   Gov. Steunenberg's assassin, Harry Orchard, implicates three leaders of the Western Federation of Miners in the plot.

The largest sawmill in the United States begins operation at Potlatch.

1907	Idaho elects William E. Borah to the U.S. Senate, where he gains an international reputation during thirty-three years of service.
1908	U.S. Bureau of Reclamation completes the Minidoka Dam.
1910	Idaho's population: 325,594.
	Devastating forest fires consume one-sixth of northern Idaho's forests, destroying many communities.
1913	Eugene Emerson establishes Northwest Nazarene College in Nampa.
1915	Arrowrock Dam complete.
	The Academy of Idaho (ISU) becomes the Idaho Technical Institute.
	Ranching community at Dempsey incorporates the town and names it Lava Hot Springs.
1917	Ricks Academy becomes a college.
1920	Idaho's population: 431,866.
	Whitebird Hill grade opens, connecting northern and southern Idaho.
1921	Neil Shipman establishes a movie company at Priest Lake.
1922	U.S. Sheep Experiment Station begins at Dubois.
1924	President Calvin Coolidge names Craters of the Moon National Monument.
	Black Canyon Dam complete.
1925	Union Pacific Railroad begins service to Boise.
1928	Restoration of the "Old Mission" Church near Cataldo begins.
	Archaeologists unearth fossils of a 3.5-million-year-old Hagerman Horse.
1930	Idaho's population: 445,032.
1934	Idaho leads the nation in silver production.
1936	Union Pacific Railroad establishes Sun Valley as a ski resort.
	William E. Borah becomes Idaho's first presidential candidate.
1940	Idaho's population: 524,873.
	January 19—William E. Borah dies.
1941	J. R. Simplot food dehydrator begins operations in Caldwell.

1942   Japanese American internment begins at Camp Minidoka near Hunt.

1944   Mountain Home Army Air Field (later Air Force Base) officially opens.

1947   University of Idaho Southern Branch at Pocatello becomes Idaho State College.

1948   Bureau of Reclamation begins plans to construct a Hells Canyon dam on the Snake River for flood control.

1949   Scientists build the National Reactor Testing Station near Arco.

1950   Idaho's population: 588,637.

1951   Scientists develop nuclear electric power at the National Reactor Testing Station.

1952   Anderson Ranch Dam complete.

1955   The Atomic Energy Commission lights Arco with electricity generated by atomic energy.

1956   Construction of Palisades Dam complete.

1959   Brownlee Dam on the Snake River complete.

1960   Idaho's population: 667,191.

1961   Oxbow Dam on the Snake River complete.

        July 2—Ernest Hemingway dies in Ketchum.

1962   Lewis and Clark Highway (US 12) in the Lochsa Canyon complete.

1963   Idaho State College in Pocatello becomes a university.

1965   Nez Perce National Historic Park established in north central Idaho.

1968   Hells Canyon Dam complete.

1970   Idaho's population: 713,015.

1971   Last log drive on the Clearwater River.

1972   Congress establishes the Sawtooth National Recreation Area, including the Sawtooth Wilderness Area.

        Sunshine mine fire at Kellogg kills 91 men.

1973   Boise State College becomes a university.

1976   Hells Canyon bill creates the Hells Canyon National Recreation Area and bans construction of hydroelectric projects in the canyon.

The 310-foot-high Teton Dam collapses in southeastern Idaho, releasing a massive flood that kills 11 and forces 300,000 people to evacuate.

1980   Idaho's population: 944,038.

Interior Secretary Cecil Andrus expands the Snake River Birds of Prey Natural Area from 31,000 to 482,640 acres.

Congress approves the Central Idaho Wilderness Act, establishing the 2.2-million-acre Frank Church–River of No Return Wilderness.

1981   Bunker Hill mine and smelter in Kellogg closes after 98 years.

1983   October 28—An earthquake measuring 7.3 on the Richter scale kills two children and causes $4 million in damage. Centered in the Lost River Valley, the quake is the largest in the continental United States in twenty-four years and leaves a ten-foot-high, fifteen-mile-long shear.

1984   Harmon Killebrew of Payette is inducted into the Baseball Hall of Fame.

1990   Idaho's population: 1,006,749. The state is 100 years old.

1994   May 30—Whitney native Ezra Taft Benson dies. He served as U.S. Secretary of Agriculture from 1953 to 1961 and as head of the Mormon Church since 1985.

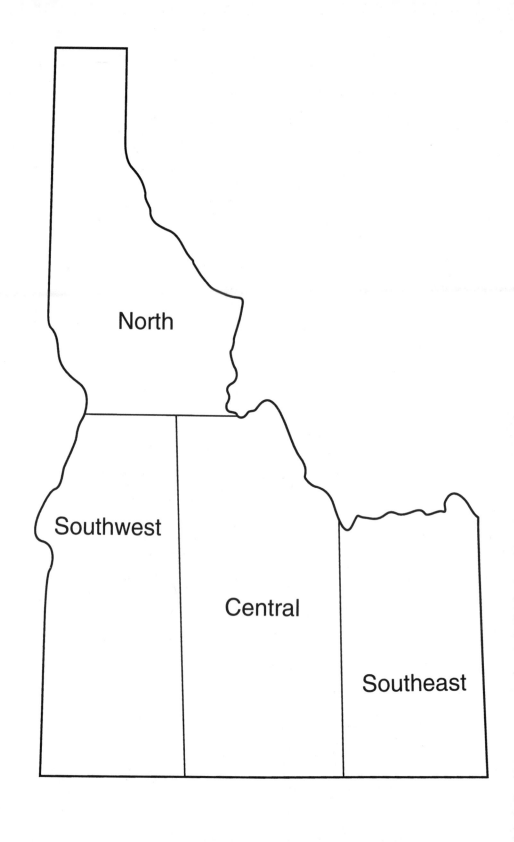

Idaho:
Gem of the Mountains

I daho is full of surprises. It has a natural and cultural diversity as great as that of any other state in the country. Drive a couple of hours in any direction and the landscape will change—from farmland to sagebrush desert to forested mountains and rippling streams. Both highlands and lowlands are dotted with country villages, sophisticated resorts, lively outposts, even ghost towns. Most of these places have an interesting story, a skeleton in the closet, or perhaps a clue to understanding the past.

This terrain, with its kaleidoscope of scenes, is a joy to travel, as more and more people are discovering. But don't expect to see the entire state in a day or even a week. At 83,577 square miles, it is larger than all of New England, but it's compressed into boundaries that give the state a unique configuration. The border with Washington and Oregon runs nearly 500 miles from north to south. The northern panhandle is less than 50 miles wide, but the southern portion of the state stretches 300 miles from east to west.

Slightly more than a million people live in Idaho—an average of about eleven per square mile. A good many live in small towns set snugly along river banks or sheltered by hills. The urban areas of Pocatello, Idaho Falls, Twin Falls, and Boise are linked by the irrigated Snake River Plain, and they contain the bulk of the population. In the forested north, towns such as Lewiston, Moscow, and Coeur d'Alene are rapidly growing.

Beneath the colorful mantle of Idaho's landscape lies the story of the cataclysmic forces that shaped it. In the panhandle, for instance, continental glaciers ground down the Selkirk and Cabinet mountains, scoured out U-shaped valleys, and left myriad lakes. Beneath the surface are old sediments deposited on the continental crust 1.4 million years ago—practically yesterday, geologically speaking. In a few places, faults and erosion expose ancient rocks dating back some 2 billion years. These rocks contain fossils of stromatolites that mark the beginning of marine life on earth.

Much of central Idaho is pristine wilderness that covers a granitic core called the Idaho Batholith. This hourglass-shaped region runs approximately

Relief map of Idaho shows the broad arc of the Snake River Plain and the predominately mountain terrain across the rest of the state. It's not easy to build freeways here. —Idaho Department of Transportation

100 miles north to south, with an average width of 75 miles east to west. Located here are the Frank Church–River of No Return Wilderness—the largest single wilderness area in the contiguous forty-eight states—as well as the Selway-Bitterroot Wilderness and the Sawtooth National Recreation Area. This wealth of high country sprawls between the South Fork of the Boise River and the Clearwater River. Historically, this area spawned the gold rush of 1861 and brought settlement to Idaho. Today it is an outdoor paradise. The only paved road that crosses this vast expanse is US 12, which follows the Clearwater and Lochsa rivers to the Montana border at the crest of the Bitterroot Mountains. Idaho 75 and US 93 skirt the fringe of the batholith on its eastern edge, and US 95 traces it on the west.

The batholith emerged from a combination of volcanic activity, plate tectonics, and other violent changes in the landscape about 100 million years ago, according to geologist Terry Maley in *Exploring Idaho Geology*. At a time when the Pacific Ocean lapped against western Idaho, exotic "terranes" from Asia floated eastward on the Pacific Plate, slammed into the Idaho shoreline (centered near Riggins), and were "sutured" in place. This horrendous collision gave rise to the Seven Devils Mountains and caused widespread compression and buckling, forcing hot magma to move upward into the continental crust and forming the Idaho Batholith. At the same time, these ongoing forces displaced sediments of an ancient seabed lying to the southeast. These sediments were pushed eastward and faulted and folded into an overthrust belt that extends in a north-south plane across southeastern Idaho (as well as into Wyoming and Utah). These 200-million-year-old marine deposits became rare phosphoria beds, the products of which are transformed into hundreds of everyday items.

Perhaps the most notable feature of southern Idaho is the Snake River Plain, which sweeps across the state from Ashton to Weiser in a great smiling arc. Along this 400-mile stretch, twenty-three dams store enough water to irrigate thousands of acres of rich volcanic soil and to generate countless watts of electricity. Maley believes that about 17 million years ago, tensions caused the upper crust to thin and pull apart along the axis of the Snake River Plain. Then intermittent lava flows—the last of which occurred as recently as 2,000 years ago—poured from hundreds of fractures to fill the depression.

Remarkable changes some 15,000 years ago took place when the great Bonneville flood drained the ancient lake that covered much of northwestern Utah and carved a deep canyon into the Snake River Plain. Mountain runoff continued to pour into this channel, and the Snake was on its way to becoming a great natural resource. A simpler story contends that Paul Bunyan, after drinking nine kegs of rum in Idaho Falls, set off across southern Idaho with Babe, his blue ox. The night was black and rainy as they wandered in a crooked path across the plain. When the trail behind them filled with water, it became the Snake River.

Giant sprinklers are a common sight in southern Idaho. This one irrigates a potato field. —Idaho Department of Agriculture

The first humans to inhabit this area apparently arrived around the time of the Bonneville flood. Evidence of human habitation over a period of thousands of years has been found in widely separated locations. These early people, who dined on giant bison and woolly mammoths, may or may not have been the ancestors of the Native Americans who greeted the first white explorers and fur traders.

When Meriwether Lewis and William Clark traveled across Idaho, they met several Indian tribes who were divided both culturally and geographically into two quite different areas. The Nez Perce, Coeur d'Alene, and Kootenai (or Kutenai) tribes lived generally north of the Salmon River and were affiliated with other plateau tribes such as the Yakima. The Shoshone (including the Shoshone-Bannocks) and Northern Paiutes roamed across most of southern Idaho and into the Great Basin country of Utah and Nevada. Before the white men came, most of these tribes had horses and ate fairly well with a diet that included game, birds, plants, and fish.

Idaho was the last state in the Union to be explored by white men. Sailors such as Capt. James Cook of the British navy approached the coasts of Washington and Oregon in the late nineteenth century and began a lucrative trade in furs. At the same time, French and Spanish traders followed the Mississippi and Missouri rivers to eastern Montana and Wyoming. But Idaho remained locked away behind the chain of the Rocky Mountains running from the Cabinets in northern Idaho to the Centennial Range in the southeast.

Lewis and Clark led the first party of white men to penetrate these borders. They crossed the Beaverhead Mountains at Lemhi Pass in 1805 and found themselves in Shoshone country. Soon afterward they crossed the Bitterroots at Lolo Pass and met the Nez Perce on Weippe Prairie. Both tribes proved helpful as well as fascinating, and the interest was probably mutual. The Indians were amazed as they surveyed the miracles of a man with black skin (Clark's servant, York) and another with red hair (Lewis). Lewis and Clark prepared a classic account of their adventure and opened the curtain on Idaho exploration.

A stream of adventurers and fur trappers followed. Of particular importance was the Wilson Price Hunt expedition, which traveled overland in 1811 en route to the mouth of the Columbia River to scout the rich beaver streams for John Jacob Astor and his Pacific Fur Company. As it turned out, the trip had greater significance as a journey of exploration than as a commercial enterprise. Hunt's party, the first group of white men to cross the Snake River Plain, inadvertently pioneered the general route that later became the Oregon Trail. A few years later British fur trappers approached Idaho from Astoria, which had fallen to them during the War of 1812.

American trappers came from St. Louis, crossed the Rockies at South Pass in Wyoming, and made their way into southeastern Idaho, where they spent nearly twenty years exploring and trapping. This reckless breed of men, folk heroes in buckskin, stayed alive in the wilderness by wit and daring. In their quest for beaver they roamed the mountains, searched out the streams, and traveled a network of trails—forerunners of the roadways that bind the state together. When the era of fur trade ended, many of the trappers turned to guiding missionaries and pioneers over the routes they knew so well.

In 1829 Bill Sublette, a partner of renowned fur men Jedediah Smith and David Jackson, brought a caravan of ten wagons—each pulled by five mules—from St. Louis to the Wind River rendezvous in Wyoming. It was the first wagon train to cross the Continental Divide. In 1836 missionary Marcus Whitman managed to bring one wagon across the mountains. By the time his party reached Fort Boise, the wagon had become a two-wheeled cart. However, this much-traveled conveyance paved the way for heavier traffic. In 1843, when Whitman returned to his mission from a trip east, he joined an early wave of the Great Migration. That year 1,000 immigrants with vast herds of horses and cattle crossed southern Idaho on the Oregon Trail. This route became part of US 30, and much of it paralleled today's I-84.

Most of the wagon trains were headed for the green Willamette Valley of Oregon, and the pioneers couldn't put the southern Idaho desert behind them fast enough. This bleak country was no place to settle—until the cry of "gold" went up, that is. From 1863 onward, prospectors trooped in from the Pacific states and British Columbia, quickly swelling the population.

From Oro Fino on the Clearwater to Placerville in the Boise Basin, miners threw up jerry-built gold towns that soon turned into permanent settlements. When the mining excitement died down, ex-miners and storekeepers turned to cattle ranching and farming. Homebuilders moved in and imbued Idaho with a culture of small towns.

When Lewis and Clark reached Idaho in 1804, it was part of the loosely defined Oregon Country, which included the entire Pacific Northwest. When Washington Territory was organized in 1853, Idaho fell within its borders. After a flood of prospectors washed in on the gold tide ten years later, Idaho became a territory in its own right. Politics ran fairly hot in those Civil War days. President Lincoln and the Republican administrations that followed him regularly sent Republican governors and staff to Idaho Territory, even though the residents were predominantly Democrats. This gave Idaho politics an ironic twist from the start—an officialdom quite at odds with the refugee rebels, the secessionists, who constituted the majority of the population.

According to legend, the name of the new territory was taken from the Shoshone word "E-da-how," roughly translated to mean "sun coming down the mountains." Over the years this interpretation has been altered to "gem of the mountains," which is both poetic and appropriate because of the abundance of gemstones—sapphire, topaz, garnet, zircon, opal, jasper, aquamarine, and others—found in Idaho. However, it seems that Idaho's name was actually taken from an early settlement in Colorado known as Idaho Springs.

As statehood approached, no serious challenge to Idaho's name surfaced, but warring factions squabbled for years over possible boundary changes. The northern part of Idaho is separated from the south by vast ranges of mountains that impede transportation and communication. Even in territorial days, northern Idaho residents groaned at the thought of throwing in their lot with the south and its faraway capital at Boise. Most of them favored annexation with either Washington or Montana, both of which lay closer geographically. A first step toward change was a bill calling for the annexation of northern Idaho to Washington Territory. It passed both houses of Congress and would have become law if not for President Grover Cleveland's pocket veto. After that close call, factions north and south decided to cooperate, do a little horse trading (the north got the University of Idaho), and move on toward statehood. Thus, the original boundaries of Idaho Territory remained intact when it entered the Union as the forty-third state on July 3, 1890.

Still, the diverse patchwork of geography led to equally diverse political and economic views. Over the years Idaho politics have proved curiously unpredictable, although the state has regularly been pegged as a conservative stronghold. Statehood had barely been achieved when the Populists reared up as a liberal element. In 1896 the Idaho legislature joined the van-

6

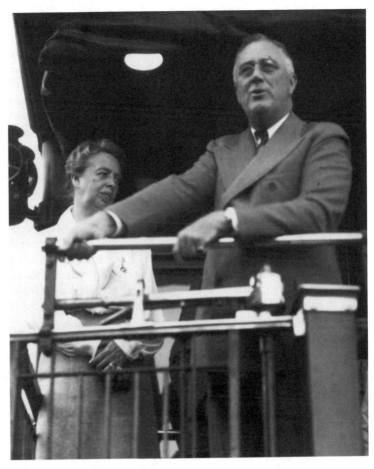

President Franklin Roosevelt and Eleanor Roosevelt on a whistle-stop tour through Idaho, circa 1939.
—Idaho State Historical Society

guard of states granting women the right to vote. Next came popular measures that provided a legal framework for initiatives, referendums, and recalls and for direct election of senators (as opposed to their appointment by the state legislature). At the turn of the twentieth century labor unions were strong in the Coeur d'Alene mines, and prior to World War I the Industrial Workers of the World (IWW) brought on a "red scare" in the northern Idaho timber industry. During this same era the Socialist Party managed to put one man—Earl Bowman—in the state senate and to capture several local offices in the southern part of the state.

For some unknown reason (perhaps to achieve a golden mean), the common political arrangement has been to match a Republican legislature with a Democratic governor. This pattern was notable during the depression years of the 1930s, when Idaho's "cowboy governor" C. Ben Ross defeated entrenched Republicans. He jumped on the New Deal bandwagon in time to bring home a good many political plums, including emergency relief, highway construction, mortgage moratoriums, and just about the biggest

Civilian Conservation Corp (CCC) program in the West. One of his political heirs, Senator Frank Church, led the charge to scuttle opposition to the controversial Hells Canyon National Recreation Area. Long-term Democratic Governor Cecil Andrus sparred for years with conservative ranchers and timber interests over how much wilderness to set aside in a state where two-thirds of the land is still owned by the federal government.

Idaho's population is about as diverse as its topography, and a wide blend of ethnic backgrounds has produced a uniquely Idahoan culture. The pioneer mining camps were a motley assortment of northern Europeans, particularly Germans, Irish, and "Cousin Jacks" from the Cornwall mines of England. Chinese arrived fresh from building the Central Pacific Railroad and added a completely different style to the boisterous gold camps. Swedish farmers settled in southern Idaho, and Finns took to the Long Valley of the upper Payette River country. Even today the pioneer homes that remain exhibit a unique style of construction, many of them including a sauna room. Priest River became the center of an Italian colony, and since early in the twentieth century southwestern Idaho has boasted the largest Basque population outside Spain.

Since the 1940s, two additional ethnic groups have become prominent in Idaho—Japanese and Mexicans. Many people of Japanese descent came to the state during World War II as part of the nation's relocation program and stayed on to farm the rich Snake River land. Mexican nationals came to relieve the wartime labor shortage. Many farmers would never have been able to harvest their beets and potatoes without a boost from south of the border. Workers stayed, became citizens, and added their colorful Cinco de Mayo celebration to the cultural milieu of Idaho.

Today Idaho is one of the fastest-growing states in the country. As its population increases, so do the opportunities for those who call it home. One wag has said that Idaho has gone from cow chips to computer chips. Certainly manufacturing companies such as Micron Technology and Hewlett-Packard play an important part in the state's economy. Agriculture remains Idaho's largest industry and it leads all other states in the production of potatoes, barley, and trout. However, some farmers are raising exotic livestock such as buffalo, ostrich, and reindeer. And a flourishing wine industry is emerging. Twelve wineries staffed with creative vintners are turning out premium chardonnays, cabernets, Johannisberg Rieslings, and pinot noirs from Twin Falls in the south to Athol in the north.

In addition, a rapidly growing tourist industry is sweeping the state. Ironically, the terrain that once deterred settlement holds the very attractions that people now seek to experience. Idaho offers spectacular mountain ranges, more than 2,000 lakes, nearly a dozen wild and scenic rivers, and incomparable deserts with scenery that ranges from moonscapes to potato fields. Plenty of space, clean air, sunny skies, and hospitable people add to Idaho's appeal.

Near Boise, Lucky Peak Reservoir during a drought year.

A long procession of settlers with spirit and vitality has left its stamp here. Countless cities, villages, mountain outposts, ghost towns, and farming communities are tangible reminders of the pioneers' influence. This roadside history delves beyond the obvious to relate everyday stories that give special identity to Idaho.

Any attempt to describe Idaho depends on one's viewpoint. In southern Idaho there are places where only a sea of sagebrush and a great dome of blue sky meet the eye. But along the Snake River Plain, fields of potatoes and sugar beets transform the desert into a vast oasis. Turn north, toward the Salmon and Clearwater rivers, and a wilderness of snowcapped mountains and white-water streams—a world unchanged for centuries—invites recreation. Still farther north, the rolling Palouse hills make for a singular picture, and their deep deposits of loess produce record crops of wheat and lentils. In the panhandle, where the climate is damp and cool, thick stands of pine, cedar, and hemlock blanket the mountains and identify this traditional lumberjack country.

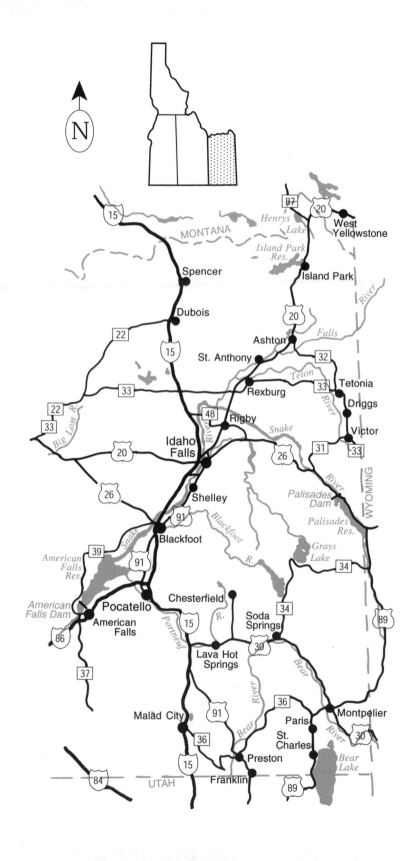

~ PART 1 ~

Southeast Idaho

Southeast Idaho lay directly in the path of early western travel. A succession of explorers, fur traders, and Oregon Trail emigrants saw the upper Snake River Plain, the Teton Valley, and the Bear Lake country long before it was settled—mostly by Mormon pioneers. Their presence is still so strong in the southeast that some of the other churches treat this area as mission territory. The Shoshone-Bannocks at Fort Hall Indian Reservation bring their own culture to the larger community, and in the major cities a variety of industries generate a complex society.

To some extent, the southeast is a microcosm of the whole state. From the hilly Bear River country in the south to Henrys Lake in the north, the traveler finds forested mountains, pristine waterfalls, fertile farmland, deserts, sand dunes, and, according to the dictates of the land, settled communities that tell the story of Idaho.

Mormon Territory

I-15
THE GOLD ROAD

For the past 130 years, a road of one sort or another has cut a vertical swath across eastern Idaho, providing a link with Montana to the north and Utah to the south. The first was an 1863 wagon track known as the Montana Trail. Later the Utah & Northern Railroad paralleled the wagon road, placing depots near the stage stops. After the turn of the century, a new macadamized road was built over the old one for the benefit of the new "horseless carriages." Finally, as interstate highways began to connect the country from one end to another, the old route was transformed into I-15. Each improvement strengthened settlements along the way and contributed to the growth of gateway cities such as Pocatello and Idaho Falls.

In 1863, when Idaho Territory was created, thousands of miners rushed to Bannack and Virginia City (now in Montana, then in Idaho Territory) "clean mad for the muck called gold." The mines were rich. Prospectors could readily sluice nuggets, but keeping their camps stocked with bacon and beans posed a problem. Gradually the territorial legislature granted franchises for a supply road. The highway left Montana at Monida Pass, crossed the Centennial Mountains, and headed south to the Snake River along a natural route used by the Indians. It followed river valleys and tortuous canyons all the way to Salt Lake City. Tolls were collected at Beaver Canyon (Spencer), Taylor's Bridge (Idaho Falls), and Portneuf Canyon (near McCammon).

A substantial amount of Montana gold passed southbound over the route via Ben Holladay stages and Wells Fargo Express while freight wagons creaked north bearing tons of food and mining supplies. The Montana Trail became a symbol of wealth not only for the fortunes in dust and bullion it carried but also for the prosperity it scattered in its wake. All along the route, new towns grew up around the stage stations; settlers moved in, ranching and storekeeping developed, and a state was in the making. Some of the early stops became permanent settlements, including Malad, McCammon, Pocatello, Idaho Falls, and Dubois. Ironically, more gold was carried over the roads radiating from Boise Basin, but those routes do not have conspicuous second lives as interstate freeways.

In pioneer times, stagecoaches spent five days and nights traveling between Virginia City and Salt Lake City. Sometimes the ride was a jolting one as the six-horse teams pulled the lurching coaches over fields of lava rock. On smooth stretches the wheels ground into soft sand, sending up stifling clouds of alkaline dust that enveloped the passenger cars. The stage stations offered as few amenities as the coaches, but discomfort was sometimes the least serious problem on the Gold Road. Travelers faced the constant threat of being robbed by road agents, who frequently targeted Wells Fargo shipments. The company routinely posted rewards for the capture of the latest scoundrel. A narrow passage through the Portneuf Canyon south of Pocatello was especially hazardous.

One beautiful July afternoon in 1865, the stage came clattering through Portneuf Canyon and was about to squeeze through the narrowest part when a voice rang out from the brush, "Boys, here they are!" A barrage of shots hit the front, back, and sides of the coach. Four passengers were killed, and the bandits made off with the treasure box that held approximately $63,000 in gold dust. By the time a posse could be organized, the robbers were long gone. They left no tracks through the rocky, lava canyon. Later the stage driver, Frank Williams, confessed to being an accomplice and was tried and hanged.

A fairly humorous holdup occurred near the Malad summit during the summer of 1870. Ed Flag and "Louisville" Stone waylaid the stage with three dummies as "accomplices." These bogus robbers were partially hidden in the sage and made to look like bona fide road agents. With this phony show of force, Flag and Stone were able to lift $36,000 from the strongbox without firing a shot.

When the stage driver galloped into Malad, he reported that five men had perpetrated the holdup. A posse soon formed and took to the trail in pursuit. They discovered Stone and Flag wandering in the sage, and a shootout followed. Flag was killed, and Stone received a wound in the leg. In this compromised situation he decided to confess but shielded himself by swearing that the three "accomplices" had run off with the money and left him penniless. Eventually the posse got the straight story and collected the reward.

Carrie Adell Strahorn traveled the Gold Road in 1878 and found few noticeable improvements, although by this time it had been in use for fifteen years. She remembered her experiences at a stage stop north of Eagle Rock, perhaps Dry Creek (Dubois). Here the stationmaster kept a cabin with combination parlor-kitchen-bedroom and attached horse stalls separated from the living area by a thin partition. While the Strahorns were eating dinner, the horses stamped and pawed and leaned so violently against the frail barrier that Strahorn thought they might kick the dishes off the table. However, the most memorable part of this stop may have been the sign over the door: "Hotel de Starvation, 1,000 miles from hay and grain, seventy miles from wood, fifteen miles from water, and only twelve inches from h-ll."

In 1869 the Union Pacific and Central Pacific railroads met at Promontory Point near Ogden, Utah, and with great fanfare drove a golden spike to bond the transcontinental connection. This event set off a fever of railroad building that included construction of the Utah Northern, which followed the Gold Road and linked Ogden with Helena, Montana. The Mormon Church organized the Utah Northern Railroad Company in the early 1870s and laid track as far as Franklin, Idaho. Mormon settlers living along the right-of-way made up the construction teams, using their own horses and equipment. But as the tracks moved farther north, these crews became fewer and fewer in number. Construction problems, plus the depression brought on by the Panic of 1873, caused the church to reconsider railroad building.

The Mormons decided to sell out to eastern financiers. Chief purchasers included Jay Gould and other Union Pacific men, such as Sidney Dillon and S. H. H. Clark. They reorganized, refinanced, and renamed their pio-

15

neering narrow-gauge railroad the Utah Northern; it later became the Utah & Northern. Construction began in Cache Valley and continued through Red Rock Pass and Marsh Valley along a natural route to the Portneuf River, where it entered the canyon at Inkom, a few miles south of Pocatello. Here it joined the route of the Gold Road, passed Pocatello station, and headed north to Ross Fork (Fort Hall Agency) and on to the Blackfoot River, where the terminus later became the town of Blackfoot.

The fact that most of this construction trespassed on reservation lands didn't seem to bother anyone except the Indians. The Fort Hall Reservation had been created in 1867. At that time the Shoshone-Bannocks owned a tract of mountains and meadows some sixty miles long and about forty miles wide—1.8 million acres—between Red Rock Pass and the Blackfoot River. As the railroad encroached on their domain they staged a mild protest, but the advancing tracks were already in place, and a negotiated settlement seemed prudent. The Shoshone-Bannocks agreed to accept 500 head of cattle (which never arrived) and free rides (which didn't last long) on the railroad in return for the right-of-way.

Construction crews laid tracks across the reservation during the winter of 1878, then moved on toward the Blackfoot terminus. A few collapsible buildings—hotel, store, post office, Chinese washhouse, Wells Fargo agency, and miscellaneous freight offices—quickly went up, creating an instant town. A complement of saloons and "wild women" followed. Citizens soon started a grammar school, and the place took on a mantle of respectability.

As a terminus town, Blackfoot was not as saturated with "sin" as some of the "hell on wheels" railroad camps. Mormon contractors set the tone by hiring their own friends and families for the construction jobs, and these folks were more apt to be drinking milk than whiskey. Local cowboys may have supplied most of the excitement.

Carrie Adell Strahorn spent a night in Blackfoot during its first winter and reported a bit of tomfoolery. A band of cowboys came into town and announced their arrival with a fusillade of shots. Whooping wildly, they galloped up and down the street and, horses and all, barged into the saloons. One saloon keeper, T. T. Danielson (also the town's postmaster), being either solicitous of their enjoyment or defensive of his property, constructed wide double doors at either end of his establishment. The cowboys could ride straight through from front to back—and perhaps leave the bar glasses undisturbed. The scene is immortalized in a Charlie Russell sketch that shows cowboys in full regalia spurring their broncs through a saloon door. Years later Russell painted a work in oil on the same theme and titled it *In Without Knocking*.

Eagle Rock also started as a railroad terminus and lived to become Idaho Falls, a major population center for eastern Idaho. Its location, however, was important long before the railroad arrived, for this is where Matt Taylor built his pioneer bridge across the Snake River. He camped on the site one night in 1863 after ferrying his freight wagon across the turbulent stream. The crossing was treacherous, and Taylor decided travelers would fare better crossing the narrow canyon on a bridge. He pulled a string out of his pocket for a makeshift measure, tied a jagged stone to one end, and hurled it across the canyon. When he reeled in the line, he reckoned eighty-three feet. From that time on he was obsessed with the possibility of bridging the Snake. He imagined a bonanza in freighters streaming past, each one paying a toll.

By the summer of 1865, Matt Taylor's toll bridge was open for business. When the Utah & Northern arrived fifteen years later, construction crews added a railroad bridge and shops. The town was ready to boom.

Beyond Eagle Rock, railroad stations moved in alongside the stage stops, and in the spring of 1880 the Utah & Northern crested the Centennial Mountains and crossed into Montana at Monida Pass.

More than 200 miles of railroad track ran parallel to the Gold Road. Long lines of creaking freight wagons became passé as the new "puffer-belly" engines pulled boxcar loads of goods and treasure. Passenger cars bumped along the narrow track, too, jostling and jolting the riders, pitching them first one way, then another. In spite of its flaws, this new mode of transportation was a success. Best of all, it became a catalyst for settlement. Mormon president John Taylor sent out a call for pioneers to come and "strengthen the cords of Zion." Railroad officials made up 30,000 brochures describing the area—glossing over the monotonous stretches of sagebrush. But the Morman Church distributed them, and a movement to colonize a 150-mile frontier began.

For new settlers and old, the coming of the iron horse brought the outside world within reach. It helped overcome isolation and loneliness, making travel and sociability easier. In *Letters of Long Ago*, Agnes Just Reid quotes a letter by her mother, pioneer Emma Just, describing the changes brought by the new railroad:

> I know you will rejoice when I tell you the youngsters have been to the circus. The first one that came through the country stopped at Eagle Rock and we all went to see it. . . . We've lived in the silent places so long that it is very hard to adjust ourselves to noise and crowds. A crowd there certainly was! Hundreds of people from hundreds of miles around! There was a time when we knew most everyone in this part of the valley but the settlers have come so fast since the railroad got here that we cannot keep track of them.

After overcoming the initial shock of empty space, the pioneers developed a kinship with the sage, knowing that where it grew the ground was rich. Agnes Just Reid wrote: "The Irish have their shamrock, the Scot his bonny heather. In Idaho it's the sagebrush that holds us all together." But times were changing.

The endless vistas of sage diminished as a system of canals brought irrigation to the land. Water worked its magic, much of the omnipresent sage was grubbed out (although it still persists around the edges), and crops were planted. Today I-15 cuts through some of the world's richest soil and the heart of Idaho's famous potato country.

I-15, Idaho 36
MALAD CITY

At the south end of the Gold Road sits Malad City, home of former govenor John Evans. According to the motto of this quiet town, "simplicity is still a way of life." Farming is the main source of income (note the giant sheaf of wheat glistening on the bank wall), and the fifteen area reservoirs that water the crops also provide recreation. Duck hunters and fishermen flock in from Salt Lake City to taste the country life.

Malad City is one of the older towns in Idaho, settled first by Mormon farmers of Welsh background. This peaceful valley lay in the path of traffic headed for the Montana mines, and a rousing frontier town developed. Freighters made this their headquarters. Mule skinners and Gentiles mixed with the more sedate Mormons, and the place grew helter-skelter. It was a successful blend, and the town became an important commercial center on the road to Montana.

Fur trappers who tramped the banks of the Malad River looking for beaver originally explored this country. The stream got its name in 1831, when a group of hungry trappers led by Joseph Robidoux camped here. They "indulged in a repast of fat beaver" that had apparently dined on hemlock plants growing near the water. The meat was tainted, and everyone in camp became ill, describing a variety of pains—"a singular fit," one of them said. From this experience they called the stream La Riviere Maladi, meaning "Sickly River." (At an earlier date fur trappers had also called Wood River the Malad, for the same reason.)

The old-fashioned Oneida Pioneer Museum tells the story of Malad City and Oneida County through artifacts the pioneers used in daily living.

I-15 and 86, US 91
POCATELLO

Pocatello is a sprawling, robust industrial, railroad, and university town pleasantly set against the base of two mountain ranges. One of the newer agribusinesses here is malting barley, which has become a major crop in eastern Idaho. When you "taste the high country," as one beer ad says, it may very well have come from Idaho malt turned out in Pocatello. Another large local industry is phosphate. Both the J. R. Simplot Company and the Farm Machinery Corporation (FMC) operate huge processing plants here that supply a national market.

Pocatello attracts both summer travelers and winter skiers. It is second to Boise in population and the only town in Idaho located at the junction of two interstate highways. The casual visitor might feel there are several Pocatellos. Most travelers first see the cluster of popular motels and visitor services at the Pocatello Creek exit off I-15. Yellowstone Avenue (the Business I-15 and US 91 route) makes for something of a restaurant-mall strip, with its north end anchored in Chubbock and its south end at Fort Hall Replica. City Center, the historic district with architectural landmarks unique to Pocatello, is yet another environment. City Center continues to thrive amid new growth and the historic preservation of districts such as Simplot Square, which has helped to revitalize this older section.

The early history of Pocatello is closely intertwined with the resident Shoshone Indians and with the coming of two Union Pacific railroads (the Utah & Northern and the Oregon Short Line), which transformed the settlement into a robust division point.

The story properly begins with an audacious Shoshone chief named Pocatello, who roamed these hills and who no doubt had a habit of pitching his tipi along Pocatello Creek. Later the Gold Road encroached on the young brave's territory when a "swing" station (where fresh horses were hooked up) was placed here. The Utah & Northern Railroad came through in 1878. Three years later the Union Pacific sent its advance man, Robert Strahorn, to report on the area. By 1881 Pocatello was already a tent town, "with all the activity, wickedness, and glaring freedom of an awakening metropolis," Carrie Adell Strahorn wrote of the place her husband visited. She added that he fought "long and desperately" before he obtained more than a squatter's right on the reservation.

With the Union Pacific in place, settlers wanted to establish a permanent town, and the Shoshone-Bannocks agreed to allow ever-widening access across their land. The right-of-way grew from a 200-foot strip for a station and railroad shops to almost 2,000 acres. An amended treaty legalized the sixty buildings "resting illegally on reservation property and adjacent to the Pocatello station," as well as a multitude of squatters who had already moved onto Indian lands. Railroad officials tended to look the other way as settlers moved in, and word went out that anyone could "make a break for Pocatello." The powerful Union Pacific lobby quickly pushed the new treaty through Congress, while in Pocatello the Indians objected to whites who built fences and homes without paying for the land.

Pocatello had carved out an acceptable townsite for itself, but it remained an island surrounded by reservation lands. Politicians and local residents began agitating to cut the entire south end of the reservation free and to open it for settlement, ignoring the "silly twaddle" about the land belonging to the "noble red man." In 1898, according to Brigham D. Madsen in *Northern Shoshoni*, 247 tribal warriors signed away 415,500 acres to the United States government at an average price of $1.45 per acre. Congress made provisions for a survey of these lands prior to opening them for settlement. Upon completion of the survey, President Theodore Roosevelt set by proclamation the date June 17, 1902, for a gigantic land sale.

Thousands of potential settlers and speculators gathered to gamble on the great rush, making Pocatello their headquarters. They came in a flood from far and near—by foot, train, horseback, and prairie schooner—and roamed about the dusty streets waiting for the land drawing. According to the rules, nobody could approach the reservation until the train whistle blew at high noon; then the throng could make a mad dash to the reservation and stake the coveted ground. The claims had to be filed at the U.S. Land Office in Blackfoot, twenty-four miles from Pocatello. If two people eyed the same piece of ground, it went to the first comer. Just about everybody expected a few brawls and minor disagreements, maybe some gunfire to back up a claim. Ray Stannard Baker observed that "more than one coat-tail covered the crook of a revolver." Baker, a nationally known muckraker, came to Pocatello for *Century Magazine*, and his story of the rush became a classic called "The Day of the Run."

When the whistle blew, a pandemonium of buggies, bicycles, and horses took off "with monstrous clouds of dust rising behind." Baker described a few phantom stragglers moving through the haze, hopelessly behind, and spied "two reeling white topped wagons, their drivers leaning out in front, lashing their horses into dusty obscurity."

The railroad company provided a special train to transport the runners to Blackfoot after they had posted their ground. It pulled out of McCammon an hour and a half into the fray, stopped at Pocatello for two minutes to allow a breathless mob to clamber aboard, and arrived in Blackfoot at 3:00 P.M. Passengers were hanging out the windows, riding on top of the cars, and standing in doorways ready for a quick jump and a race to the U.S. Land Office as the train rolled in. At the Blackfoot station the train unloaded in a flash, and a close-packed line formed in front of the Land Office. A day and a half passed before the last runner had filed his claim. No shootings occurred, but there were plenty of disputes to keep the trail to the attorneys' offices hot.

After the land sale, the Shoshones and Bannocks crowded onto a smaller reservation that offered a poorer quality of life. But the town of Pocatello was set to boom. It was the headquarters of the Union Pacific system in Idaho and a major junction between Omaha and Portland. Eventually it grew into a forty-track yard to accommodate the 700,000 railroad cars that passed through annually.

The rush to stake a piece of land during the 1902 allotment at Pocatello.
—Idaho State Historical Society

In those days, Pocatello was a traditional railroad town, a wild "sin city" full of whiskey, prostitutes, drifters, and brawls—a place the good Mormons had best be leery of. But it outgrew this phase, became a university town, and developed a cultural climate with a diversity of people and ideas. Manufacturing joined railroading as an important enterprise, and the processing of phosphate from nearby mines added a significant industry. The trucking business, food processing, and a major medical complex all contributed to a diversified economy and population. The variety of jobs attracted union workers of many backgrounds, including a sizeable Greek population, migrant Hispanics, and an African-American community that produced a distinguished mayor (Les Purce) despite making up less than 1 percent of the electorate.

From the beginning, the town took on a liberal twist. Even so, conservatives such as George Hansen occasionally slipped into office. He served a troubled stint as a U.S. representative from 1975 to 1985 and eventually served a prison term. He was indicted under a 1978 ethics law for making false statements on his financial disclosure reports from 1978 through 1981.

One of the most colorful political personages to launch his career from Pocatello was Senator Glen Taylor, the "singing cowboy," who served from 1945 to 1951. Some people thought the image he projected—twanging his guitar on the steps of the Capitol building and crooning, "Oh give me a home near the Capitol dome . . ."—was hardly senatorial, and his ideas were twenty years ahead of their time. His stand on social issues, poverty, civil rights, and foreign affairs belonged more to the 1960s than to the Truman era. F. Ross Peterson, Taylor's biographer, quotes John Gunther as saying, "Taylor, no matter what people in Boise or Pocatello, Idaho, may tell you, is not a clown, not a hillbilly, not a buffoon. On the contrary he is an extremely serious man. He has a nice dry wit, abundant common sense, fertility of mind and a sense of showmanship." Gunther was right on all counts. Eventually Taylor gave up politics, moved to California, and got rich manufacturing toupees.

Idaho State University

The school that began as the Academy of Idaho in 1901 eventually grew into an impressive campus. Its modern curricula range through such diverse fields as pharmacy, advanced nuclear engineering, and vo-tech, in addition to a broad spectrum of offerings in the humanities. The Idaho State Civic Symphony and Theater ISU (in existence since the 1930s) represent the performing arts.

The Museum of Natural History, located on the ISU campus and easily accessed from I-15 exit 69, showcases replicas of Idaho's prehistoric animals. On display here are fossil replicas (the real ones are in storage) of mammals that lived in southeastern Idaho during the Pliocene and Pleistocene periods, from perhaps 5 million years ago to about 10,000 years ago. These include huge mammoths, prehistoric horses, ground sloths, saber-toothed tigers, and giant bison. The bison skeleton, with a horn spread of eight feet (see American Falls Reservoir), is part of the large and impressive collection of giant bison fossils located at this university.

The museum also holds a few fossil remains of the ceratopsian, a bona fide Idaho dinosaur that lived during the Cretaceous period, as well as other dinosaurs such as triceratops, which are not found in Idaho. A replica of the prehistoric horse found in large numbers near Hagerman is also on display here. A 3.5-million-year-old specimen of the Hagerman Horse was designated by the 1988 legislature as the state fossil. The museum includes a children's hands-on exhibit rich in pioneer and Indian lore.

Stanrod Mansion

This French Renaissance mansion is now owned and managed by the city of Pocatello, but when the Stanrod family lived here this house witnessed some of the town's finest social events. A turn-of-the-century showpiece, it was built primarily of native sandstone hauled to the site by wagon and cut in the backyard. Drew W. Stanrod was an attorney, banker, and district judge who served on the drafting committee for the Idaho constitutional convention in 1889.

Ross Park

Named for former Governor C. Ben Ross, this park is unequaled among the thirty-two public tracts of land in Pocatello. It is most easily reached from exit 67 (Fort Hall) off I-15, or through town via Yellowstone Avenue. The park contains two sections divided by a line of basaltic cliffs. Picnic facilities and a zoo lie below the cliffs, and a complex of buildings with a historical orientation sits atop them.

Bannock County Historical Museum

On a bluff overlooking the Portneuf Valley is an impressive building constructed by private donors. It is a Lasting Legacy project for Bannock County honoring the 1990 Idaho Centennial. One unique feature of the museum is a wall of colorful murals where historic scenes are incised in granite tiles. Exhibits tell the story of this region, with emphases on railroads, Indians, and pioneers. The transportation area features a restored Ben Holladay stagecoach that used to travel the Gold Road.

North of the museum is Pocatello Junction, a re-creation of the early-day town. Here a cluster of vintage-looking buildings with authentic facades represents such historic structures as a livery stable, a train depot, and a saloon.

Fort Hall Replica

This building is a re-creation of historic Fort Hall, which was built in 1832 approximately seventeen miles northwest of Pocatello along the Snake River. The original site now lies within the Fort Hall Indian Reservation. John K. Townsend, who was on hand when the new structure was built, says the original fort stood nine miles above the mouth of the Portneuf River in an area of many springs and luxuriant grasses later known as the Fort Hall Bottoms.

Nathaniel Wyeth built the fort out of frontier necessity. It was an accident of history as well as a significant Idaho event. Wyeth, a successful Boston businessman eager to gain a foothold in the Rocky Mountain fur trade, came west with a band of New England trappers in 1832 to attend the rendezvous in Teton Valley. While there he contracted to bring a load of supplies to the 1834 rendezvous on the Green River in what is now Wyoming. He arrived at the appointed time and place with a stock of goods worth $3,000, but the mountain men repudiated the contract, and Wyeth was left in the lurch. He decided to move farther west and set up a trading

Mountain man Gordon Perry on duty to explain the intricacies of the Indian trade at a Fort Hall Replica celebration in Pocatello.

post. Fort Hall—a wilderness bastion and "store" with a stock of goods to trade for furs—grew from that post.

While the fort was under construction, a hunting party of twelve men went out for provisions. After riding about forty miles from camp, they encountered "a rich and open plain of luxuriant grass, dotted with buffalo in all directions . . . a picturesque hill in front and a lovely stream of cold water flowing at our feet." They stayed for two weeks, feasting on fresh roasted meat and drying quantities of it on scaffolds built over low fires. Later they baled the jerky and packed it in buffalo skins prepared specifically for the purpose. When they finished, they had more than a ton of meat, notes Townsend in *Narrative of a Journey Across the Rocky Mountains to the Columbia River*: "Each bale contains about a hundred pounds, of which a mule carries two; and when we had finished, our twelve long-eared friends were loaded."

When the hunters arrived back in camp, Fort Hall (named for one of Wyeth's business associates) stood completed and ready to begin its watch over the wilderness. Jason Lee, the popular Methodist missionary who had

Fort Hall replica, Pocatello.

traveled west with Wyeth, delivered one of the earliest sermons in the Northwest at the fort. He addressed Wyeth's men and about thirty of Thomas McKay's Hudson's Bay trappers and associated Indians who happened to be present. This sermon to the Indians, "who were remarkably quiet and attentive, and sat upon the ground like statues," marked one of the earliest attempts to Christianize natives in the Northwest. Lee pushed on to the Willamette Valley in Oregon. But other missionaries—including the Whitmans, the Spaldings, and Father Pierre Jean De Smet—came to Idaho and continued the work Lee had begun.

On August 5, 1834, the fort was officially launched. The Stars and Stripes waved atop the flagstaff, and the men fired a salute as Wyeth opened a keg of whiskey in celebration. It was a wet christening, with plenty of "gouging, fighting, and fisticuffing." Townsend wrote in his journal with apparent relief, "Night at last came and cast her mantle over our besotted camp."

That fall a welcoming band of Bannocks came and pitched 250 lodges nearby. Business seemed off to a good start as they traded "a considerable quantity of furs, a large supply of dried meat, deer, elk and sheep skins."

The Oregon Trail. Sesquicentennial wagon train crosses Idaho during the summer of 1993.
—Larry Jones photo

However, the business was doomed. After McKay left Fort Hall, he established Fort Boise to compete with Wyeth for the Indian trade. Backed by the huge but hungry Hudson's Bay Company, McKay undercut Wyeth's prices. Within two years he drove the American out of business and purchased Fort Hall for the British.

Neither fort proved very profitable, however. By the 1840s the fur trade had dwindled, and both Fort Hall and Fort Boise served mainly as wagon stops on the Oregon Trail. For more than twenty years both outposts flew the Union Jack while hosting a flood of American emigrants in covered wagons who pulled in to rest and buy supplies. The overwhelming majority of those overland pioneers continued on to settle in the Willamette Valley, where they soon outnumbered the British subjects and helped to win Oregon for the United States.

Over the years many distinguished visitors stopped at Fort Hall, but perhaps none were more interesting than two scientists who traveled west with Wyeth to study the new varieties of flora and fauna. One was John K. Townsend, an ornithologist whose journal provides an insightful glimpse into early Idaho. He first described and named several species of birds, including Townsend's warbler. The second scientist, Thomas Nuttall, was a distinguished botanist who headed the Harvard herbarium and who also taught botany there. Nuttall discovered several previously unknown species of native plants, many of which appear in all major field guides to Rocky Mountain wildflowers. One plant he first collected and named is the white

Fort Hall, as sketched by William Tappan in 1849. Taken from the report of Quartermaster General Osborne Cross, 1850. —Idaho State Historical Society

wyethia (*Wyethia helianthoides*), which honors the leader of the expedition. Other now widely known wildflowers he found include the leopard lily (*Fritillaria atropurpurea*), Rocky Mountain iris (*Iris missouriensis*), and anemone (*Anemone globosa*). His mark on American botany survived the ridicule of fur trappers who ribbed him for hiking mountains and meadows to pluck flowers for his press, completely oblivious to the wilderness dangers of hostile Indians, grizzly bears, heat, thirst, hunger, and other perils.

Little trace remains of the original Fort Hall except a monument marking the site. The area is restricted and can be reached only through the Fort Hall Indian Reservation. Fort Hall Replica—open from Memorial Day to Labor Day—includes a museum, authentic tipi, historic implements, blacksmith shop, and living quarters like those the traders used.

I-15, US 91
FORT HALL RESERVATION

A trading post complex welcomes visitors to the reservation ten miles north of Pocatello. Among its attractions is a museum featuring Native American artifacts and exhibits curated by Idaho State University. Special tours may be arranged at the museum to visit the monument at the original site of old Fort Hall.

The Fort Hall Reservation is home to some 3,500 Shoshone-Bannock Indians, many of whom perform ceremonial dances around the state during times of celebration. During the second weekend in August, the tribe hosts a festive powwow at Fort Hall. Rhythmic drums, dancing feet, jingling bells, and swirling colors make this a memorable occasion for first-time visitors and old-timers alike. Auxiliary events include a parade and a rodeo.

Historically the Shoshone and Bannock, different tribes with different languages and customs, traveled and hunted together. They also intermarried, and over the years they became known as the Sho-Bans. Today the two tribes exist as a nation that governs itself through an elected tribal council, which administers separate divisions of government such as education, land use, economics, health and nutrition, and law and order. The Indians are no longer "wards" of the government; they lead their own affairs.

Early in the reservation system, when the Fort Hall Reservation was called Ross Fork (after a stream by that name), the United States agreed to furnish food and clothing if the Indians stayed within a specified boundary. Unfortunately, the reservation did not contain adequate forage to sustain life, and the government agent placed in charge often had no food to distribute, especially when Congress failed to appropriate money for supplies.

Indian dancers at the Sho-Ban powwow, Fort Hall Reservation north of Pocatello.

The Indians' early attempts at farming failed, mostly due to a lack of water for irrigation and an abundance of grasshoppers. Consequently, the hungry Sho-Bans sometimes left the reservation to hunt and fish, much to the consternation of white pioneers.

By 1878 the Indians became increasingly restless. A thousand or more packed up and rode their ponies over to Camas Prairie (near Fairfield) to dig bulbs, only to find the settlers' hogs rooting out this staple of their traditional diet. In desperation, they went on the warpath. Within three months they had been defeated and had returned to the reservation.

Twenty years later economic conditions were still uncertain, and two small bands continued to live apart. One of them lived in the Bliss area. An agent from the reservation made a visit to persuade them to move to Fort Hall. Brigham Madsen tells the story in *Northern Shoshoni:* "Old Tom and Captain Jack, the headmen, were emphatic about not going to a reservation, chiefly because there was no hunting and the rations issued were sufficient for only two days a week. As they expressed it, 'Two days eat, five days no eat.'" No reservation!

Times are better now, and the Sho-Bans are again a proud people who nurture and cherish the old traditions in their language, ceremonial dances, Native American church, and tribal values. They struggle to live in two worlds—to tread the fine line between the ways of their ancestors and the restrictions imposed on them by the modern white society.

I-15, US 26 and 91, Idaho 39
BLACKFOOT

Blackfoot is located at the confluence of the Snake and Blackfoot rivers in the heart of potato country. Five local plants process potatoes nine to ten months of the year, and some thirty fresh potato warehouses distribute the tubers to a worldwide market. Russets are the main variety; more of them are produced in Bingham County than in any other county in the nation.

Blackfoot developed from modest beginnings as a stage stop on the Gold Road and later as a train stop for the Utah & Northern Railroad. The community grew slowly at first and was overlooked when the coveted railroad shops and roundhouse moved from Eagle Rock to Pocatello. A scheme to move the capital from Boise to Blackfoot quickly went awry. In response to this "ridiculous" idea, the *Boise City Republican* declared, "Blackfoot is several degrees nearer hell than any other town in Idaho"—and had more wind and mosquitoes, to boot.

Undeterred, some shrewd Blackfoot politicians maneuvered to bring home the county seat for the new Bingham County when it might have gone to a more heavily Mormon town. In an article about his hometown, Dr. Davis Bitton quoted the fuming Salt Lake City press: "One is almost tempted to think that the Idaho Legislature perpetrated a huge burlesque when they made this settlement the capital of the newly organized county. . . . If the saloons, gambling halls and bawdy houses were removed the town would be so insignificantly small that it would require a keen eye to find even a single building remaining."

The courthouse remained, and Blackfoot residents shrugged off their town's critics. They proceeded to acquire the state insane asylum, the U.S. Land Office, and the Eastern Idaho Fair, all of which shored up the economic base as the agricultural community developed. They built canals to channel water to their fields of wheat and potatoes, and they made the desert bloom. With commendable local pride, the citizens spruced up their community by planting gardens and so many trees that for years Blackfoot was known as "The Grove."

Fred Dubois, a consummate Blackfoot politician, boosted his hometown and championed Idaho. As a U.S. senator, he sponsored Idaho's statehood bill and urged President Benjamin Harrison to sign it immediately so the new member of the Union could officially celebrate statehood on July 4, 1890. A talented manipulator, Dubois cast a wide political net in Idaho. At one time or another he controlled the Republicans, anti-Mormons, Silver Republicans, and Democrats—most of them at the same time. The town of Dubois is named for him.

Idaho World Potato Exposition

The Idaho World Potato Exposition is an unusual museum all about potatoes. It traces the famous tuber from ancient Peru, where it was first cultivated about 200 B.C., to modern times. The early Peruvians worshiped a potato god and prepared knobby little spuds in a variety of ways. In one process it was cooked, mashed, dried, frozen, dehydrated, and reconstituted when needed for food. Spanish conquistadors found the Indians eating this homely vegetable and carried it back to Spain, along with much fancier loot.

Europeans eyed the curious "batata" with suspicion. It is related to the deadly nightshade family of plants, which they feared. It had too many eyes, all evil. Marie Antoinette wore potato blossoms in her hair, and for a time the tuber was thought to have medicinal powers useful in curing everything from rheumatism to warts.

Eventually, the potato gained acceptance as a table food. The Irish thrived on it. Chefs vied for gourmet recipes, and soon vichyssoise was all the rage. The potato came back to America with a group of Irish settlers bound for New Hampshire, and in 1872 Luther Burbank began experimenting with a variety he found in New England and developed the Idaho Russet. Since then Idaho and potatoes have enjoyed a symbiotic relationship that has brought fame to both. The state's volcanic ash soil, clean air, abundant sunshine, and plentiful irrigation water make for a superior tuber.

One of the highlights of the Idaho World Potato Exposition is a poster of Marilyn Monroe wearing her famous potato sack and infusing it with glamour. Browse the gift shop, where everything is spudly: "free taters for out of staters," cookbooks, fudge, ice cream, hand cream, t-shirts, and jewelry.

The Idaho World Potato Exposition, located in downtown Blackfoot at the old Union Pacific depot, is easily identified by the huge butter-dripping plastic potato out front. It is open May through September, closed Sundays.

Bingham County Museum

The native lava rock mansion that houses this museum was built in 1905 by John G. Brown. He brought his wife and family here from Tennessee along with servants, a chauffeur, and a Chinese cook. In its heyday, the marvelous structure served as the social center of Blackfoot. Today the special collections inside include relics of Native Americans and pioneers, dolls, and family histories.

US 91

SHELLEY

At Blackfoot, interstate highway travelers have the option of continuing on I-15 to Idaho Falls or taking US 91 through the prolific potato country to the town of Shelley, seventeen miles away. Although farmers here also grow alfalfa, grain, sugar beets, and fruit—as well as fine horses and other livestock—they take the tuber most seriously. When harvest season is in full swing, the town hosts multitudes of revelers at the Idaho Annual Spud Day.

Long ago the editor of the *Shelley Pioneer*, having observed Peach Days, Watermelon Days, and Strawberry Days elsewhere in the United States, wondered: "Why not Spud Day?" The town got behind the idea, and since 1927 volunteers have baked spuds with all the trimmings and have handed them out to thousands of people during the celebration. A recent chairperson for the event said the organizers baked 5,000 potatoes and ran out early. However, anyone who arrives late for the bakers can still make the Dutch oven cook-off.

After dining come the contests. People arrive from far and near to have fun and to compete for prize money in french fry eating, spud picking, spud peeling, and various other tests of skill. One year Marj Killian and her team of five peeled 850 pounds of potatoes in forty-five minutes, which may qualify as a Guinness world record.

Sixty-fourth Idaho Annual Spud Day at Shelley. —Bob Carlson photo

I-15, US 91 and 20
IDAHO FALLS

This energetic city is a retail hub for approximately 200,000 people in the upper Snake River Valley. Much of the economic base is traditional agribusiness and food processing. Anheuser-Busch brought in a new enterprise when it opened a malting house. However, the chief factor in the economy is the Idaho National Engineering Laboratory, located west of town in the Arco desert. This facility is a major employer and adds millions of dollars annually to the collective purse.

Major destinations such as Yellowstone National Park and Jackson Hole are within a few hours' drive of town, and Idaho's own Henrys Lake country and the Teton Valley are even closer. Idaho Falls, however, is a destination in and of itself, especially for those interested in the Mormon Temple, a mecca to the faithful. In addition, the town boasts many parks and an excellent aquatic center with an Olympic-sized pool. Educationally, Idaho Falls offers Eastern Idaho Technical Institute and University Place, where the University of Idaho and Idaho State University offer a substantial variety of courses.

Urban sprawl has affected Idaho Falls as it has many other western communities, although the downtown core here remains very active and attractive. Modern landscaping, corporate offices, banks, brokerage houses, boutiques, and public buildings hint at the prosperity of the region. The city library, an elegant structure with three floors of open space tied together by a winding ramp, is a case in point. This modern facility offers users thousands of books and other media while providing a comfortable environment and serving as a well-used social center.

The Regional Chamber of Commerce (take I-15 exit 118 to Lindsay Street), an excellent first stop for visitors, offers essential maps and other information. It also has an excellent archaeological exhibit, curated by the Museum of Natural History at Idaho State University and featuring artifacts from the Baker Caves site. The relics include many bison remains as well as points, scrapers, drills, fragments of sagebrush rope, stone pipes, and an array of beads made from bone and shell. A peek into the life of these ancient campers is awesome.

Riverside Parkway, a block from the chamber, offers a riverside drive along the greenbelt, which showcases the "Idaho Falls," a great place to jog, feed the ducks, or relax to the rumble of tumbling water. A cluster of popular motels and restaurants are at the east end of Riverside Parkway, along with a bridge that leads to Memorial Drive, the Mormon Temple, and downtown. The Idaho Vietnam Memorial is located adjacent to the greenbelt in Freeman Park.

Thousands of years ago, the Idaho Falls area was home to roving bands of Shoshone and Bannock Indians who eked out their subsistence by hunting ancient elephants and bison. At the Wasden site in the desert west of Idaho Falls, Owl Cave has revealed remains of ancient bison, mammoths, and camels, as well as smaller animals. Archaeologist Suzanne Miller, who worked at the site, says these fossils have been carbon-dated at 10,500 to 11,000 years old. All of the remains show signs of apparently being butchered with Folsom points found at the earliest level in the cave. Although the mammoths and camels died out about this time, the bison lived on to modern times. Owl Cave is especially significant for its long record of human habitation.

Miller speculates on these early times: "It is interesting to think of the people who lived and hunted these extinct animals and the exciting things they witnessed, especially the volcanic activity going on around them." Floods of lava poured intermittently across the Snake River Plain, and while these early hunters pursued their prey, they no doubt kept a watchful eye on the eruptions along the Great Rift. Big Southern Butte west of Idaho Falls was already ancient, but seething hot lava still gushed from the fault line and spilled across the landscape in what must have been a frightening stream of molten rock. (See Craters of the Moon.)

The first pioneer to settle near Idaho Falls was Harry Rickets, who built a ferry nine miles upriver to cash in on the thousands of gold miners and freighters headed for Montana in 1863. Two years later, Matt Taylor built his famous toll bridge at the site of Idaho Falls. First called Taylor's Bridge, then Eagle Rock, the growing settlement took the name Idaho Falls in 1890, hoping to project a more dignified image. In 1912, a small dam to generate electricity was built above a series of riffles, and this created the falls we know today.

The early town prospered as a stage stop and train station along the Gold Road, but it went into a slump when the Utah & Northern shops moved to Pocatello. However, Mormon pioneers came to settle and farm, and with irrigation the volcanic soil yielded good crops of wheat, potatoes, and especially sugar beets. In 1903 the first sugar factory in Idaho was built at Lincoln, a short distance from Idaho Falls. It has long since shut down.

Tourism blossomed along with the potato crop. As early as 1890, Idaho Falls profited by catering to travelers heading for Yellowstone National Park, Henrys Lake, and other upper Snake River attractions. Railroad passengers detrained here and headed for Dan Clyne's livery to hire out a horse and buggy or to sign on with the tourist stagecoach for a jaunt into Yellowstone. The biggest factor in the growth of Idaho Falls, however, came much later, with the establishment in 1949 of the National Reactor Testing Station, known today as the Idaho National Engineering Laboratory (INEL).

In the early days of INEL, forecasters predicted the nearby town of Arco would boom. Instead, Idaho Falls took in the bevy of scientists and staff who built and sustained the engineering facility. Thousands of them commute daily to the desert labs fifty miles away. These professionals have high expectations for a quality lifestyle and have contributed much to the economic and cultural environment of the city.

Mormon Temple at Idaho Falls, located in a greenbelt along the Snake River across from the man-made falls.

Mormon Temple

The temple at Idaho Falls is one of more than fifty Mormon temples worldwide. Built in 1945 in an interesting Mayan style, with a ziggurat tower ascending twelve stories high, the exterior is finished in blocks of crushed onyx that sparkle in the sunshine and show impressively against the green landscaped park (which features 600 varieties of trees and shrubs, all labeled). The temple itself is open only to church members, who arrive constantly in groups of two or three or more to pass through the portals and receive a special blessing. The adjacent visitor center is open daily and welcomes guests.

Bonneville County Museum

The exhibits here relate the story of the county from the days of prehistoric elephant hunters to the nuclear age, conveying information on Indians, fur trappers, miners, and agriculture. At the mock-up of pioneer Eagle Rock, one can stroll down the boardwalk and peer into old-fashioned stores such as the millinery, photo shop, jail, blacksmith, country grocery, and apothecary. There is also a reading and reference room and a gift shop. The museum is located in the refurbished Carnegie Library building at Elm and Eastern streets.

Idaho National Engineering Laboratory

INEL is located on US 20 west of Idaho Falls, surrounded by 890 square miles of sagebrush desert. In this great, isolated expanse, research and development in nuclear and non-nuclear energy proceeds. The scientists who work here also expend considerable effort on chemical and biological research and on storage of nuclear waste from other sites. The controversial issue of spent-fuel storage has erupted time and again here. At stake is the Snake River aquifer, the region's primary source of underground water, which is covered only by a fragile, porous shield of desert mantle.

Part of the site (570,000 acres) is designated a National Environmental Research Park, where universities and research foundations conduct ecological studies. This is the largest undisturbed area of sagebrush vegetation in the Intermountain West. To the casual observer it appears barren, but more than 400 species of plants grow here, and a wide variety of animals— including elk, deer, and pronghorn antelope—inhabit the region.

Access to the installations at INEL is very restricted. However, the old 1951 Experimental Breeder Reactor (EBR-1) has been declared a National Historic Landmark and is open for tours during the summer and by special appointment at other times. In 1955 the town of Arco was lit up for two hours by one of the reactors here, the first usable electricity generated by atomic power. To get to INEL, take US 20 west about fifty miles from Idaho Falls.

DUBOIS

In the forty-eight miles between Dubois and Idaho Falls, the highway skirts three protected wildlife zones—Camas National Wildlife Refuge and the Mud Lake and Market Lake management areas. The lakes, ponds, and marshes here attract great numbers of migrating waterfowl. Wintertime brings elk, antelope, and a few moose. Wildlife biologists seed some areas to provide additional food and cover. In times past, both Indians and fur traders valued this region as a rich hunting ground where they restocked their larders.

Trapper Osborne Russell, on his way to Fort Hall in 1834, noted thousands of buffalo in this area. After a hard march he stopped to recuperate in celebration of the Fourth of July. He noted in his journal, "The next day being the 4th, I lay all day and watched the buffaloe which were feeding in immense bands . . . as far as the eye could reach." Later a band of friendly Bannocks came to hunt with bows and arrows and killed "upwards of a Thousand Cows . . . without burning one single grain of gun powder." When the hunt ended, Russell camped among the Indians' 332 lodges and watched the women prepare the meat and dry it over scaffolds that "bent beneath their rich loads of fat Buffaloe meat." After a couple of days, the young trapper left the village and proceeded on to Fort Hall "with a good supply of buffaloe tongues and the necessary directions and precautions from the old chief."

Nearby Market Lake got its name during pioneer times because settlers spoke of "going to market" here for their supplies of meat. The big game are no longer as abundant, but this habitat still witnesses a spectacular spring migration of waterfowl. During the last two weeks of March, as many as a million ducks and geese stop by to feed and rest en route to the north country. Altogether some 175 species inhabit the area, making this a prime location for bird watching and photography. Mud Lake is also a recreational area, with swimming, water skiing, camping, hiking, fishing, hunting, and snowmobiling among the most popular sports.

The isolated little town of Dubois got its start as a stage station on the Gold Road. Later it became a stop on the Utah & Northern Railroad. The abundant surrounding rangeland made it a natural center for cattle and sheep ranchers and led to its being selected in 1922 as the location for the U.S. Sheep Experiment Station (USSES), which continues today. A highly trained staff of geneticists works on new strains of breeds that develop superior fleece and meat. The center has achieved outstanding success with the Columbia, Rambouillet, Targee, and, lately, the Polypay strains. These are bred for multiple births (three to five), and lambing is regulated so that "spring lamb" can be marketed year-round.

Visitors, scientists, veterinarians, and ministers of agriculture from around the world come here to learn new techniques for an industry as old as Abraham. They find a fringe benefit in the unique guard dog program initiated by Dr. Jeffrey Green in 1977. He places Komondor and Great Pyrenees puppies among the sheep to begin a bonding process. By the time the pups are grown, they move with the flock as though born into it. Light in color, they blend in so well that coyotes and other predators are tricked into thinking they are sheep. These are not the usual "round 'em up Shep" dogs; they work on their own initiative, flushing out intruders with barks, threats, and hot pursuit. They rout bears, foxes, and eagles but are especially hard on the sheepmen's nemesis, coyotes.

Each spring crowds of farmers, ranchers, and hangers-on come to watch the station's authentic old-time sheep auction. Only the breeds are new. The proceeds of this lively sale add to the economic base of the USSES, which is a joint venture between the United States Department of Agriculture and the University of Idaho. Visitors are welcome, although a full tour should be arranged in advance.

Dr. John Stellflug and friends at the United States Sheep Experiment Station. These sheep of Polypay lineage replicate their numbers quickly, as multiple births of three to five lambs are common. This is only one of several breeds that have been developed since 1916.

Spencer lies on the Idaho-Montana line, in the wide-open spaces between Dubois and Monida. Livestock companies originally founded this community as a shipping center on the Utah & Northern Railroad. Today it is better known for the Spencer opal deposits. The best known site is the Deer Hunt mine, which has been popular with rock hounds around the world. For many years anyone could prospect in this open-pit mine and hope to pick up gem-quality opals for the price of a permit. In 1996, however, the mine plans to become a strictly commercial operation and will no longer be open to the public. The Spencer Opal Mine Shop downtown is a good place to see some opals.

The opals occur in a Tertiary-age rhyolite flow. Eons ago, gas bubbles formed in fluid magma and hot water loaded with silica percolated into these cavities. The silica was deposited in thin layers. Over time it became opalized. Idaho "fire opals" sparkle from refracted light in shades of green, yellow, pink, blue, and red.

From Spencer one can proceed north to Montana via I-15 or return to Dubois and take County Road A2 to Island Park. This road goes by Camas Meadows, which is one of numerous sites managed by the Nez Perce National Historic Park. It is also a National Historic Landmark. The Nez Perce camped here on their flight to Montana during the 1877 Nez Perce War. The road winds through miles of astonishingly beautiful high prairie grassland sheltered by the Centennial Mountains. It is approximately fifty miles to Island Park. Some travelers might prefer to travel from Spencer to Idaho Falls on I-15 and take US 20 from there to Island Park and Henrys Lake.

Henrys Fork Country

US 20, Idaho 48
RIGBY

About halfway between Idaho Falls and Rexburg is the little town of Rigby, distinguished as the hometown of Philo T. Farnsworth, the inventor of television. He worked out the basic formula when he was a high school student here and went on to perfect a working model as an adult. Farnsworth appeared on a United States 20-cent postage stamp honoring inventors. He patented more than 300 inventions in television and related fields and is best known for the first all-electric television transmission, which occurred in San Francisco on September 7, 1927. The downtown Jefferson County Historical Museum showcases this story in a Philo T. Farnsworth room.

The obscure settlement of Annis, five miles northwest of Rigby, is the birthplace of Vardis Fisher, a distinguished Idaho writer who also graduated from Rigby High School.

US 20, Idaho 33
REXBURG

Rexburg is located near the mouth of Henrys Fork of the Snake River, between the Teton River and the South Fork of the Snake, a spot with enviable recreational opportunities. This environment has allowed the town to make a good living by catering to "sunbirds." Every summer the population increases by about 1,500 as overheated southwestern residents come to town to rent student housing and to vacation here. The Tetons, Yellowstone, Craters of the Moon, and Henrys Lake are all easily accessible by day trips. And if these fail to please visitors, Rexburg itself provides a pleasant atmosphere. It has a solid agricultural base, a flourishing college, and an increasing tourist trade. The attractive little city is laid out in a grid pattern characteristic of Mormon towns. It has wide streets, attractive parks and playgrounds, and an air of wholesomeness about it that would rival that of a Norman Rockwell cover.

Porter Park

This nice city park is worth a stop, if only to ride the antique wooden carousel (summers only), a rare piece of art dating from the early 1900s. The 1976 Teton Dam flood caused serious damage to the old structure, so several local families each adopted a horse and helped restore these snorting beauties to their original glory. Now they glide to the tinkle of vintage carousel tunes that virtually nobody can resist.

Teton Dam Flood Museum and Rexburg Tabernacle

Displays here show the course of the 1976 flood, from the breaking of the dam to the recovery. A number of additional exhibits include pioneer relics and World War II items. Several unique films about the area are available for viewing, and the museum features a gift shop with an excellent choice of Idaho books.

The disastrous Teton Dam flood necessitated the rebuilding of a substantial part of Rexburg. The earth-filled 310-foot dam had barely been finished in 1976 when it broke. A wall of water gushed across the valley, sweeping up houses, cattle, trucks, refrigerators, and everything else in its wake. Tim Palmer describes the calamity in *The Snake River: Window to the West:*

> The dam failure killed eleven people, scoured 100,000 acres of farmland, obliterated thousands of buildings, drowned 16,000 head of livestock, flushed away toxic chemicals stored on the floodplain, and forced 25,000 people from their homes... [It] made mud-splattered carnage out of Sugar City, battered nearby Rexburg and Roberts along the Snake River, then inundated parts of Idaho Falls and Blackfoot.

The local civil defense organization, police, and volunteers worked frantically to alert people. National Guard helicopters came from Mountain Home Air Force Base to provide aerial surveillance and were able to pluck up at least one person clinging to a treetop. Ricks College, which was high and dry, opened its cafeteria to flood refugees and for a while fed approximately 36,000 people daily. Many families lost all they had—stores, homes, cattle, and even land that was gouged by the force of the water. Local resident Keith Walker observed, "Some of the big white houses and stuff that came from over above Smith Park floated on down Main Street. Logs, cattle and everything else floated by." The rampaging waters were finally contained at American Falls Dam.

A break in the Teton Dam poured tons of water into Rexburg and neighboring towns. The deluge raced across the wide valley floor until it stopped at American Falls Dam. —Rexburg Standard Journal

This historic building was originally the Rexburg Tabernacle, built in 1911 from native stone. Today it is launched on a second life as the town's civic center.

Ironically, one purpose of the dam was to control floods as well as to store irrigation water and to generate electric power. Few traces of the flood remain in Rexburg today. The town is so completely restored that the casual observer would never know a painful disaster struck here.

The Teton Dam Flood Museum is housed in the basement of the former Rexburg Tabernacle, an impressive structure on the National Register of Historic Places now on its second career as a cultural center. The building was built in 1911 from stone slabs quarried near Rexburg and laid up in an Italianate design with twin towers, rose windows, and Romanesque arches—hardly a typical country church. The auditorium is large and airy with superior acoustics, making it a natural location for community concerts, recitals, and lectures.

Ricks College

This delightful campus lies within three blocks of the city center. With approximately 7,000 students, Ricks is the largest private two-year college in the country. Each summer it hosts a number of Elderhostel programs and sponsors the widely acclaimed Idaho International Folk Dance Festival. Each August teams from around the world turn Rexburg into a folk village, with an eight-day fest of public performances, barbecues, hoedowns, and general fun. The college was founded in 1888 as an academy and was named after Thomas Ricks, a Mormon pioneer and one of the chief founders of Rexburg.

US 20
ST. ANTHONY

The Henrys Fork River runs through the middle of St. Anthony and provides a handy island for an attractive city park, the Keefer Memorial. The Targhee National Forest office is an excellent stop for travelers seeking information about the area.

St. Anthony's location made it a good bet for irrigated agriculture and commercial growth. In 1893, when the city center consisted of a mere two buildings, the town nabbed the county seat of giant Fremont County (before it was divided). Long before this it was an Indian and buffalo ground.

The Henrys Fork takes its name from fur trader Andrew Henry, who built a fort here in 1810, the first American post west of the Continental Divide. Henry and his band of trappers packed their gear and quit the Three Forks of the Missouri after losing several men in a skirmish with the Blackfeet Indians. They crossed the Rocky Mountains at Targhee Pass and traveled along the Henrys Fork, stopping near the present site of St. Anthony, where they erected cabins and spent the winter of 1810. Cold weather drove the friendly Shoshone Indians and buffalo farther south (perhaps to the Portneuf River), so the Americans spent an uneventful season living on horse meat and trapping a few beaver. In the spring they returned east of the mountains, leaving the deserted cabins to shelter one more famous band of adventurers.

Wilson Price Hunt and his party of Astorians took possession of the abandoned huts on a cold October day in 1811. They were traveling overland to scout opportunities for beaver en route to the Oregon coast while their supply ship, the *Tonquin*, sailed around Cape Horn. The two groups would rendezvous at the mouth of the Columbia River, where John Jacob Astor proposed to build Fort Astoria as headquarters for his Pacific Fur Company.

As soon as Hunt's weary travelers (who had departed from St. Louis the preceding fall) settled in on the Henrys Fork, they began building canoes in which they planned to glide down the Snake and Columbia rivers to their destination. They would leave their seventy-seven horses at the fort with two friendly Shoshone Indians. In seven days the eager trappers built fifteen canoes, loaded them with supplies, and prepared to embark on the uncharted stream. The French-Canadian voyageurs among them were ecstatic. They scorned overland travel and looked forward to this day when they could skim over the water, paddling to the cadence of rousing boat songs.

For approximately 150 miles, with only an occasional portage, the Astorians rode uneventfully along the Snake's swift flow. Then they came to the Devil's Scuttle Hole and Caldron Linn. This raging stretch of froth wrecked their canoes. Antoine Clappine drowned, "much goods" were lost, and the men decided to abandon the idea of floating to the Columbia. They dug sixteen caches in which to store their remaining supplies, and Hunt divided the travelers into three groups. At this time they numbered fifty-three persons including Marie Dorian, the Indian wife of interpreter Pierre Dorian, and her two children.

Each group made its way separately across the southern Idaho desert in an epic of hardship and disaster. By February 15 most of them had straggled into Fort Astoria. One man, Jean Baptiste Prevot, drowned while fording the Snake River near Homestead, Oregon. The Ramsey Crooks party, which wintered in the Blue Mountains, did not arrive at the fort until mid-May.

St. Anthony Sand Dunes

St. Anthony is probably best known for its sand dunes, which begin about twelve miles west of town. The dunes run for about fifteen miles, and some reach heights of 500 feet. It's a fascinating area for sightseers, picnickers, and folks who just want to dig their toes into soft sand. Wade Brown, a recreation planner for the Bureau of Land Management, says many visitors are curious about the dunes: "Busloads of them make their way out here just to look and to walk about in the sand." He adds with a sense of wonder, "The dunes are incredible. They don't seem to sit with the rest of the landscape"—which, incidentally, is spectacular itself, with the Tetons looming on the far horizon.

The dunes are part of the Sand Mountain Wilderness study area. Covering 10,000 acres, with an additional 10,000 acres of sage and juniper on the perimeter, this is a wintering range for 1,500 deer and 2,500 elk. Migrating geese and ducks stop at two seasonal lakes within the area, which come and go with the rise and fall of the water table. Because of its importance to wildlife, the area is closed during winter.

In spite of its mile-high altitude and short, eighty-six-day growing season, Ashton lies in the center of a rich farming area. Grains and seed potatoes thrive here, along with the inevitable sagebrush that creeps in around the edges. On this bountiful prairie between Falls River and the Henrys Fork are some sixty potato farms that raise certified seed stock for the famous Russet Burbank spuds. If you'd like to visit one of these potato farms, the staff at the Ashton City Building on Main Street will gladly arrange it. Planting usually takes place in May, harvesting in September and October.

Like many southern Idaho communities, Ashton traces its beginnings to the railroad and the rise of tourism. In 1905 the St. Anthony Railroad Company began an extension (later purchased by the Union Pacific) from Ashton to Yellowstone National Park and imported a bevy of Japanese and Greek tracklayers to get the job done. They earned $2 per twelve-hour day. By 1908 the woodlands between Ashton and Yellowstone (and north to the Montana border) had been set aside as the Targhee National Forest. The trains stopped running along the fifty-five-mile line years ago, and now the old roadbed serves as a trail for snowmobilers and cross-country skiers.

One of the ways Ashton capitalized on the railroad in the early days was by hosting an annual dogsled race, the Dog Derby, which began in 1917. Mushers came from far and near to compete for the $3,000 prize. Originally the race began at West Yellowstone and ended at Ashton, but one winter a blizzard almost buried the drivers and their dogs. The following year a twenty-two-mile course was laid out in a figure-eight pattern, which took the teams through Ashton twice but eliminated Yellowstone. Several times Tud Kent from Island Park won the money.

The derby occasionally had female competitors. An attractive young driver named Lydia Hutchinson scooped modern Iditarod musher Susan Butcher by almost seventy years. Lydia, or "Whistlin' Lyd," mushed her dogs through several races and helped gain a national audience for the Dog Derby. The Union Pacific promoted the event across the country by touting the pretty girl from Ashton who could compete with the best of them.

Mesa Falls Scenic Byway

Idaho 47 is the route to take if you enjoy looking at the landscape. This twenty-five-mile route leads to Upper and Lower Mesa Falls on the Henrys Fork River. At the falls, pristine water roars across the wide sweep of a cliff with a 114-foot drop. Clouds of swirling mist add a gossamer touch but cannot mask the thunderous power of the water that falls here. The Lower Falls drops 65 feet in a series of cascades easily seen from an overlook at

Grandview Campground. At the Upper Falls, a mile upstream and less than a mile off the highway on a well-maintained road, a 1907 lodge is being restored for use as an interpretive center. From the Upper Falls it is approximately twelve miles to US 20 and Harriman State Park.

Thunderous water at Upper Mesa Falls on the Henrys Fork of the Snake River north of Ashton.

HARRIMAN STATE PARK

This lovely place may be the crown jewel of the state park system. It encompasses 15,000 acres of forests, meadows, lakes, and streams that were once the playground of the Guggenheims and the Harrimans. A short drive past Silver Lake leads to an outdoor visitor center and the historic ranch buildings.

The Henrys Fork winds nine miles through the park, providing natural beauty as well as world-class fly-fishing. Hiking, horseback riding (the only such concession in an Idaho state park), and photography are also popular. Spectacular wildflower displays adorn the meadows, which are frequented by deer, elk, and moose. Bird watchers come to see the rare trumpeter swans, pelicans, eagles, ospreys, ducks, geese, and dozens of other species.

The park is open year-round, and in the wintertime eleven miles of groomed trails await cross-country skiers. Many vacationers prefer the quiet beauty of winter to the bustle of the busier summer season. This is a day-use-only park, except that groups of fifteen to forty people can rent the old ranch cookhouse and dormitory. Campgrounds and lodges are available in the adjacent Island Park area.

Back in 1902, this area was owned by the Island Park Land and Cattle Company, later called the Railroad Ranch. The Guggenheims, who made their fortune in mining, owned most of the shares in the enterprise. But the Harrimans, best known as shareholders in the Union Pacific Railroad, and a latecomer, Charles Jones, of Atlantic Richfield Oil Company (now ARCO), also had interests in the ranch. The property doubled as a working ranch and vacation haven. In *Harriman*, Mary Reed and Keith Peterson's history of the family, Roland Harriman recalls, "It was a matter of love at first sight for all of us. The glorious scenery and weather, the fishing, the hunting, the horseback riding and learning the lore of cattle handling, all combined to lure us back there summer after summer." Friends were often invited. In 1913 naturalist John Muir spent ten idyllic days here. He was delighted with the serene landscape and especially the river, "winding in shimmering ripples through the broad meadows."

As the years went by, the owners thought more of conserving this favored spot as a wildlife refuge and less of trying to make it pay as a working ranch. Eventually, Roland and Averill Harriman acquired all shares in the operation. Neither could face the prospect of relinquishing the land as an uncontrolled real estate development "with hot dog stands and cheap honky tonks." So they began negotiating with Governor Robert Smylie to transfer their ownership to the state. In 1961 Roland and Gladys Harriman and Averill Harriman provided by will that the coveted Railroad Ranch would go to the state of Idaho, with several stipulations. One called for the preservation of a safe habitat for trumpeter swans, and another required the development of a professionally-staffed department to manage the park. The latter condition sparked the 1965 legislation that created the Idaho Department of Parks and Recreation.

The Harrimans continued operating the ranch until April 1, 1977, when they presented the park by gift deed to the state. A week later the Department of Parks and Recreation sent Gene Eyraud in as park manager and enlisted former ranch hand Rand Sandow as his assistant. Together they studied the area and planned how best to blend this natural resource with the considerable number of people who would come with the opening of the park. Both state and federal conservation grants facilitated their work. In 1982 Harriman State Park opened to the public.

US 20
ISLAND PARK

Island Park is one of those places with nebulous boundaries that often confuse visitors. In the late 1890s, Island Park became a rest stop for the Yellowstone stage, which pulled up in a natural clearing that resembled an island in the midst of the heavy forest. A small village grew here along the stage road. When the modern highway came through in 1916, the route changed slightly, and the village moved to the present site of Pond's Lodge but kept the name Island Park. Over the years the community witnessed an accretion of stores, campgrounds, and motels, until today the town's main street stretches out for some twenty-five miles along the Henrys Fork. Generally speaking, it begins below Harriman State Park and continues to Henrys Lake.

This whole area shares a common geology, the Island Park Caldera. As Terry Maley explains in *Exploring Idaho Geology*, two major cycles of volcanic activity began about 2 million years ago. In each cycle, hot spots about six miles below the surface of the earth filled with boiling magma. The episodes climaxed with an eruption of molten material that spewed out of a dome-shaped chamber. When it was about empty, the dome collapsed, leaving a huge double crater. After each cycle, a series of lesser eruptions partly filled the caldera and built up a lava plateau. Eventually, the waters of the Henrys Fork established a path through the caldera floor, which is approximately eighteen miles wide and twenty-five miles long. Evidence of the craters is not obvious to the casual observer except at the north end of the valley, where a piece of the old crater rim forms the mountain backdrop for Henrys Lake. Four miles south of the lake, another section of rim stands free as Sawtell Peak, just a whisper under 10,000 feet.

Island Park has several centers of activity where gas, groceries, restaurants, camping, and all kinds of rental gear are available. Most of these facilities are located along US 20, although the side roads feature several hunting and fishing lodges and campgrounds. Stop at the Island Park forest service office for directions.

Island Park Reservoir, a popular spot for boating, fishing, and water skiing, is accessible from County Road A2 about a mile beyond Pond's Lodge on the Buffalo River. Buffalo Campground near Pond's Lodge offers fishing for handicapped individuals.

US 20, Idaho 84
BIG SPRINGS

Considered part of the headwaters of the Henrys Fork (which actually begins at the lake's outlet twelve miles upriver), Big Springs emerges from the Yellowstone aquifer. Each day, 420 million gallons of water flow from the springs at a constant temperature of 52 degrees Fahrenheit, creating a perfect environment for the giant rainbow trout that live here. Visitors are fascinated with these beauties, but leave your pole in the car—fishing here is illegal. Johnny Sack's hand-built cabin stands in rustic splendor across the

Johnny Sack's cabin and pump house at Big Springs in Island Park. The abundance of clear spring water and the rustic cabins continually draw visitors. This young boy particularly likes the schools of eighteen-inch trout that make their home here.

pond, and its miniature copy—a pump house with a waterwheel alongside—sits close by the water's edge. Virtually nobody leaves without shooting a roll of film.

Johnny Sack was a favorite local character in the first half of the twentieth century. He was a bachelor "with a heart of gold." Estelle Irving Phillips wrote in her diary (quoted in *Snake River Echoes*) that he was "a queer little man, Rumplestiltskin I call him to myself. . . . He was about five feet tall, gray and grizzled, with a wild, snapping pair of blue eyes, and the longest arms and the loudest voice one could imagine." After about thirty years, Johnny became pretty disgusted that so many people were moving into Island Park and threatened to leave: "Nothing but a lot of hard roads for automobiles and you hardly ever see a horse anymore; the creeks all fished out and a lot of dude camps stuck around on the best places and women and kids yelling all the time just spoiling everything so there ain't room for a man no more. So I am a'gitten out!"

Instead of "a'gitten out," he built a home at Big Springs in 1932. It became something of a tourist mecca, along with the springs. His guest book listed thousands of visitors from every state. They were enchanted with this place, his house, and the unique furniture he made. Johnny might have complained about being crowded out, but he enjoyed company, had scores of friends, and even hosted a few famous guests (such as film star Wallace Berry, who was a frequent visitor).

After Johnny died in 1957, the Forest Service considered tearing down his cabins to carry out a policy of obliterating human development in the forest. However, thanks to a determined local outcry and the good offices of Senator James McClure and Dr. Merle Wells at the Idaho Historical Society, Johnny's place gained a spot on the National Register of Historic Places and was saved.

US 20, Idaho 87
HENRYS LAKE

Henrys Lake sits at the base of the Henrys Lake Mountains at the north end of Island Park, five miles from the Montana border and fifteen miles from Yellowstone National Park. Over the years it has been a favorite fishing and camping location, enhanced by the addition of Henrys Lake State Park on the south shore. This day-use and overnight facility offers fishing, boating, water skiing, and bird watching, among other activities.

The south shore borders a wide-open prairie called Henrys Lake Flat, where herds of antelope come and go and where wildflowers ripple across the plain in the springtime. On the north and west, the lake is bordered by the Targhee National Forest. Idaho 87 leads to the wooded north shore, winding past several fishing lodges and a state fish hatchery. Beyond Wild

Rose Ranch the highway goes on to Montana at Reynolds Pass. Forest Road 055 continues around the northwest shore to Staley Springs, about eight miles from US 20. A loop can be made by continuing on FR 055 until it joins FR 053, which returns to US 20 after an additional twelve miles.

The lake bed formed perhaps 10,000 years ago when glaciers covered the old caldera lava and gouged out a depression that later filled with water. From early times, both the Shoshone-Bannock and Blackfeet Indians camped here. It was not only an important fishery for them but also a gateway to the buffalo country via Targhee Pass (named for a Bannock chief) and the Three Forks of the Missouri. One trail traversed the length of Island Park to where the reservoir now stands, then continued west across Shotgun Valley to Dubois and the Montana Trail; another continued south from Island Park to the Teton River country.

The first white men known to have traveled these Indian trails were Andrew Henry's Missouri Fur Company trappers, who left the upper Missouri in a hurry ahead of Blackfeet warriors in the fall of 1810. They crossed Targhee Pass and traveled down the northern fork of the Snake to the Teton River, where they built Fort Henry (see St. Anthony). They soon moved on, but Wilson Price Hunt and the overland Astorians followed in their wake, naming both the river and the lake after Henry. Legions of fur trappers followed and crisscrossed southeastern Idaho in search of beaver, making the river trail a major thoroughfare.

As the years went by, many notables graced the shores of Henrys Lake, including Jesuit missionary Father Pierre Jean De Smet, who performed mass here with a delegation of Flathead Indians in 1840. Chief Joseph and hundreds of Nez Perce Indians rested here briefly on their historic flight from the U.S. Cavalry in 1877. Yellow Wolf remembered, "It was, I think, twelve suns from the [Battle of the] Big Hole [August 9, 1877] that we camped on the southwest side of a fine lake. Camped for about one sun then we went through a gap [Targhee Pass] into the Yellowstone Park." Their pursuers, Gen. O. O. Howard and his cavalry troops, lagged a few days behind, but when they made Henrys Lake, they, too, stopped here to bivouac.

The first settler at Henrys Lake was Gilman Sawtell, whose name is given to the peak that dominates the landscape south of the lake. He came in 1868 and claimed choice ground around Staley Springs. Among his early guests were photographer William Henry Jackson and a small detachment from the Hayden survey party. This famous group had camped on the Wyoming side of the mountains to document the wonders of the Yellowstone country prior to its becoming a national park. Jackson also wanted to see the country west of the Tetons and received permission for a three-week leave. In August 1872, the surveyors landed at Henrys Lake fresh from a photo opportunity in the Teton Valley. During their visit with Sawtell, Jackson took the first known pictures of Henrys Lake and the pioneer ranch.

Island Park sourdoughs at the Sawtell Cabin, 1872. —William Henry Jackson, National Archives

Sawtell was a stockman, but he also earned money from the natural bounty in the lake. He harvested thousands of fish and marketed them via the Utah & Northern Railroad (probably out of Spencer) to the mining camps at Virginia City and Helena, Montana. According to Charles Brooks in *The Henrys Fork*, an 1890s settler named Joe Sherwood estimated that 90,000 pounds of fish were taken from the lake each winter. Sherwood operated a general store, hotel, and post office known for years simply as "Lake." Many significant artifacts from his businesses are now kept by the Idaho Historical Society.

Young Harry Gordon arrived at Henrys Lake in 1889 and wrote to his brothers in Michigan about two fellows who were landing 1,000 trout a day. Harry decided to join the fishing fraternity. Eventually the catch dropped to only about 50 per day, so Harry concocted a scheme to harvest greater numbers. He rigged up "a wire gaff hook" and, to keep others from doing the same, pretended it was something special he had ordered from back east. "A luminous bait," he called it, and it worked like a charm. While his fishing buddies remained in the doldrums, he pulled in 300 to 400 fish per day and sold them for a nickel a pound. Two years later he was still catching 300 per day, and the market price had increased by three cents.

The fishing at Henrys Lake lasted a remarkably long time, considering the influx of settlers and the numbers of tourists who pounded the waters. Yellowstone cutthroat were prolific in the early days. Other native fish included sculpins and Rocky Mountain whitefish. Today most of the fish are planted, and the prize to catch is a Henrys Lake rainbow-cutthroat hybrid. Many fisherman have long considered these the best trout fishing waters in the country. In *The Henrys Fork*, local resident and writer Charles Brooks says: "It is perhaps the finest trout fishing lake in the contiguous forty-eight states. One says, 'perhaps' because these things cannot be measured like a piece of string."

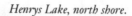

Henrys Lake, north shore.

In recent years, when it looked as if the quality of the fishery was in decline, Brooks spearheaded the establishment of the Henrys Lake Foundation. This organization works in cooperation with the state Fish and Game department and local ranchers to manage not only the lake but also the snow-fed streams flowing into it. The growing success of the foundation has become a happy story of people working together to defend a unique piece of nature's handiwork.

US 20

YELLOWSTONE NATIONAL PARK

The western edge of Yellowstone National Park lies in Idaho, and the town of West Yellowstone, Montana, lies just fifteen miles from Henrys Lake. Given the crowds that surge into the park every summer, the lake is a good choice for overnight lodging.

The days when Harry Gordon lived here are long gone. After a trip to Yellowstone in July 1891, he wrote home that he was amazed to see "48 tourists there over Sunday." Larger crowds were not long in coming. After the turn of the century, long lines of stagecoaches rolled in from Virginia City and Salt Lake City loaded with sightseers. Tourists then and now marvel at the grandeur of the mountains, the curiosity of the geysers, and the smell of boiling mud pots. Some early travelers, however, also experienced the excitement of stage robberies.

One of the most ambitious stickups occurred during the summer of 1908, when seventeen stages were robbed in the same heist. The coaches were spaced about 100 feet apart because of the dust that rolled up between them. When the robber stopped the first one, the whole line came to a standstill. The coaches in the rear had no idea what the delay was until a masked bandit appeared with his helper, a frightened lad from the first stage. He carried a pillowcase, holding it open wide so the passengers could deposit their money and valuables. "The trembling boy and the desperado moved down the line of seventeen coaches and collected $1,369.95 in cash and $730.25 worth of jewelry," wrote H. Leigh Gittins in *Idaho's Gold Road*. "That evening at the Lake Hotel, the 152 holdup victims called it the greatest stagecoach holdup and robbery of the 20th Century. The bandit was never caught."

A few years later, another string of coaches was quietly robbed in a similar manner, this time with distinguished persons aboard. One was U.S. Senator James H. Brady from Pocatello, and the other was Bernard Baruch, an adviser who served several presidents. He threw his money in the pot and later said, "It was the best $50 I ever spent."

Teton Valley

US 26, Idaho 31, 32, and 33
TETON SCENIC BYWAY
SWAN VALLEY, VICTOR, AND DRIGGS

The Teton Valley can be approached from Idaho Falls, Rexburg, or Alpine, Wyoming, although the Idaho Falls route is perhaps the most frequently used. Leave Idaho Falls heading southeast on US 26, and at Swan Valley turn north on Idaho 31, the Teton Scenic Byway.

About forty-five miles from Idaho Falls, US 26 crosses the Snake River and enters the small settlement of Swan Valley, named for trumpeter swans. The town's fly shops and fishing lodges cater to those who seek access to the Teton River and some of the country's finest wild trout fishing. If you continue along US 26, you will travel a scenic stretch of roadway that skirts the Palisades Reservoir before reaching Alpine, Wyoming, after about twenty-eight miles. High mountains, green forests, and groves of aspens make this drive special any time of the year.

The Teton Valley begins about twenty miles north of Swan Valley at the town of Victor and continues for twenty miles across spectacular country to Driggs and Tetonia. The valley was originally called Pierre's Hole. The

A field of potatoes in the Teton Valley, where many of the Idaho spuds are grown for seed. —Idaho Potato Commission

Skiing Grand Targhee in the Tetons near Driggs.
—Grand Targhee Resort

early fur traders who named the landscape often called valleys "holes." This valley honors old Pierre Tevanitagon, an Iroquois trapper and one-time Hudson's Bay Company employee who made a lasting contribution to the fur trade. He was an old hand at fighting the Blackfeet. However, he saw one skirmish too many and "went under" near the headwaters of the Jefferson River while en route to Cache Valley (Utah) with a party of American trappers in 1828.

The grandeur that attracted the fur traders to this spot still inspires travelers and modern settlers. Rarely does a mountain range rise up so dramatically from a flat valley floor. The astonishing three Teton peaks pierce the clouds at 13,000 feet. The Jedediah Smith Wilderness blankets their western slopes, and the valley is intersected by the Teton River and other small streams, completing a vista of singular beauty. More and more people discover this quiet refuge each year.

Teton County includes the whole valley, with Driggs as the county seat. It is the largest of the valley towns, which altogether number fewer than 3,500 people. Since the earliest settlers came, the economy has depended on agriculture, especially cattle ranching, grains, and seed potatoes. But that's changing now as tourism grows in popularity and more people enter this high country in need of services. Crowds flock to the Grand Targhee Ski Resort twelve miles from Driggs. Three hundred miles of forest trails attract hikers and mountain bikers. Fishing, hunting, sightseeing, and special events bring still more visitors. One resident says, "We are no longer a little laid-back farming community. We have lots of people from New York and California. Some from the Midwest are beginning to come—Wisconsin, Minnesota. We are becoming a melting pot. A mixture of city folks, ski bums, and farmers."

This area has always been a popular place to live. Before white settlers arrived, the Teton Valley was home to the Shoshone Indians, although the Montana Blackfeet visited often to fish, hunt, or raid whoever else might be here. The first white man known to have entered the valley was John Colter, who came west with Lewis and Clark. As the expedition returned east, Colter remained in the mountains and was the first to report on the wonders of Yellowstone. Few believed his wild tales, and the place he spoke of was called "Colter's Hell." In 1807 he joined forces with fur trader Manuel Lisa, who built a post on the Bighorn River and soon afterward dispatched Colter to visit the Indian tribes—Flatheads, Crows, Shoshone-Bannocks, even Blackfeet—and to bring them in to trade. During this trek, Colter traveled through Jackson Hole and crossed the mountains into the Teton Valley, probably during the spring of 1808. He mapped his journey, and the Teton geography was later included on Capt. William Clark's map of the far west.

Colter's most famous adventure took place east of the mountains, near the Three Forks of the Missouri. He and his partner, John Potts, were trapping in Blackfeet country during the fall of 1808. As they ascended the Jefferson River, each in his own canoe, a group of Blackfeet appeared along the bank and signaled them to come ashore. Potts refused and was killed. Colter landed, and the Indians stripped him naked and challenged him to outpace their arrows. The prize for the warrior who killed him would be his scalp. Colter misled them into thinking he was slow of foot, so his captors sportingly gave him a head start. He took advantage of the lead and sprinted toward the Madison River, some five miles away, across a plain covered with grass and prickly pear. The pack of warriors followed in hot pursuit, but Colter stayed well ahead of all but one brave.

After about four miles, desperately tired and bleeding from his nose, Colter heard the footsteps of his closest pursuer. Since he could go no faster, he stopped suddenly and faced the equally exhausted warrior. This surprised the Indian and caused him to miss his footing as he lunged to spear the white man. Colter grabbed the weapon, pinned his adversary to the ground, and safely made for the river. Unable to continue running and with no inviting place to hide, he plunged into the water near a pile of driftwood and hid beneath the shelter of debris. He stayed in the icy water until nightfall while his angry pursuers scoured the riverbanks looking for him, sometimes standing on top of his cover. He managed to escape after dark and in the next eleven days traveled more than 250 miles to Lisa's fort at the mouth of the Bighorn River.

Both British and American trappers knew the Teton Valley well, but it was the Americans who used it for their famous rendezvous. The British traveled in large "brigades" that the Hudson's Bay Company outfitted from permanent supply depots such as Fort Spokane. The Americans, however, from 1824 to 1838 relied solely on caravans of goods packed into the mountains from St. Louis. Suppliers, trappers, and Indian allies met annually at designated locations for great trading fairs. The mountain men exchanged furs for tobacco, gunpowder, whiskey, trade beads, new blankets, and other necessities. Beaver pelts provided the currency, and trade was conducted in a mixture of dialects. This was the social event of the year, a great bash with games, races, yarn spinning, and whiskey drinking. A trapper might spend a year's worth of skins at a rendezvous and be dead broke after ten days of revelry.

The largest and most picturesque rendezvous was held in Pierre's Hole in July 1832. Many men brought Indian wives and mixed-blood children, and new groups straggled in each day until perhaps a thousand people (according to famed mountain man Joe Meek) were scattered about, each group in its own camp. William Sublette's supply caravan from St. Louis arrived first, along with Nathaniel Wyeth and his band of greenhorns. Parties of the Rocky Mountain Fur Company and American Fur Company mingled with free trappers and Flathead and Nez Perce allies. Lodges lined the streambanks. Young Indian women wore their finest buckskins awash with shells, feathers, beads, and froufrou in anticipation of the party.

This colossal gathering was distinguished by some memorable events. One was the late arrival of Thomas Fitzpatrick, who appeared like an apparition, battered and weary from a harrowing encounter with the Blackfeet. Rendezvous 1832 is also remembered for the Battle of Pierre's Hole. When the liquor was gone and the trade goods had been distributed, the various groups broke camp. Milton Sublette, the Wyeth party, and a few independent trappers set out first. They traveled about eight miles, then made camp near the present site of Driggs. The next morning, they watched a line of Gros Ventres ease their way down a pass into the valley. The chief advanced holding a peace pipe, apparently wanting to parley. Antoin Godin and a Flathead companion rode out to meet him. When the chief extended his hand in friendship, the Flathead raised his rifle and shot him, and Godin snatched the scarlet blanket he wore. This was blood revenge for Godin, whose father had been scalped by Gros Ventres. The triumphant pair rode off unscathed, but the Battle of Pierre's Hole was on.

The beleaguered group sent a runner back to the main camp for reinforcements. Soon, according to Zenas Leonard's narrative, "200 whites, 200 Flatheads and 300 Nez Perce" joined them. Greatly outnumbered, the Gros Ventres retreated to a willow thicket behind a breastwork of logs. Daredevils such as William Sublette and Robert Campbell advanced perilously close to the enemy's fortifications, making oral wills as they went. Fitzpatrick was also in the thick of it, along with old hands Milton Sublette, Joe Meek, and Zenas Leonard, all of whom escaped in one piece. William Sublette was shot in the arm. Sniping continued all afternoon, but during the night most of the Gros Ventres stole away to lick their wounds. Zenas Leonard reported, "5 whites, 8 Flatheads and 10 Nez Perces killed, besides a large number of whites and Indians wounded." Gros Ventres losses were estimated at 26.

The trappers dressed their wounds and prepared to leave the Teton Valley to set their traps in Rocky Mountain streams. William Sublette, with about sixty men, returned to St. Louis loaded with 169 packs of beaver pelts that would sell for approximately $60,000. Washington Irving witnessed their return to western Missouri two months later and reported that the cavalcade stretched out single file for half a mile, its members looking "like banditti returning with plunder." Sublette still wore his arm in a sling.

Teton Valley Events

The Teton Valley Balloon Festival is one of the biggest celebrations of the year. Thousands of visitors gather to watch as balloons with names such as Stardrifter, Diamond Clipper, and Windsong ascend in a symphony of color against this unique mountain backdrop. Participants come from throughout the West. The event takes place annually in Driggs on the Fourth of July weekend.

The colorful August Rendezvous recreates the historic days of Indians and fur traders, with just about all the trappings of that wild frontier. Among the many activities are black-powder shoots, campfires, flint knapping, and a John Colter footrace commemorating his escape from the Blackfeet. Plenty of trading posts are on hand, too.

Pierre's Playhouse, a summer theater at Victor, has delighted theatergoers since the 1960s. Villainous hiss-and-boo melodramas such as *Lily the Virtuous Seamstress* are favorites. Make reservations early.

TETONIA

The Teton Scenic Byway continues to Tetonia at the north end of the valley. Here one can head west on Idaho 33, which passes close to the site of the failed Teton Dam and leads to the city of Rexburg, or continue the scenic byway on Idaho 32, which leads to Ashton and Mesa Falls.

The drive between Tetonia and Ashton is one of scenic splendor. The road crosses miles of rolling hills, none of which are large enough to obscure the view of the Tetons at ten or twenty or even fifty miles. Northbound travelers may have to stop frequently and look back, but on the trip south from Ashton the mountains are always in view. In the spring, green fields of wheat and barley blanket the hills just about as far as the eye can see. At harvest time their rounded contours make golden waves across the landscape, a marvelous sight under a great blue dome of sky with the Tetons on the far horizon.

During pioneer days many little villages lay scattered among these hills. Severe winters demanded that a country store and post office be within easy reach by team and sled. With the advent of modern transportation and communications, however, these hill towns dwindled away. Now snow-crazed recreationists come here because of the long winters.

The Teton Scenic Byway meets US 20 at Ashton, where drivers can proceed north to Island Park and Yellowstone or south to Rexburg, Idaho Falls, and Pocatello.

Portneuf Valley

US 30
LAVA HOT SPRINGS

Pocatello is the main gateway to the southeastern corner of Idaho, which includes the Portneuf Valley, Lava Hot Springs, and the Bear River country. Drive south on I-15 through the Portneuf River canyon. Take exit 47 at McCammon and follow old US 30 along the river to Lava Hot Springs. US 30 is a historic route that generally follows the Oregon Trail across southern Idaho, sometimes merging with I-84 or I-86, and sometimes standing alone, as it does in the extreme southeast.

Forbidden dip at Lava Hot Springs, circa 1920. —Idaho State Historical Society

Lava Hot Springs is a charming resort situated along the Portneuf River. A scallop of mountains cuts the sky behind Main Street and shelters the fabulous hot springs complex, where travelers and locals alike "take the waters." Lately the business community has accelerated as urban and suburban people have arrived to share in the wonderful rural lifestyle. One of these newcomers, a corporate dropout, takes pride in the new sidewalks and street lamps and in the restoration of many downtown buildings. All this reflects the prosperity generated by outdoor recreation.

In this year-round playground, the hot pools are always popular. Fall brings elk and deer hunters, and winter brings snowmobilers, who come to enjoy the 250 miles of trails. Cross-country ski trails are accessible from town, and downhill skiers can drive just 35 miles to the slopes at Pebble Creek. Lava's primary attraction, however, is its complex of pools for swimming and soaking. The geothermal waters are odorless, colorless, and constantly flowing; they have been for 50 million years. Originally the hot springs were part of the Shoshone-Bannock reservation set up in 1867. When the southern part of the reservation was taken in 1902 (see Pocatello), the springs were deeded to the state of Idaho. Over the years the state-directed Lava Hot Springs Foundation has developed this world-class facility.

A cluster of four soaking pools (two with jets) is open year-round. These bone-warming beauties keep constant temperatures of 104 to 110 degrees Fahrenheit and are aesthetically placed at the base of a lava cliff, where landscaped terraces form the backdrop. At the other end of town, an award-winning Olympic-sized swimming pool and its AAU companion are open May to September. The Portneuf River flowing through town is a first-class trout stream and an enticing summer float, especially for kids. Other local attractions include the Mountain Man Rendezvous and the Pioneer Days gala, held every July.

The Portneuf River (named for Joseph Portneuf, a French-Canadian trapper) figured prominently in the fur trade. The stream was rich in beaver, and British and American trappers visited the area many times. A generally mild climate made this valley popular as a winter campground for Indians and trappers alike. Capt. Benjamin Bonneville spoke of camping on the Portneuf one winter with a band of Bannocks and mentioned the "fine springs of water and grass in abundance . . . and large trout darting about in the transparent water." Early one winter, William Sublette and party came to "lay in a supply of buffalo."

Olympic-sized pool at Lava Hot Springs.

Steam rises from one of several hot pools in the Lava Hot Springs complex.

61

Joe Meek and a band of Rocky Mountain fur men left the Snake River, where "fuel war scarce," and moved into the Portneuf Valley during the winter of 1832–33. Cold weather plagued them here, too, but it also provided a classic bear story. In *River of the West*, Frances Fuller Victor recorded Meek's recollections of the bitter weather that winter, when frost hung in skeins from the roofs of their lodges "and our blankets and whiskers war white with it." Food was scarce; hunting parties usually returned to camp with nothing but jackrabbits. Meek tells of tramping the mountainsides for days and seeing nothing of consequence until they came upon a set of grizzly bear tracks.

The "bar" had obviously come out of a nearby cavern to test the weather, sniffed a frigid blast, and returned to the den. The trappers followed the tracks and parleyed long about who was "up to bar." Finally Meek and two others agreed to venture into the murky cave and drive the grizzly out. The rest of the party would sit above the cave entrance and shoot the bruin when it emerged. The men entered the cave and found a mother with two half-grown cubs, drowsy from hibernating. Wanting only to escape the clamor let loose by the intruders, the bears bolted one by one out the front door, where the hunters shot them down. Upon hearing the dispatch of gunfire, one of the men inside the den began shouting with delight, "We're Daniels in the lion's den!" Soon they all took up the euphoric chant. Joe Meek later added, "Of course, it war winter and the lions war sucking their paws." The elated hunters rigged sleds made of mountain willows and hauled the meat to the hungry camp in the valley below.

One of the last fur trappers in the area was Jack Dempsey, who made his camp close to the site of Lava Hot Springs. He did a brisk business in horse trading with Oregon Trail emigrants who left the main trail at Soda Springs and struck off for California on Hudspeth's Cutoff. This route of the '49ers led directly to "Dempsey's Hot Tub." As ranchers took up land in the Portneuf Valley, a community developed at Dempsey. In 1915 the town was incorporated and named Lava Hot Springs.

The handsome South Bannock Museum provides excellent interpretive displays of local history, with exhibits on Indians, mountain men, pioneer trails, railroads, and the famous hot springs.

Chesterfield

A side trip to Chesterfield requires leaving US 30 about five miles east of Lava Hot Springs. Turn north on East Road and continue fifteen miles. This isolated settlement near the headwaters of the Portneuf River represents the dashed hope of some Mormon settlers who expected the place to become a town of size and importance. Instead it was plagued by grasshoppers and cold winters, which reduced it to a near-abandoned state. Today the well-preserved nineteenth-century village of brick and stone buildings is on the National Register of Historic Places and is well worth the drive.

Daughters of the Utah Pioneers operate a museum (open only on special occasions) at the hilltop chapel, dedicated in 1892.

Bear River Country

SODA SPRINGS

Soda Springs, near the junction of the historic California and Oregon trails, presents a modest appearance at first glance. A bit of nosing around, however, reveals some unusual features behind an ordinary facade. This is an important phosphate center and the only town in Idaho with a geyser in its backyard. It also enjoys a crossroad location at the top of the Bear River loop. Idaho 34, a gateway to the Teton Valley, connects Soda Springs with Preston and Franklin via the Pioneer Historic Byway. The Caribou Scenic Byway takes a more easterly direction and leads to Montpelier and the Bear Lake settlements. Don't look for caribou along this route. The name comes from "Caribou" Fairchilds, a prospector who was famous for telling tales about his experiences in the Caribou mines of British Columbia.

Indians called the area around Soda Springs "Tsoiba," or "sparkling waters," because of the dozens of bubbling fountains and mineral springs dotting the landscape. Fur traders called it Beer Springs and never missed an opportunity to camp here. Captain Bonneville made note of one "beer frolic" when his party stopped here in 1832. According to Washington Irving, writing in *The Adventures of Captain Bonneville,* "In a few minutes every spring had its jovial knot of hard drinkers, with tin cup in hand, indulging in mock carousel, quaffing, pledging, toasting, bandying jokes, singing drinking songs and uttering peals of laughter."

When Soda Springs became a key point on the Oregon Trail, thousands of emigrants stopped here long enough to camp and partake of the waters. In *Historic Sites along the Oregon Trail,* Aubrey L. Haines quotes observations from several diaries. One passage, written by William J. Scott on August 14, 1846, reads: "The Sody Springs is aquite acuriosity thare is agreat many of them Just boiling rite up out of the ground take alitle sugar and desolve it in alitle water and then drink up acup full and drink it before it looses its gass it is furstrate. I drank ahol gallon of it." Another traveler recommended adding lemon syrup "to render it perfect soda water." Perhaps most unusual was the comment of Sarah White Smith, quoted in David Crowder's *Tales of Eastern Idaho:* "We find it excellent for making bread. No preparation of the water is necessary, take it from the fountain & the bread is as light as any prepared with yeast."

The main route of the Oregon Trail entered Idaho near Montpelier and followed the Bear River to Soda Springs. With the discovery of gold in California, '49ers joined the Oregon-bound emigrants and traveled the same route until they reached Soda Point, two miles west of town. Here the trail to California veered south toward Raft River, Salt Lake, and the Sierras. Thus, Soda Springs became the junction of two great western trails.

In the early years of emigration, Indians tended to let pioneers pass unmolested. But when the trickle became an endless column of covered wagons, trailed by herds of livestock that grazed the country bare, the Shoshone-Bannock turned unfriendly. They preyed on stragglers and small groups, killing the people and plundering their goods. Near the site of Soda Springs, a family of seven was killed during the migration of 1861. Later travelers discovered the bodies and conducted a funeral service, interring a man, a woman, and their five children in their wagon box. A monument to the "wagon box grave" stands a short distance from town.

Such attacks led the government to establish a military fort at Soda Springs. In 1863 Col. Patrick E. Conner arrived from Utah with a detachment of troops and 100 Morrisites, dissenters from the Mormon Church who hoped to establish homes. However, both the fort and the Morristown settlement were soon abandoned. A successful colony finally took root when Brigham Young, Charles C. Rich, and other Mormon leaders came to lay

Phosphate mining at Conda early in the twentieth century before the open-pit method was used. Old style shaft and tunnel techniques required a lot of underground work. —Idaho State Historical Society

the groundwork. The place flourished and took the name Soda Springs. When the Oregon Short Line Railroad came to town in 1882, its future was assured.

By the beginning of the twentieth century, Soda Springs had become a major shipping center for sparkling water, wool, and livestock. Agriculture was the mainstay, but the economy began to change after the Anaconda Copper Company opened its Conda phosphate mine in 1906. Boyd Cooke, ranger for the Caribou National Forest, says deposits extend over an area of approximately 100 miles in a geologic formation called the Overthrust Belt. The phosphorite deposit extends into Utah, Wyoming, and Montana, although most of it is in southeastern Idaho. Called the Western Phosphate Field, it contains about 45 percent of total U.S. reserves.

Five major companies—Simplot, Monsanto, FMC, Conda Partnership, and Rhone-Povlenc—operate mines and/or processing plants around Soda Springs, providing the main economic base for the town. The local payroll

Phosphate mine near Soda Spings. Phosphate-rich sediment was deposited in a shallow sea perhaps 250 million years ago in Permian times. As a result of tectonic activity and crustal folding, the mineral lies in long, relatively shallow beds, as shown here.

*As mining progresses, dirt stripped from the surface
is continually backfilled for contouring and planting.*

In twenty years' time, a restored phosphate site blends in with the landscape.

for mining, processing, and distribution of phosphate and associated products is estimated to be nearly $15 million annually, and the reserves are projected to last another hundred years.

Phosphate sediments consisting of minute shells and other organic material accumulated on the floor of a shallow sea during Permian times, some 250 million years ago. Mountain-building events approximately 150 million years ago caused this ancient seabed to break along fault lines, tilt upward, and fold over onto itself. This accounts for the 200- to 300-foot depth of the deposits. The phosphate is recovered in open-pit mines—long, linear trenches that follow the strike of the fold.

These pits have the potential to disturb the natural environment. However, a cooperative effort between the mining companies, the Bureau of Land Management, and the Caribou National Forest has been successful in restoring the appearance of the land. Around Soda Springs this team is setting the national standard for the reclamation of all surface-mining areas. The companies constantly backfill the pits, add topsoil, and plant native grasses and shrubs, which achieve a respectable ground cover in six to eight years. When the growth is substantial, the leased land is returned to the Forest Service as grazing and wildlife habitat. An "original growth" look requires about twenty years.

Phosphates are a critical natural resource used extensively in agriculture and in hundreds of consumer products. One processing technique results in elemental phosphorus, which goes into everything from plastics to toothpaste, enamels, dental cement, even soda pop and fire retardant. A second method yields farm fertilizer and the phosphorus in the NPK formula (nitrogen, phosphorus, potash) familiar to gardeners.

Soda Springs Town Geyser

This miniature Old Faithful was accidentally uncorked in 1937 by well drillers digging for geothermal water to supply the local swimming pool. The gusher used to spout off irrepressibly, but today it is capped and regulated by a timer. It releases a 150-foot jet every hour on the hour. If the breeze is right, everything in sight gets a sprinkling, including the tourists.

Hooper Spring, another noteworthy local attraction, offers the same effervescing soda water that fascinated fur trappers and Oregon Trail pioneers. It has delighted casual travelers for decades. Hooper is merely a remnant of an extensive field of artesian springs and rumbling waters that have disappeared below the Soda Point Reservoir. Located two miles west of town, the reservoir is a popular recreational site. It lies near a nine-hole public golf course where ruts from the Oregon-California Trail can still be seen.

History buffs may want to visit the Pioneer Museum, which is operated by the Daughters of the Utah Pioneers.

The town geyser at Soda Springs generally spouts every hour on the hour.

Idaho 34
HENRY

Twenty miles north of Soda Springs, Henry consists mainly of a single country store. This old-fashioned community gathering place has a pot-bellied stove and an atmosphere of rural sociability. The store has been operated by the Chester family since 1892, although the present building dates only from 1908 and is a replacement for the original. Henry (named for John Henry Schmidt, who started the store about 1884) has long served as a center for the sheep and cattle ranchers in the area.

| *The pioneer Henry store north of Soda Springs.* | *The Henry store is a bit ragged now but is still a hub of activity in the Grays Lake region.* |

Idaho 34
GRAYS LAKE NATIONAL WILDLIFE REFUGE

Grays Lake is twenty-seven miles north of Soda Springs. The name of the lake honors a fur trapper named Ignace Hatchiorauquasha, an Iroquois mercifully dubbed John Grey by his friends. Over the years the spelling has changed to "Gray." This natural lake is actually a shallow marsh, most of the water having been drained off by canal into the Blackfoot Reservoir. Nevertheless, it is a haven for wildlife. The refuge hosts one of the world's largest nesting populations of greater sandhill cranes. More than 200 pairs nest here annually. As many as 3,000 cranes can be seen in late September and early October prior to their migration to Arizona and New Mexico.

Early travelers found whooping cranes abundant at Grays Lake, but through habitat destruction and overhunting they have been reduced to near extinction. For several years the refuge staff participated in an experimental project to save the whoopers. They transported eggs from nests in Canada's Wood Buffalo National Park and placed them with setting sandhill cranes at Grays Lake. These foster mothers hatched and nurtured the young whoopers. High mortality plagued the project, although some 30 whooping cranes survived and continue to live at Grays Lake, migrating with the sandhills. Whoopers are still very rare, numbering only about 150 worldwide.

A visitor center is located three miles off Idaho 34 on Grays Lake East Road. Idaho 34 skirts the southern edge of the lake and proceeds east to Freedom, Wyoming. This road is part of the longer Pioneer Historic Byway, which begins at Franklin. Those coming from Montpelier to Wyoming joined the pioneer road at Soda Springs. Mormon lore has it that during the days of polygamy a man could keep a wife on both ends of the road, with little chance that the law would nab him across state lines—and that's how Freedom got its name.

At Freedom, turn north on US 89 for a connection with the Teton Valley via Alpine, Wyoming, or return to Soda Springs and proceed to Montpelier.

US 89 and 30
MONTPELIER

Montpelier is the commercial center of the upper Bear River Valley. Restaurants and comfortable motel accommodations make it a good headquarters from which to explore the Paris–Bear Lake area, less than twenty miles away.

The Oregon Trail first entered Idaho near the Montpelier Creek Crossing. In keeping with this background, the town gears up annually for an Oregon Trail Rendezvous Pageant. Held toward the end of July, this celebration brings together mountain men, Indians, fiddlers, square dancers, and assorted colorful characters. Also, the Rails and Trails Museum is an excellent place to learn more about the Indians, trappers, pioneers, miners, and railroaders who left their footprints here.

As the fur trapping era drew to a close around 1840, the flood of emigrants had just begun. For some thirty years, thousands of covered wagons trekking along the Oregon Trail paused in this valley. It provided a luxuriant resting place between two difficult landscapes, the Rocky Mountains behind and the Snake River desert ahead. Here the travelers relaxed while their livestock (sometimes totaling thousands of head) grazed on the rich valley grasses to fatten up for the journey ahead.

John C. Frémont and his government surveying expedition (guided by veteran trappers Kit Carson and Thomas Fitzpatrick) followed in the wake of the Great Migration of 1843. Frémont reported on at least one encampment in this valley:

> The edge of the wood for miles along the river was dotted with the white covers of emigrant wagons collected in groups at different camps where

the smoke was rising from the fires, women occupied in preparing the evening meal, children playing, herds of cattle grazing . . . a rare sight for the traveler in such a remote wilderness.

While the Oregon Trail traffic was still at its peak, ex-trapper Thomas "Peg Leg" Smith built a trading post five miles south of Montpelier in a choice spot along the Bear River, near the present-day settlement of Dingle. Peg Leg had participated in the glory days of the fur trade and in 1828 attended the Bear Lake Rendezvous, stumping around on his new hand-carved wooden leg. Two years earlier, his leg had been shattered close to the ankle by a shot from a Crow ambush on the Platte River. After the battle, his companions thought he would surely die from loss of blood. Undaunted, Smith tied a buckskin thong around the leg for a ligature, called for a sharp knife, and, assisted by Milton Sublette, amputated the offending part. He recovered against all odds, and his courage became legendary throughout the early West.

Pioneer diaries dating from 1844 have preserved glimpses of this genial horse thief, fur trapper, and womanizer at home on the Bear River. In *Historic Sites Along the Oregon Trail*, Aubrey L. Haines quotes many of these sources, each one describing a different aspect of Peg Leg's post. Peter Decker, who came by in 1849, observed several Indian lodges pitched near the "fort." Ruben Cole Shaw described Peg Leg's dwelling, which was made of sun-dried bricks and stood fourteen feet by twenty feet with walls six feet high. The interior had only a dirt floor, but a stone fireplace graced one end of the room "furnished" with buffalo robes and deerskins—a snug place on the far edge of civilization.

Further comment comes from P. A. Reading, whose *California Pioneers* includes observations of Peg Leg's herds of oxen, milk cows, beef cattle, and pigs. Emigrants dropped off their travel-weary stock, and the animals, when fattened on the river-bottom grasses, gave variety to Peg Leg's cuisine. Guests were impressed with his spread of garden vegetables, beef and pork, cold buttermilk, sweet cake, and brandy.

However, Smith himself may have been the most fascinating aspect of the Bear River camp. One diarist saw him as "jovial, red-faced and a braggart full of good humor and an apparent load of whiskey, inside and out. . . . Smith has but one leg, is quite fleshy and appears happy as a Lord. And why not? If what he tells us is true he gains over $100 per day in wealth."

Historian Merle Wells says the latest scholarship on this wily opportunist reveals that he was a secret agent for the Hudson's Bay Company, working in opposition to American trappers such as Jim Bridger and Louis Vasquez. He reported their activities to the company and directed trade to the British-held Fort Hall.

Smith kept between 300 and 500 fine horses that he or his partner Walkara had taken in raids from Spanish California. These formed a base for his Oregon Trail trade. The horses grew fat on Bear Valley grass, and emigrants eagerly bought them in exchange for their footsore stock. Peg Leg also supplied basic staples that had to be packed in from Missouri or, after 1847, from Salt Lake City. Occasionally he visited Fort Hall, trading horses for his immediate needs, and on one occasion he purchased a "plump young Bannock woman" named Mountain Fawn, his fifth wife. Smith brought polygamy to Bear Valley long before the Mormons arrived, having after this transaction three Ute wives, one Crow, and one Bannock.

It is difficult to say whether it was the lure of gold in California or trouble on the domestic front that caused Peg Leg to pull up stakes and head for the sunny south. His Crow wife stabbed Mountain Fawn to death in a fit of jealousy, and the other wives returned to their people. Smith headed for California with Mountain Fawn's son Jimmy and arrived there in 1850, leaving further development of Bear Valley to the Mormons.

A group of pioneers arrived from Utah in 1864 to form an agricultural community. They named their settlement Clover Creek, then changed it to Belmont, and changed it again when Brigham Young paid a visit. He expressed a desire to name it Montpelier, after the capital of his native Vermont. And Montpelier it has been ever since.

The town flourished as a sedate Mormon village until the Oregon Short Line Railroad arrived in 1882. This railway connected southern Idaho with the Union Pacific system, and Montpelier became a division point, radically changing the town's history. Trains were serviced and crews were changed here, bringing an influx of workers who tainted the settlement with Gentiles and whiskey. A new "downtown" mushroomed along the tracks, where the non-Mormon element thrived on a mix of commercial enterprises and saloons. A fence went up to separate the "wicked" downtown from the "righteous" uptown, but eventually the barrier came down and the two sections integrated.

In the summer of 1894, the townsfolk rallied to support a fragment of Coxey's Army that rode into town on the train. The protesters were hitching a ride to Washington, D.C., via boxcar. Like some twenty other "armies" across the nation, they intended to join Jacob Coxey and his group at the White House to petition President Grover Cleveland for jobs. Most of the men were peaceful, but the idea of protest unnerved the federal authorities, who were generally hostile toward the Coxeyites.

The men who landed in Montpelier had come from the West Coast, hiking and riding as they could. Union Pacific officials generally ignored the fact that several hundred protesters occupied the boxcars. But by the time they arrived at Montpelier, the officials decided they had made a mistake in giving this motley bunch a free ride. The train was sidetracked, and when the men got out to stretch, they discovered they were stranded.

Mass confusion reigned for a few days. Two sets of Coxeyites fired up engines standing in the roundhouse and steamed out of town. U.S. Marshall Joe Pinkham arrived from Boise with irate railroad officials. Montpelier's

On the Oregon Trail, circa 1890. By this time traffic had thinned considerably as people could come west via the Union Pacific Railroad, moving their household goods in boxcars. —Idaho State Historical Society

mayor called a town meeting, where the citizens declared support for the Coxeyites. During a melee at the railroad yard, Jack Westfall, the local sheriff, was arrested and hauled off to Boise along with 157 other prisoners—mostly Coxeyites and several local citizens who had defended the protesters during the Montpelier town meeting. A two-week trial opened on May 28, with federal Judge James H. Beatty deciding whether the men had violated his earlier injunction enjoining them from riding the Union Pacific trains. Guilty parties would be cited for contempt and sentenced to prison.

Westfall and three other Montpelier citizens served thirty days in the Bingham County jail at Blackfoot. Two Coxeyite leaders served six months in a variety of county jails. The rank and file Coxeyites, who numbered almost 150 (plus 30 would-be train stealers from Nampa), served time at Camp Pinkham, Idaho (also called Camp Despair)—a barracks hastily constructed along a depressing stretch of the Snake River near Huntington, Oregon. Federal troops guarded the prisoners throughout the summer. Beatty released them gradually until the last ones left on September 1, 1894, ending southern Idaho's part in the nationwide drama.

Montpelier long remembered its participation in this remarkable avant-garde protest of the nineteenth century. Politically, the town still has a liberal touch. The Democratic ticket is reported to have a fifty-fifty chance here, whereas other Bear Lake settlements vote solidly Republican.

One of the practical attractions of today's Montpelier is Butch Cassidy's Restaurant and Saloon, which lights up like a beacon for the hungry and the curious. Sure enough, the romanticized outlaw and his "Wild Bunch" left their mark here. On a hot August afternoon in 1896, Butch rode into town with Bob Meeks and Elza Lay. They moseyed down Washington Street leading a little sorrel pack mare, tied their horses to the bank's hitching post, and sauntered in. Cassidy quickly whipped out his gun and lined banker G. C. Gray and his assistant up against the wall, along with two or three banking patrons. Meanwhile, Lay cleaned out the cash drawers, raided the vault, and toted the loot out front, where Meeks waited with the horses. Calmly, Lay tied the bags of gold and silver to the pack mare's saddle and threw the sack of currency across his own. Cassidy joined the two of them after bowing good-bye to the bankers with a warning to wait ten minutes before calling for help.

The "cowboys" calmly rode out of town with the valuable little mare trotting behind. As the posse formed, the "Wild Bunch" rode east with $7,000 and vanished among the high ridges. A local constable gave chase on his bicycle, but, as someone said, "Who could catch Butch Cassidy on a bicycle?"

US 89
PARIS AND THE
BEAR LAKE SETTLEMENTS

Paris is a rural town set amid small family farms with fields of alfalfa and meadow grass rolling off toward the hills, where livestock feed along the ridges and rocky outcrops. A number of other villages share this valley, but from the earliest days Paris has been the leader among the Bear Lake settlements. Writer and historian Bernard De Voto must have been fascinated with the idea of Paris. When his wife suggested a trip to Europe, De Voto is reported to have said, "Why should I go to Paris, France, when I haven't seen Paris, Idaho, yet?"

Today Paris is best known for its Romanesque-style tabernacle. The six-story pink sandstone structure dominates the landscape. In the early days it made Paris something of a cathedral town. It is the personal handiwork of nineteenth-century Mormon pioneers who built it to house the Bear Lake Stake, the administrative center for Bear River church congregations. In 1884 drovers began hauling the rose-colored sandstone from the east side of Bear Lake—by wagon in summer and over ice in winter. After 1,200 loads reached the site, Jacob Tueller and Sons, stone masons from Switzerland (later known for contributing the French Mansard style to Paris architecture), began cutting, dressing, and laying up the blocks. Other workmen of equal skill fashioned hand-hewn doors, carved intricate designs for the ceilings, banisters, and balcony, and hand-cut the roof shingles to exact measurement. Most of the brethren and sisters (as they called themselves) throughout the valley contributed in some way to the massive undertaking. Individual work, however, as in the building of medieval churches, was rarely recognized or signed. When authorities dedicated the church in 1889, it was the largest in Idaho. Time has not dimmed the luster of this remarkable building, open from Memorial Day to Labor Day.

The tabernacle inspired a spate of residential building that sprinkled the town with a variety of architectural styles. French Mansard, Greek Revival, and Queen Anne are all represented, as are some interesting "polygamous designs" intended to house multiple families.

Long before the Mormons came to Bear Lake Valley, Shoshone-Bannocks claimed this territory. Then the fur trappers discovered its many streams fringed with willows and cottonwoods that made for prime beaver habitat. The first white men known to have seen this valley were Astorians Robert Stuart and Ramsey Crooks. They traveled near the site of Montpelier in 1812 en route from Fort Astoria to New York City with messages for John Jacob Astor. They did not stop to trap or trade, but their significant journey forged the basic route that later became the Oregon Trail.

During his Snake River foray of 1819, Donald McKenzie of the North West Company made a detour to Bear Lake (which he called Black Bear Lake) and was much impressed with the prospect of finding beaver here. With every step he lamented that he and his trapping brethren had been "so long deprived of the riches of such a country."

American trappers from St. Louis soon followed. They found their way across the Rocky Mountains at South Pass (Wyoming) in 1824 and spilled over into this beaver-rich valley, much to the consternation of the British. Here came Jedediah Smith, Jim Bridger, David Jackson, William Sublette, Thomas Fitzpatrick, and a host of others who became celebrated heroes in buckskin. They challenged the British presence west of the Rockies and heightened the competition for both beaver skins and territory in the Northwest.

Before the white men came, Bear Lake was a traditional summer ground for bands of Shoshone-Bannock Indians. They lived well on the ducks and geese that inhabited the marsh at the north end of the lake, and on the elk and deer that ranged nearby. Jedediah Smith and company crisscrossed the valley many times, tending their traps and camping with local Indians. According to Osborne Russell's *Journal*, the trappers often joined the Bear Lake Shoshone in their lakeside villages of three to four hundred lodges.

The Indians were generally hospitable during the 1820s and 1830s. They wanted the white men's trinkets and had struck a treaty of trade and friendship with the Canadian Donald McKenzie, representing the British North West Company, during his 1819 tour. Because the Shoshones did not always differentiate the white men's countries of origin, legions of American trappers benefited from McKenzie's diplomacy. The Blackfeet, by contrast, stood uniformly against all intruders; their raids sharpened the trappers' marksmanship and caused many a mountain man to "go under."

As Robert Campbell's group of eighteen trappers headed for the 1828 rendezvous on the south end of Bear Lake (in Spanish territory), it met a party of Blackfeet warriors. In *Jedediah Smith*, Dale Morgan tells how the trappers took refuge behind a rocky outcrop and defended themselves in a hot five-hour contest. One American was killed, and Jim Beckwourth, the "gaudy liar," no doubt told the truth when he said, "Never in my whole life had I run such danger of losing my life and scalp."

The era of fur trapping declined after 1840. By then, beaver hats had gone out of style and beaver populations had diminished severely. Fast on the heels of the trappers, however, came thousands of emigrants traveling along the Oregon Trail. After the initial onslaught of the Great Migration, the Indians might have reclaimed their space, but in 1862 Congress passed the Homestead Act. This opportunity to take up land claimed by the government turned Mormon eyes toward the Bear Lake country, for the Utahans were eager to establish colonies along their northern perimeter. At first they held back, fearing Indian opposition. That obstacle soon came down when Gen. Patrick E. Conner and his California Volunteers broke the power of the Cache Valley Shoshone in a bitter attack during the winter of 1863.

In the summer following this massacre, Indian representatives signed the Treaty of Box Elder at Brigham City, Utah. Although it made no reference to the prospect of pioneer settlement, the July 1863 treaty provided safe passage for stagecoaches and emigrants across Shoshone territory. That started a land rush. By August, Brigham Young announced his plan to colonize the Bear Lake Valley.

Pioneers handpicked by the church founded the town of Paris first. Prior to settlement, Brigham Young himself designated Charles C. Rich—a tested pioneer, man of the faith, and member of the Twelve Apostles—to lead a scouting party. He was to select a site and negotiate for peace with Chiefs Washakie and Tighi. The Indians were reluctant to share their hunting and fishing paradise, but during the parley Rich pointed out to them that it would be foolish to fight the white men; like the waves on Bear Lake, they would keep coming.

The Indians finally agreed to let the Mormons settle at the northern end of the lake while they kept the southern end as a summer campground. In return, the Mormons agreed to share their crops whenever the Indians passed through the country. This provision upheld Brigham Young's belief that it was "less expensive to feed and clothe them than to fight them." For many years thereafter, housewives dished out hot bread and buttermilk, and often a sack of wheat and joint of meat as well, to passing Indians.

Permanent settlers followed in the wake of the scouting party, arriving in the fall of 1863 under the leadership of Thomas Sleight. They traveled by horseback and wagon from Franklin through Cache Valley to Paris, eight miles north of Bear Lake. The colonists built temporary housing the first winter, but this was no haphazard affair; Mormon leaders envisioned an orderly place, like the ideal City of Zion. In the spring, Brigham Young arrived from Salt Lake with Frederick T. Perris, who came to survey the new townsite. He laid it out in a grid pattern, like a miniature Salt Lake City, with streets 132 feet wide. There were twenty-three blocks of sixteen acres apiece, each block containing ten lots. The inhabitants were so pleased with his work that they named their town after him. However, over time the spelling became "Paris," rather than "Perris."

With the help of Charles C. Rich, Young distributed the town lots and the surrounding farmland. As in New England settlements, the inhabitants lived in the village, which would provide sociability as well as protection. Maintaining homes here was a difficult assignment. The short summers and deadly winters made pioneering tough, but the Mormons stayed and prospered.

As Paris took shape, more settlers streamed in from northern Utah to establish nearby communities. During his 1864 visit, Brigham Young gave names to several of these fledgling settlements—Montpelier, Bennington, Bloomington, St. Charles, and Fish Haven. He encouraged the colonists to build substantial homes, schools, and other public buildings. Paris, particularly, took this counsel to heart. It was to become a geographic and spiritual center, the leading Mormon stronghold in the valley.

Paris grew and attracted settlers of diverse backgrounds and practical skills. During one especially hard winter, the citizens petitioned church leaders in Salt Lake City for help. Instead of sending food and clothing, however, they sent "millers, sawyers, weavers, candlemakers and brickmakers." Lize Reitzes, who has written extensively about Paris, says, "These calculated migrations of craftspeople were the essence of the Mormon expansion system." The Mormons drew many converts from western Europe and urged these people to bring the tools of their trades with them.

A small emigrant train that detoured from the main Oregon Trail into Bear Lake Valley during the summer of 1864 apparently met some of these new converts. Years later, emigrant Arabella Fulton remembered the beauty of the country, the irrigated gardens, and the generous people who shared their produce. The settlers likely remembered the Oregon-bound travelers for a long time, too. Fulton wrote, "Almost at once we were surrounded by a motley crowd, most of them being foreigners of the Holland type, dressed in old-country style, and stomping around in their flat, wooden shoes. They

Elegant architecture near Paris. From the early days of settlement, Brigham Young advised the colonists to build "commodious habitations" of stone or brick. This handsome old derelict is a stone structure built in the French Mansard style, probably a Jacob Tueller design, circa 1884.

were as much of a curiosity to us as we were to them and the treat seemed to be mutual."

At one time, Paris—whose founder, Charles C. Rich, had six wives and fifty children—was known as the "hotbed of polygamy" in Idaho. Even the tabernacle is featured in some of the polygamous lore. While it was still under construction, stake president J. U. Stucki and Bishop C. W. Nibley had to make a run for the church tower one night to hide from the anti-Mormon deputies.

Prior to 1882 the polygamous brethren carried on with little interference. The old laws were difficult to enforce. But after Congress passed the Edmunds Act in 1882, convictions came easily and something of an open season on polygamists followed. The penalty was a $500 fine or five years in jail, sometimes both. With such dire consequences, it is not surprising that the Mormons devised some fascinating ways to evade the law.

By 1890 polygamous families in Idaho had declined to 3 percent. Presumably Paris also followed this pattern. Those few men who still had multiple wives were often the community leaders, prosperous and respected persons who were readily protected by their neighbors. The state penitentiary overflowed with polygamists, but few of them were from Paris. Lawmen entering Bear Valley by train had to get off at Montpelier, ten miles from Paris, and complete their journey by horse. By that time one of the many lookouts would have spread the word. In Paris someone was always on duty to sound the alarm. In *Folklore in Bear Lake Valley*, Bonnie Thompson tells of the morning the deputies arrived at 2:00 A.M., and the entire town, except the polygamists, was on hand to greet them.

Most polygamists had a safe retreat and could disappear at a moment's notice into the willow patches along the creek, a safe house with secret passages, or perhaps a cell beneath the living room floor. One hapless fellow dived into a large flour barrel in the pantry but, alas, his pursuer lifted the lid.

Like other Bear Lake settlements, Paris looked to Utah for guidance and in its early years led rather a double life. It was located in Idaho but assumed it belonged to Richland County, Utah. Not until the Idaho-Utah boundary

Historic Mormon architecture at Paris. Identical front doors and windows suggest a multiple-family dwelling with separate but equal facilities for the wives. —Idaho State Historical Society

survey was accepted in 1872 was it definitely established that the town fell on the Idaho side. The change in allegiance came slowly. In the mid-1870s Charles C. Rich held a seat in the Utah Territorial Assembly while his son, Joseph C. Rich, sat in the Idaho legislature in Boise.

More than a century has gone by since the founding of Paris, and it is still largely an ethnic, agricultural community. Only eight miles away is Bear Lake, where tourism is growing rapidly. Real estate developments and an influx of summer residents forecast changes ahead.

St. Charles

The village of St. Charles sits near the northern end of Bear Lake and provides access to Bear Lake State Park. Mile-long stretches of sand provide a generous playground here. Joining the park on the north is the Bear Lake National Wildlife Refuge. This marshy area where the lake flows into Bear River has been a traditional habitat for moose, elk, and many varieties of birds. The refuge office is in Montpelier.

St. Charles, named for Charles C. Rich, founder of Paris and a leader in the Bear River settlements, is best known as the birthplace of Gutzon Borglum, the sculptor who carved the colossal presidential group at Mount Rushmore in the Black Hills of South Dakota. Although little is known about his early life, historian Merle Wells reports that Borglum's Danish immigrant parents arrived in Salt Lake City about 1865 and his father worked for the church. The elder Borglum proved too independent for the Saints, however, and soon brought his family to the Bear Lake Valley, where Gutzon was born, perhaps in 1871. While still very young, his family moved to Ogden and then to Omaha, where Gutzon grew up. A monument honoring the sculptor stands on the Mormon church grounds at the north end of St. Charles.

Ten miles west of St. Charles on Forest Road 412 is the popular Minnetonka Cave. The Forest Service offers guided tours of the half-mile-long cavern daily during the summer. It features fascinating deposits that have formed stalactites and stalagmites.

Two miles south of St. Charles, on the west shore of Bear Lake, is Fish Haven, long known as a lakeside retreat. The waters here were once famous as the home of the Bear Lake Monster, a serpent supposedly no less than a hundred feet long. Said to move with incredible speed, lashing waves while standing on its hind legs and spouting water from multiple mouths, the beast was believed by some to be a leftover from ancient Lake Bonneville; others reckoned it came through an underground tunnel from Loch Ness in Scotland. Sightings of the monster went on for years, and witnesses swore they had seen the frightful thing in one guise or another. Actually, it sprang to life from the fertile pen of Joseph C. Rich, who wanted to make Bear Lake famous and have some fun at the same time. He was eminently successful. West Coast newspapers carried stories of each new sighting, and more than a hundred years later the Bear Lake Monster still rises to the surface occasionally.

Bear Lake itself is a turquoise blue gem, twenty miles long and seven miles wide. Its northern half is in Idaho while its southern half extends into Utah. In addition to recreation, the lake provides water for irrigation and is a source of hydroelectric power. A series of man-made canals connects the river and lake, which also functions as a reservoir. Six power plants (five in Idaho, one in Utah) tap the energy of the river as it flows first north to Soda Springs and then, after leaving Alexander Reservoir, flows south to the Great Salt Lake. This is the only river in Idaho that is not part of the Columbia River drainage system.

Bear Lake is exceptional in many ways. Formed some 28,000 years ago, for approximately the last 8,000 years it has been separated from its natural tributary, the Bear River. Sediment built up between the lake and river, creating a swampy causeway and isolating the lake in a unique environment. The extremely pure water is low in nutrients and high in limestone, a combination that gives Bear Lake its profound blue color. But the lack of nutrients also limits the varieties of fish that flourish there. Four rare species found nowhere else in the world have adapted to this environment—the tiny Bonneville cisco, Bear Lake whitefish, Bear Lake sculpin, and Bonneville whitefish. One of the delights of winter is the cisco run. At the peak of the season, thousands of cisco approach the shallow, rocky shore-

Moose at Strawberry Springs near Bear Lake. —Rick Just

81

lines to spawn. Fishermen by the hundreds don waders and head for the icy waters with buckets and dip nets to scoop up the tasty fry. Cisco are the only fish in Idaho for which a regular dipnet season has been established.

Cache Valley

US 91 begins its northward trek through eastern Idaho at Franklin, across the northern reaches of the Wasatch Range from Bear Lake and about seven miles south of Preston. When settlers from Utah first began to spill over the Idaho border, they came to this sheltered spot on the Bear River. The area had long been popular with Indians and fur trappers, who found the river, with its tributary streams and protected valleys, a favorable place to rendezvous. Trappers often cached, or stored, their furs around here in underground pits until they could pack them off to market in St. Louis—thus the name Cache Valley.

Franklin, at the southern end of the valley, is well known as the oldest town in Idaho. Brigham Young organized the colonizing expedition that founded the community in 1860. As the town grew, it became a supply center and gateway for Mormon settlers branching out in a fringe of northern colonies. The wilderness route they took—through Franklin and Cache Valley, along Bear River to Soda Springs, and on to settlements in Wyoming—is today designated the Pioneer Historic Byway, Idaho 34.

The Franklin pioneers chose a townsite near Bear River, where both the valley and the river straddle the Idaho-Utah line. Thinking they were in Utah, they selected a wooded spot along the Cub River, a tributary of the Bear. Here they marked off a sixty-by-ninety-rod enclosure to contain inward-facing cabins, making a kind of fort for protection from the local Indians. They surveyed the land and their leader, Thomas Smart, supervised the apportionment of lots. Each adult male received a one-and-a-quarter-acre building site in the village and a ten-acre farm plot in the country. Grazing lands still farther out were held in common.

The colonists plowed and planted and harvested, and the Utah legislature incorporated their village. Much to their disappointment, an 1872 boundary survey revealed they were actually located in Idaho. With the exception of Henry and Eliza Spalding's 1836 mission at Lapwai, far to the north in Nez Perce country, the Franklin community started Idaho's first school, first lumbermill, first railroad, first gristmill, and first telegraph. In *Tales of Eastern Idaho*, historian David Crowder says the news of Custer's Last Stand was relayed to the world through Franklin. Telegraph lines at Bozeman, Eagle Rock, and Blackfoot were down, so the news was sent by stagecoach to Franklin, where the telegraph operator transmitted the message to Salt Lake City. The next day, the news from the Little Big Horn made headlines throughout the country.

Agriculture, particularly dairy farming, has long been the sustaining business of Franklin, but residents also grew potatoes at an early date. During the community's first spring, some settlers built log houses while others dug irrigation ditches and prepared fields for crops. Goforth Nelson planted potatoes that first year and harvested thirty-three bushels in the fall of 1860, three years before Idaho became a U.S. territory.

Pioneer Relic Hall and Hatch House

The Pioneer Relic Hall tells the story of early Mormon settlement in this region. It is open by appointment or during the Pioneer Days celebration, held annually in August.

Hatch House is adjacent to the museum. This classic three-story building, designed in the Greek Revival style, is crafted of hand-dressed native stone quarried in the early 1870s. Originally it housed the Hatch family. Lorenzo Hatch, a substantial leader in the community, was a bishop of the church and the first Mormon representative in the Idaho legislature (1872–73). His large family included several wives, twelve sons, and twelve daughters.

US 91
PRESTON

Preston, a tidy town laid out in the grid pattern characteristic of early Mormon communities, boasts wide streets, lots of trees, safe playgrounds, and pretty parks. Located at the north end of Cache Valley, this prosperous farming and recreation area lies in the shadow of the Wasatch Mountains to the east, the Portneufs to the north, and the Bannocks to the west.

Settlers began building homes in this area about 1877, and early in its history Preston became a center of education. Its Oneida Academy building, which still stands, is an unusual Romanesque-style historic structure built between 1890 and 1894 of volcanic rock. A number of prominent Idahoans received an education here, including Ezra Taft Benson, who grew up as a farm boy in nearby Whitney. He became secretary of agriculture under President Dwight Eisenhower and later achieved high honors as president of the Mormon Church.

Battle Creek Massacre National Historic Landmark

Five miles north of Preston on US 91 is a monument commemorating a tragic battle during which some 400 Shoshone Indians died. Before white settlers came, Cache Valley was home to a band of Shoshones who lived in migratory groups and moved "as the season walked around." In spring and summer they gathered seeds, roots, and berries across southern Idaho. Toward fall they traveled to the fishing grounds along the Salmon River, but in the wintertime their home was Cache Valley. The forest of willows and brush along the Bear River sheltered the Indians from wind and snow, and they took advantage of the area's plentiful hot springs.

For some years Chief Bear Hunter and his local band hosted an annual two-week campout for the Shoshones under Chief Washakie and the Shoshone-Bannocks under Chief Pocatello. Many hundreds of Indians gathered to sing and dance, tell stories, and socialize. At this time of year the tribes performed the Warm Dance, an encouragement to Mother Nature to turn up the heat. One such meeting took place in January 1863. After the last story had been told and the goodbyes had been said, the guests folded their lodges and returned home while the local Shoshone families settled into their winter camp along Bear River.

Meanwhile, trouble was brewing over several altercations between white settlers and a few renegade Indians. When word of these confrontations reached Gen. Patrick E. Conner at Fort Douglas, Utah, he set out on a winter campaign to exterminate the Cache Valley Indians. His soldiers came upon Chief Bear Hunter's camp in full battle charge and indiscriminately slaughtered men, women, and children "like wild rabbits," the Indians later said. Bodies lay everywhere. The snow turned brilliant red with blood. Only a few Indians escaped this single largest massacre of Native Americans by U.S. troops west of the Mississippi. Their defeat assured the expansion of pioneer settlements.

Red Rock Pass

Twenty miles north of Preston on US 91, Red Rock Pass marks the spot where the waters of ancient Lake Bonneville overflowed about 15,000 years ago. This enormous lake covered about half of present-day Utah and extended into eastern Nevada and southern Idaho. At Red Rock Pass, before there was a pass, the water worked its way through a weak spot in the terrain. The trickle quickly turned into a torrent as Lake Bonneville drained in a roaring deluge. Highlands channeled the cataclysmic flow along the route of the Portneuf River and then westward across the Snake River Plain. At the Portneuf Narrows, forty-five miles to the north, the geologic record shows that the flood reached a depth of 400 feet.

The powerful rush of water that passed through Red Rock Pass deposited rocks and gravel for many miles along the Snake River. The swift current tumbled huge basalt boulders, breaking them down and wearing them smooth until the rapids could no longer move them. Geologists aptly named one type of these rocks "melon gravel" after Ferris Lind (of Fearless Ferris Stinker Stations) placed a highway sign along one such deposit that read, "PETRIFIED WATERMELONS, Take One Home to Your Mother-in-Law." This unexpected call roused many a sleepy desert driver.

Over the next few thousand years, as the climate became hotter and drier, what remained of Lake Bonneville receded; we call its remnant the Great Salt Lake. Red Rock Pass marks the divide between the Bear River–Bonneville Basin watershed, which drains only into the Great Salt Lake, and the Snake River–Columbia Basin watershed, which drains into the Pacific Ocean. Thirteen miles beyond Red Rock Pass, US 91 joins I-15, and thirty-five miles beyond there lies Pocatello and I-86.

Eastern Snake Plain

I-86, Idaho 37 and 39
AMERICAN FALLS

American Falls is a processing and shipping center for Idaho potatoes, although it is equally well known for its giant reservoir, which stores irrigation water for thirsty acres. American Falls Reservoir is fed by the Portneuf and Snake rivers and a series of freshwater springs, making it an excellent rainbow trout fishery. The visitor centers at the dam, the fish hatchery, and the hydroelectric plant are all worth seeing. The city values summer recreation and maintains several nice parks and a good marina with a sandy beach.

American Falls was a famous landmark for fur trappers and a favorite camping spot for emigrants on the Oregon Trail. Many travelers commented on the spectacular cascade of froth and foam and the thundering waters that could be heard for many miles. In *Tales of Eastern Idaho*, David Crowder quotes Charlotte Stearns Pengra, who camped here in 1853 with a wagon train and observed the water "tumbling, and rumbling, and whirling and boiling, and bubbling and foaming, clashing and dashing to the depths below."

When the dam was constructed in 1927, the falls disappeared under the reservoir. The whole town moved to higher ground, house by house, store by store, and church by church, over a two-year period. As the reservoir filled, it inundated the entire old settlement except "the lonely grain elevator sticking up like a tombstone for the town."

More recently, some fascinating archaeological features have come to light. A team from Idaho State University unearthed the skulls of giant bisons that lived here 10,000 or more years ago. An ISU student noticed what appeared to be the tip of a horn sticking out of a bare cliff near the reservoir's high-water mark. The wash of the water eroded the old river bank and exposed long-covered fossil deposits, including one almost perfectly preserved bison skull with an impressive set of horns. The discovery crew named it "Mary Lou." Other bison fossils and parts of a ground sloth have also been uncovered here. The relics found a home in Pocatello at the ISU Museum of Natural History, an institution known for its large collection of giant bison fossils. The buffalo-like image has fittingly become the museum's logo.

The late Earl Swanson determined that the ancient peat bogs along the edge of the reservoir are rich in plant fossils, too. These ancient flora are remarkably similar to a thousand or so plant species that still grow at the north end of the reservoir in the Fort Hall Bottoms, an unusual environment fed by spring waters. It supports a unique biotic community of rare fish, plants, and birds, making it an irreplaceable natural resource.

Aberdeen Research Station

Idaho 39 crosses the nine-story American Falls Dam and leads to an expanse of grain and potato and sugar beet fields that reach nearly as far as the eye can see. The fifteen miles to Aberdeen pass quickly. Here, on 460 acres, the Aberdeen Research Station scientists and support technicians study grain genetics and breed new varieties of potatoes. This work has been going on since 1910 as a cooperative effort between the University of Idaho, the Soil Conservation Service, and the U.S. Department of Agriculture.

The facility has become the center for the National Small Grains Collection, which has acquired approximately 150,000 types of seeds and bits of germ plasm. The Small Grains Collection library has a sample of every known variety of genetic plasm from wheat, barley, oats, and rice. Horticulturists from around the world use this facility to promote genetic diversity.

The Aberdeen Research Station divides eighty different fields into five-acre experimental plots planted with potatoes and grains. It usually takes about fifteen years of breeding, cross-breeding, and experimentation to develop a new variety of potato. Some of the qualities or characteristics the scientists work toward include disease resistance, size, shape, or maturity. Examples of recent releases are the Frontier, designed for an early market, and the Ranger, which is a full-season spud. The research station welcomes visitors year-round.

Massacre Rocks State Park

This historic site ten miles west of American Falls on I-86 has an excellent visitor center with interpretive displays on the geology of the area and on human activity at Massacre Rocks.

Volcanic formations highlight this unusual setting overlooking the Snake River. Scattered throughout the park are polished stones and huge boulders rolled into place by the ancient Bonneville flood (see Red Rock Pass). Many trails wander through the juniper and sage, making the area easy to explore. In the spring, colonies of sego lilies and lupines soften the rough landscape, and some 200 species of birds have been sighted here.

The Silver Fox (note headgear) in handmade mountain man regalia at the annual Mountain Man Rendezvous, Massacre Rocks State Park. In real life the Silver Fox is Assistant Ranger Chuck Bartroff.

The place called Devils Gate, or the Gate of Death, was a landmark on the Oregon Trail. Here the route passed through remnants of an extinct volcano, and a narrow break in the rocks barely permitted wagons to squeeze through. The modern name of Massacre Rocks is a misnomer. No documented massacre occurred here, although the terrain looks ominous and a massacre did occur several miles away in August 1862. In that incident, Indians attacked two wagon trains and killed several people. More men died in a skirmish the following day when a relief party of thirty pursued the Indians. Within a day or two, a total of five separate groups of emigrants gathered at Massacre Rocks to defend themselves against potential attacks and to bury their dead. The five wagon trains regrouped here and resumed their journey west together for safety.

Register Rock is a point of interest at the west end of the park, about two miles from the visitor center. A basalt boulder sheltered by a pavilion bears pioneer names either carved into the rock or painted on with axle grease.

Each June a crowd gathers for the Massacre Rocks Rendezvous, a recreation of nineteenth-century lifestyles that features black-powder shoots and trading posts.

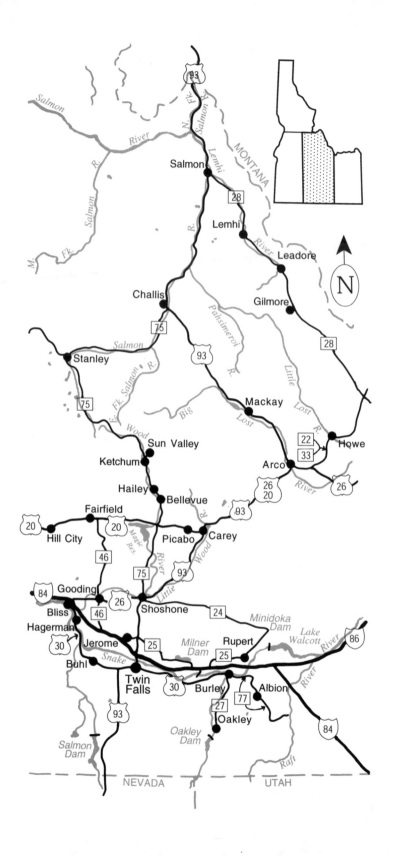

~ PART 2 ~

Central Idaho

C entral Idaho runs from the Utah-Nevada border on the south to the Salmon River in the north. The northern part of this region is dominated by several national forests and the Frank Church River of No Return Wilderness. The Salmon and its many tributaries provide 425 miles of free-flowing water. The middle area of central Idaho is shrouded in mountains—notably the Sawtooths, the Boulders, the Smokies, the Pioneers, and the Lost River Range. Interspersed between the mountains are ghost towns such as Leesburg, Gilmore, Sawtooth City, Vienna, Bonanza, and Custer—specters that once rode a wave of prosperity. In the southern part of the region, the Snake River Plain is known by another name, Magic Valley, the heart of a prosperous agricultural region. Here more than 2.5 million acres produce beans, sugar beets, potatoes, hay, grain—just about any crop that grows in a temperate climate. And fish farms in this area make Idaho the nation's leading producer of commercial trout. The centerpiece of the valley is the Snake River, whose generous groundwater aquifer and many storage dams bring life-giving water to the desert.

~

Magic Valley

I-84, Idaho 24 and 25
RUPERT

Five miles east of Rupert, I-86 ends at its junction with I-84, which continues west across the Snake River Plain. The highway cuts across a large agricultural area known as Magic Valley, which has a rich historical heritage and many recreational opportunities.

91

Rupert is part of the Minidoka Irrigation Project, where reclaimed sage-brush land has become famous for production of sugar beets and potatoes. A cluster of nearby smaller communities—Paul, Acequia, Heyburn, and Declo—contribute to the local economy. Both Rupert and Heyburn house Simplot potato processing plants. Sugar beets go to the Amalgamated refinery at Paul. See the chamber of commerce for information about a self-guided agricultural tour. Another local attraction, the Minidoka County Museum, features an early train depot, steam engine, 1926 ice cream parlor, household items, and other displays that tell the local story.

More than a century ago this farm and ranch country was part of a vast open desert that both white men and Indians crossed quickly en route to better locations. The Oregon and California trails diverged about twelve miles east of town at Raft River, near the eastern edge of the Minidoka Wildlife Refuge. At this junction, settlers bound for California left the main trail and traveled up the Raft River to make a connection with Hudspeth's Cutoff, which took them to the City of Rocks and the California Trail.

The town of Rupert developed after the Minidoka Dam brought water to the land, spurring the growth of farms. Bureau of Reclamation engineers surveyed the townsite in 1905 and designed it to be a model city for other

Roadside travel included most any mode of transport during the Great Depression of the 1930s. —Idaho Department of Transportation

reclamation projects. They included a central park, which today is known as Rupert Square, a focal point for local celebrations.

Lake Walcott, the body of water formed by the Minidoka Dam, makes Rupert a center for water sports recreation. An adjoining 25,000-acre wildlife refuge appeals to bird watchers and photographers. This is an important stop along the Pacific flyway for tundra swans and other waterfowl and is a major nesting spot for white pelicans.

Walcott Park, a picnicking and boating area near the dam, has trees that have been growing since construction began on Minidoka Dam. During the Great Depression, a Civilian Conservation Corps (CCC) camp was set up here, and the boys repaired miles of irrigation ditches. They also planted additional trees, added stonework, and enlarged the park, which today remains essentially unchanged.

Minidoka Dam, completed in 1906, was an early project of the U.S. Bureau of Reclamation. The entire Minidoka Project eventually grew to include five upstream dams that store enough water to irrigate a million acres. In 1908 a hydropower plant was added to the dam to provide power for the pumping stations. Both the dam and power plant are included on the National Register of Historic Places. The power plant still operates much as it did in the early 1900s, and guided tours are available to show visitors an era of power generation long gone.

To get to the power plant, Walcott Park, and the refuge, take Idaho 24 north from Rupert to County Road 400. Follow directional signs for about thirteen miles.

I-84, US 30, Idaho 27
BURLEY

Burley hugs the river's edge, where twenty miles of shoreline along the Snake River make recreation an important factor. However, agriculture plays the major role in the local economy, with a strong food-processing industry driven by gigantic corporations such as Amalgamated Sugar, Del Monte, J.R. Simplot, Kraft, Ore-Ida, and others. One of the more recent players in the agricultural field, Adolph Coors, maintains a 9-million-bushel storage facility here for malting barley. A representative of the Idaho Barley Commission says the Magic Valley usually contributes about 24 percent of Idaho's malting barley crop.

Thousands of Oregon Trail pioneers passed very close to the site of Burley, but the town did not begin until the Minidoka Irrigation Project brought water to the south side of the river early in the 1900s. The Cassia County Historical Museum displays pioneer trail maps that show the routes of the Oregon Trail, the California Trail, the Kelton Road, Hudspeth's Cutoff,

On the Oregon Trail with former governor John Evans, whose family were pioneers in southeastern Idaho. Evans and friends participated in the Sesquicentennial celebration, which in 1993 recreated the Oregon Trail passage. Here the wagons have reached Declo in southern Idaho.

and the Salt Lake Alternate, all of which were interconnected. Other exhibits interpret the history of Burley and Cassia County.

Another local attraction, the Idaho Regatta, is a national powerboat race that occurs annually in June, churning up both water and excitement on the river.

Idaho 27 and 77
OAKLEY, CITY OF ROCKS, AND ALBION LOOP

Oakley, located seventeen miles south of Burley, is the gateway to the City of Rocks and a worthy destination in itself. This village of 800 thrives on agriculture (made possible by the nearby Goose Creek Reservoir) and on the stone quarries that produce the distinctive Oakley stone, a popular material for home construction that is shipped throughout the country.

Victorian mansion at Oakley.

This country village has a surprising abundance of Victorian architecture. Many of the homes are built of local brick and feature verandas, turrets, balustrades, and gingerbread to celebrate its link with the past. Each year, on the third Saturday in June, the Historic Oakley group hosts a tour of several of these old structures. The whole town has been designated a National Register Historic District.

The nearby City of Rocks National Preserve, a National Historic Landmark, is a strange Precambrian colony of granite shapes covering some 14,000 acres of weathered towers and turrets. More than 100,000 visitors a year find their way to this remote spot, which is protected by the National Park Service.

City of Rocks is a mecca for climbers, who come from all over the world. Some stay for weeks at a time to explore the thousand "routes," marked by bolts anchored to assist climbers. Ned Jackson, a ranger at the interpretive center in Almo, says, "We are written up in international rock climbing guides so they all know about this unique park area."

In the midst of the City of Rocks National Historic Landmark.

Rock climbers at the City of Rocks. —Rick Just

Visitors find few amenities here—some primitive campgrounds and a picnic table or two—but the serenity, unique geology, and infusion of history keep people coming. The "city" is about eighteen miles from Oakley on a good gravel road and twenty-seven miles from Albion on pavement.

This isolated corner of Idaho has fascinated travelers since 1843, when Joseph Walker led the first wagon train from Raft River through the City of Rocks and on to California. Eventually 250,000 emigrants passed through on the California Trail, and many of them stopped at this strange formation to rest and recuperate. They wrote their names in axle grease on Register Rock and marveled at the wild and romantic scenery, "naked and piled high in the most fantastic shapes." Some of these shapes were given imaginative names such as Devils Bedstead, Giant Toadstool, and Elephant Head.

The City of Rocks is part of the Cassia Batholith, a granite dome that has been eroded to create a valley setting. After the surrounding surface weathered away, only the fantastic shapes made of harder stuff remained. Of particular interest are the Twin Sisters, about two miles south of the main "city." The elder of these 600-foot towers is about 2.5 billion years old; the age of the younger sister is calculated to be a mere 25 million years. Additional information is available from the ranger station in Almo, at the eastern edge of the reserve.

Emigrants on the California Trail wrote their names in axle grease at Register Rock.

The Twin Sisters in the City of Rocks. Thousands of '49ers passed by this landmark on their way to the California gold rush.

Almo sits near the old City of Rocks stage station, which was on the road between Kelton (Utah) and Boise. Turn north at Almo and drive through valleys fenced with rugged mountains to Elba. Along the way, clumps of poplars and remnants of hand-hewn log cabins mark the homesteads of Mormon pioneers. Off to the west, if the light is right, a cluster of peaks shimmers like a fairyland castle. This is Castle Rocks, 500 acres of Gothic spires inaccessible to travelers except on foot.

Four miles beyond Elba the secondary road meets Idaho 77, which leads to Albion, a picturesque little town between the Snake River Plain and the southernmost spur of the Sawtooth National Forest. To the north, fields of potatoes and beans stretch to the far horizon; toward the south, Mount Harrison rises above rolling ranch land covered with sagebrush, grass, and fat cattle. The town has long been a ranching center, but in recent years a recreation industry has developed around Pomerelle Ski Area and Lake Cleveland in the mountains south of town.

In its early days Albion was a stage and freight stop on the Kelton-Boise run. The first store was established in 1869, and ten years later Albion became the seat of Cassia County. Albion State Teachers College trained many southern Idaho teachers between 1894 and 1951, when it was closed by legislative decree. Most of the campus now stands silent and empty. A few buildings remain in use, and the original structure of locally quarried stone is being restored.

The county seat went to Burley a long time ago, and today Albion is a quiet place brimming with history. The old Cassia County Courthouse and Jail still stands as a reminder of one of the most bizarre criminal cases to have come before the Idaho bar. "Diamondfield Jack" Davis spent several years in this prison serving time for murder—after someone else had confessed to the crimes in question. Jack's trial was a sensation. James H. Hawley, a future Idaho governor, defended him while William E. Borah, future U.S. senator, headed up the prosecution. From start to finish, Davis was caught between the bitter political maneuvering of powerful sheep and cattle interests.

In the early days Cassia County extended east and west for about a hundred miles and north to south from the Snake River to the Utah-Nevada border. The western part of the county was cattle country; sheep ranchers claimed the eastern part. Diamondfield Jack was a cowboy for the Sparks-Harrell outfit of Nevada, whose many cattle ranches spilled over into Idaho. His job was to keep sheep off the cattle range. To back up his authority, he went armed with a .45 revolver.

In February 1896 two herders were seen grazing their sheep well into the cattle domain. A few days later a camp visitor discovered their bodies, each one with a .44 slug through the heart. Diamondfield Jack became the

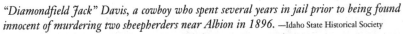

"Diamondfield Jack" Davis, a cowboy who spent several years in jail prior to being found innocent of murdering two sheepherders near Albion in 1896. —Idaho State Historical Society

favorite suspect. Not only was he known to poke around the sheep camps, he was also a swaggering storyteller, a braggart, and a blowhard.

Jack was charged with the murders and brought to trial in the Cassia County Courthouse at Albion. The evidence was circumstantial, but the jury (made up predominantly of farmers from the sheep ranching end of the county) found him guilty. The judge, who later became a sheep rancher, sentenced him to hang. The case was appealed to the Idaho Supreme Court, which upheld the guilty verdict.

Hawley continued to work in Jack's defense, and finally two cowboys came forth and confessed to the murders. They were speedily tried and acquitted on grounds of self-defense. Inexplicably, Diamondfield Jack continued to languish in jail. Early in 1899 officials built a gallows in preparation for Jack's hanging, but just in the nick of time Hawley's law partner galloped into town waving a reprieve. The U.S. Circuit Court of Appeals reaffirmed the death penalty, and another hanging day arrived during the

James H. Hawley, attorney (and later governor) who twice finagled a last-minute stay of execution to save "Diamondfield Jack" Davis from hanging. —Idaho State Historical Society

summer of 1901. The gallows was ready; a crowd began to gather. But Jack was destined for better things. Once again a horseback rider streaked into town with a reprieve.

An enormous body of evidence pointed to Jack's innocence. But, as historian David Grover has written in *Diamondfield Jack*, "a curious alliance of the sheepmen, the Democratic state administration, the Republican *Statesman* and Borah seemed determined that Jack Davis would still hang." Grover says that Governor Frank Steunenberg (a member of the three-man pardon board) was involved in sheep ranching, which may account for some of the bias. A new administration under Governor Frank W. Hunt came in, and Diamondfield Jack was pardoned and set free in 1902.

Jack returned to Nevada, where his old friend and employer John Sparks had become governor. Sparks helped him make a fresh start. Jack turned to mining and eventually became both wealthy and respectable. However, as if this run of good fortune was too much for the fates to allow, he was struck by a taxi in Las Vegas in 1949 and died with his boots on after all.

Continue north from Albion on Idaho 77. At Declo turn west on Idaho 81 and go nine miles to Burley, to finish the loop.

I-84, US 30 and 93
TWIN FALLS

US 30 generally follows the Oregon Trail across Magic Valley and runs parallel to I-84. The interstate is faster, but sightseers might prefer US 30, which meanders past well-tended farms and fields of potatoes, corn, and beans. It also passes several historic sites. Of particular interest are the Milner Historic/Recreation Area and Caldron Linn, located near Milner Dam midway between Burley and Twin Falls.

One of the main features of the historic/recreation area is a one-mile interpretive nature trail that includes a section of Oregon Trail ruts. Visitors can also hike on bits and pieces of the trail that run throughout the area. The Milner ruts are one of the component sites of the Oregon National Historic Trail. In addition to history, the visitor will find picnic tables and a boat launch for the Snake River and Milner Lake. Directional signs point the way. From I-84, take the Ridgeway Road exit.

Caldron Linn is eight miles downriver from Milner Dam. Five years after Lewis and Clark left Idaho, the overland Astorians led by Wilson Price Hunt (see St. Anthony, in Southeast Idaho) passed this way. They made canoes from standing timber, then skimmed along the river for some 150 miles, first on the Henrys Fork and then on the main Snake. They expected to boat all the way down to the Columbia River, but Caldron Linn changed their plans. Here the river roared through a narrow chute and dropped into a swirling vortex. In *On the Oregon Trail*, Robert Stuart quotes one party member as saying the violent stretch of water "beggars all description. . . . Hecate's caldron was never half so agitated when vomiting even the most diabolical spells, as is this Linn in a low state of water." And beyond this "frightful abyss" the river kept raging and roaring on until lost to sight.

One of the Hunt canoes overturned in this churning water, and Antoine Clappine, an experienced Canadian boatman, drowned. After this disaster the gloomy party made plans to pack up their supplies and strike off on foot across the desert, but not before they named this awesome spot. They called it "Caldron" because the swirling waters reminded them of a boiling pot and added "Linn" from an old Gaelic word meaning "waterfall."

Today a marker identifies the spot, but there is no easy access to it. Caldron Linn is almost dry anyway, as the upriver dams rob it of the water that used to churn through here. However, during the irrigation off-season, sufficient water still comes down to float advanced kayakers, who enjoy the fourteen-mile stretch to Twin Falls. Downriver from Milner Dam, the Snake is largely replenished by tributary streams running in from the mountains and from the Snake River aquifer. Upriver from Milner, virtually all the water is appropriated.

Twin Falls is the burgeoning center of a rich agricultural area. The volcanic soils sustain sizable quantities of sugar beets, potatoes, and corn, as well as more bush-type garden seed beans than anywhere else in the country. Seventy-five percent of the country's commercially raised trout comes from nearby spring-fed fish farms and are processed here. A thriving tourist industry also has developed. Twin Falls is within an easy drive of Sun Valley and the Sawtooth Mountains and lies midway between Boise and the major southeastern Idaho cities. A commercial "strip" testifies to new growth. The old town is a charming complex of shops, trees, flowers, pathways, and benches. Visitors will find an interesting cultural mix of theater and music (weekly concerts in City Park) and several municipal parks.

Settlement first came to the Twin Falls area in the 1870s, when gold was discovered in the Snake River gravel. Helter-skelter camps grew in the canyon at Springtown, Dry Town, and Chinatown, and solitary miners scattered for a distance of fifty miles up and down the river. Springtown, half a mile below Hansen Bridge, was the main metropolis. Supplies came in from Rock Creek Station and were carried by burros down the canyon wall along an old Indian trail.

Charlie Walgamott arrived on the scene in 1875 and wrote a rare account of life in these camps. Charlie became a full-fledged miner for a while and worked a strip of "pay gravel" with a partner. The gravel was located about 300 feet from the river. Charlie, the junior partner, was chosen to pack the rock to the river's edge, where his partner ran it through the sluice. "Four hundred buckets of dirt were considered a day's work," he wrote in *Six Decades Back*.

Charlie gives us a glimpse of social conditions, too. He says of Springtown, "Few lasting acquaintances were made and few men knew their neighbors excepting by their given name—Tom or Bill, with usually a nickname attached, such as 'Fat Bacon Tom' or 'Sourdough Bill,' to designate them from other Bills and Toms. This was all done in good humor." By spring, the miners were hungry for some kind of fresh greens, having eaten bacon and beans all winter. Charlie was much impressed by the dry beans his Chinese neighbors so cleverly turned into green sprouts and willingly shared.

The placers yielded fine stuff called flour gold. Each fall it was pretty well played out, but the spring runoff brought a fresh supply, so it seemed inexhaustible. However, one year nothing came down but mud. Most of the prospectors pulled up stakes and flocked to the new Wood River mines in 1879.

About the time gold prospectors moved into the Magic Valley, so did cattlemen. During the 1870s thousands of Texas cattle arrived to graze on the Snake River Plain, where nutritious grasses grew alongside the sagebrush. However, permanent settlement and a substantial population came only with the magic of irrigation.

I. B. Perrine came to the area in 1884 and began to develop his picturesque Blue Lakes farm. In this sheltered retreat he cultivated small fruits, vegetables, and orchards that turned out prize-winning produce. Perrine gained a national reputation as his fruit captured gold medals from such prestigious fairs as the Paris Exposition and the St. Louis World's Fair of 1904. Today the canyon ranch is the private domain of the Blue Lakes Country Club.

Once he learned the value of irrigation and the richness of the desert soil, he was driven by a dream to bring water to the surrounding sagebrush land. When Congress passed the Carey Act in 1894, it seemed made-to-order for prospective irrigators. This bill provided that a million acres of public land would be granted to each arid state that could make the desert productive. Once water was available, settlers could gain ownership of the land by filing on it for a nominal fee, planting crops, and establishing a residence.

In 1900 Perrine filed for 3,000 cubic feet of Snake River water per second and made plans to build the Milner Diversion Dam. He enlisted the support of Stanley B. Milner of Salt Lake City; Frank Buhl, a Pittsburgh millionaire; Peter Kimberly; and others who were willing to risk their fortunes in this grand venture. Early in 1903 they formed the Twin Falls Land and Water Company (today's Twin Falls Canal Company) and signed a contract with the state of Idaho to develop 276,000 acres of land under the Carey Act. In *Idaho*, Merle Wells and Arthur Hart reckon, "No gravity system so ambitious had been developed since Babylonian Times."

The company, which developed only the south side of the river, was incorporated in 1903 and sold 240,000 shares at $1 per share. These develop-

Grubbing sagebrush, a common site around Twin Falls, circa 1905.
—Idaho State Historical Society

ers bought land from the state for 50 cents an acre and sold it to the settlers for the same price, but they charged $25 per acre for water, delivered within half a mile of each farm.

Perrine and company began work on Milner Dam in 1903, and two years later irrigation water was splashing over the thirsty land. Eventually 100 miles of main canals and more than 1,000 miles of laterals were constructed within Twin Falls County. When completed, it was the largest project of its kind in the United States. Today the historic Twin Falls Canal Company remains a successful user-owned irrigation system.

The Twin Falls townsite was laid out in 1904 on a flat stretch of sagebrush. Legend has it that while inhabitants were still sparse, coyotes were occasionally seen chasing rabbits down Main Avenue, and sometimes the dogs chased the coyotes while everyone watched the fun. Settlers filled up the irrigated land, and the town grew as the leading commercial center for Magic Valley.

Herrett Museum and Twin Falls County Historical Museum

The Herrett Museum, an excellent facility on the campus of the College of Southern Idaho, houses Norman and Lillie Herrett's collection of pre-Columbian artifacts. Their holdings range from 12,000-year-old projectile points to contemporary Hopi kachina dolls. The museum also showcases an important gem and mineral collection as well as a variety of art exhibits. The push to fund a new wing to house the Herrett Planetarium is gaining momentum. For many years the Herretts operated the facility as a public service, bringing the starry skies within reach of the community. It was located adjacent to the family's jewelry store in downtown Twin Falls.

The Twin Falls County Historical Museum, housed in the old Union School three miles west of Twin Falls on US 30, features antique machinery, clothing, photographs, Indian relics, a completely furnished pioneer house, and (perhaps most critical of all) a sagebrush grubber.

Perrine Memorial Bridge

This impressive structure on US 93 at the northern entrance to town makes for a memorable introduction to Twin Falls. It spans the Snake River Canyon from rim to rim at a height of 480 feet and replaces an older, equally commanding structure also named for I. B. Perrine, who helped create an irrigated empire in the desert by bringing water to more than 250,000 acres of sagebrush land.

Evel Kneivel attempted to leap the mile-wide canyon in his rocket-powered motorcycle in 1974 about three miles upstream from the bridge.

Shoshone Falls

Leave Blue Lakes Boulevard (US 93) at Falls Avenue and travel five miles east to the falls. Here cascading waters lit with misty rainbows roar over a 1,000-foot-wide horseshoe rim, 212 feet high—at least, sometimes. During the irrigation season only a trickle drops over the edge. Even then, the grandeur of the canyon and the beauty of the rock formations make the trip worthwhile. A small park and picnic site lie alongside.

Shoshone Falls on the Snake River near Twin Falls. At 212 feet, they are higher than Niagara Falls and are a spectacular 1,000 feet wide when the river is running full. —Idaho Power

Shoshone Falls during the irrigation season, when the amount of water falls to a trickle. Even then the geological formation is quite astonishing and worth a visit.

Emigrants traveling the Oregon Trail missed the falls by about ten miles, as did most early travelers and explorers, including John C. Frémont. However, some of the fur traders saw them. Thomas Farnham noted in 1843 that the roar of the waters could be heard from three miles away.

Bishop A.M.A. Blanchet's party of priests and aides first put a name to this grand sight in 1847. They were traveling overland to a pioneer bishopric at Fort Walla Walla and were fascinated by the grand sight the falls presented. In his *Journal of a Catholic Bishop*, Blanchet says, "We gave it the name Canadian Waterfall because it is known almost only to Canadians who pass on the right with pack horses for the Hudson's Bay Company." When Americans later passed this way, they objected to the name. Two men from the Regiment of Mounted Riflemen under Major Osborne Cross (who came to protect the hundreds of emigrant wagons rolling west) investigated these rumbling cascades and renamed them the Great Shoshone Falls in honor of the local Indians.

Thirty years later young Charles Walgamott saw commercial potential here: He and his partner decided to run stagecoach tours from the new town of Shoshone to the falls. Touring groups came to Shoshone on the new Union Pacific Railroad, then completed the journey by stage "over the roughest road any mortal ever traveled." Once at the falls, they were ferried to the southside "hotel," which then consisted of two tents. When the crowds numbered thirty or forty people, Walgamott and his partner Joseph B. Sullaway were hard-pressed to furnish enough beds. They solved the problem by buying hammocks. Tourists sometimes balked at this arrangement but eventually came around. In *Six Decades Back*, Walgamott writes, "[M]y partner was a good storyteller, and every night before bedtime he would tell stories of rattlesnakes crawling into people's beds. A few stories of this kind usually created a demand for hammocks."

Sullaway also contrived to eliminate the possible loss of the bed pillows they furnished. He tied the corner of each pillow to the frame of the cot with a piece of string. Walgamott says, "I asked him why, and he said, 'In case some tourist gets one in his ear we can get the pillow back.'"

In 1883 Walgamott sold out to a syndicate of capitalists from Omaha and W. A. Clark of Butte (later a U.S. senator from Montana), who thought they could make a big-time tourist attraction out of the falls. They put up a frame hotel on the north side of the river and spent a fortune building roads to their "Niagara of the West." The hotel burned in 1910 and was never replaced. As the city of Twin Falls developed, so did hydroelectric projects. An electric streetcar was built to connect the town with Shoshone Falls. People then took the "Sunday Special," a day trip that allowed them to enjoy the falls and lunch in the shade of the cottonwoods.

Many influential people saw the falls, including Jay Gould, Teddy Roosevelt, and Andrew Mellon. Edward Harriman, president of the Union Pacific Railroad, made a trip west by special car, bringing with him a party of 100 assorted scientists and literary persons. They detrained at Shoshone and connected with the falls via a procession of wagons, buggies, and saddle horses. National publicity followed, and an attempt was made to make this stretch of the river into a park. In *The Snake River*, Tim Palmer says, "In 1901 a congressional bill would have designated a Snake River Canyon National Park here, but the bill died and the irrigation systems were built instead."

Twin Falls, from which the town takes its name, was once a spectacular double cascade a few miles upriver from Shoshone Falls. It, too, has been reduced to a trickle by irrigation and hydropower projects. Some of the locals facetiously call it "Double Drip."

Rock Creek Station and Stricker Ranch House

To reach this historic site, drive east of Twin Falls on US 30 about eight miles to Hansen, then south on County Road G3 for five miles. Follow the signs.

For many years Rock Creek Station was a busy site along the Oregon Trail; the abundance of water made it a favorite stop for emigrants. In 1865 pioneer James Bascomb built the eighteen-by-twenty-foot, one-room log store, which still stands. Ben Holladay stages used this site as a "home station." After 1869 it was a major stop for freight wagons that hauled goods from the railroad at Kelton, Utah, to the gold camps in southwestern Idaho.

Herman and Lucy Walgamott Stricker bought the store in 1884 and prospered with it and an adjoining ranch. They built the two-story Stricker House, which has been preserved through the efforts of the Friends of Stricker Ranch and the Idaho State Historical Society, owner of the site. The store operated between 1865 and 1897 and was an important supply point between Fort Hall and Boise.

Rock Creek Station became a social center for the early pioneers, and its store served many colorful personalities. One of these was a horse thief named Bill Dowdle, whose story has become legend. Charles Walgamott, whose sister ran the station, spent a good deal of time at the station and has preserved the story in *Six Decades Back*.

In 1874 Charles and Irene Walgamott Trotter managed the station with the help of a young man named Wilson. Dowdle reined in one day, and both Trotter and Wilson recognized his horse, which belonged to a friend in Boise. As Dowdle tried to ride off, Wilson jumped him and, after a scuffle in the sagebrush, clamped him in irons. Dowdle finally went off to Boise for trial, swearing vengeance on everybody at Rock Creek.

Three years later, fresh out of the territorial penitentiary, Dowdle returned to Rock Creek to settle the score with his enemies. He was enraged to learn that Wilson had moved on and that Trotter was in bed with typhoid fever. He drank a few whiskeys to relieve his frustration, then went outside and began firing indiscriminately. One shot dropped the blacksmith, and when the boy in charge of the store appeared in the doorway to see what was going on, Bill fired again and hit the door casing (the hole is still there). The boy grabbed his gun and returned the fire. Dowdle fell, mortally wounded, exclaiming, "Such is the life, boys, in the days of Forty Nine."

Dowdle's burial in the Rock Creek cemetery was something of a celebration. With no clergyman present and no hymnbooks, the crowd took its cue from Bill himself and sang an old California refrain, "The Days of Forty Nine." No matter that it was a doggerel song written for some unfortunate named "Lame Jess"—they substituted Dowdle's name for that of Jess, who was a kindred spirit, anyway. The service was conducted at night so the freighters could attend, and on their march to the graveyard, Walgamott says, the procession sang:

> Old Bill Dowdle was a hard old case; he never would repent.
>
> He never was known to miss a meal, or ever pay a cent.
>
> Old Dowdle Bill, like all the rest, he did to death resign—
>
> And in his bloom went up the flume, in the days of Forty-Nine.

Dowdle was the third person consigned to the Rock Creek cemetery. All three had died with their boots on.

I-84, Idaho 25

JEROME

Jerome is a growing community with a flourishing dairy industry and thriving bean and potato fields. A more unusual business, the Jerome Bird Farm, raises ring-necked pheasants and chukar chicks. Visitors are welcome.

The Jerome County Historical Museum offers a good range of exhibits, including an account of life at the Hunt Relocation Center and the story of the Carey Act irrigation projects. On the first Saturday in August, the museum sponsors "Live History Days," which includes everything from stagecoach rides to butter churning demonstrations. The county historical society has started an ambitious new project—the Idaho Farm and Ranch Museum—on a ninety-acre site at the intersection of I-84 and US 93. The historical society intends to recreate an authentic pioneer farming operation.

Jerome and Wendell, as well as smaller communities such as Eden and Hazelton, developed as a result of the North Side Irrigation Project. In some respects it repeats the success of the South Side Project at Twin Falls. Chief developer Frank Buhl encountered many delays and financial problems, but water from the Minidoka Project (at Jackson Lake Reservoir in Wyoming) eventually reached the land, along with "natural flow" from the diversion dam at Milner. Town lots in Jerome went on the market in 1907, and the community appropriately took its name from one of the irrigation financiers, Jerome Kuhn.

Among those who claimed land on the newly irrigated north side of the Snake River were Charles and Annie Greenwood, who settled around 1910 on a hardscrabble farm near Hazelton, a few miles east of Jerome. The area was sparsely populated when they arrived, with neighbors far apart. In *We Sagebrush Folk*, Annie wrote of "miles and miles of wilderness, and not a sign of habitation; no tree, no green, only the gray of pungent sagebrush. And, everywhere, leaping jack-rabbits."

It took years of rabbit drives to make a dent in their tremendous population. One winter Annie looked out her window and saw "a river of rabbits, running from west to east, the loosely packed little animals moving like rippling water." By summer the hungry herds had often nibbled away most of the crops—unless the dust storms blew them away first. Greenwood spoke of the fields being "literally transferred by the power of the winds."

The farmers battled white fly in the sugar beets; the wheat crop fell from rust; and sometimes potatoes brought only 45 cents per hundred pounds.

Yet there were good times, and when Annie Greenwood viewed her domain she probably expressed the views of a good many of her neighbors. "I loved Idaho, I loved the vast, unspoiled wilderness, the fabulous sunsets, lakes of gold, and the dreamy purple mountains that appeared in the sky along their rims; and when these gradually dimmed and vanished, a million stars in the dark-blue sky—a million stars seen at a breath."

Most of the early settlers lived on the poverty line, although the Greenwoods were probably better off than some, as Annie took the job of country schoolteacher. The schoolhouse became a social center for the community, a place where farm families gathered for a spell-down or an evening of songs and recitations. Getting there was not always easy, Annie recalled: "Some of the farmers and their families came for miles around, driving through the bitter, biting cold in wagons bedded with straw, old quilts drawn over the family, the driver muffled to the eyes." They brought with them the same lanterns they had used in their evening milking and hung them on nails around the bare board walls of the schoolhouse. On one memorable occasion, the local folk celebrated the arrival of a new Edison phonograph with a music night:

> In the rough, brown-planked school-house, sitting two to a seat, a baby on each desk, my work-worn, shabby farmers and their wives; children standing in aisles; the big boys lounging against the walls; every face intent; not a sound except the music from that morning glory horn. These farm people had felt so much, had suffered so much, . . . had been so isolated from the world—this music, austere, classical though it was, voiced the emotions of their hearts.

About 1916, a new schoolhouse named the Greenwood School was built six miles east of Hazelton in Jerome County. The old two-room school still stands, abandoned, across from the former Greenwood property. Years later another band of pioneers would come, but not by choice. One of the momentous events in Jerome took place in the summer of 1942. In the wake of Japan's attack on Pearl Harbor, more than 110,000 persons of Japanese ancestry were suddenly expelled from their homes as a "security measure." Not one of them was accused of any crime or given due process of law. Approximately 10,000 of these displaced persons landed at Jerome and were taken to the hastily constructed Minidoka Camp fifteen miles east of town. Today only a few tangible fragments of the camp remain—the ruins of a stone wall, the chimney of the guardhouse, and the trace of a street whose barbed-wire-enclosed barracks once stretched across the desert for two and a half miles.

Most of the internees came from the Seattle area, where the land was cool and green. Minidoka was a different world. During the first summer they scorched in 110-degree heat on the bleak sagebrush landscape in crude barracks. In *Executive Order 9066*, David Takami recorded the impressions of one young man: "Some people just broke down and bawled. . . . There

Japanese American internees arriving at the Minidoka internment camp at Hunt in the summer of 1942. They lived here in tar-paper shacks for the duration of World War II. —National Archives

are many rattlesnakes and scorpions and besides these there are black widows, bull snakes, beetles, horned toads and of course the very persistent mosquito." Like Annie Greenwood, one of the girls remembered sandstorms and swirling brown dust that enveloped everything and seeped into the living quarters. Winter brought relief from the heat and dust, but then bitter winds blew in icy blasts against the thin barracks, where potbellied stoves fired with sagebrush provided the only heat.

Eventually community life emerged in the form of schools, newspapers, sports teams, and a library. The Japanese staffed their own hospital and formed an outstanding choir, which, because of its excellence, was permitted to perform concerts in neighboring towns. As time went on, some of the internees made beautiful gardens of desert shrubs and wildflowers. Woodcarvers fashioned lamps and lacquered pins from gnarled greasewood. George Nakashima, who built furniture from wood scraps, went on to become a renowned furniture designer. Kenjiro Namura, already a brilliant painter whose work had been exhibited at the Museum of Modern Art in

Children in the elementary school at the Minidoka internment camp.
—National Archives

New York City, created signs for the restrooms and mess halls. On the northern edge of the camp, some of the internees dug a seven-mile irrigation ditch. When finished, it brought water from the Minidoka Canal to irrigate 1,000 acres of vegetables.

Life went on, with weddings, births, graduations, deaths. Some of the internees even came to terms with the harshness of the desert. Monica Stone, echoing Annie Greenwood, called it a "strange, gaunt country, fierce in the hot white light of day, but soft and gentle with a beauty all its own at night."

Many of the men joined the army. One Minidoka internee said, "If we are to be embodied in the American grain so conclusively that we can never again be smeared and reviled by bigots ... there is no course for the eligible among us but to get into the uniforms of Uncle Sam's fighting forces." More than 300 young men volunteered from Minidoka and joined battalions later distinguished for bravery in World War II.

The traumatic experience of these 10,000 citizens was over in August 1945. They scattered to new locations to reconstruct their lives and, in time, to enter the mainstream of American life. Virtually all that remains of the old camp is a sad memory. In this silent place even the desert has vanished, and rich fields of beans and potatoes grow.

I-84
MALAD GORGE STATE PARK

This 652-acre park is located off I-84 at Tuttle (exit 147). What appears to be an ordinary desert stop becomes a dramatic experience when the churning Devils Washbowl comes into view. The waters of the Malad River (a different stream from the river of the same name in southeastern Idaho) thrash wildly in a churning pool that makes a chasm 250 feet deep and 140 feet wide. The source of this two-and-a-half mile-long river is a curiosity. The stream bubbles up from underground and meets the Big Wood River (which ends at the crest of the falls) coming in from above. Numerous springs along the gorge produce ponds and brooks that can be viewed from hiking trails along the canyon rim.

The geology of the gorge is uncertain, but the melon gravel on the canyon rims indicates that the Bonneville flood, which gouged everything in its path, rushed through here. In historic times fur trappers came this way and named the Malad River. Lalia Boone, in *Idaho Place Names*, credits the name with a group of trappers who stopped here with Donald Mackenzie in 1819. They became ill after eating beaver trapped in this stream and understandably called it Malade, the French term meaning "sick." The name originally included all of the stream known today as the Big Wood River before it empties into the Malad at the Devils Washbowl.

Niagara Springs and Crystal Springs, former units of Malad Gorge State Park, became Niagara State Park in 1993. They are some of the least developed springs in the Thousand Springs complex still available to the public. Niagara Springs, which discharges up to 300 cubic feet of water per second, is a Natural National Landmark. Take the Wendell exit (157) and head south toward the park for nine and one-half miles.

Snake River Country

US 30
BUHL AND THE
THOUSAND SPRINGS SCENIC BYWAY

The Thousand Springs Scenic Byway follows the Snake River. It begins in Twin Falls and passes through the towns of Filer, Buhl, Hagerman, and Bliss along the old Oregon Trail.

The attractive town of Buhl is best known today as the trout capital of the world. Clear Springs Trout Farm, the largest fish ranch in the state (some say the world), is located here. Fish are raised, processed, frozen, and shipped from this facility to all parts of the United States and some foreign countries. At the farm's visitor center, a seven-foot sturgeon swims in its own private pool. This one is merely a youngster. Its predecessor, the eighty-year-old Kanaka, was a ten-foot giant that weighed in at 600 pounds.

A classic dairy barn near Buhl.

Buhl began early in the twentieth century as a community of dairy farmers, some of whose gambrel-roofed barns still stand. Many of these were built by German pioneers and serve as a reminder of their practical old adage, "the barn builds the house." The town was named for Frank Buhl, one of the financiers of regional irrigation projects.

Balanced Rock

This basaltic monolith stands twenty-two miles southwest of Buhl. Leave Buhl on the Castleford Road (also 1400 East Road). It leads to the Balanced Rock Road and Salmon Creek Canyon, with its sculptured rocks and pillars of stone. Balanced Rock is beyond the creekside park. Perched atop the rimrock, it resembles something halfway between a giant mushroom and a question mark. It stands forty-eight feet high and is nearly as wide at the top. This amazing piece of geology balances on a three-foot stem of lava.

Thousand Springs Valley

Eighteen miles downriver from Buhl, the Thousand Springs emerge in instant waterfalls from the north side of the canyon wall. In earlier times this unexpected gush of water seemed magical. However, today's geologists know that the springwater percolates through the porous Snake River aquifer. Forty percent of this underground water comes from the upper Snake River Plain above Idaho Falls. The Big and Little Lost rivers, which sink away near Howe, account for a large percentage of it, and the rest is from rain, snowmelt, and irrigation water. Altogether this is one of the largest groundwater systems in the world.

Oregon Trail emigrants were fascinated by the sheet of cascades that poured from the canyon wall. The name Thousand Springs graphically described the sight, and it became a milepost marking 1,363.5 miles from Independence, Missouri. Today most of the water that "fell in a white foam" has been siphoned off for hydropower and fish farms. Only one of the major falls remains in its natural state, although several small cascades can still be seen pouring from the rimrock.

After its journey beneath the Snake River Plain, the underground water, filtered to crystal clear, emerges year-round at a temperature of 58 degrees Fahrenheit—perfect for raising trout. Early settlers were quick to see the possibilities. The industry began in 1928 with the Snake River Trout Company. Today the fish farms that dot the river between Twin Falls and Bliss furnish 75 percent of the commercial trout eaten in the United States.

In addition to the cascades, underground springs, both hot and cold, bubble up throughout the valley. Geothermal swimming pools can be found at the historic Banbury Hot Springs, Miracle Springs, and Sligar's, all of which are in the falls area.

This thundering cascade traveled through the Snake River aquifer and emerged as part of the famous Thousand Springs near Buhl. The water is used for power generation at the nearby Idaho Power hydroelectric facility and is then recycled, splashing down the canyon wall.

US 30
HAGERMAN

For years Hagerman was known for its beautiful valley, the choice farmland confined within the walls of the Snake River Canyon, and the clumps of poplar trees that marched in phalanxes up the valley, marking the old homesteads. Today one hears more about the Rose Creek Winery, the fossil beds, and the fish hatcheries.

The historic U.S. Bank structure is recognized for its pioneering lava-rock construction and interior grillwork. Inside, the years roll back, and visitors feel they are back in the Wild West. Tellers work behind antique grillwork at a counter supported by walnut paneling complete with a brass footrail. Some historians consider the original portions of grillwork to be among the finest examples of its kind in the West. Completed in 1887, the old building has served a variety of purposes and now holds a spot on the National Register of Historic Places.

Vineyard culture is relatively new to Hagerman Valley. The downtown Rose Creek Winery uses a substantial portion of local grapes to supplement those imported from Washington. Johannisberg Riesling is popular, as are blends with good Idaho names such as Basque Red, Rose Creek Mist, and Thousand Springs.

Several shops along Main Street specialize in historic crafts. These include Advance to Go, a stained-glass store and workshop that also displays local art; the Tepee Shop, which sells Sioux-type tepees (from which the Nez Perce and Northern Shoshone adapted theirs); and Joe's OK Saddlery, where young cowboys can watch demonstrations of this old-time western skill.

The nearby National Fish Hatchery and Idaho State Fish Hatchery, which includes a thirty-five-acre natural preserve along the river, are both popular with visitors. These facilities produce a variety of fish for eventual distribution to streams. The U.S. Fish and Wildlife Service's Tunison Laboratory conducts sturgeon research aimed at restoring this historic fish to its natural Snake River habitat. If this experiment succeeds, can caviar be far behind?

At Thousand Springs Farm, an historic 427-acre site, the pristine Minnie Miller Springs gush from the canyon wall. For seventy-five years, Minnie Miller and the Judge Willis Ritter family defended the springs against development. Consequently, these springs (running at 800 cubic feet of water per second) are the only major ones in the Thousand Springs complex that have not been channeled into some sort of commercial enterprise. Today the farm and the surrounding land are owned by the Nature Conservancy and operated as a natural preserve. The site is open to visitors during the summer season.

Early in the twentieth century Minnie Miller operated a classic dairy farm here, and her prizewinning Guernsey stock was known far and wide. In 1944 the farm was featured in *National Geographic* as one of Idaho's most spectacular areas. The stately farmhouse, built around 1920 from local lava rock, now serves as an interpretive center. Still to be developed are the dairy museum and an aquarium depicting the unique characteristics of Thousand Springs. The farm is adjacent to a historic hydroelectric plant.

The Hagerman Valley Historical Society Museum showcases many pioneer relics important to the area, but the most unique display is the 3.5-million-year-old Hagerman Horse (*Equus simplicidens*), which comes from the Hagerman Fossil Beds National Monument. After this deposit was discovered in 1928, the Smithsonian Institution sent a team of archaeologists to investigate. They uncovered the remains of saber-toothed cats, mastodons, camels, the famous horse, and a number of smaller species. More

117

than 150 individual horse fossils were found, plus thousands of additional specimens representing more than ninety distinct species. These treasures from the Pliocene epoch brought worldwide fame to the quarry, although it did not achieve national monument status until 1988.

The fossil beds lie along the west side of the canyon near Bliss. Large numbers of animals once lived here in a countryside that was dotted with lakes and marshes. Lava flows came from the east, inundating the swamps and entrapping the animals. The results of this volcanic activity can be seen in the lava walls on the east side of the canyon. Across the river, on the western side, are the sedimentary bluffs that yield the fossils. The visitor center on Main Street in Hagerman brims with information, and a paleontologist is on duty to field hard questions.

Hagerman History

The Hagerman Valley has had a variety of tenants, including Indians, emigrants, settlers, farmers, and ranchers. The riverside location provided a favorite fishing spot for generations of Shoshones, who came to Fishing Falls (today's Kanaka Rapids) and wintered near the valley's numerous hot springs. In 1812 Robert Stuart (one of Hunt's Astorians who returned east with messages for Astor) saw about 100 lodges here, with Indians busily catching and drying salmon. When the fish began to jump soon after sunrise, the Indians took to the water. They swam to the center of the falls and pulled in fish by the hundreds using sharp, straight spears made of elk horn and willow poles. Apparently they hit the mark most of the time. According to Kenneth Spalding in *On the Oregon Trail*, fur trapper Joseph Miller told Stuart he had seen the Indians "in a few hours kill some thousands of fish."

When the Oregon Trail was booming, lines of covered wagons often pulled up at the falls, where the emigrants rested and bought fish from the Indians. The place must have taken on the aspect of a trading post. Daniel Hutchinson and Larry Jones in *Emigrant Trails of Southern Idaho* quote Joel Palmer, who wrote in 1845: "[T]he Indians have an abundance of them [fish], which they very readily dispose of for hooks, powder, balls, clothing, calico and knives, and in fact for almost anything we have at our disposal."

In 1871 M. E. Payne established a ferry below the falls to capture the stage and freight business on the Kelton Road as well as the diminishing Oregon Trail traffic. W. W. Dawson, who spent some childhood years here, remembered the ferry and the variety of livestock and wagons it carried. In James Huntley's *Ferry Boats in Idaho*, he recalled: "I saw many emigrant teams cross the ferry—some wagons were drawn with horses or mules and some with oxen and cows, and some even with a horse and cow hitched together."

The town of Hagerman was settled in 1892 when Stanley Hagerman opened the first store to serve the incoming settlers. Eventually the town also attracted artists, craftsmen, writers, and musicians. Aldrich Bowler's Snake River Pottery, with its wheel-turned earthenware, is the oldest pottery factory in Idaho. The late novelist Vardis Fisher and the landscape painter Archie Teater, both nationally known Idaho natives, found inspiration in the natural beauty of the canyon country. Fisher once said that eastern publishers and friends felt sorry for him because he lived in Idaho—and in Hagerman, of all places. But when they visited and saw the unique landscape, the abundant springs on the Fisher place, and the unusually mild climate, they are captivated and no longer pitied "poor Vardis."

Fisher became Idaho's preeminent man of letters, publishing, on average, a book a year for thirty-five years. These included both western fiction and nonfiction as well as his monumental Testament of Man series. All his works are nourished by a strong inclination to scholarship and his keen observation of nature.

The late Archie Teater and his wife Pat also fell in love with this landscape. They settled near Bliss after Archie had painted his way around the world, producing pictures that hang in many distinguished collections. They spent their later years here in a pink sandstone house that cantilevers over the edge of the canyon off highway 30. This gem of a house, the only one in Idaho designed by architect Frank Lloyd Wright, is on the National Register of Historic Places.

US 30
BLISS

The tiny settlement of Bliss began as a stage station in 1879 and still functions as a stop for travelers. US 30 joins I-84 here. From this crossroad one can proceed to southwestern Idaho or take US 26 to Shoshone and the Sawtooth Scenic Byway, which leads to the central Idaho mountains.

Sawtooth Scenic Byway

Twenty-one miles north of Twin Falls is a major junction for central Idaho, providing access to the extreme southeast, Craters of the Moon, and the Lost River country. It is on the northern fringe of Magic Valley and marks the beginning of Idaho 75, the Sawtooth Scenic Byway. This 116-mile route runs from the lava fields near Shoshone to an alpine setting in the midst of the Sawtooth National Recreation Area at Stanley.

Irrigation has made Shoshone a modern agricultural center, but it origi-nated as a stop on the Oregon Short Line Railroad (an offshoot of the Union Pacific). The first train came through in March 1883, when the town was a rough-and-tumble terminus. Carrie Adell Strahorn remembered guns go-ing off at all hours of the night, fights in the streets, and ten or fifteen arrests per day. The only jail was a hole in the ground. Guards were posted around, and any head that raised up was a likely target.

The railroad gangs moved on, and Shoshone quieted down to become a shipping center for the Wood River Valley. Freight wagons hauled supplies from here to build the infant city of Twin Falls, which sat marooned on the desert with no railroad. The Union Pacific made Shoshone a crossroads for travelers. In the early years, visitors came from far and near to view the spectacular Shoshone Falls on the Snake River. They arrived by train, then transferred to a stage for a bumpy ride across the desert to reach the "Niagara of the West." Years later, J. P. Morgan, William Paley, and a galaxy of Hol-lywood stars brought excitement to Shosone. After Union Pacific officials closed the spur line to Ketchum, such visitors detrained here and rubbed elbows with the locals until they could catch the Sun Valley special (bus or sleigh, depending on the season).

The Shoshone Ice Caves, seventeen miles north of Shoshone, are Idaho's most famous underground caverns. The largest sustains a living glacier underneath an arid lava desert. An ice block inside the cave measures 1,000 feet in length and varies from 8 to 30 feet in depth. For a period of some fifty years after the mid-1880s, this natural refrigerator provided a welcome source of summer ice for neighboring towns. The cave is open from May 1 to October 1 for guided tours.

The ice cave is in the midst of a giant lava flow that spread over much of southern Idaho. Geologic features such as caves and tunnels, hot springs and cold springs, and the Craters of the Moon stem from this volcanic ac-tivity. The mantle of gray-green foliage that borders highway 75 covers a sea of lava that has been dusted over with windblown sand and anchored down with sagebrush.

Twelve miles north of the Shoshone Ice Caves, at the junction of Idaho 75 and US 20, turn east on US 20 for a forty-four mile trip to Craters of the Moon.

Idaho 75
BELLEVUE

Bellevue lies in a green valley rimmed by the gentle folds of the Pioneer Mountains, beyond both the lava fields and the agricultural lands of the Snake River Plain. An occasional break in the hills shows the distant Boulder Peaks, and across the valley a fringe of willows marks the course of Big Wood River. This ranching country is fast turning to tourism as the popularity of Sun Valley spills all the way down the Wood River Valley. Bellevue lies within easy reach of Sun Valley, Silver Creek, Camas Prairie at Fairfield, and Craters of the Moon National Monument.

Established in 1880, Bellevue was the first town founded in the Wood River Mining District. It was named for the beautiful scenery, although detractors from the rival town of Hailey tried to pin the name "Biddyville" on the place. Hailey and Bellevue were the largest of several now-forgotten mining camps in the Wood River Mining District. In *History of Alturas and Blaine Counties*, historian George McLeod says there were "several thousand mining locations of record." Most of the working mines operated stamp mills that crushed the ore before it was hauled to the closest town for processing. Ore from the Minnie Moore mine came to the smelter at Bellevue, and for a time wealth in silver, lead, and gold flowed through the town.

The mining days ended when the price of silver dropped during the Panic of 1893, and the Wood River country turned to cattle and sheep ranching.

Idaho 75
HAILEY

Change is coming rapidly to Hailey. Condominiums now stretch out along the Wood River Valley, linking Hailey with Ketchum and Sun Valley, twelve miles away. Downtown services are good, and several turn-of-the-century buildings give it an authentic western look. The Blaine County Courthouse dates from 1883, and the residential section boasts two Gothic Revival gems: St. Charles Catholic and Emmanuel Episcopal churches.

Also of interest is the home in which Ezra Pound was born in 1885. His father was employed as manager of the federal Land Office in Hailey, and when Ezra was two years old the family moved on. His biographers say that as the years passed, the idea of Idaho as a background of vitality and energy became important to him and had some influence on his writing. He lived abroad as an expatriate for most of his life and was in disrepute for pro-Mussolini sympathies. Although many Idahoans have been negative about the famous poet, a new generation of readers is warming to him as the "father of modernism." Idaho claims him along with literary giants Ernest Hemingway and Vardis Fisher. The Blaine County Museum has a good display of Ezra Pound memorabilia, along with a collection of Indian artifacts and an early telephone switchboard. The building itself is a pioneer structure dating from 1882.

Hailey developed with the growth of the Wood River mines and in 1883 beat out Bellevue for the county seat of huge Alturas County. When the county was divided, Hailey became the seat of the new Blaine County. The town is named for John Hailey, Idaho's "Stagecoach King," who platted the townsite in 1880. A year later the place had eighteen saloons and a dozen casinos where, night and day, miners gambled away their take at faro, poker, and roulette. The town also turned out three daily newspapers and installed Idaho's first telephone exchange on September 17, 1883.

Idaho 75
KETCHUM

The Sawtooth Scenic Byway (Idaho 75) follows the Big Wood River, with its green corridor of aspens and cottonwoods, all the way to Ketchum. This stretch of meadow and river nestled between the Pioneer and Smoky mountains once attracted fur traders and ranchers. Now it lures developers and home buyers who seek a lifestyle enriched with blue sky, clean air, and sparkling water.

Ketchum is a colorful resort town bustling with boutiques and art galleries, a public health spa, and all the accoutrements dear to the hearts of travelers. It even has KART—Ketchum Area Rapid Transit—which offers free rides around town, to the ski lifts, and to Elkhorn and Sun Valley. The Ketchum Community Library, an unusually attractive facility, houses a wide-ranging collection, including an impressive regional history section. The library is known for its wildflower garden and is a successful promoter of beautification.

Many elegant homes line the creeks and stairstep up the hillsides. Real estate agents and land developers continue to multiply, and a steady influx of tourists keeps the town humming. For all that, Ketchum retains the facade of a small western town. Cowboys mix with the uptown crowd at the local watering places, and the look of old Leadville still clings to some of the architecture.

Ketchum Wagon Days, an annual Labor Day weekend celebration, mixes Old West revelry with modern festivities. One big feature is the parade of museum-quality carriages, buckboards, and coaches. The high-sided Lewis ore wagons (from the Horace Lewis Fast Freight Line), which once hauled silver and lead ore to the smelters, carry memories of old Ketchum. Classic cars, peddlers, antique dealers, Olympic skaters, and concerts add to the smorgasbord of entertainment. Check with the downtown visitor information center or the Ketchum District Ranger Station on Sun Valley Road for maps, activities, and brochures.

The town takes its name from David Ketchum, who built a cabin nearby on Wood River in 1879. A year later the mining rush began. Rich ledges of lead and silver ore were scooped out of the nearby hills, and soon the Pittsburg Mining and Smelting Company set up a smelter at the mouth of Warm Springs Creek. Naturally, the miners called their settlement Leadville. However, the postal service requested a change in name because a number of "Leadville"s already existed. The town became Ketchum in honor of its first settler, who had already pulled up stakes and departed. The original name lives on at the Leadville Saloon.

After about ten years the mining boom ended, and those who stayed on turned to ranching. Soon thousands of sheep and cattle dotted the valleys, far outnumbering the inhabitants. Ketchum shrank to about 250 persons. The old town relaxed like a burro at the hitching post and hardly twitched a muscle until 1936, when Averill Harriman came to town. He touched off a new bonanza in Sun Valley gold, and nothing around here has been the same since.

Sun Valley

"The Valley," as locals call it, is one mile west of Ketchum on the Trail Creek Road or Forest Road 408. It has become a self-contained four-season resort with numerous condominiums and an expanded village for upscale shopping. However, none of this new development has displaced the venerable lodge, Sun Valley Inn, or opera house, which are still the heart and spirit of the place. Creekside paths meander through the aspens, giving the landscaped grounds a natural, enveloping beauty. Bald Mountain furnishes the backdrop.

Although Sun Valley premiered as a ski resort, it has become equally popular as a summer destination. Families enjoy the wide range of daily activities. An active schedule in music, art, and dance offers a counterpoint to hiking, riding, swimming, and other outdoor sports. The Sun Valley Center for the Arts and Humanities schedules classes throughout the summer, and in August arts and crafts are showcased at the inn. An annual July-August music festival features classical, jazz, and folk performers.

Another highlight of the summer season is the July-August Sun Valley Ice Show, where delighted audiences crowd onto the lodge terrace to watch skaters from all over the world. Such Olympic notables as Katarina Witt, Nancy Kerrigan, and Scott Hamilton have performed here, along with youngsters from the local summer skating school. A unique feature of the show is the outdoor arena, where the skaters perform under the stars.

Sun Valley Lodge with Bald Mountain in the background.

Sun Valley was the dream of Averill Harriman. The dream come true is recounted by Dorice Taylor, longtime Sun Valley publicity director, in her fascinating book *Sun Valley.* Harriman wanted to create an American ski resort in the grand style of those he had seen in the Austrian and Swiss Alps. He also wanted it to be accessible via the Union Pacific Railroad, of which he was then chairman of the board. Early in 1936 he invited his friend, Count Felix Schaffgotsch of Austria, to scout the West for a site along the Union Pacific right-of-way. Harriman started him off in a private railroad car that took him to California, Nevada, Utah, Colorado, and Wyoming. The right spot eluded him until, in desperation, he took the spur line to Ketchum. When he stepped off the train, he thought, "This is the place."

The count later said it was "God's own choice for a ski resort." He saw a magical valley surrounded by high mountains and blessed with powdered snow, blue sky, and sunshine. The count sent for Harriman, who came out to look the place over, bringing along UP publicity agent Steve Hanagan, who had recently turned an unknown sandbar into Miami Beach.

On Dollar Mountain and Bald Mountain, UP engineers designed and installed the first chairlifts in the United States, and Hanagan advertised the whole shebang worldwide. Construction began immediately on the lodge, which exuded rustic charm. A flock of delightful Austrian ski instructors came to teach railroad magnates, cowboys, and movie stars the art of downhill skiing. Daringly, they rode up the mountain in the new chairlift. A summer-winter ice rink under the stars, swimming pools, and moonlight sleigh rides contributed to the fairy-tale success story.

Soon after Sun Valley's Christmas opening in 1936, *Life* magazine featured an eight-page spread on the new resort under the headline "East goes West to Idaho's Sun Valley, Society's Newest Playground." Soon it glittered with Hollywood stars as well as Rockefellers, Fords, and Greek shipping barons. Ernest Hemingway finished *For Whom the Bell Tolls* in suite 206 at the lodge. Gary Cooper came to hunt, Marilyn Monroe to film *Bus Stop*, Lowell Thomas to broadcast the national news from the Harriman cottage. Even Virginia Hill, Bugsy Siegel's moll, created quite a stir at one time. Eventually the Kennedy clan came to ski on Bald Mountain, as did the Shah of Iran.

As Sun Valley grew, the hometown folks could hardly believe the transformation from bacon and beans to high society. Many of them perceived that the luxurious lodge was not very welcoming of the locals. The late Dick d'Easum related an incident in *Sawtooth Tales* that is said to have cured the problem:

> A man in sheepskin and wool pants seated himself in the lobby by the fireplace where he watched comings and goings while stropping a knife on his boot. The clerk presently asked if he was comfortable. He said things were tolerable. Then the assistant manager stepped up. He inquired what room the man had. He was not registered. The assistant manager sent the bellhop to proceed further.
>
> "Staying here, sir?"
> "No."
> "Having dinner?"
> "No."
> "Do you have money?"
> The man folded his knife, slipped it into his pocket and hauled out a fat wallet.
> "A little," he said. "How much do you want for the place? Better make a deal now. It's the last time I'll sit in one of your chairs."

After this incident, so the story goes, the management extended a warm welcome to all comers. Today the lodge continues to offer a comfortable blend of many different peoples.

During World War II, Sun Valley closed and became a navy convalescent center. Eventually the Union Pacific Railroad sold out to the Janss Corporation, which in turn sold to Earl Holding in 1977. He took an environmental approach and immediately planted two thousand trees. Robert Trent Jones designed a golf course that incorporated Trail Creek into the design, adding another thousand trees.

Many changes have come to Sun Valley over the years, but its charm is still irresistible. In every season, sunshine and blue sky combine with the ineffable alpine mystique to captivate visitors and residents alike.

Ernest Hemingway Memorial

This tribute to Idaho's most famous writer is about a half mile east of Sun Valley on Trail Creek Road. A popular hiking path parallels the road all the way to the Trail Creek Cabin (a Sun Valley property used for special occasions) and passes the memorial en route. This setting is always beautiful, colored with wildflowers in the summer and aspens in the fall. The snows of winter transform it into an entirely different view seen primarily by Nordic skiers. It is a particularly appropriate setting for a tribute to Hemingway.

Hemingway and his wife, Mary, bought a house in Ketchum. The writer died there in 1961. He loved to hunt, drink with his cronies, and tramp the big open country along the Wood River. He is buried in the Ketchum cemetery.

Trail Creek Summit

This drive parallels Trail Creek before climbing to the spectacular summit, with its wide vistas of mountains and valleys. The road is high, wide, and safe, although flatlanders may flinch a bit. It follows an old Indian trail that fur trappers also used between the Big Wood River Valley and the Big Lost River country. Alexander Ross and his Hudson's Bay men made their way down the grade in September 1824. A year later Peter Skene Ogden and his Snake brigade of trappers climbed up. When the mines were active, wagon loads of ore traveled over this route between Challis and the smelters at Ketchum. Farther east, the Trail Creek Road (FR 408) connects with US 93 on the Big Lost River between Mackay and Challis. (See Mackay.)

Sawtooth National Recreation Area

The Sawtooth Scenic Byway parallels the Big Wood River to the Sawtooth National Recreation Area (SNRA) headquarters, seven miles north of Ketchum. The headquarters building—an extravagant structure of wood, glass, and peaked roofs that in a man-made way almost does justice to the majestic mountains around it—offers some excellent dioramas and an outstanding display of photos highlighting human history in the Sawtooths and providing insight to the area's wildlife.

This 756,000-acre paradise encompassing the Boulder, White Cloud, Smoky, and Sawtooth mountains was created by Congress in 1972. This extraordinary land of lakes (300 of them), rushing streams, glacial basins, and grassy meadows provides unlimited outdoor recreation. During the summer months, cattle and sheep graze in the valleys. The most restrictive part of the SNRA is the 216,000-acre wilderness area that straddles the Sawtooth Mountains. In this roadless area, visitors must travel by foot or horseback to reach sparkling lakes, alpine peaks, and hidden recesses.

Heading north from SNRA headquarters, the Sawtooth Scenic Byway follows the Big Wood River to the base of Galena Summit. This 8,700-foot pass divides the Wood River Valley from the Sawtooth Valley. The summit presents a spectacular vista. Two thousand feet below, the headwaters of the Salmon River flow across a magnificent valley with the serrated Sawtooth Mountains for a backdrop.

Alexander Ross and his band of Hudson's Bay trappers crossed this ridge from the Wood River drainage in September 1824. They doubtless felt the thrill of space and grandeur as they eyed these wild and scenic Sawtooths for the first time. Other trappers crossed the valley occasionally, but it took the gleam of gold and silver to induce settlement. In the 1880s a small community began near the summit, close to a cluster of mines and smelters. It took its name from the lead-silver ore found here, called galena. Several saloons, stores, eating places, a stage line to Hailey, and a post office thrived at Galena despite almost unbelievable winter snows. During the 1930s, long after the mining days were over, Pearl Eva Barber ran a country store here and found keeping supplies on hand to be a perennial problem. The road across the summit had undergone some improvement by then, although it was still narrow, steep, and treacherous. Model T Fords went up in reverse.

For a closer look at the headwaters of the Salmon River, drive along the western base of the summit for a mile or two. A dirt road leads through a sprinkling of sage, pine, and aspen to a wet meadow cut by the tiny stream, which can be crossed in a single stride. There's little promise here of the white-water rafting so popular thirty miles downstream. The grasses that grow in this valley make good sheep range, so don't be surprised to see a herder's chuck wagon parked beneath a stand of aspens and a band of woolies grazing nearby.

A quarter mile west of the Smiley Creek store, travelers may opt to leave Idaho 75 for a side trip to old Vienna. Follow Smiley Creek Canyon for about seven miles (summer only) to what remains of this old mining camp. Between 1880 and 1887, about 800 people lived here, and the city boasted all the trappings of a frontier gold and silver town, including Chinese laundries. Local writer Esther Yarber says that one mill was equipped with twenty stamps and a 200-horsepower Corliss steam-fired engine. It could process fifty tons of ore in twenty-four hours—a modest but, in view of the terrain, admirable operation. Not much remains of the old townsite—a few foundations, rotting logs, and whatever excitement the imagination can conjure up.

Approximately one mile past the turnoff for Vienna (mile 167), you may opt for a side trip to Sawtooth City. Take the Beaver Creek Road and drive three miles to the old townsite. It has all but vanished. Only one cabin remains, propped up by the surrounding trees.

Home on the range. This Peruvian herder in the Sawtooth Mountains plays his guitar to while away the lonely hours in camp.

A band of sheep in the Sawtooth Valley. Although the range sheep industry has diminished, a few bands can sometimes be spotted on the side roads as the camp tender moves them to a new location.

Sawtooth City flourished in the same decade as Vienna. They shared many common hardships when, according to writer Dick d'Easum, "the snow laid eye-deep to a Swede." In *Sawtooth Tales*, d'Easum relates a unique culinary story from the wilds of Sawtooth City. It seems restaurant owner Harry Giese became offended when a customer failed to finish eating his codfish balls, which came as part of the house special. Giese demanded that the finicky diner clean up his plate, but the man refused. So Giese whipped out his gun and shot him in the leg. At the ensuing trial, the jury declared Giese innocent, citing the principle, "If you order codfish balls you eat codfish balls."

After returning to the Sawtooth Scenic Byway and continuing up the valley, watch for signs to Pettit and Alturas lakes. The water in these two glacial basins glistens a dozen shades of blue. Both are easily accessible, two and three miles, respectively, off the highway. No commercial activity is allowed.

The Sawtooth Scenic Byway continues another eighteen miles to Stanley. The Boulder Mountains lie to the east, and an occasional White Cloud peak shines through. But the real fascination is to the west. Here the clustered pinnacles of the Sawtooths present a unique study in mountain sculpture. Down the length of the valley their domes, spires, scallops, and minarets shape the western skyline in an ever-changing panorama.

The Sawtooth fish hatchery—built to rear chinook and sockeye salmon and steelhead trout to bolster the diminishing number of wild fish—is at milepost 184. Daily tours are offered during the summer months. In season, visitors can observe hatchery workers hand-spawning the chinook, which is a *threatened* species while the sockeye is *endangered*. Both of these ocean-going strains of salmon travel 900 miles to the Pacific, then try to return to spawn in their home waters. Few make it all the way back, however, because of the many dams and locks that have been built on the lower Snake River. About ten miles downriver from the hatchery, wild chinook can still be seen spawning in August.

Redfish and Little Redfish lakes were named for the spawning salmon that once returned in incalculable numbers. Old-timers used to describe the streams as "teeming with redfish." In those days so many fish covered the pebbly streambeds that riders threw rocks ahead of their horses' hooves to scatter the fish and clear a path. These lakes are now part of the Sawtooth National Recreation Area. Snowcapped Mount Heyburn furnishes a dramatic background and, with the dense pine forests, creates a memorable setting for the many campgrounds camouflaged among the trees. The only commercial venture here is the historic Redfish Lake Lodge and store. Bob Limbert built the lodge in 1929, and the basic log structure is still in use today. The See family has owned it for many years.

The Redfish Lake visitor center is an excellent place to obtain information on such widely diverse subjects as ghost towns, hiking, and kayaking. A

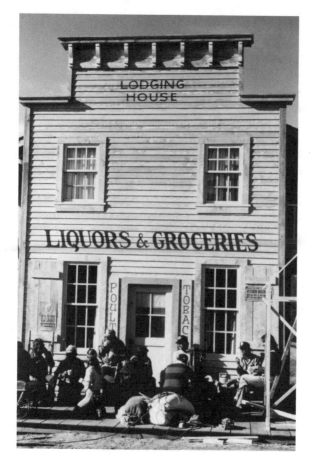

Time out for lunch on the set of Pale Rider, *a Clint Eastwood picture, filmed in the Boulder Mountains north of Sun Valley.*

series of colorful dioramas interprets life in the Sawtooth country. Evening programs take place at the amphitheater.

Idaho 75
STANLEY

At Stanley three scenic routes converge: the Sawtooth Scenic Byway; the Ponderosa Scenic Byway, which connects with Boise; and the Salmon River Scenic Byway, which leads to Salmon City and Montana.

Stanley is an alpine village set in the midst of marvelous snowcapped peaks. As the only town in the Sawtooth National Recreation Area, it is the headquarters for floaters planning trips down the Salmon River and for hikers and campers who come to enjoy the heart of the Sawtooths.

When summer green changes to dazzling winter white and the thermometer hits 30 degrees (or more) below zero, Stanley becomes the hub of a vast, snowy playground. This world offers long weeks of Nordic skiing, long evenings of fireside conversation, and 1,000 miles of groomed snowmobile trails that wind through the forests of central Idaho.

Considering its size, this mountain town generates a lot of action. It claims the largest general store in Idaho, as well as good accommodations and restaurants. Traditionally, this is the place to be on a Saturday night. In several local bars, happy crowds stomp to country-western music, and by 10:00 P.M. the party spills out onto Ace of Diamonds Street, where the packed boardwalk becomes a thoroughfare of blue jeans and cowboy boots. The nightlife is good, but Stanley offers entertainment by day, too. The Stanley Museum displays artifacts and photographs illustrating the settlement of Sawtooth Valley and Stanley Basin. Another attraction, the annual Mountain Mamas Arts and Crafts Fair, draws visitors from town and country, near and far. This annual mid-July event features old-time fiddling, barbecues, and pancake breakfasts.

This has long been a popular spot. Before the white men came, the Shoshone Indians made forays into the Sawtooth Valley and Stanley Basin to fish for salmon and hunt big game. Fur trappers later came in search of beaver. The long, cold winters and short growing season deterred settlement, but when the cry of "gold" was raised, the importance of staying comfortable suddenly diminished.

In 1863 a prospecting party discovered placer gold in Stanley Basin (named for miner John Stanley), and the following year miners stampeded to the nearby Salmon River. Eventually small placer operations were strung out for a hundred miles. By 1875 boomtowns such as Custer and Bonanza on Yankee Fork Creek (a tributary of the Salmon) had sprung into existence. When the mines played out, a few hardy souls remained to homestead and permanently settle these high valleys. Today there is more recreation than ranching, and any direction from Stanley will lead to a superlative day's outing.

Stanley Lake

One would expect to have to labor up a hard wilderness trail to discover such a dramatic expanse of water as Stanley Lake, shimmering at the base of majestic McGowan Peak. So visitors are pleasantly surprised to find a good road to the lake. Drive five miles northwest of town on Idaho 21 to the Stanley Lake sign, turn left on a gravel road, and drive two and a half miles. Somewhere along Stanley Lake Creek, John Stanley and company struck pay dirt in 1863 and sparked settlement of this valley, which holds some of the oldest ranching operations in the state.

Spring fishing at Stanley Lake in the Sawtooth National Recreation Area.

Salmon River Scenic Byway

Scenic US 75 and (after Challis) US 93 follow the Salmon River for 100 miles between Stanley and the city of Salmon. One of the first attractions for east-bound travelers is the Land of the Yankee Fork State Park.

LAND OF THE YANKEE FORK STATE PARK

Leave Idaho 75 at Sunbeam, fourteen miles north of Stanley. Look closely at the turnoff for remnants of the old Sunbeam Dam in the Salmon River. It was built in 1910 to generate power for the Sunbeam gold mine and mill. However, mining activity ceased before the dam was finished, and the salmon runs were hindered for no benefit. Hecla Mining Company has resumed operations at the site, enlarging and modernizing the Sunbeam facility. It may be the largest gold and silver mining operation ever undertaken in Idaho. Over a ten-year period, they hope to squeeze out 831,000 ounces of gold and 16 million ounces of silver.

This old Yankee Fork dredge once scooped up tons of gold-bearing gravel. Now settled into its pond near Custer, it is part of the Land of the Yankee Fork State Park. —Rick Just

The road follows Yankee Fork for about ten miles to the celebrated Yankee Fork gold dredge and the ghost towns of Bonanza and Custer. This historic mining area is the heart of the state park created in 1990 as an Idaho Centennial project. However, local volunteer organizations worked for years in cooperation with the U.S. Forest Service to preserve this remnant of Idaho history.

Several miles of dredge piles herald the approach of the Yankee Fork gold dredge, which did not enter the mining scene until 1939. Now this 988-ton monster, one of the largest of its kind, sits like an abandoned ship in the waters of Jordan Creek. Its seventy-one buckets once gouged the earth to a depth of thirty-five feet. The processed gravel yielded about $11 million in gold between 1939 and 1952. Its last owner, J. R. Simplot, donated it to the Forest Service, and in 1979 the dredge became a museum. Guided tours are offered throughout the summer.

Gold was first discovered on Yankee Fork in 1866, but few prospectors worked the stream before 1875, when Bill Norton staked a claim called the "Charles Dickens." His lode yielded rich gold quartz. For a time he pounded the ore in a hand mortar, then panned the fine dust. In this laborious way, he and a friend recovered $11,000 in thirteen days. In 1876 another party located a spectacular lode and dubbed it the "General Custer," for the un-

General Custer Mill in the Yankee Fork Mining District, 1876. —Idaho State Historical Society

fortunate leader of the 7th Cavalry who died that summer on the Little Bighorn in Montana. Miners flocked in to work in the quartz mills. Additional mines were located, and the towns of Custer and Bonanza took root in the wilderness.

A number of Chinese immigrants moved in and found niches as miners, cooks, chore boys, gardeners, and laundrymen. Their exotic style set them apart. In *Land of the Yankee Fork*, Esther Yarber says, "As a rule they wore fingertip coats made of brocade or black poplin which they called mandarins. And on their heads they wore tight-fitting skull caps to match their coats . . . their hair long and tightly braided hung down their backs."

The remnants of these old towns are popular tourist spots. Custer has a museum featuring historical items that highlight the golden days of Yankee Fork. At Bonanza one can pay respects at the old cemetery half a mile up the hill. However, greater drama revolves around Boothill, half a mile farther on.

A rickety picket fence marks the burial site of Richard King, Agnes Elizabeth King, and Robert Hawthorne—the only graves in the cemetery. Their

Custer Museum in the Land of the Yankee Fork State Park. The park encompasses a ninety-three-mile loop that links Custer and Bonanza with the interpretive center at Challis on the Salmon River Scenic Byway.
—Rick Just

135

story reads like a classic Greek tragedy and may or may not have happened exactly as told here. Elizabeth and Richard are happy lovers. Enter a mysterious assailant, who kills Richard at high noon. The mourning Elizabeth finds consolation in the company of dashing Robert Hawthorne. The new lovers pledge undying love just in time to receive a mysterious pair of fatal bullets. None of the "honest folk" want to be buried alongside the scandalous King-Hawthorne trio, so they plat a new cemetery. To this day, only the three sinners occupy Boothill.

Another twist was added to the story years later. Charles Franklin, a reclusive Stanley Basin bachelor, was found dead in his cabin—with "Lizzie's" locket clutched in his hand.

Bonanza was laid out in 1877 in a precise rectangular grid, and two years later the town of Custer, a haphazard one-street affair, mushroomed two miles away at the Custer mill site. The street extended for half a mile, with the mill at one end and the Nevada Hotel at the other. Chinatown, with a population of about thirty, was, predictably, just beyond the pale.

Bonanza was the scene of some excitement in 1879 when six half-frozen Chinese miners straggled into town to tell a grisly tale. Bandits had attacked their winter camp on Loon Creek, killed their nine companions, plundered the camp of provisions (5,000 pounds of flour and 4,000 pounds of beef, rice, and beans), and set the wreckage on fire. The deed was blamed on a band of mountain Shoshones commonly called the Sheepeaters, al-

The town of Custer about 1880. —Idaho State Historical Society

CUSTER, IDAHO—1880.

136

though some believed that the real murderers were white men masquerading as Indians. Nevertheless, the army was alerted, and the unique Sheepeater campaign began.

Gen. O. O. Howard dispatched two detachments of cavalry, a few mounted infantry, and assorted Umatilla scouts to chase the Sheepeaters around the Salmon River wilderness north of Custer. Col. E. F. Bernard complained of the steep terrain, saying, "This country is made up of streams and mountains. All except the streams are set up on edge, causing the traveler to go over two sides of it instead of one."

According to Brigham D. Madsen, writing in *The Lemhi: Sacajawea's People*, the army became somewhat embarrassed over the less-than-efficient campaign. After four months both the pursuers and the pursued were exhausted. The Indians agreed to go to Fort Hall, and General Howard wrote glowing reports of the expedition. Actually, it took on a comic aspect when heads were counted. The entire band of Sheepeaters amounted to fifty-one persons, mostly women and children. There were only fifteen warriors, and they conducted their entire defense (even winning several skirmishes) with four carbines, three rifles, and one double-barreled shotgun. This motley campaign ended the Indian wars in Idaho.

Bonanza and Custer were linked to the outside world by a twisting toll road that climbed the mountains to Challis. It was a thirty-five-mile trip and took five days. In several places the pitch of the grade was so steep that the teamsters snubbed their wagons to trees to keep them from plunging downhill. In good weather one can still travel the old toll road, now called the Custer Motorway. However, it is rough and narrow and best traveled by high-clearance vehicles. Trailers are not recommended. Return to Idaho 75 for a riverside drive to Challis.

US 93, Idaho 75
CHALLIS

The highway follows the main Salmon River through its colorful canyon. Then the mountains recede, and the valley widens to accommodate a greenbelt of pastures and small farms that contrast with the convoluted outcroppings above. By the time Challis comes into view, the landscape has changed to high prairie country dominated by Mount Borah and the Lost River Range.

Challis is a mile high in elevation and has the least precipitation of any place in Idaho (7.5 inches annually). Cattle and sheep flourish on the surrounding grasslands, and a rich mineral belt has provided jobs over a long period of time. Mineral resources include gold and silver, and for several years Challis has been the center of a large molybdenum operation.

Tourism also figures prominently, as Challis is a wilderness gateway for trips into the Salmon River country and the Lost River Mountains. The Challis National Forest headquarters is located here, as is the interpretive center for Land of the Yankee Fork State Park. This facility, located at the junction of Idaho 75 and US 93, highlights the area's rich mining heritage, as well as the local geology that made it possible. The center also provides maps and information on local activities and services.

White men first explored this area in 1822, when Michel Bourdon and a Hudson's Bay brigade came searching for beaver. The British were still on the prowl eight years later, when John Work and his party camped at the site of Challis. Work's field journal, *The Snake Country Expedition of 1830–31*, tells us "30 beaver were taken" and, a few miles to the south, his men "had a fine hunt in the afternoon after a herd of buffalo several of whom they killed."

Permanent settlers arrived in Challis long after the buffalo hunters were gone. Cattle ranchers began moving onto the grasslands in the mid-1870s, and a few years later mining activity started to boom on the Yankee Fork. Jerry-built towns mushroomed, and suddenly Bonanza, Custer, Bayhorse, Clayton and various mountainside camps needed a supply base. Alvah P. Challis scented an opportunity here and laid out the town of Challis in 1876.

Challis Buffalo Jump

This site, west of the intersection of Idaho 75 and US 93, includes a fifty-nine-foot cliff over which prehistoric hunters drove herds of buffalo. Behind the cliff, small piles of stones mark a drive lane to the brink. The animals tumbled over the edge and rolled down a talus slope to a flat landing below, where the butchering took place. The site was excavated in 1971 by Robert Butler, curator of archaeology at Idaho State University. He found fragments of bison bones, numerous projectile points, and skinning knives. His evidence revealed that the jump had been used some 800 years ago. Even more surprising, a nearby rock overhang provided clues showing intermittent use dating back as far as 5,000 years.

Challis Hot Springs

This hot-water spa once catered to central Idaho miners, and today the fourth-generation owner offers a lot of hospitality to casual passersby. The wide choice of activities ranges from rock hunting to photo excursions to river rafting. Riverside campgrounds and limited bed and breakfast accommodations are available. The spa is located four and a half miles off US 93 on Hot Springs Road.

Idaho 75 ends at Challis, and the Salmon River Scenic Byway continues on US 93 along the Salmon River to the city of Salmon. This little town of 3,500 people is the getaway for the largest wilderness area in the lower forty-eight states—the Frank Church–River of No Return Wilderness. The Salmon and Lemhi rivers meet here, and with the Bitterroot Mountains to the east and the Salmon River Mountains on the west, it is a singularly attractive place. Pickups and packhorses, hikers, bikers, and rafters crowd the streets, and the main attire is likely to be cowboy boots and a plaid shirt.

The Lemhi County Museum tells the local story, with particular emphasis on early gold mining. It also displays an unusual collection of Asian art and textiles acquired during the 1920s by a local pioneer.

Certain distinctions of location and history have long made Salmon a special place. It enjoys a choice location along the banks of the Salmon River, the longest free-flowing waterway in the continental United States. Not far from here on August 11, 1805, Capt. Meriwether Lewis and a band of men from the "Corps of Discovery" crossed the Continental Divide at Lemhi Pass, now a National Historic Landmark. They planted the U.S. flag for the first time west of the Rockies. Two days later, Lewis and Clark and their men camped with a Shoshone Indian village on the banks of the Lemhi River, not far from the future site of Salmon. These were Sacajawea's people, who, after their initial fright, gave Lewis and Clark a warm welcome. Their hearty embraces were almost too much. Captain Lewis wrote in his journal, "We were all carresed and besmeared with their grease and paint till I was heartily tired of the national hugg."

Lewis observed how the Shoshones mixed traits of mountain and plains culture, living part of the year on salmon and roots from the valleys, then crossing Lemhi Pass to hunt buffalo on the western fringe of the plains. Yet the captains found them in "a wretched stait of poverty." They were, however, cheerful and generous with what little they possessed, "extreemly honest and by no means beggarly."

These natives knew the country well and advised Lewis and Clark not to attempt going down the Salmon River. However, before giving up the idea of traveling by canoe, Captain Clark, accompanied by an Indian guide and several of his men, went downriver on a reconnaissance trip. They reached Pine Creek, two miles below present-day Shoup, where Clark cast his eyes on some of the most rugged and difficult country in the Rocky Mountains. He found the river almost one continuous rapid, the water confined "between hugh Rocks and the Current beeting from one against another." The guide told Clark this was nothing compared with what would come farther downriver, where the water goes "foaming and roreing through rocks in every direction" and the mountains are "like the Side of a tree Streight up." Eventually men would shoot these rapids in wooden boats and rubber rafts, but in 1805 this activity was out of the question.

Prudently, the captains decided against the Salmon River route, and on a frosty morning in late August they headed north toward present-day Gibbonsville. They crossed the Bitterroot Range at Saddle Mountain west of Lost Trail Pass, which brought them to the headwaters of the Bitterroot River in present-day Montana. They followed the Bitterroot Valley to the Lolo Trail, now a National Historic Landmark. There, they recrossed the Bitterroots into Idaho and continued their journey to the Pacific.

Twenty-five years after Lewis and Clark camped at the site of Salmon, both British and American fur trappers came to winter in the shelter of the aspens and cottonwoods growing along the river. The huge party of 1832 and 1833 brought together a roll call of famous mountain men. The participants included Jim Bridger (with a newly placed Blackfoot arrow in his back), Thomas Fitzpatrick, and Kit Carson; a remnant of the American Fur Company, fresh from a scrape with the Blackfeet, where they lost the gallant Vanderbaugh; and the band of trappers led by Capt. Benjamin Louis Eulalie de Bonneville, on leave from the U.S. Army. This medley of campers settled in with villages of friendly Nez Perce and Flathead Indians. According to Bonneville, some three hundred lodges of Pend d'Oreilles (Flatheads) stopped to visit en route to the Bitterroot Valley.

Because of the large crowd, food became scarce for both man and beast. The luxuriant bunchgrass that covered the lower mountain slopes soon disappeared as hundreds of horses were turned out to graze. Early in the winter the party broke up, and many of the trappers moved to the Snake and Portneuf river valleys. However, Captain Bonneville and his men stayed on the Salmon and camped with the Nez Perces, as Washington Irving relates in *The Adventures of Captain Bonneville*.

They moved up the North Fork of the Salmon River, where elk and mountain sheep were abundant, and settled down to a pleasant existence: "The hunt, the game, the song, the story, made time pass joyously away." In this idyllic situation, Bonneville decided he needed only a companion to make his life complete, and he approached the Nez Perce headman. "I want a wife," he said. "Not a young, giddy-pated girl that will think of nothing but flaunting and finery, but a sober, discreet, hard-working squaw." In good time the chief produced a woman, and amid solemn pipe-smoking ceremonies with his new relatives, Bonneville claimed her allegiance.

The spot where the Lemhi River joins the Salmon might have remained just another pretty valley but for the discovery of gold at Leesburg. Prospectors struck paydirt on Napias Creek in the summer of 1866, and after they had traveled to Virginia City to bring in supplies, news about the new diggings traveled fast. Miners soon lined the trails to Napias Creek, and a camp mushroomed at Leesburg. This was a fairly remote wilderness, and it sparked the growth of Salmon as a supply point for the mines.

George L. Shoup, a young merchant from Virginia City, and some of his associates platted the townsite of Salmon. As the population grew, it became the seat of Lemhi County. The idea of being one of the first storekeepers in the new settlement appealed to Shoup, and his place flourished from the beginning. He sold everything from cookstoves to lanterns, including whiskey, beans, rice, and canvas pants. At first he packed in supplies from Montana via Lemhi Pass, but when the Union Pacific arrived in Utah, the town of Corinne became the new supply center. Goods were shifted from boxcars to wagons and hauled north along the Gold Road (I-15) to the Lemhi Valley (Idaho 28).

In addition to running his mercantile business, Shoup amassed a fortune in land and cattle before going into politics. He became Idaho's last territorial governor and its first U.S. senator. Idaho became a state July 3, 1890. When the first state legislature convened in January 1891, one of its primary duties was to elect U.S. senators. Political maneuvering threatened to deadlock the process until the legislature finally selected three senators: George Shoup, William J. McConnell, and Fred Dubois. Shoup and McConnell finished the term that ended March 3, 1891, at which time they drew lots to see who would serve the regular four-year term commencing on March 4, 1891. Shoup won the four-year term while Fred Dubois won the six-year term commencing on the same date. Shoup became the first of two Idahoans to be memorialized in Statuary Hall in the United States Capitol. Senator William E. Borah is the second Idahoan so honored.

Salmon flourished as a center for mining, as quartz lodes containing gold, silver, and trace metals were discovered throughout the area. These, in addition to sheep, cattle, and agriculture, produced a stable community long before recreation entered the picture.

Much of Salmon's history is tied to the river and those who used it. One of these was a local character named Harry Guleke, who made a commercial success of freighting on the Salmon beginning in the 1890s. For years he shot the rapids with boatloads of bacon and beans for the pioneer placer miners and homesteaders who dotted the sandbars between Salmon and Riggins. Guleke was their lifeline and their communication with the outside world. As word of the daring adventurer spread, Guleke acquired a national reputation as a river guide. Over the years a good many passengers signed on for the "wildest boatride in America," including politicians, millionaires, and, in 1935, a *National Geographic* expedition. In spite of the popularity of the ride, Guleke's main business was not recreation but freight.

When Guleke began making the risky downstream trips, the Salmon was truly a "river of no return." Having floated down, no wooden boat could beat its way back upstream, so Guleke constructed a new one for each voyage. He would build a scow at Salmon, float downriver to Riggins, sell

Representatives of the National Geographic Society explore the Salmon River with Harry Guleke in one of his famous wooden boats on their Salmon to Lewiston trip, 1935. —Idaho State Historical Society

the boat, and return home by stage or train, both of which took circuitous routes. Sometimes he walked. With each new launch, half the population of Salmon turned out along the riverbank to send him off.

Guleke's boats were made of rough, green lumber spiked together in scow fashion. They were flat bottomed and usually took one or two weeks to complete. He waterproofed the seams with hot tar and double-lined the bottom of the boats with two-by-fours. R. G. Bailey caught a ride downriver in 1903 and described the craft as being eight feet wide, thirty-two feet long, and three feet deep. The steering mechanism consisted of two oars, or "sweeps," one placed on either side of the boat, fore and aft. The sweeps were eighteen feet long, with a blade attached to the end of each one. These blades measured six feet long, eighteen inches wide, and two inches thick—certainly a cumbersome arrangement. However, the success of these boats made them the standard, with variations in size, for all craft that headed downriver. In all his years of boating, from the 1890s to the 1930s, Guleke never lost a life, although a few supplies got churned up in the rapids.

One famous person who signed on for the wild ride was Eleanor Medill Patterson (better known as "Cissie," and for a time as the Countess Gizycka). She was an adventurer, society figure, and, as owner-editor of the *Washington Times Herald* and part owner of the *Chicago Tribune* and *New York Daily News*, probably the most powerful woman in the United States. Her exposure to the Salmon River wilderness gave Idaho a great deal of publicity. Patterson was awed by the canyon and its wildlife and by the way Guleke's home-made boat performed. Robert G. Bailey, in *River of No Return*, says she described it as an "unlovely but capable little scow" that drew only six inches of water. "It swims unresistingly along like a cork over the rocks and through the monstrous swirling rapids, shooting sometimes clear out of the river as it drops down the bigger falls."

142

In these wooden boats Guleke hauled tons of bacon and beans, sluice boxes, picks and shovels, farm machinery, and mining equipment. The owner of the Painter mine, two miles above Mackay Bar, hired Guleke to float down nine boatloads of heavy machinery. A boat was assembled and used for a time; ninety years later, it stands on a lonely shelf along the river, much to the amazement of today's river rafters and jet boaters.

North Fork, Shoup, and Corn Creek

The favorite launching site for rafters on the main Salmon River is at Corn Creek, forty-three miles below North Fork, which has always been a junction for downriver traffic and continues to hum with the activity of sportsmen and travelers. From here, a good secondary road follows the Salmon River all the way to Corn Creek. Many people who do not intend to float make the journey for the stunning scenery and for interesting stops like Shoup. Although now diminished to a single store, the town has seen livelier times, as the remnants of abandoned mines and mills suggest. Across the river from Shoup are the tantalizing remains of the old Clipper-Bullion mine. For a closer look, cross the river a mile or so below Shoup and hike back upriver to the rusting stamp mill and bunkhouses.

The remains of this old five-stamp mill lasted longer than the ore did at the Clipper-Boullion mine on the Salmon River near Shoup.

Corn Creek is at the end of the road and is generally popping with activity. Rafts line up along the shore, adventurers stow away freight for the downriver float, and hangers-on watch the excitement. Close at hand lie the Corn Creek campground and, across the river, the Salmon River Lodge. Jet boats and rubber rafts ply the water, which flows through one of the deepest gorges in North America (second only to Hells Canyon). Salmon River Canyon is part of the Idaho Batholith, where mile-deep canyon walls slice through solid granite and, to use William Clark's phrase, rise "like the side of a tree, streight up."

Although some visitors come only to shoot the rapids, they are soon caught up in the story of humans in the canyon, for this is a float through history. From the red ochre rock paintings and petroglyphs to the sagging pioneer homesteads along the terraces and river banks, one senses the whisper of the past. At the Jim Moore place, nine hand-hewn cabins have been restored and added to the National Register of Historic Places. Moore came to the canyon about 1898. He staked a mining claim but stayed on to grow fruit, vegetables, and beef for prospectors on their way to Thunder Mountain. Farther downriver the restored Polly Bemis cabin makes for a nostalgic stop, and Buckskin Billy's "fortress" is a delight. Stories of these two are especially fascinating and have been broadcast nationwide. Polly Bemis's life is retold in *Thousand Pieces of Gold*, and Sylvan Ambrose Hart, better

Red pictographs in the Salmon River Canyon.

The Jim Moore place about 1897.

The Jim Moore place after preservation and restoration.

known as Buckskin Billy, is remembered in *The Last of the Mountain Men* (see Riggins, in North Idaho).

Elk, bighorn sheep, black bear, and deer are often seen on journeys downriver, although not in the great numbers of former years. Robert Bailey claimed that during his 1903 float, "for a distance of 100 miles along our route there was never a half hour that some kind of game was not in sight." Deer and elk, particularly, frequented the hot springs, where alkaline residues made good salt licks. Bailey's party watched the deer around one spring and counted seventy-two females in the lick at one time.

Old hiking trails that brought miners and packers to the Salmon River Canyon and to mining camps such as Leesburg, Warren, Dixie, and Thunder Mountain lace the wilderness. For those who want to go on foot, an excellent guide to this backcountry is Margaret Fuller's *Trails of the Frank Church–River of No Return Wilderness*.

Leesburg

At the picturesque ghost town of Leesburg, a few of the original cabins built in 1866 still stand. To get there, take US 93 approximately six miles south of Salmon to the graveled Williams Creek Road, which arrives at Leesburg about eighteen miles distant. Gold was discovered here on Napias Creek in the fall of 1866, setting off a new stampede. Miners flocked in from Virginia City and then from every direction, and soon some 2,000 prospectors were digging up the creek beds with picks and shovels. Supplies came in on a steady stream of pack animals (in trains up to sixty mules long) outfitted across the mountains in Montana.

During the first winter most of the miners left for lower country, but some 500 men decided to tough it out in camp. A severe winter came on, and only travel by snowshoe kept up communication with the outside. With drifts piled four to twenty feet high, almost nobody wanted to venture out. Supplies began to run short, and a correspondent to the *Montana Post* suggested medical aid was needed: "We have two men with ax cuts in their feet; two frozen men; one gunshot wound, and any quantity of coughs and colds, together with some rheumatism, and there is no physician nor a particle of medicine in the camp."

In these straits, a team of miners decided to shovel out a "toll" trail. They started early in February and by March 8 had cleared a slot through the worst of the snow wide enough for a pack animal. Needless to say, the camp was overjoyed when the first batch of supplies came down this narrow channel—and nobody complained of the toll. Idaho historian Merle Wells counts this as "one of the exceptional ventures in the history of mining transportation."

The Leesburg population stabilized at about 2,000 for three or four years. The discovery party and other early arrivals were Southern sympathizers and named the camp after Gen. Robert E. Lee. A Northern contingent set

Remains of old Leesburg, which was founded on Napias Creek in 1866. This mining camp stimulated the growth of the more durable Salmon City, which originally grew as a supply center. —Idaho State Historical Society

up a rival camp about a mile down the trail and named it Grantsville, but for all practical purposes it was all one camp with a long main street. The name Leesburg stuck, and people soon forgot about Grantsville.

The trail to the Leesburg area was never easy. After the turn of the century some of the creeks in the basin were dredged, and years later Frank Bryant, a young mining engineer, recalled the skill and horsepower it took to bring in the machinery. In Wells's *Gold Camps and Silver Cities*, he recalled how his friend Doc Hudkins, "a big, red-complected man and 'boss freighter'" hauled in a load—most of it uphill.

> I saw him pull the spud of a dredge twelve miles from Salmon to Bohannon Bar. The spud weighed thirty-six thousand pounds. He put it on a special wagon with thirty-two head of horses hooked onto it. . . . He climbed aboard the near wheeler and called, "Yeah Blue." Every horse leaned into the collar and the spud moved off. He hauled that tremendous load to the dredge site in one day.

The Leesburg rush was significant because it led to the development of Salmon as a service community and to the exploration of a large undeveloped area of Idaho. Mining continued off and on for years, and today there is new interest. According to Virginia Gillerman of the Idaho Geologic Survey, a recent discovery at the FMC mine near Leesburg is projected to be the biggest single gold prospect in the state's history.

Lemhi and Birch Creek Valleys

These two valleys merge to make up one long, narrow, northwest-trending valley between the Bitterroot and Beaverhead mountains on the east and the 100-mile-long Lemhi Range on the west. Similar valleys—the Little Lost River–Pahsimeroi Valley and the Big Lost River Valley—lie west of the Lemhis. All of these are a part of the basin-and-range province, formed when heat and pressure inside the earth pushed the mountains up along fault lines and dropped the valley floors. This is big country. The long, linear valleys range from 75 to 100 miles in length. The mountains are high and settlement is sparse, with more livestock than people.

People have lived here a long time. The Birch Creek studies of the late archaeologist Earl Swanson indicate that ancestors of the Shoshone Indians inhabited this area more than 8,000 years ago.

Idaho 28
LEMHI PASS

Travel south of Salmon on Idaho 28 for nineteen miles, turn east at Tendoy, and go about eight miles on a good dirt road that leads to Lemhi Pass. This marks the spot where Lewis and Clark first crossed the Continental Divide and entered Idaho. It is easily accessible yet high enough in altitude to present a panoramic view of the valley and the mountains beyond. Captain Lewis may have felt discouraged as he reached this spot and looked across the valley to see "immence ranges of high mountains still to the West of us." Descending the divide, he found a "handsome bold running Creek" and happily drank for the first time "the water of the great Columbia river."

On the Montana side of the divide, the attractive Sacajawea Park provides a good picnic site. On the Idaho side, those who want to hike in the footsteps of Lewis and Clark will find markers pointing out the descending trail. Return to Idaho 28 at Tendoy.

Lemhi Valley

This valley was the traditional home of Sacajawea's Shoshone band. When white settlers came to the area they established a store, a school, and a post office at Tendoy. These have faded away, but the site is interesting for the name, which honors a favorite chief of the Lemhi Indians. Sacajawea's people welcomed Lewis and Clark, and later, under Tendoy's leadership, achieved a good record of friendship with their white neighbors. In 1907 this Shoshone band moved to the Fort Hall Reservation near Pocatello.

While the Indians still roamed free, Brigham Young decided to send a missionary group among them. In 1855 this band of pioneers arrived to settle the Lemhi River country. They immediately built a combination fort-

148

stockade within which cabins were erected. They named the enterprise Salmon River Mission. As the years went by, Gentiles called it Lemhi—a misspelling of King Limhi, a figure from the Book of Mormon. Lemhi became the accepted name, and soon it also was attached to the local Indians, the river, a range of mountains, and the adjacent valley.

As soon as they arrived, the Mormons set about building irrigation ditches and planting wheat and potatoes. Some of them learned the Shoshone language, and at church services the Indians gathered around to sing hymns. Many of them joined the Mormon Church, and the mission flourished. Back in Salt Lake City, Brigham Young was so pleased with reports from this field that in 1857 he personally led wagonloads of church officials to visit the mission. The settlement seemed to be succeeding beyond all expectations, and for the first time ever he allowed the brethren to marry Indian women (only three did).

By late 1857, however, it became widely known that 6,000 federal troops were marching on the Mormons in Utah to enforce anti-polygamy laws. To some, this seemed to imply government consent to attack all Mormons. Consequently, early in 1858, some Shoshones attacked Fort Lemhi. Two Mormons were killed and 250 head of cattle were driven off. The settlers quickly abandoned the place and withdrew to Salt Lake City. They left little to mark their sojourn here except a tale of rugged pioneering, the name Lemhi, and an irrigation ditch that is still in use.

After the gold rush started at Leesburg in 1866, sheep and cattlemen moved into the Lemhi country. Emma Yearian came in 1887. While most of her peers were busy at the kitchen range, Emma was busy becoming "The Sheep Queen of Idaho." She acquired a 2,500-acre ranch and 5,000 head of sheep. Her husband raised cattle, and she spoke fondly of "*my* sheep and *our* cattle." The story goes that once, during lambing season, she was inspecting her sheep and found the herders playing cards in the bunkhouse. She fired them all on the spot (which may have been one reason for her success). Although she had her ups and downs in marketing, she is said to have made $85,000 in one year—and that was when a dollar was worth a dollar.

Shortly after 1900 the Gilmore & Pittsburg Railroad came to the Lemhi Valley. It fulfilled the dreams of homesteaders eager to get their produce to market. However, the mines played out, and decline set in during the Great Depression. While World War II was still in progress, the rails were lifted to become part of the government's scrap-metal drive. Today the old roadbed is becoming a "rails to trails" hiking path.

In its heyday the train was something of a galloping goose. Locals dubbed it the "G & P," or "Get out and Push." It crossed the Bitterroots at Bannock Pass and connected Armstead, Montana, with Leadore in the Lemhi Valley. From here it branched, one track going north to Salmon and the other south to Gilmore.

Leadore is a business community and gathering place for the cattle ranchers scattered throughout the Lemhis. It is the only town along the 150-mile stretch between Salmon and Arco (except for the post office–store at Howe). When the Gilmore & Pittsburg Railroad came to town, Leadore expected to grow on the strength of freight and passenger service. However, the lead mines shut down, the railroad proved to be unprofitable, and Leadore settled back to being a cow town.

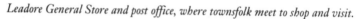

Leadore General Store and post office, where townsfolk meet to shop and visit.

Historic twenty-mule team hauling lead ore in the Lemhi Valley.

Idaho 28
GILMORE

Gilmore, a ghost town within sight of Idaho 28, is located on the south side of the Continental Divide between Lemhi Valley and Birch Creek Valley. As ghost towns go, it is rather large and interesting, despite the fact that it was not laid out until 1910. Lead ore was discovered here in the surrounding gulches about 1890, but not much profit was realized until the Gilmore and Pittsburg Mining Company began to ship out wagonloads of ore in 1903. The ore was hauled from Gilmore to the Utah & Northern Railroad at Dubois and sent on to a smelter in Pennsylvania. The shipments of ore, "galena that sparkled like diamonds," were so large and profitable that mining officials were able to persuade the Northern Pacific Railroad to build the Gilmore and Pittsburg branch. In 1910, the company began shipping direct to Montana on the G & P.

The place flourished for about twenty years, and some of the men involved in mining also turned to ranching. The late Pearl Oberg, Birch Creek historian, said one of the biggest outfits belonged to the Wood Livestock Company, which ran about 10,000 head of cattle and more than 20,000 head of sheep. Many big ranches owned sizable chunks of the countryside. Cowboys could claim a 640-acre homestead and sign the deed over to a large ranch company, which paid the patent fee. It didn't take many of these transactions to create giant ranches.

When the mining days were over at Gilmore, the ghosts set in. Today it is an interesting piece of memorabilia and the gateway to Meadow Lake, which lies about five miles from Gilmore at the end of a high and twisting road. The sight of this glacier-fed pool is worth the effort. A wall of white granite rises up behind it, and down a short path the rocky terrain opens to a small meadow with a stream whose banks are luxuriant with mountain flora. Meadow Lake is one of the few easily accessible lakes in this part of Idaho.

Charcoal Kilns

Turn off Idaho 28 at milepost 61 and follow the signs toward the western foothills for six miles. This strip of dirt road can be a hazard in wet weather, but when dry it is suitable for all vehicles.

The kilns look like giant beehives, lonely sentinels set down amid a quiet stretch of sage where the only sign of life is likely to be a herd of antelope galloping across the hillside. However, during the 1880s this place was fairly lively, with a colony of Irish and Italians who cut wood and stoked the kilns. At that time sixteen of these great brick ovens stood in a row. Now there are four, the others having been raided like the structures of ancient Babylon for building bricks. Those that remain are protected by the Targhee National Forest.

One of four charcoal kilns that stand like giant beehives in Charcoal Kiln Canyon, ten miles from the lead smelter at the site of Nicolia.

A massive amount of wood was slow-burned here to make charcoal for the lead smelter at Nicolia, ten miles across the valley. In its prime, each kiln held thirty to forty cords of wood and produced about 1,500 bushels of charcoal per load. Filling one usually required a full day, and it took a week more for the wood to burn and cool. Hundreds of woodcutters were hired to bring wood down from the mountainsides. It is estimated that they hauled 150,000 cords of wood for the brick kilns and an even greater amount for some forty open-pit kilns. When the kilns were abandoned in 1889, forty acres of cordwood lay stacked and ready to burn.

The charcoal was hauled to a lead smelter near the Viola mine, ten miles across the valley from the kilns. During its heyday this mine was the largest producer of lead ore outside the Coeur d'Alenes. A lively little settlement called Nicolia developed here. Today, only ghosts remain.

At the time Nicolia flourished, neither workers nor their families were protected from the poisonous smelter fumes. Inhabitants were frequently sick from lead poisoning. However, the ten saloons, two wholesale liquor establishments, and a skating rink must have provided at least a few lighter moments. Historian Pearl Oberg said, "Some men stood it for two years but the lead always got them finally. . . . One Chinaman who was afflicted cut his belly open to let out the pain." Children were particularly susceptible, and lead poisoning attacked livestock, too. Herds of cows that grazed around the smelter would die within three weeks. It was equally dangerous for dogs, cats, and horses. Only hogs seem to have been immune.

Lost River Country

Idaho 22 and 33
HOWE

At the junction of Idaho 28 and 22, drivers have the option of traveling east to make a direct connection with I-15 in approximately thirty miles or going west for twenty-three miles to Howe and the Little Lost River Valley.

A store and post office have been located at Howe since the cattlemen moved in during the 1890s. Cattle still graze the foothills and range up the length of the Little Lost River and Pahsimeroi valleys, but the roadside fields at Howe mark it as Simplot country. Here resident farmers grow great sweeps of hay and grain on 3,000 acres. The fields run back to the foothills, and a quick eye may catch a band of antelope coming in for dinner. Accord-

Herd of antelope in the Lost River country.

ing to the ranch foreman, the herds are growing because they get plenty of alfalfa to eat.

The Little Lost River Valley, like the Lemhi Valley, is one of the elongated crevices in the basin-and-range province. Only a few miles from here, the fabled Big Lost River disappears into the Big Lost River Sinks. Along with waters from the Little Lost River and Birch Creek, it travels unseen through a vast, porous honeycomb of basalt called the Snake River aquifer, emerging 150 miles away at Thousand Springs (see Hagerman).

Donald Mackenzie and a brigade of British fur trappers were the first white persons to come into this valley. In the summer of 1819, they traveled from the Columbia to the Snake River and on to Little Lost River searching for beaver. The cottonwood-lined streams here were full of beaver, and, in addition to conducting a good hunt, Mackenzie bargained an important peace treaty with several bands of Shoshone Indians.

When they first arrived here, the trappers had narrowly escaped being drawn into a rather serious Indian war. As they advanced up the Snake River, it seemed that perils were everywhere—a war party of Blackfeet in front of them, Nez Perce behind, and hostile Snakes (a common name for various Shoshone bands) all around. As the trappers were deciding which way to jump, the Nez Perce suddenly wheeled their horses around and took off for the hills, leaving the Blackfeet and Snakes to fight it out.

Prudently, the fur trappers withdrew. When it was all over, the Snakes had won and proceeded to observe their victory in a frenzy of dance, song, and drumbeat, all the while exhibiting their prized Blackfoot scalps. Alexander Ross in *Fur Hunters* may have exaggerated when he said they numbered 5,000 to 6,000, but it was no doubt a large group, representing many different bands: "Their huts, their tents altogether resembled a city in an uproar; and their scattered fires and illuminations, during the nights, exhibited rather an awful spectacle."

Mackenzie and his party, which included 55 men and some 150 horses, waited eighteen days for the victorious Indians to wind down. The trappers were eager to move on to the Little Lost River to begin the fall hunt. When the men dispersed to set traps, Mackenzie left to explore the Bear River country. While there he met a large band of Snakes, who traveled back with him to the Little Lost River and accepted his suggestion to participate in a grand peace council. Two important Snake Chiefs, Pee-eye-em and Ama-qui-em, attended with fifty-four others who represented many of the Shoshone divisions—the "buffalo hunters," the "salmon eaters," and the "sheepeaters."

Mackenzie promised to begin a profitable trade with them if they would establish peace with the Nez Perce and the trappers. A settlement with the Blackfeet was out of the question. The Snakes were eager for guns, knives, and trinkets, so it took only a week to thrash out an agreement. Mackenzie presented each of the two main chiefs with a flag, and the peace was sealed. Thus began a long period of generally good relations between the Indians and the British fur trappers. American trappers, less skilled in diplomacy, sometimes cashed in on this peace settlement since the Indians did not always distinguish between British and American men.

When the ceremonies concluded, trade began. The Shoshones sold horses for an axe apiece. Beaver skins went for a brass ring worth less than half a cent, or for a knife or an awl. Mackenzie said, "Our people might have loaded a seventy-four-gun ship with provisions bought with buttons and rings." Pee-eye-em, a prominent Boise Shoshone, is buried at Table Rock in the capital city. A curious sidelight on the negotiations was the size of two of the principals. Mackenzie, known as "Perpetual Motion," was the stoutest of the trappers, weighing in at 312 pounds, yet Pee-eye-em was of an even greater girth. Mackenzie's waistcoat was too narrow by fourteen inches to button around the big chief.

The 1819–1820 season was successful all around. When Mackenzie's brigade left the mountains, it took 154 horses loaded with prime beaver skins.

Arco is located on the Big Lost River at the junction of several roads that connect the southeast and central parts of Idaho with the southwest; in fact, its original name was Junction. Today it serves a large ranching area. With the growing popularity of nearby Craters of the Moon National Monument, tourism has also become a large part of the economy.

US 20 traces a historic route used by many explorers and trappers traveling from Fort Hall to Boise. Donald Mackenzie and his brigade of trappers came through here in 1819, following an old Indian trail. Alexander Ross and his Hudson's Bay men came this way in 1824. Nearly a decade later the Nathaniel Wyeth party traveled northwest from newly built Fort Hall, crossing the desert past the Three Buttes to the present site of Arco. Here they turned west to cross Camas Prairie, taking the future highway 20 all the way to the Boise River.

Many pioneers on their way to Oregon used this route from Fort Hall as an alternate to the Oregon Trail, which stayed closer to the Snake River. In 1862 emigrants who were afraid of the increasingly hostile Indians on the main trail asked Tim Goodale, a seasoned mountain man, to lead them from Fort Hall to the Salmon River mines near Riggins. When all the wagons were gathered the group numbered 795 men and 300 women and children. He led them safely past Big Butte to the extensive lava flows along the northern fringe of Craters of the Moon, then across Camas Prairie to rejoin the main Oregon Trail a few miles west of Mountain Home. After this success, wrote Hutchinson and Jones in *Emigrant Trails of Southern Idaho*, the new emigrant road became known as Goodale's Cutoff.

The town of Arco began in 1879 as a stage station to serve travelers headed north for Challis and the Yankee Fork mines, as well as those headed west toward the Wood River country. The early stage station apparently offered no overnight accommodations. Carrie Adell and Robert Strahorn arrived here late one night in 1880. When Robert inquired about a room he was told, "Well, great God, man, you've got the whole territory of Idaho spread out before you. Ain't that enough?" The Strahorns ended up sleeping on the floor of the station with twenty-six other travelers.

Several months later they returned to find no improvements and again rolled up in blankets on the floor with a number of other travelers. Mrs. Strahorn wrote:

> We chose our corner and settled ourselves as well as we could, and it was not long before there was a chorus of snores such as Sancho Panza never heard when he said, "God Bless the man who first invented sleep." . . . The whole scale of sounds was there—one man ran the whole octave and then

let go like the escape valve of a steam engine, another gave the squawk of a guinea hen and a third struck a note on a high key and gave a chromatic descendo of four or five notes, as if his body might be crushed by a wedge."

Needless to say, it was a night not soon forgotten.

A few years later Arco moved to a new site three miles away and enjoyed something of a boom. In 1909 the Enlarged Homestead Act opened 80,000 acres to settlement. In contrast to the wild 1902 land rush at Pocatello, the process here was an orderly one, as prospective landowners (many of them from Nebraska and Iowa) lined up to register for the land drawings.

Another period of growth came in 1949 when the Atomic Energy Commission constructed the National Reactor Testing Station twenty-five miles from town. After reorganization, the name changed to the Idaho National Engineering Laboratory. Today the main focus is on research for peaceful uses of nuclear energy and the safe storage of nuclear waste. To demonstrate the more peaceful side of the atom, Arco was lit up by electricity generated by atomic power for about an hour in 1955, a world first.

Prospective ranchers waiting to file claims during the Arco land allotment, 1908. —Idaho State Historical Society

This little town hunkers down in the middle of the Big Lost River Valley, with the towering Lost River Range on the east and the White Knobs on the west. Most of the inhabitants are cattle ranchers, and Mackay is their service center. The river provides a greenbelt through the town, and outlying areas are rimmed by fields of hay and grain that receive water from the nearby Mackay Reservoir. The contrast between the harsh, bare mountains and the green valley is stunning.

Mackay began in 1901 at the door of the Big Copper Mine and was named for promoter John W. Mackay. Over time, the mines dwindled and the town depended on ranchers for support. In the early days sheepherders outnumbered cattlemen. The Thalman family came to the valley in 1898 and settled fifteen miles north of Mackay at a forgotten spot called Chilly. They ran about 10,000 head of sheep on the open range, as did half a dozen other outfits. In *Hard Work and Guts*, Ray Thalman said the sheep raisers and cattlemen operated under the priority system: "If the sheep were there first it was sheep range, and if the cattle were first it was cattle range."

The two types of ranchers coexisted in relative peace until big outfits from New Mexico began trailing sheep in to summer on this northern domain. They added an extra 50,000 to 60,000 head to compete with the cattlemen for the Lost River grasslands. This riled the cowboys. Finally, some of them contrived to shoot a sheepherder of Mexican descent. The herder survived, but no charges were filed because the herder could not identify any of the cowboys who had shot him. Later a U.S. marshal turned up in the valley and lived incognito for several months while he learned the intricacies of local society. He arrested five cowboys who were taken to Pocatello for trial. Thalman wrote: "No one went to jail, but it cost the Copper Basin Cattle Association $70,000, and an appeal brought another $75,000. The herder, living in Los Angeles, finally sent word that he would settle for $12,500 and it was sent post haste. Too late to save several cattle outfits that had already gone bankrupt over the proceedings."

Ray Thalman remembered Mackay as a wide-open town where a lot of hell was raised. It tamed down considerably after the mines closed and Prohibition came in. Even so, whiskey was never in short supply—it just wasn't sold over the counter. Stills dotting the isolated gulches churned out moonshine, some for personal use, some for sale. In one way or another, spirits passed from hand to hand, and country dances were often enlivened by a fifty-gallon wooden keg fitted up with a spigot and a tin cup.

Federal officials had an inkling of the traffic in whiskey, but anytime they arrived in town not a bottle was to be found. Wrote Thalman: "It seemed that any time a Fed got on the train at Blackfoot for Mackay the word reached Mackay long before the train did. I do not remember of a single time when anyone got caught."

Idaho 51
MOUNT BORAH

About fifteen miles north of Mackay, US 93 meets FR 208. This stunning thirty-six-mile drive offers sweeping vistas along the Big Lost River before twisting down the spectacular Trail Creek grade to Sun Valley.

The country north of Mackay along US 93 is very dramatic. Some of the highest mountains in Idaho rise up on either side of the valley, with several peaks cutting the sky at 12,000 feet. The highest peak in Idaho, 12,662-foot Mount Borah, towers over them all. This colossus is named for William E. Borah, an Idaho political giant. When the U.S. Geographic Names Board met in 1929, he was an internationally known statesman, chairman of the Senate Foreign Relations Committee, and widely known at home and abroad. In recent years Mount Borah has become somewhat famous in its own right, drawing 300 to 400 expert mountain climbers each summer.

On a quiet fall morning in 1983, Mount Borah was the epicenter of an earthquake that registered 7.3 on the Richter scale and sent shock waves through most of the northwestern United States and Canada. People in the vicinity of Mackay claimed to have seen the ground rolling like the waves of the ocean. When it was over, the valley floor west of the fault line had dropped 7.5 feet, and the eastern side, including Mount Borah and the Lost River Range, had gained one foot of elevation. Fault scarps now run for a distance of twenty miles along the western base of the mountains. Look for the interpretive sign along the highway.

Fortunately, this severe jolt occurred in a sparsely populated area, and casualties were kept to a minimum. In Mackay and Challis several buildings were seriously damaged. In Challis, a Main Street store collapsed on two children, killing both. Damage amounted to about $15 million. The quake also brought many changes in hydrology, not only locally but as far away as Yellowstone, where the quake altered the timing of Old Faithful.

Cinder cones at Craters of the Moon National Monument. A climb up the cone presents a sweeping view of the lava fields and a look at the perpetual ice in the heart of the crater.

Land of Lava and Camas

US 20
CRATERS OF THE MOON
NATIONAL MONUMENT

Craters of the Moon is like a newly minted creation. Some sections are geologically young, with lava having erupted perhaps only 2,000 years ago. The basalt here looks newly hardened, stark, and bare. In older areas, where soil has had time to develop, communities of sage, bitterbrush, limberpine, and quaking aspen soften the appearance of the land. Bluebirds flit through the trees, picas scurry among the rocks, and a living environment has evolved.

Climb the smooth, cindery slope of the Inferno Cone and from its breezy summit look down on a vast panorama. To the north and west, the dark upheaval rolls away toward the Pioneer Mountains. To the east, a chain of spatter cones marks the path of the Great Rift. This line of weakness in the earth's crust can be traced for sixty miles across the Snake River Plain. It is the longest rift system in the United States and is designated a National Natural Landmark. Here the earth spewed out fire and fumes some 15,000

160

years ago. Beyond the cones, toward Idaho Falls, stands the 300,000-year-old Big Southern Butte, a grand sentinel of the Snake River Plain.

Take in the Devils Orchard, where a thin forest of limber pine grows along with bitterbrush and sage. In early summer, pink monkeyflowers bloom like miracles in the cinders, and persistent blossoms of buckwheat and paintbrush work their way through the narrowest of crevices. Squirrels and picas skitter through the brush, and toward evening deer may come to graze. This harsh environment relies on a delicate balance between the lava microclimates, soil and moisture, flora and fauna.

No river or stream flows through Craters of the Moon, but many of the caves, tubes, and depressions hold winter moisture and become water holes. For the native Shoshones, this may have been the region's best feature. When they traveled across the lava beds, they prudently picked a trail that took them from one water hole to the next.

Early explorers and westbound pioneers avoided this alien landscape. Most of them shared the view of Capt. Benjamin Bonneville, who described it as "an area of about 60 miles in diameter, where nothing meets the eye but a desolate and awful waste, where no grass grows nor water runs, and where nothing is to be seen but lava." Early wagon roads skirted the fringe

Stream of lava at Craters of the Moon.

Lava in ropy pahoehoe formation at Craters of the Moon.

of the lava beds along old Indian trails, and today's highways follow essentially the same routes.

Interest in the area was slow to develop. The craters were not explored to any extent until 1921, when Robert Limbert and W. C. Cole took a harrowing eighty-mile trek across the lava beds. Limbert followed this with a series of magazine articles and photos that captured the interest of President Calvin Coolidge, who declared the craters a national monument in 1924. Only a small section was originally set aside, but it was subsequently increased to eighty-three square miles.

The National Park Service has developed only a corner of this gigantic area. A seven-mile paved loop brings visitors close to some of the most spectacular sights. A vast, primitive territory awaits beyond—sixty-eight square miles of relatively unexplored volcanic terrain. In this designated wilderness, hikers need maps and a compass. So harsh is this part of the craters that astronauts came here to study the terrain before taking off on their moon shots. Check with the visitor center for a wilderness permit. The visitor center also provides video presentations that explain the volcanic forces that created this moonscape.

Triple Twist Tree at Craters of the Moon National Monument. The tree has 1,350 growth rings, and the Park Service estimates another 150 were destroyed by rot before the count was taken. It is older than the lava around it.

CAREY, PICABO, AND SILVER CREEK

Carey sits in a fertile valley that bears little resemblance to the harsh lava terrain east of it. Cattle graze on the hills here, and the irrigated fields support crops of hay and grain that are stored for feedlot use during the long winters.

Seven miles from Carey stands the venerable country store and post office at Picabo. According to Vardis Fisher, the name comes not from the child's game of "peek-a-boo" but from an Indian word meaning "come in." Anyway, this country store watches the famous Silver Creek flow past its front door. Fly fishermen come from around the world to cast a line in these legendary trout waters. This unique stream is not a rushing brook urged on by spring runoff. It is fed by a network of artesian springs that gently bubble up from mysterious subterranean depths. The slow-moving water keeps a year-round temperature of about 52 degrees and provides an ideal habitat for trout and the aquatic insects they thrive on.

Birds find a haven here, for the creek provides wetland conditions in an otherwise desert habitat. Thousands of ducks and geese gather during the winter months. Sandhill cranes and long-billed curlews feed in the meadows, and great blue herons nest in the clumps of aspen. Eagles fly overhead, and along the creek muskrat, beaver, and fox thrive.

Eight hundred acres along Silver Creek have been set aside as a Nature Conservancy preserve, and the agency administers an additional 2,000 acres in the area. The field station turnoff is about half a mile west of Picabo. This has become a popular classroom. Teachers and scout leaders bring youngsters to study the unusual streambank habitat. Hikers and bird watchers love it too, and canoeists find these quiet waters superb.

According to Jones and Hutchinson in *Emigrant Trails of Southern Idaho*, emigrants traveling this way were fascinated by Silver Creek. Annie Jane Biggers Foster saw the creek in the fall of 1904 and wrote:

> But the prettiest sight we seen was at the Silver River [Silver Creek] . . . the water was ten or twelve feet deep and clear as a cristle. Under the bridge the fish lay on the bottom of the river side by side looked like they do when packed for sardines. We all laid down on the bridge and watched them. . . . They wouldn't bite a hook or pay any attention."

Many of today's fly fishermen would maintain they still don't pay any attention.

US 20
FAIRFIELD

Fairfield lies on the southern flank of the Sawtooth National Forest at the northernmost edge of the Snake River Plain with the Camas Prairie as its front yard. Ski lifts at Soldier Mountain have introduced a winter industry, but most of the economy still centers on hay, grain, cattle, and the increasing cross-state traffic on US 20.

The Camas County Museum, a developing facility housed in the old Union Pacific Railroad depot, displays local memorabilia, textiles, pioneer medical equipment, telegraph machines, and additional items from the depot. Another historical attraction, the Manny Shaw Memorial, is located near the visitor information center. Look for an antique railroad car at the entrance to town on Idaho 20. For many years Manny promoted old-time fiddling and helped form the Idaho Fiddlers Association. He spread the joy of fiddling like a contagion and became "everyman's" fiddler.

Winters on Camas Prairie are long and cold, but when the mountains are still capped with snow, spring brings patches of blue camas that color the odd corners and decorate the fencerows. These are remnants of great camas fields so thick with shimmering blue flowers that from afar they were mistaken for lakes. The seas of camas lilies are diminished now, but the vision still lives on in the name Fairfield.

For centuries, camas bulbs were a source of food for the Indians and occasionally for white travelers as well. Nathaniel Wyeth's party made camp

Manny Shaw, who spent his life on Camas Prairie at Corral. He was "everyman's" fiddler and worked to promote this old-time art throughout the Northwest. There is a memorial marker at Fairfield.

here in 1834, and according to John Townsend, "all hands took kettles and scattered over the prairie to dig a mess of kamas." It struck them as tasting something like the common potato. These enormous bulb fields were a natural commissary for the Shoshone-Bannocks, who came here each summer to camp and prepare the bulbs for winter storage.

During 1878 rations at Fort Hall were notoriously skimpy. The Indians were hungry, unhappy, and restless. In a disgruntled mood, several hundred of them packed up and rode over to Camas Prairie for the annual bulb harvest. When they arrived, they found a settlement of farmers. Horses and cows grazed on the prairie grass, and hogs were rooting out the camas bulbs. This was the last straw. The Indians thought the prairie had been set aside by treaty for them. It had been, but because of an error in the paperwork, the place was called Kansas Prairie instead of Camas Prairie. The error was never corrected, and the Shoshone-Bannocks lost out.

In response to this and other grievances, Chief Buffalo Horn organized a fight known as the Bannock War. His plan was to terrorize the settlers and proceed cross-country toward the Owyhee Mountains and Steens Mountain in southeastern Oregon. He sought to pick up Paiute allies along the way, hoping their combined forces would defeat the U.S. Cavalry. However, Gen. O. O. Howard remembered the Nez Perce fiasco and quickly put men in the field. By the time the Battle of Steens Mountain was finished, both Buffalo Horn and the Paiute chief Egan were dead. The leaderless bands soon dispersed and made their way back to their reservations.

When old Indian fighter Gen. George Crook made an inspection of Fort Hall during the hostilities, he was asked why the Bannocks had gone on the warpath. "Hunger, nothing but hunger," he responded.

US 20
HILL CITY

Hill City, a sleepy little settlement with no services on the western edge of the prairie, may be the best place to see remnants of the historic camas fields. The settlement has gained stature with the development of the Camas Prairie Centennial Marsh, and magnificent vistas of blue camas have become its hallmark. Spring snowmelt cascades from the Soldier Mountains to a 3,000-acre marsh below, making a perfect habitat for camas and a prime resting place for migratory birds. A dirt road bisects the reserve, making viewing easy. There are two entrances to the marsh, one at Hill City and another about five miles east toward Fairfield.

Camas Prairie ends west of Hill City, but US 20 continues along the historic Goodale's Cutoff to make a connection with Mountain Home and I-84.

GOODING

Gooding is located on the Little Wood River in a green oasis of prosperous farming country. First called Toponis, it was founded in 1883 when the Union Pacific Railroad came through. However, because Frank Gooding donated the land for the townsite, the name was later changed to honor him. He owned a sheep ranch here and later became governor of Idaho and a U.S. senator.

Bands of sheep can still be seen grazing on the hillsides, but more surprising is the revival of buffalo at the France ranch. As many as 600 to 1,000 of these historic critters can be seen here.

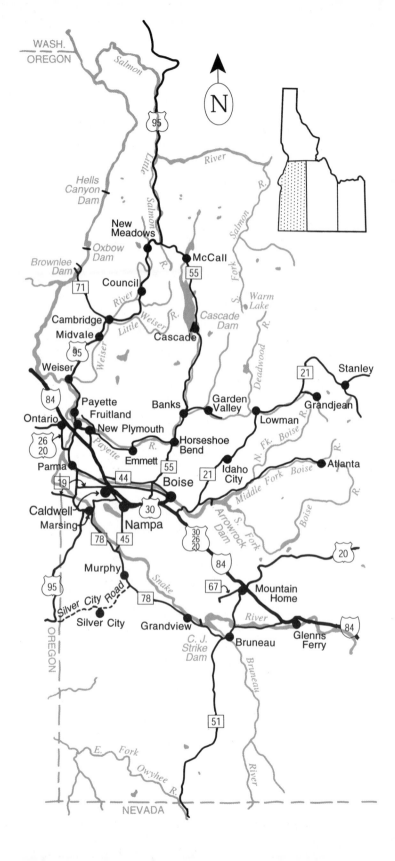

PART 3

Southwest Idaho

As the Snake River crosses southwestern Idaho, its broad plain gradually tilts toward the west. In far western Idaho, near Weiser, the valley narrows. After following its gentle, smiling arc across the southern part of the state for more than 500 miles, the river radically changes direction. At Farewell Bend it turns sharply north and begins its plunge through Hells Canyon. For more than 100 miles the canyon marks the state boundary: Idaho lies to the east, while Oregon and Washington lie to the west.

The lower elevation of the southwestern valleys provides a mild climate with a 180-day growing season. This "banana belt" holds a major share of the state's population. In many locations, galleries of rock art remain as silent reminders that others passed this way long ago. In historic times, fur traders and prospectors left remnants of camps and towns tucked away in the hills. By the beginning of the twentieth century, farming, ranching, and the timber industry were well established, and, more recently, technology-related industries have contributed to southwestern Idaho's growing economy. Land in this area has been booming for decades, as parcels rapidly change hands to accommodate all the newcomers.

~

The River and the Desert

I-84
GLENNS FERRY

The outstanding feature of Glenns Ferry is its location along the banks of the Snake River. This lifeline supplies water to thousands of acres of land surrounding the town and gives it a prosperous agricultural base. Even the plateau lands high above the river are not beyond the reach of water—it is pumped some 550 vertical feet to reach thousands of acres of beans, potatoes, alfalfa, and mint.

Gus P. Glenn established a ferry here in 1869. It served Oregon Trail wagons and freighters hauling goods from the railroad at Kelton, Utah, to the Boise Basin mines. The ferry was used extensively until the Union Pacific Railroad built the Oregon Short Line across southern Idaho in 1883 and 1884. Railroading soon became the leading industry here, although Glenns Ferry also developed as a supply center for area farms and ranches.

Recently, vineyards have taken root in the valley to supply the Martell family's new Carmela Winery. The Martells' own sixty acres of grapes grow on a hillside overlooking the river, a scenic spot that lends itself to social and recreational activities as well as to wine making. A new golf course is developing here with fairways that wind picturesquely beside fruity stretches of Johannisberg Rieslings. The winery offers wine tasting and has a gift shop and restaurant.

Three Island State Park

Thousands of Oregon Trail pioneers used Three Island Crossing beginning about 1840, and the state park commemorates this bit of history. The site includes a visitor center, a small herd of buffalo, longhorn cattle, historical displays, and a self-guided tour of a segment of the Oregon Trail.

Each year the town of Glenns Ferry remembers the Oregon Trail by reenacting the Three Island Crossing. This feat required a treacherous venture into the river, but it landed the wagons on the north bank and set the pioneers on the short route to Fort Boise. In *Emigrant Trails of Southern Idaho*, Daniel Hutchinson and Larry Jones record the description of George T. Newby, who was with an 1843 wagon train. At the second island, Newby said, "we tied a string of waggons to gether by a chane in the ring of the lead cattles yoak & made fast to the waggon of all a horse. . . . We carried as many as fifteen waggeons at one time. . . . The water was ten inches up the waggeon beds in the deepe plaices."

The household effects might get wet, but to cross without additional mishap was good fortune indeed, as people occasionally were swept away by the river and drowned. Even the seasoned adventurer John C. Frémont lost a howitzer to the river, barely saving the two mules that pulled it.

I-84, US 20, Idaho 67
MOUNTAIN HOME

This desert town thrives as the commercial center for the Mountain Home Air Force Base. In the early years, sheep and cattle ranching sparked the economy. During World War II, it became an Air Force town. Today the air force base, ranching, and recreation support a lively business center.

Mountain Home has been a major base since World War II and is currently home to the 366th Tactical Fighter Wing. Planes such as the F-16

Fighting Falcons train over practice bombing ranges in the great spaces of the Owyhee Desert. The 366th is prepared to go anywhere in the world on a moment's notice. The base and the town of Mountain Home enjoy a symbiotic relationship, which is expressed in two annual celebrations: Mountain Home Air Force Appreciation Day in mid-September, and Community Appreciation Day and Air Force Open House in October.

Mountain Home lies in the midst of a sagebrush plain in high desert country that marks the northern edge of the Great Basin, which extends southward into Nevada and Utah. It developed from an old stage stop located next to the hills on Rattlesnake Creek, nine miles northeast of the town's present location. This was near the point where Goodale's Cutoff joined the main Oregon Trail. Originally called Rattlesnake, the station later became known as Mountain Home. When the Union Pacific came through in 1883, the settlement was doomed because the railroad tracks and the new depot bypassed it by nine miles. The railroad station out on the desert acted as a magnet, and soon the townsfolk moved to the new site. But they kept the name Mountain Home.

The Elmore County Museum preserves a good deal of local history, featuring pioneer relics, genealogy materials, Native American artifacts, and Chinese memorabilia from the gold rush days.

Anderson Ranch Reservoir Recreation Area

Take US 20 out of Mountain Home to the Anderson Ranch turnoff at milepost 117. After about five miles, be ready to shift down for the two-mile plunge to the dam and its scenic gorge. Once across the dam on the north side, visitors can drive along the shoreline for twenty miles beside the languid waters of the South Fork of the Boise River. The road snakes around the base of wooded mountains, following mini-fjords, where scalloped inlets and quite waters invite a lazy day of trolling, picnicking, or sightseeing.

The tiny settlement of Pine lies at the north end of the reservoir. Ten miles to the north is Featherville, a mountain town with an Old West personality, haphazardly tucked in among the pines. In the early days the stage stopped here on its way to the mining camp of Rocky Bar. During the 1920s, Featherville was the center of a dredging operation that recovered an estimated 33,000 ounces of gold. Today the old town is a focal point for families headed for the many campgrounds along the South Fork. Food, gas, and groceries are available.

Owyhee Country

The extreme southwestern region of Idaho, south of the Snake River, is hardly a place one would expect to be named for an exotic Hawaiian island, but here it is: Owyhee. After John Jacob Astor established a fur trading post at the mouth of the Columbia River in 1811, his ships stopped at the Sandwich Islands, more commonly known as Hawaii, for supplies before continuing on to the Oregon coast. They also picked up native Hawaiians who later joined the trapping fraternity. Over the years the islanders became an interesting ingredient in the history of the fur trade.

In 1818, several years after the British North West Company took over Astor's fort, three of the Hawaiians signed on with Donald MacKenzie for an expedition to the Snake River country. They separated from the main party to trap an uncharted tributary of the Snake. Two years later, when the expedition was ready to return to Astoria (which had briefly been renamed Fort George after the British took possession), Mackenzie sent men to bring in the three Hawaiians. They found an empty camp, and the horses had been stolen, the Hawaiians killed. Mackenzie named the stream in their honor. Spelled phonetically and garbled a bit, it has ever since been Owyhee.

Owyhee County was the first one created by the new territorial legislature in 1863. In those days, everyone lived high on Silver City mining excitement and a growing cattle industry. Big trail herds from Texas came bawling across the range all the way to the Snake River Plain and the foothills of the Owyhee Mountains. Perhaps as many as 200,000 head ranged here prior to the rugged winter of 1888. There was plenty of room to roam in a county that contained more than 7,500 square miles—roughly the size of Connecticut, Rhode Island, and Delaware combined. Even today nobody is hemmed in—with about 8,500 inhabitants, the county has slightly more than one person per square mile. Most of them are concentrated in scattered towns along the Snake River (Grandview, Marsing, Homedale), where the magic of irrigation allows for abundant crops and prosperous farms.

Off toward the west, vast open spaces and sprawling ranches lie beneath the snowcapped Owyhee Mountains. In this high aerie lie the remains of Silver City. Known as "Queen of the Owyhees," the town became famous for rich mines that once rivaled the Comstock Lode. In the southern part of the county the desert presents a sweep of limitless space. Here a world of grass and sage runs for 100 miles north to south along Idaho 51, from Mountain Home to the Duck Valley Indian Reservation on the Nevada border. The east-west distance of this desert is even greater.

172

Wild horse round-up in the Owyhee Mountains. When the herds are bigger than the range can support, the horses are corralled and offered for "adoption." —Bureau of Land Management

In this ranching country, large operators calculate their holdings in square miles. Scattered springs support herds of cattle and offer a haven for wildlife, which carries on daily living much as it did centuries ago. The desert holds one of the largest herds of bighorn sheep in the country, along with healthy stocks of antelope, elk, mule deer, chukars, and quail. For decades, Owhyee wild horses have been a colorful aspect of this desert.

Both men and animals have inhabited the Owyhee country for eons, and the county is rich in archaeological sites. One of the most startling discoveries came from the former Mark Hoagland ranch in the Reynolds Creek area. A few years ago Hoagland discovered weird teeth, six inches long and three inches wide, sticking up out of the soil, and he called in an archaeologist to investigate. The teeth proved to be from an ancient elephant that roamed the Owyhees approximately 15 million years ago. According to paleontologist Greg McDonald, who is with the National Park Service at Hagerman, these remains are "probably tied in with the earliest appearance of this animal on the North American continent." The elephant-like *Gomphotaherium obscurum* entered the New World roughly 15 million years ago via Siberia and Alaska. McDonald says it is an ancestor of the true mastodon found at Hagerman (dated at 3.5 million years old) and of the younger mammoths found in southeastern Idaho (dated at 1.8 million years old).

Additional fieldwork in the Owyhees revealed the remains of an ancient rhinoceros. These were found in scattered outcrops of the Chalk Hills formation and dated at approximately 6.8 million years old. Ancient camel bones from the same period were also found, along with the remains of a three-toed horse. In the dim past, when these exotic beasts were cavorting about the countryside, Owyhee had a balmy climate and the desert was a grassy savannah.

People have lived in Owyhee country a surprisingly long time. Archaeological materials from the southern part of the county show that people have lived here intermittently for the past 11,000 years. Researchers have discovered a complex of buffalo jumps that were used over a period of 7,000 years. These occur on the high desert of southern Owyhee County, where the 5,900-foot elevation would have provided a relatively cool summer range. One complex had five drive lanes into which the buffalo were funneled and driven to the brink of a cliff. The panic-stricken beasts crashed over the edge and were dispatched. According to Larry Agenbroad's *Buffalo Jump Complexes in Owyhee County*, other cultural features at the site include more than 200 projectile points of various ages and design. The site seems to have been abandoned about 1700 A.D. Horses became available about this time, and the local inhabitants probably gave up driving buffalo on foot in favor of mounted pursuit. The jumps prove that buffalo herds ranged to the extreme western borders of Idaho and that prehistoric people here used all the classic strategies found in the buffalo jumps on the Great Plains.

Today the Duck Valley Indian Reservation, which spills over from southern Owyhee County into Nevada, occupies 250,000 acres on land. The small band of Shoshone-Paiutes who live here graze their cattle and farm with irrigation water from the Wildhorse Reservoir.

Idaho 51 and 78
BRUNEAU

The village of Bruneau depends almost entirely on farming and ranching. Water, both hot and cold, is abundant here. C. J. Strike Reservoir supplies irrigation water, and geothermal wells supply naturally hot water to grow hydroponic vegetables year-round.

The name Bruneau applies to the town, the river, the valley, and the gemstone Bruneau jasper. They all take their name from J. Baptiste Bruneau, a French Canadian who trapped for the North West Company and, after 1821, for the Hudson's Bay Company. The area was not known for an abundance of beaver. Even the seasoned trappers in Peter Skene Ogden's brigade found slim pickings in the Bruneau drainage. The Bruneau River itself was almost inaccessible because in many places its high-sided canyon cuts 2,000 feet into the desert floor. The fur traders called these narrow chasms the "cut rocks." Capt. Benjamin Bonneville, who traversed the country in 1833, said, "[T]he basaltic rocks rise perpendicularly so that it is impossible to get from the plain to the water or from the river margin to the plain."

The sixty-seven-mile long Bruneau River Canyon in the Owyhee country, where the river cuts a 1,200-foot wall with a perpendicular drop.

The earliest settlers came to the Bruneau Valley because the vast range-lands seemed ideal for herds of cattle and sheep. They called it Valley of the Tall Grass. In the late 1860s and early 1870s, a few enterprising men such as David Shirk, Henry Miller, and Con Shea became legendary characters for herding thousands of Texas longhorns to Owyhee County and the Bruneau Valley.

Some of the Bruneau settlers, such as the Wilkins family, went into the horse business. This industry eventually spawned two nationally renowned Idahoans. The Wilkins family settled here with a small band of horses in 1880. By the early 1900s, daughter Kitty Wilkins and her brother John had their diamond brand on some 16,000 head, which they marketed across the country. Kitty, a charming and educated young woman, enjoyed good press and became famous as the "Horse Queen of Idaho." It took a lot of wranglers to keep track of her thousands of horses, all of which were sold as "broke." Taming the mustangs gave the hired hands plenty of bucking practice, and one of them, Hugo Strickland, jumped into the big time. Strickland could ride just about any horse on the range. Well experienced in bronco busting, he left Bruneau to follow the rodeo circuit and in 1916 won acclaim as the world champion saddle bronc rider. He gained the title repeatedly through the 1920s and performed many times in Madison Square Garden.

Kitty Wilkins, "Horse Queen of Idaho." —Idaho State Historical Society

Bruneau Dunes State Park

This popular early spring and fall destination offers picnicking, hiking, fishing, and even skiing down the steep, sandy slopes. A grassy park has been developed along the shore of the lake, and a visitor center spells out the geology of the dunes and the prehistoric life of the desert. The dunes boast several unusual features. The largest dune, at 470 feet in height, ranks as the largest single standing dune in North America. The big dune and another imposing sand ridge cover more than 600 acres. The two lakes that have formed at the base of the dunes are inconsistent with the desert setting. They first appeared during the 1950s when nearby farms began using irrigation water from C. J. Strike Reservoir. The water table rose, and subsurface seepage created the lakes. This moisture encouraged the growth of vegetation and wildlife, contributing much to the beauty of a unique landscape.

The formation of the dunes themselves may be a one-of-a-kind story. When the Bonneville flood occurred some 15,000 years ago, the wildly churning waters of the Snake River cut a new channel, and the former

Bruneau Dunes State Park. Mountains of sand aren't the only attraction here. The lakes that lap at the base of the dunes attract a variety of waterfowl as well as fishermen.

riverbed was left dry. In a basin of this old riverbed, now called Eagle Cove, sands from the Owhyee Desert began to swirl and settle. They were blown by winds that tended toward the southeast 28 percent of the time and toward the northwest 32 percent of the time. Over the centuries, the opposing wind directions have given form and shape to the dunes. And the incessant process continues.

Nomadic Indians apparently visited the dunes for thousands of years, as many arrowheads and other artifacts have come to light here. Oregon Trail pioneers passed this way, too, and later on settlers in the Bruneau Valley drove to the dunes by horse and buggy to picnic and see the sights.

Idaho 78
GRANDVIEW

Grandview is a picturesque little town on the Snake River in the midst of farm and ranch country. The nearby C. J. Strike Reservoir assures an ample supply of water for its agricultural base and also attracts water-sport enthusiasts. The J. R. Simplot feedlot and the Triangle Dairy, one of the largest dairy operations in the West, both carry sizable local payrolls.

Grandview grew at the site of the Dorsey brothers' ranch, which was established about 1870. The Dorseys also ran a popular Snake River ferry, which became the nucleus for a settlement called Dorsey. In 1888 it was renamed Grandview. A series of pioneer irrigation projects began in 1887, creating an agricultural base for the community. One of the chief crops in the early days was alfalfa hay, which fed the thousands of sheep that wintered in the valley.

Idaho 78
MURPHY

With a population of fifty, Murphy may be one of the smallest county seats in the country. Even so, it is far from unknown. News of its one parking meter has traveled far, and its excellent Owyhee County Historical Complex and Museum is as well known as any in Idaho. The museum retells the story of Owyhee County in exhibits on mining, ranching, homesteading, and ethnic populations. It also maintains a research library and substantial photograph archives.

Each spring the Owyhee County Historical Society hosts the popular Outpost Days, a favorite country soiree that brings in large crowds for food, fun, and entertainment. This event has been a leader in demonstrating lost arts such as saddle making, flint working, and blacksmithing.

The settlement of Murphy traces its beginnings to a private railroad. Wealthy mine owner Col. William Dewey dreamed of a fast connection between his Owyhee mines and the outside world. The dream took form when he built his own railroad—the Boise, Nampa and Owyhee. The tracks reached Murphy (named for the construction boss) in 1899 and went no farther. However, Murphy benefited as the county's only railroad terminal and became a busy place, handling passengers, freight, mail, sheep, and cattle. Early in the twentieth century, this isolated spot shipped more livestock than any other place in the Pacific Northwest.

Idaho 78
SILVER CITY

The turnoff for Silver City is five miles south of Murphy on Idaho 78. The twenty-three-mile fair-weather dirt road leading to Silver City is generally suitable for sedans, but local conditions can vary, so it is advisable to inquire at Murphy.

Outside of Murphy the sagebrush hills rise higher and higher, finally merging with the wild Owyhee Mountains. Winding around, climbing up, plunging down, the route places some of the pioneer accomplishments in perspective. Thousands of people and tons of freight came up this circuitous route by pack train or stage. Most surprising, they succeeded in establishing high-mountain towns that boasted not only the bare necessities but also schools, churches, drama, music, newspapers, and all the accoutrements of "society."

Several high-altitude mining camps—Wagontown, Ruby City, De Lamar, Dewey—developed in the Owyhee Mountains, but the metropolis was Silver City. Today it is a ghost of its former self, yet not entirely a relic of the past. People summer here and continue to patch up the old place, so it teeters on the brink of coming alive again. Ground squirrels skitter across the dusty streets between weathered buildings whose ranks have thinned. The structures seem haphazardly placed on the hillsides—one here, one there. This is a far cry from the old days, when close-packed houses stairstepped up and down the hills. According to Mildretta Adams, "A man couldn't step out on his doorstep to spit tobacco juice without puttin' out the fire in his neighbor's chimney."

The old schoolhouse has become a museum housing Silver City relics, and the picturesque little Catholic church (originally Episcopalian) holds

It took a lot of freight wagons to supply high-altitude camps like Silver City.
—Idaho State Historical Society

179

Restored charmer, now a summer home at Silver City.

Silver City, "Queen of the Owyhees," circa 1880. Idaho Hotel is at lower left.
—Idaho State Historical Society

services occasionally. The sagging Idaho Hotel still stands, a faded dowager now, and close by is the building that once housed the *Owyhee Avalanche*, one of the hottest newspapers in the territory—especially when William J. Hill was in charge.

Wit and humor and mining news made the *Avalanche* a popular paper, and old Hill himself became a household name in the territory. He was also known for engaging in journalistic feuds, especially with Milton Kelly, editor of the *Boise Tri-Weekly Statesman*. One time he fairly ground Kelly to bits in a famous retort: "Come now, speak the truth for once in your life, you spawn of iniquity! You louse on the body politic. . . . You maggot squirming in corruption!—you fester!—you itch!—you gangrene!—you deformity!" And finally, spitting scorn, "You Kelly."

Ordinarily Hill was quite congenial. His wide range of friends included just about everyone from the Chinese miners to the governor, and his 1873 wedding to Belle Peck was practically an affair of state. No personal invitations were issued; everyone was invited. He rented the Idaho Hotel and the Masonic Hall for the celebration, and Governor Bennett braved the lurching stage ride from Boise City to preside over the ceremony.

The original Masonic Hall still spans Jordan Creek. It is used occasionally, and folks can still walk from one end of the building to the other to accomplish the biblical feat of "crossing the Jordan."

The famous Idaho Hotel at Silver City, now dimmed by time and the elements. Hosea Eastman first built the hotel at nearby Ruby City, but when Silver City began to grow, he moved it up the hill in sections by ox team and reassembled it on Jordan Street, where the old dowager has been ever since.

Chinatown stood across Dead Man's Alley from the town proper. Here some 700 "Celestials" scurried about in their loose black jackets and wide coolie hats, pigtails swinging behind. Their presence was not always appreciated by white society, but their services were willingly accepted. Most were laundrymen, houseboys, or water carriers. The latter shouldered a yoke from which two five-gallon cans swung, delivering one load of ten gallons to each patron daily—with an extra turn on Monday, which was wash day.

Nature has reclaimed the once colorful Chinatown, a welter of shacks once identifiable by the smell of dried fish, herbs, and other exotics that wafted on the air. The settlement included a joss house elegant with tapestries, restaurants and gambling places ringing with the sing-song chant of Cantonese, stores with lichee nuts and opium and candied ginger, and great dragon kites that floated high on windy days. The Chinese residents loved celebrations, and even a funeral could be most colorful. The late Lem York, a Silver City native and publisher of the *Owyhee Avalanche*, recalled the funeral of a well-known merchant, Song Lee. Before Lee was laid to rest in the Chinese cemetery, a hog roasted with various delicacies was served to a large group of friends, both white and Chinese. After much revelry they formed a procession, and the town band hired for the occasion struck up a popular tune, "There'll Be a Hot Time in the Old Town Tonight." A Chinese band chimed in with a piccolo and symbols, which added a proper Oriental touch. Once at the graveside, the band (apparently full of Irishmen) obliged with another tune, "Down Went McGinty."

The pioneer cemetery on the hillside north of town reveals a few nuances of Silver City history, too. This is no Boothill. The haphazard assemblage of headstones portrays solid citizens who built a permanent community in a hard spot.

Silver City began in 1863 when Michael Jordan and a party of prospectors from Boise Basin headed for the Owyhees. They struck pay dirt on Jordan Creek. When word of the new diggings leaked out, some 2,500 men poured out of Boise Basin overnight and tramped the sagebrush trail to Owyhee. Some were disappointed and scattered like mercury for the next strike. However, many of them stayed, and several small camps mushroomed— Ruby City and Booneville first, Silver City the following year.

The new town stretched out along Jordan Creek and up the mountainside, thriving on rich veins of ore deep within the earth. These required the building of shafts and tunnels and the installation of heavy machinery for mining and milling. The most prominent mines became famous, and their romantic names—the Ida Elmore, Golden Chariot, Morning Star, Belle Peck, and Poorman, to name a few—rolled off tongues all the way from San Francisco to London. Most of the mines produced $2,000 to $6,000 worth of precious metal per ton, predominately in silver. The Poorman, ironically, was the richest of them all. During its ten-year career (1865-1875), it yielded up a treasure worth $4 million.

Mining activity at Silver City tapered off in 1875. Banks failed, the price of silver declined, and the richest ores had been skimmed off. However, during the 1880s, the whole business boomed anew when William Dewey developed the nearby Black Jack and Trade Dollar mines. These were rich enough to attract eastern money and investors from London. They also paved the way for Capt. Joseph DeLamar, who bought several claims and consolidated them into one district named for himself. DeLamar spent a fortune building a mill and a town complete with hotel, stores, and red-light district. His gamble paid off, and in 1891 he sold out to a British company that kept the mines open until 1910.

Over the years the district has come to life intermittently, and today the DeLamar Silver Mine is active in open-pit mining. Since 1976 it has produced 390,000 ounces of gold and more than 24 million ounces of silver. This amount surpasses the total previous production of DeLamar and is more than half of the total previous production of all the Owyhee mines combined.

Idaho 55 and 78
WALTERS FERRY

Idaho 78 passes two historic sites between Murphy and Marsing: Walters Ferry and Givens Hot Springs. The ferry was established in 1863 to accommodate miners, stagecoaches, and pack trains traveling the Boise–Silver City route. It was used until the days of the Model T Ford, when a steel bridge was built across the river in 1921. Today the old ferrymaster's house near the riverbank is the central feature of a private museum complex. It includes pioneer artifacts, an impressive clock collection, and a section devoted to medical history. All of this is the work of Cleo Swayne and the late Dr. Samuel Swayne, who developed the museum over a period of thirty years.

The historic steamboat *Shoshone* briefly plied the river between Walters Ferry and Farewell Bend (near Huntington on the Oregon border). It steamed up the river for the first time in May 1866 and tied up at the ferry landing. The coming of the *Shoshone* was a major event. In *Old Fort Boise*, Annie Laurie Bird writes that several of the territory's most prominent people arrived by stage "just in time to hear the music of the steam whistle reverberate for the first time along the sage brush solitudes of the Snake." Alas, there was too much sagebrush and not enough timber. After a few runs the supply of wood to stoke the boilers ran out, and that ended the career of the *Shoshone* on the middle Snake River (see Parma).

Prehistory buffs might want to see the petroglyphs downriver from Walters Ferry. These appear on rocks in two different areas, but most people come to see the curious Map Rock. This huge boulder, probably deposited by the Bonneville flood, is fully inscribed with rock art. No one has made a definitive translation, but some authorities believe the pictures tell stories of hunting grounds, Snake River geography, and perhaps prehistoric visitors. Turn at the sportsman's access east of the Walters Ferry bridge. The inscribed rocks are seven and eight miles respectively from the bridge.

Idaho 78
GIVENS HOT SPRINGS

To reach Givens Hot Springs, take Idaho 78 along the west side of the river. This route is part of the south alternate of the Oregon Trail, which generally followed the course of Idaho 78 from Glenns Ferry to Homedale, where it met the main trail.

In the summer of 1851, Lucia Williams, Oregon Trail emigrant, wrote of the hot springs, "It was such a beautiful water that many of our company alighted to drink but on a near approach they were satisfied with jerking their hands away. . . . the water was hot enough for cooking." When pioneer Milford Givens came to settle in 1881, he saw commercial potential and developed the springs as a resort. Since that time the Givens family has continuously operated a swimming pool and camping facility here.

The story of the hot springs goes back a long time, as Indians came to this favored spot long ago. Archaeological excavations along the river have uncovered 4,500-year-old pit houses as well as points, scrapers, and other objects of daily living.

Idaho 55 and 78
MARSING

Marsing sits in a picturesque valley. The Snake River glides past the front door, and Lizard Butte, a giant basaltic reptile, stands guard from a nearby hilltop. The Owyhee Mountains frame the southwest, and toward the north, waves of vineyards and apple orchards cover the rolling hills.

The settlement here dates from the turn of the century, when the Gem Irrigation District attracted farmers to the area, then known as Henderson Flats. The new bridge across Snake River became the catalyst for town building. Marsing was platted as the bridge was finished in 1921.

Idaho 78 ends two miles south of Marsing at US 95, which proceeds to Homedale, nine miles away. Idaho 55, which is Marsing's main street, crosses the Snake River into Canyon County and the Sunny Slope region of orchards and vineyards. Vintners at Weston Winery, Hells Canyon Winery, and Ste. Chapelle Winery transform a variety of grapes into thousands of cases of premium wines. Wine makers extol the volcanic ash soils, long sunny days, and cool nights characteristic of this area. Over the years, Ste. Chapelle has won many medals with wines made from locally grown grapes. In 1994 their Special Harvest Johannisberg Riesling Champagne won two medals in national competitions: a gold medal at the American Wine Competition and Best of Show at the American Wine Society.

The senior (since 1976) and most elegant winery is Ste. Chapelle, perched on a hillside overlooking a mosaic of vines and orchards that sweep away in all directions. The graceful design is patterned after a medieval chapel, with a Gothic upthrust in the tall arched windows. Each one frames a picture, a grand spread of hill and valley, sky and distant mountain—and each day brings another scene, a new mood, a changing season.

Idaho 55 bisects the agricultural land of Canyon County and meets I-84 near the outskirts of Nampa.

Ponderosa Pine Scenic Byway

The Ponderosa Pine Scenic Byway, Idaho 21, links Boise with the town of Stanley and the beautiful Sawtooth Mountains. This excellent highway winds beside Mores Creek in the Boise River drainage and along the South Fork of the Payette River through 130 miles of upland forest. The route eventually crosses Mores Creek Summit, Beaver Creek Summit, and Banner Summit, topping out at more than 6,000 feet each time and dipping down to river grade between the heights. From the mountaintops dramatic vistas of peaks and ridges appear, with phalanxes of ponderosa pine defining their contours. An understory of chokecherry and syringa blankets the hillsides next to the road. The byway presents a number of interesting stops, beginning with Idaho City, a remnant of the boom days in Boise Basin.

Idaho 21
IDAHO CITY

Idaho City still maintains an aura of the Old West—wooden sidewalks, dusty streets, false-fronted buildings, and sometimes a few cowboy types

On the boardwalk in Chinatown, Idaho City. —Idaho State Historical Society

idling in front of the Miners Exchange Saloon. Several nineteenth-century buildings face Main Street, and a line of weathered houses haphazardly climbs the ravines. Buildings of special interest include the Boise Basin Mercantile, the oldest general store in Idaho; the *Idaho World* building, rebuilt after the 1865 fire; and, up on the hillside, St. Joseph's Catholic Church (1867) outlined dramatically against the sky. Close by is the oldest Independent Order of Odd Fellows (IOOF) lodge in Idaho (1865).

Surprisingly, this slice of western Americana is still the county seat of Boise County. The larger and more accessible Horseshoe Bend protests occasionally, but so far nostalgia wins out. The county business supports a colony of year-round residents. June brings summer travelers, winter the Nordic ski crowd.

Idaho City dates from the fall of 1862, when two miners set off from Pioneerville (Hog'em) to see what lay over the mountain. They found rich prospects along Mores Creek, but upon returning to camp they said the only thing they had seen on the other side was a bear. When they next crossed the mountain, however, several curious fellows from Pioneerville tagged along to see the "bear"; the secret was out, and the stampede to Idaho City was on.

Soon Mores Creek boasted forty-one saloons, thirty-six grocery stores, twenty-three law offices, sundry other establishments, and the name of Bannock, which was later changed to Idaho City. With a population of 6,000 people, it had become the largest city in the territory and the center of one of the richest gold strikes in the West. Altogether Boise Basin yielded up an estimated $24 million in gold during its first three years. Over time this figure extended to $100 million.

Historian H. H. Bancroft preserved a rich Idaho City story told by prospector Sherlock Bristol. Some of the men were unwilling to walk to the creek for water and decided to dig a well in the center of town. About eighteen feet down they struck bedrock and the glitter of gold. A bucketful of soil panned out at $2.75. "By nightfall," Bristol said, "I could not have bought the claim on which my house was built for $10,000. It proved to be worth $300,000." Later on, almost every house in town was jacked up while the

St. Joseph's Catholic Church still overlooks Idaho City. The church opened for service in 1863 under Father Toussaint Mesplie and was rebult after the 1867 fire.

earth beneath was washed for gold. One could even say the streets were paved with it, as gold tailings were laid down for a roadbed.

Idaho City claimed the first newspaper in southern Idaho, the *Idaho World*. Its presses came in on the backs of mules and for a few months printed the only paper within 300 miles. Elegant theaters, lodges, churches, and even a circulating library also flourished in this mountain community. Episcopalian bishop Daniel S. Tuttle came over from Boise City to size up prospects for a church and found that pandemonium reigned in the streets, even on Sunday. Wagonmasters unloaded freight with a great deal of clatter, hun-

One-time home of the Idaho World, *a pioneer newspaper established in Idaho City, 1863. Current editor Chris Smith has collected most of the original printing equipment and still puts out a weekly edition of the venerable old paper.*

dreds of men gathered around to bet on a horse race, music tinkled from the hurdy-gurdy houses, and faro games prospered extravagantly behind swinging doors.

The earth yielded up its treasure, and both miner and businessman seemed to be on the road to prosperity. Then a great calamity struck. On May 18, 1865, a disastrous fire swept the city. Eyewitness Charles Teeter described the scene in "My Adventures in the Far West," published in the Idaho Historical Society's thirteenth annual report on December 31, 1932. It began about 9:00 P.M. in one of the hurdy-gurdy houses and quickly spread from one street to another. Most of the storekeepers were burned out, and looting was rampant.

However, out of the smoke and cinders emerged a hero. As soon as the fire started, George Dwight hurried to Craft's store to help salvage merchandise but was pressed into service as a banker of sorts. Craft opened the door of his safe and took out more than 100 pounds of gold dust laid out in buckskin pouches, each stamped with the owner's name. They stuffed the pouches into a gunnysack and tied the top shut. Dwight then shouldered the load and disappeared into the night. A few minutes later the store went up in a burst of flame.

Dawn came and most of the town lay under a bed of hot ashes. Of about 300 businesses, only a few on the outskirts remained. Downtown, dozens of men wandered about in a daze, poking at the debris, while an uneasy group gathered around Mr. Craft to inquire about their gold deposits. Finally, George Dwight walked in with the sack of dust secure on his shoulder. "Ho for Diogenes!" they shouted. Craft distributed the pouches, and the men had some fun kidding him: Did he prefer to sit up all night with 100 pounds of gold dust or a pretty girl?

Within ninety days of the fire Idaho City was humming again, a more substantial town than before. A number of brick buildings now graced Main Street, but they were no insurance against fire. The place burned again in 1867, 1868, and 1871. Each time it rose from the ashes, seemingly indestructible.

Boise Basin Historical Museum

The Boise Basin Historical Museum's collections showcase life in the old mining camp with the tools of daily living—remnants of a stamp mill, primitive telephone switchboards, and account books dating from the days when ten pounds of bacon sold for $2. The museum is the center of a complex that includes the city park and an outdoor display of antique mining equipment. Close by is the territorial-era Boise County Jail, whose prisoners spent most of their time escaping. Across the street the Masonic Hall, Lodge No. 1, which dates from 1865, still gets occasional use.

The pioneer cemetery provides a picturesque storybook of early Boise Basin history. A pine forest guards the markers, scattered helter-skelter throughout the burial ground. Some are set off by elegant wrought-iron fences, others by wooden ones, weather-bleached and standing askew. The Pinney plot may be the most elegant, but when it came to last rites J. Marion More may have eclipsed them all.

More came to Idaho before it was a territory and staked a claim to fame and fortune. He struck it rich, first in Idaho City and then in Silver City, where he owned an interest in the Golden Chariot mine. Hard words were uttered during a claim-jumping dispute with the Ida Elmore owners, and More fell victim to a gun blast in front of the Idaho Hotel at Silver City in February 1868. The Masons brought his body here for burial. According to legend, the funeral procession was the longest one ever seen in Idaho Territory. When the hearse pulled up beside the open grave, the last buggy in line had not yet reached the hot springs three miles west of town on Mores Creek Road (Idaho 21).

Idaho 21, Forest Road 307
PLACERVILLE

The remains of this old camp are about ten miles across the hills from Idaho City. There is still life in the old place, with a handful of year-round residents living the good life here and more summer people coming in all the time. Several turn-of-the-century homes remain, and a number of business buildings date from the gold rush. Unlike the usual haphazard mining camp, Placerville was carefully planned, with a town square and a community well. The old Masonic lodge, post office, Boise Basin Mercantile, and Magnolia Saloon still sit at right angles to each other on the square. The Merc is open for business, and a few museum displays can be seen at the saloon and city hall. The most fascinating site of all may be the pioneer cemetery, with its record of hardy families written in epitaphs on ornate headstones.

One can still take the prospectors' route from Placerville to Garden Valley, then head west to Banks and Idaho 55 or return to Idaho City and the Ponderosa Pine Scenic Byway.

Idaho 21, Forest Roads
ATLANTA

The old mining camp of Atlanta is located high in the mountains on the Middle Fork of the Boise River. Historically it belongs to the South Boise Placer District rather than Boise Basin, but road conditions make the approach from Idaho 21 the logical route. Seventeen miles east of Idaho City, the highway intersects with a complex of Forest Service roads that provide access to Atlanta some thirty miles away. Although the roads are maintained during summer, at some places they narrow to a single track and require additional caution. Signs mark the route to Atlanta, though you may also wish to obtain a map for the Boise National Forest.

Long before the town comes into view, its presence is heralded by the imposing hulk of Greylock Mountain. The original name of this granite peak was "Greyrock," a graphic description, but Chinese miners from nearby China Basin could not pronounce the "r," so it has ever since been "Greylock."

The town is almost hidden in the mountain terrain but gradually materializes as a vertical collage of weathered buildings, summer homes, and watering places. This tiny resort town has only a sprinkling of year-round residents. Outdoor recreation is popular, as the community sits on the fringe of the Sawtooth National Forest, and many trails lead into the Sawtooth Wilderness Area. The Atlanta Historical Society Museum, featuring the restored jail and exhibits of early Atlanta and Rocky Bar, is open by appointment.

From these heights it is easy to appreciate the muscle necessary to build a mountain community. During the early years (1864–1878), all goods (including the stamp mills) came in from the south by pack train over a narrow trail from Rocky Bar. Ironically, after that stupendous effort most of the gold was lost in the milling. An efficient process was finally developed in 1932, and the Atlanta lode became Idaho's major gold mine. It eventually produced more than $16 million in gold and silver.

The name Atlanta represents a bit of the Old South in Idaho. It first applied to a mineral lode, christened by Confederate miners who were celebrating General Hood's victory over Sherman in the Battle of Atlanta. News finally reached the mountains that Sherman had actually won the fight, but the miners kept the name anyway and later bestowed it on the town.

Idaho 21
LOWMAN AND GRANDJEAN

Lowman consists of a scattering of summer homes along the South Fork of the Payette River and a general store that provides travel services. The town's location makes it something of a backcountry junction. From here one can gain access to Garden Valley and Horseshoe Bend or Bear Valley and Cascade. East of Lowman, Idaho 21 follows the turquoise waters of the South Fork of the Payette River to the Grandjean turnoff, twenty miles away.

At Grandjean, the pioneer Sawtooth Lodge stands on the western fringe of the Sawtooth National Recreation Area. Dozens of trails lead into this unspoiled wilderness. The place is named for Emile Grandjean, who was born in Copenhagen, Denmark, to a French Huguenot family. When he arrived in this country, he joined the Wood River mining boom of the 1880s and later tried his luck in the gold mines of Alaska. By the turn of the century, he was back in Idaho and became a pioneer supervisor for the Sawtooth, Payette, and Boise national forests. He loved this pristine land, and it seems fitting that his name has become as natural to the landscape as the mountains, trees, and water.

Idaho 21
STANLEY

The serrated peaks of the Sawtooth Mountains in the Sawtooth National Recreation Area dominate the landscape on the eastern end of Idaho 21. They cut the sky at about 10,000 feet, announcing a spectacular alpine country of pristine lakes, clear streams, and mountain meadows.

At Stanley, the Ponderosa Pine Scenic Byway meets the Salmon River Scenic Byway and the Sawtooth Scenic Byway. (See Stanley, in Central Idaho.)

Roadside travel had its inconveniences well into the twentieth century. Rarely could one travel a hundred miles without engine trouble or a flat tire or two. Here a 1923 Model T Ford and a 1923 Dodge have broken down along the Ponderosa Pine Scenic Byway. —Idaho State Historical Society

Payette River Scenic Byway

HORSESHOE BEND, BANKS, AND GARDEN VALLEY

This much-used route from Boise leads to the Payette lakes and the resort town of McCall. Most of the scenic drive follows the Payette River, which in spring cuts through its canyon in a roar of white water. By October the brawling stream is more sedate, and low water exposes a gorge of jumbled rocks worn smooth by eons of spring runoffs. The river landscape makes this drive something of an annual pilgrimage for many local travelers.

Idaho 55 joins the Payette River at Horseshoe Bend. This small settlement dates from the gold rush days, when prospectors thronged in from all directions to climb the hills to the Boise Basin mines. William J. McConnell and his partner John Porter came from the Oregon coast to strike it rich—not in gold nuggets but in onions, potatoes, sweet corn, and watermelons. They staked a camp on the Payette close to the horseshoe bend near the trail to Placerville. Out came the irons for the plow, garden seeds, potatoes, and "a milk pan full of onion sets secured from an old lady in Yamhill." The garden flourished under tender care and irrigation water. Soon the entrepreneurs were able to harvest a hundred bunches of green onions, which McConnell tied on his packhorse and carried up the hill to Placerville. He went down Granite Street, where a motley assortment of steep-roofed buildings faced each other across the square. The green onions created quite a commotion. Prospectors who hadn't seen a fresh vegetable this side of the Willamette clamored for them at a dollar a bunch. Legend has it that they sat around on flour barrels munching the juicy "fruit" with tears running down their cheeks, as happy as if they were at home in the old apple orchard. The adventuresome young McConnell went on to a career that took him from farmer to vigilante, merchant, and eventually, in 1893, to governor (see Moscow, in North Idaho).

At Banks one can turn off Idaho 55 and take South Fork Road to Crouch and Garden Valley. These picturesque settlements lie along the South Fork of the Payette River in a meadow ringed by high mountains and tall timber. Beyond Garden Valley the road climbs to the high country and meets Idaho 21 at Lowman, twenty-three miles away.

Today the Crouch–Garden Valley area is popular for recreation home sites, but in the beginning farmers settled here. Like McConnell, they sold their produce to the Boise Basin miners. Later on, loggers came to cut timber from the surrounding hills, and the river was used as a highway to float the wood downstream to sawmills at Emmett. Crews sawed logs most of

Prospectors on the South Fork of the Payette River. —Idaho State Historical Society

the winter. In the spring, when the river was in a terrible mood, daring men rode the logs downstream, shooting the rapids, breaking up jams, shepherding the valuable cargo all the way to the mill.

A few miles north of Banks, Idaho 55 passes Smith's Ferry, better known today as Cougar Mountain Lodge. Here, at a broad arc in the river, Clinton G. Meyers established a pioneer ferry in 1867 and a small log house where travelers could gather for food and warmth. James Smith later bought the business and gave it its name.

The old ferry is long gone. Herds of sheep and pigs no longer wait to crowd on board, and bears rarely make nighttime visits, but travelers still gather for food and warmth at Cougar Mountain Lodge near the old ferry site. The main focus now is on recreation, with fishing, hunting, and snowmobiling high on the list of priorities.

Idaho 55
CASCADE

The town of Cascade is situated on the shore of Cascade Reservoir, which stores Payette River water to irrigate farmland in the lower valleys. The river's tumbling waters gave the city its name. The reservoir now covers

Settlement of Crawford, now beneath the waters of Cascade Reservoir.
—Idaho State Historical Society

most of these rapids, as well as a few ranches, hot springs, and the former pioneer towns of Crawford and Van Wyck.

This is ranching and timber country, but the Boise Cascade sawmill has long sustained the local economy. The county seat is also here, and the town offers access to the lake and the surrounding recreation area. Fishing goes on year-round, and the winter landscape offers hundreds of miles of trails for Nordic skiing and snowmobiling.

Snowbank Mountain

The main feature of a drive to Snowbank Mountain is the panorama from the top. Mountains descend, ridge upon ridge, from incredible heights to the wide valley floor below. The road is well maintained because a federal aircraft tracking station stands at the summit.

The Snowbank Mountain road goes by way of Cabarton (named for early-day banker C. A. Barton). The town started in 1921 as a shipping center for the Boise Payette (now Boise Cascade) sawmill at Emmett. Its population peaked at about 300 persons before the community faded into oblivion. The company moved its operation on to stands of virgin timber close to New Meadows, and the population flocked to a new bonanza. Now ranch land spreads across the valley in a storybook setting.

*Soaking up summer
at Warm Lake.*

Idaho 55, Warm Lake Road
WARM LAKE

This popular mountain hideaway twenty-six miles from Cascade boasts two rustic lodges and several campgrounds. Bill and Molly Kesler were pioneers in the tourist industry here. With little but their own hands and a team of horses, they blazed a road into the lake and built the Warm Lake Hotel. It soon became a haven for backcountry travelers and fishermen. Molly herself became known as something of a character. For more than thirty years she made things lively and generated a number of Warm Lake stories.

A favorite one took place on a winter night in 1935 when an errant Boeing airliner roared across the sky in a blizzard, 140 miles off course. Molly heard the plane's engine fade away toward the Sawtooth Range and then return. After listening to the aircraft wander around up there, she alerted Boise airport officials. Ruth T. Knight of Boise picks up the story, which made newspaper headlines at the time:

Molly pulled on her shoes and threw a coat about her. With a lantern in her hand she went out into the night, the wind and snow impeding her steps as she groped her way down to the lake where she built a flare on the ice. Back at the telephone again she succeeded in raising some of the other subscribers along the line and flares were built to guide the plane to a good landing field at Cascade. Here the townspeople were aroused and with their cars surrounded the landing field, flooded it with light. The plane was landed safely, the passengers never having been aware of the danger.

Landmark Junction is nine miles east of Warm Lake. From there, the road leads north to the mountain town of Yellow Pine and south to Deadwood Reservoir and Bear Valley, which connects with the Ponderosa Scenic Byway at Lowman on Idaho 21. The highway from Warm Lake to the junction is high and winding but excellent. In the early days, when the road was merely a trail in the wilderness, a largely forgotten spot called Knox grew up on Cabin Creek two or three miles above Warm Lake. The town lived on the elusive hopes of gold and silver. Nothing much happened in the way of mining, and today it is remembered primarily for the company that dropped in one winter evening.

Sailing at Warm Lake.

Mel Able lived in a remote section of today's Frank Church–River of No Return Wilderness (at that time called the Primitive Area) until someone murdered him at his ranch on Big Creek in the dead of winter. The late Earl Wilson of Yellow Pine told how, after the murder was discovered, the Masonic Lodge at Cascade paid a team of volunteers to snowshoe in to recover the body. They made the 230-mile round trip in nineteen cold, miserable days.

Once at their destination, the team wrapped the frozen corpse in clean sheets and fresh deer hides, then headed for home. When they reached Cabin Creek Summit, Dan Drake told the others he would go ahead of the entourage and arrange for warm beds and a hot supper at Knox. He left the summit before the main party, but a couple of its members soon passed him. They had tried to wrangle the corpse down the steep mountainside, and the heavy, frozen body just about got away from them. As it started to plunge, the mountaineers jumped aboard and rode it to the bottom. By the time Drake arrived at Knox, the drop-ins had already spoken for bed and board.

Idaho 55
McCall

Between Cascade and McCall, Idaho 55 passes through Donnelly, which gives access to the north end of Cascade Lake and the old Roseberry townsite.

The historic Methodist-Episcopal church is one of the few buildings left at Roseberry, and it houses the Long Valley Museum. Displays here feature the old townsite, agriculture, mining, lumber, and the Finns, who settled in Long Valley about 1890. They enriched the local culture with their unique method of constructing log houses, their saunas, their Finn bread, their music, and other traditions that are still celebrated annually on St. John's Day. Today most of the remaining Finnish people are settled around Lake Fork five miles south of McCall.

From McCall, located on the south shore of Payette Lake, visitors can view shimmering blue water enclosed by a round sweep of forested mountains. About 2,500 residents live here year-round, but the population swells to about 8,000 when the summer residents come in. The mainstay of the town used to be the Brown Tie and Lumber Company, but today recreation drives the economy. The building boom seems perpetual. The place is alive with summer and winter crowds, yet the old resort has not outgrown its charm. The air is pure and piney, and each season brings its own special activities.

Winter Carnival is a bright spot during the long winter. Held for ten days in late January and early February, it has gained wide acclaim for its ingenious ice sculptures. Brundage Mountain offers a long ski season, and

The sawdust burner, once a favorite landmark at the Brown Tie and Lumber Company in McCall. Condominiums now occupy this choice site on Payette Lake.

spring brings a variety of arts and crafts fairs, rendezvous, rodeos, antique car shows, and celebrations that keep the calendar lively. If these fail to excite, one can always take to the woods. Nature has provided an outdoor paradise of some 130 lakes and 150 streams within a radius of thirty-five miles. For additional information, check with the Payette National Forest office in McCall.

McCall began when Tom McCall moved here with his family in 1891 and built a home along the lakeshore. He had the townsite surveyed, built a hotel that catered to backcountry travelers, and opened for business. Other settlers followed, and in 1914 a branch of the Union Pacific Railroad was extended from Cascade to McCall, bringing the outside world a bit closer. Carl Brown went into the lumber business with H. R. Hoff, and for nearly seventy years Brown and Hoff (later Brown Tie and Lumber Company) furnished the main payroll for the town. The sawmill was located at the site of present-day Mill Park.

In the early days, the lake and the many adjacent streams made this prime fishing territory. Betty O'Reilly writes in *The Magic of McCall* that locals caught trout and salmon in abundance from the lake. Particularly popular were the "silver sides" (red-meated kokanee salmon) and a whitefish that residents seined in the fall and salted down for the winter.

McCall eventually attracted Hollywood moviemakers and actors, who came to town in 1938 to film *Northwest Passage*. Their coming generated more excitement than the place had ever seen. Locals rubbed elbows with Spencer Tracy, Robert Young, Walt Brennan, and a host of lesser lights.

Mountain hideaway near the resort town of McCall.

Most of the filming was done around a set of rustic forts on the lakeshore. The story centered on Roger's Rangers, a superb team of eighteenth-century guerrilla fighters whose handbook was still in official use during the Vietnam War. A part of the old set has been incorporated into Jack Simplot's summer home.

Ponderosa State Park

This 840-acre park lies two miles north of McCall on a peninsula shaped long ago by glacial action. The approach across a sagebrush flat gives little indication of the beauty that is in store: a stand of 500-year-old ponderosa pines, sandy beachfronts, exhilarating overlooks, and a sizable wilderness area laced with hiking trails.

High Llama Ranch

This unusual ranch on the Farm to Market Road transplants a little bit of the Andes to McCall. Dozens of llamas live here adjacent to a wilderness area, where they are carefully trained by Cutler and Nancy Umbach and their crew. Some of these beauties will be show-stoppers, some barnyard pets, but most will become pack animals prized for their gentle dispositions and their ability to walk the forest trails without a trace. Today the Forest Service often uses a pack string of llamas rather than horses to carry gear into remote regions.

Idaho 55, Warren Wagon Road
BURGDORF AND WARREN

The road to Burgdorf and Warren follows the historic Warren Wagon Road, which began along the west shore of Payette Lake. The Burgdorf junction is thirty miles from McCall, and the "town" is two miles beyond that on a good fair-weather road.

The old Burgdorf Hotel, brown with time, rises up in the middle of the settlement like a cathedral in a medieval village. It faces west across an expanse of meadow toward the famous hot springs and the enclosing mountains. At their base a row of rustic cabins seems to have taken root among the pines. The present owners are rehabilitating the picturesque old resort and plan to offer overnight accommodations and swimming in the warm-water pool. Here mineral waters, gushing in at a "just right" temperature, circulate, drain, and constantly replenish.

The resort was the work of Fred Burgdorf, who joined the rush to Warren's Diggings in 1864. A year later, on a tip from a Chinese miner, he inspected the hot springs and staked a claim of 160 acres. Burgdorf quit the goldfields, stocked his meadows with cattle, and soon reaped his own bonanza selling beefsteaks and hot baths to the miners. Fred and his warm springs generated a lot of good humor. One yarn the "rusticating" prospectors spread was that Fred skimmed the water after they had finished bathing and gathered enough gold dust to make a living.

From the beginning, this was more than just a resort. Friends met here often, coming to the springs from far and near to share the hospitality of Jeanette and Fred Burgdorf. In winter they came on webs or skis or by dogsled. When the hotel came in sight they were greeted by a scramble of noisy dogs and rows of skis standing on end under the porch roof. In *Memories of an Old-Timer*, Adelia Routson Parke recalls a Christmas party with the Burgdorfs as a storybook affair: "There were mistletoe and holly and evergreens; a large tree with real candles; and from the ceilings hung red tissue-paper bells . . . tinsel and glitter everywhere." Equally astonishing was John, the black cook, who wore a white coat and a chef's hat. After dinner he made a spectacular entrance holding aloft a flaming, holly-decked plum pudding. Most of the guests had never eaten such a dish, much less seen one served in such elegant style.

The Burgdorfs lived in relative isolation on the fringe of the frontier, yet they lived graciously. Parke remembered an interior decor rich with oriental rugs, paintings, books, and unique furniture. Now the old settlement is on the National Register of Historic Places, its plush days only a fleeting whiff of nostalgia.

Warren is twelve miles from Burgdorf. Wind through the Sesesh Meadows at river level, then climb the ridge and enjoy the easy downhill ride to Warren. The town, a remnant of the gold rush days, has several historic buildings that are still in use and a handful of year-round residents who brave the snowbound winters. During that harsh season, mail, groceries, Christmas presents, catalog orders, and everything else has to come in by ski plane from Cascade.

The settlement at Warren began when a party of miners swarmed down from the Florence placers in 1862. James Warren, generally described as the most shiftless man of the lot and a petty gambler to boot, struck pay dirt, and the stampede was on. Two colonies—one Rebel, the other Yankee—mushroomed near the mouth of Slaughter Creek (a tributary of the Salmon River). The Confederate sympathizers called their camp Richmond, which offended the Union men, who moved down the gulch and built their own town, calling it Washington. Richmond was dug up for the placer ground beneath it and soon disappeared, whereas Washington (at first known as Washington at Warren's Diggings) took the name Warren. As the camp grew it captured the Idaho County seat, and the records were moved from Florence in 1868. (The seat of county government later moved to Mount Idaho and finally to Grangeville.)

The placers here proved to be quite rich, and after the initial excitement died down the population settled at about 500 miners. The district was opened to the Chinese in 1870. According to Elsensohn in *Idaho Chinese Lore*, the census for that year listed 213 white men, 12 white women, 16 white children, 343 Chinese men, and one Chinese woman. It is interesting to speculate whether this lone Chinese woman might have been Polly Nathoy.

Polly came to Warren as a slave girl about 1870, and her experiences have been intertwined with a variety of tales. One of these made her famous as Idaho's "poker bride." The story goes that Charlie Bemis, owner of a local saloon, won Polly on the turn of a card in a poker game. Sister Alfreda Elsensohn writes in *Pioneer Days in Idaho County*: "One night Charlie Bemis the gambler was playing cards with a Chinaman. For Charlie his money was at stake and his saloon; and for the Chinaman it was his slave girl and a little bit of gold." Bemis won.

In 1890, several years after the alleged poker incident, Bemis got into an argument with a gambler named Johnny Cox. Described as "a hard case from Lewiston," Cox shot Bemis in the face. Dr. Bibby from Grangeville came to dress the wound but expected it to prove fatal. However, Polly took charge of the sick man, picking out pieces of shattered cheekbone with her crochet hook and nursing him to recovery. In 1894 they were married and moved to the Bemis ranch on the bank of the Salmon River. They became well-known pioneers, and interest in Polly's fascinating life continued to grow.

The Chinese at Warren were scattered throughout the district, occupied in mining as well as a variety of other jobs. One of their much-appreciated activities was gardening, as the miners were always keen for fresh produce. A tangible bit of Chinese life can still be seen at the Celedon Slope Garden and its interpretive center, Hays Station, eight miles east of town. The garden has recently been recovered under the U.S. Forest Service Cultural Resource Management Program.

On a sloping mountainside above the Salmon River, a group of industrious Chinese made three large terraces on which they cultivated approximately twelve acres of vegetables for the Warren market. They used the site from 1870 until about 1902. Records are sparse, although the U.S. Census for 1880 lists four farmers and three gardeners among Warren's Chinese residents. Celedon Slope, the remnant of one terrace, covers about an acre. Here, notes Lawrence A. Kingsbury in *Celedon Slope Garden*, archaeologists have recovered fragments of porcelain, coins, opium pipes, and the celedon ware for which the site is named.

Hays Station is easily accessible on the main road. A visit to the garden site involves a steep downhill hike toward the South Fork of the Salmon River.

In the days when conveniences were few, a Chinese cook was a great boon to the pioneer household. —Idaho State Historical Society

YELLOW PINE AND STIBNITE

Yellow Pine lies fifty-four miles east of McCall on the Lick Creek Road (Forest Road 48), a good fair-weather route. Yellow Pine can also be reached from Cascade and Landmark Junction via FR 413, but truck traffic from the Stibnite mine may be heavy here, so Lick Creek Road is preferable. Beyond Lick Creek summit, the road drops down to the stream and winds through a scenic basalt canyon where shrubs and flowers vie for growth on vertical slabs of rock. Lick Creek runs into the Sesesh River, and the road follows its contours until its merger with the East Fork of the Salmon River, which flows all the way to Yellow Pine.

This tiny settlement still bears the look of the Old West in its dusty streets, frame buildings, and board sidewalks. It is a homey place where residents get the local news off the bulletin board in front of the general store. There are no telephones. The annual harmonica contest in August brings in thousands of spectators. Summer visitors come to camp along the waters of the East Fork of the Salmon River. Winter visitors bring their snowmobiles. One resident remarked, "I've seen 150 snowmobiles sitting on Main Street on a Saturday night."

Yellow Pine has just about come full circle in the last 100 years. It began as a stopover for miners on their way to the Thunder Mountain mines, and today it is a stopover for miners on their way to Stibnite, four miles from Yellow Pine near the old Thunder Mountain District. The Minvin gold mine at Stibnite is going strong, with the prospect of long-term production.

Open-pit mines were developed at Stibnite during the 1930s, but the real boom came during the World War II pinch for strategic minerals. The U.S. Bureau of Mines sent in drillers, who found much-needed mercury and tungsten. Stibnite became something of a boomtown, emerging as the leading tungsten producer in the United States and runner-up in the production of mercury.

These mountains witnessed Idaho's last placer mining excitement, and the story reads like fiction. In the summer of 1896 the four Caswell brothers (Dan, Lou, Ben, and Cort) prospected up Monumental Creek. They had poor luck and prepared to pull out, but they had to track down one of their stray mules first. The animal led them along an unnamed creek, and there they discovered fabulous outcroppings of gold ore. Appropriately, they named their find the Golden Reef—and each spring they took out a water bucket full of nuggets.

In 1900 the Caswells sold the Golden Reef for $100,000 to Col. William Dewey of Nampa and Silver City. He paid them with a single check, and the *Idaho Statesman* ran a picture of it on the front page. This was all it took

The Caswell brothers at home on Thunder Mountain. They prospected successfully for gold here and precipitated the Thunder Mountain Stampede of 1902.

to spread Thunder Mountain gold fever. Miners swarmed in from all directions to look for a fortune in this wild and rugged country. They came on foot, horseback, and muleback, with endless pack trains struggling up one side of Monumental Summit and down the other. A good many of them camped at the base of the summit, where Mule Creek met the crashing waters of Monumental Creek. Here the lively settlement of Roosevelt grew. It was a typical mining camp, full of gambling, saloons, and high-priced flour. Food prices soared, and men made good money ($30 a sack) packing in flour over the sixty-mile trail between Warren and Thunder Mountain.

Most of the rich ore came in ledges rather than in simple placers. Mining this material required a large expenditure for heavy machinery, whose every nut and bolt was packed in on the backs of mules. Colonel Dewey brought in a ten-stamp mill and apparently met with success. Most of the $350,000 worth of gold taken from the region came from his mine.

By 1907 a majority of the inhabitants had drifted away, and during one wet spring the whole town of Roosevelt disappeared. A landslide moved down the mountain and dammed the waters of Monumental Creek, forming Lake Roosevelt. It gradually drowned the town and sparked an unusual form of "fishing." Household goods began to float about the lake, and from a makeshift raft one could hook a pot, pan, or shaving mug from the submerged town. Adelia Routson Parke remembered that the most cherished mirror on their Big Creek ranch was fished from Lake Roosevelt.

Writer Zane Gray became so fascinated with the story of Roosevelt that he used the setting for a novel called *Thunder Mountain*.

Big Creek

Big Creek is a tiny settlement on the fringe of the wilderness. During the 1920s a hand-hewn cabin was built here to serve as the U.S. Forest Service's headquarters. Later, new buildings were constructed for the Forest Service half a mile away, and the original building became Big Creek Lodge. Today it is a private home. Nevertheless, Big Creek still serves as a popular launching point for visitors to the Frank Church–River of No Return Wilderness, the largest single roadless area in the United States outside Alaska. Deer, elk, black bear, mountain goats, and more than 150 other species roam this natural environment little disturbed by twentieth-century technology.

Idaho writer Vardis Fisher saw this awesome expanse from the air some sixty years ago, and his description from *Idaho, A Guide in Word and Picture* still fits:

> In any direction for a hundred miles there is only an ocean of thousands of zeniths. . . . From peak to peak, from backbone to backbone, the landscape lifts and falls until it shimmers in the distance. . . . In the far southeast are the Sawtooth spires; in the far northwest is the tumbled blue cloudland of the Seven Devils . . . there are lakes of utmost loveliness and serenity, or impassable jungles of fir and lodgepole and pine, or meadows where wild flowers grow dense and knee-deep, or river gorges dropping sharp and sudden to the white-capped waters below.

This is the incomparable Salmon River drainage: isolated, rugged, and still relatively inaccessible. The gorges of the main Salmon and the Middle Fork are two of the deepest in North America. Primitive populations found shelter here some 8,000 years ago. They hunted elk and wild sheep and left traces of their culture in paintings and petroglyphs on the walls of their caves. Eventually a small band of Shoshone Indians called the Sheepeaters inhabited this wilderness until they were dislodged in the Sheepeater War of 1879 (see Custer, in Central Idaho).

Just before the dawn of the twentieth century, the Salmon River country began to settle up. Every meadow that could support a few acres of hay became a prospective homesite in a backcountry where everything came in on muleback. In *Memoirs of an Old Timer*, Adelia Routson Parke recalled the adventure of moving to the Caswell ranch on Big Creek in 1910. The family was on the trail six days. Adelia, then a ten-year-old, well remembered the narrow, frightening places, especially Jacob's Ladder and the Devil's Elbow, "where many horses had fallen off, rolling into the dashing torrent below." Her father, John Routson, rode at the head of the procession leading a bell mare. Next came her mother on a saddle mule, with the baby lying on a pillow across the front of her saddle. Two younger children followed, riding double on a gentle mule. Adelia rode last in line to keep an eye on the seven mules that carried their precious supplies. They walked ahead of her in single file, their high packs swaying as they plodded up the precarious trail.

The Routson family lived in the backcountry for more than twenty years, ranching and mining; their sojourn is preserved in the geography (Routson Creek and Routson Peak). The children were home schooled and grew up with books, music, and adventure. Along with a sprinkling of other settlers, they survived weather, fires, bears, accidents, heroic deeds, and the rigors of pioneer living. Their life in this primitive area will not likely be repeated.

Today the old settlers are all gone, but the wilderness remains as rugged as ever. A few airports dot the mountain meadows. Hunters and fishermen fly in to meet their outfitters; then, like the pioneers, they pack up their gear and head for the trail on foot or horseback.

The Treasure Valley

I-84, US 20/26 and 30
Idaho 21 and 44
BOISE

Boise lies in a greenbelt along the Boise River, where sagebrush plains merge with forested mountains. This fertile area, thick with cottonwood trees, was a delight to the early fur trappers. When the French Canadians among them saw the green river banks, they are said to have exclaimed, "Les bois! Les bois!" meaning, "The woods! The woods!" The name Boise comes from this expression and is pronounced, "Boy-see." Coming off the desert on I-84, the unexpected sight of the green valley below is as welcoming today as it must have been in 1820.

This city of some 135,000 people has grown into a cultural, educational, and artistic center. It is also a focal point for business and industry. The skyline is sprinkled with corporate headquarters of national and international giants such as the J. R. Simplot Company, Albertsons, Trus-Joist/MacMillan, Morrison-Knudson, Boise Cascade Corporation, and Ore-Ida Foods. Yet the town continues to be a rare blend of urban and rural.

Jack Simplot in the early years of his potato processing empire, circa 1940. Now the company is a diversified one that includes ranches, frozen foods, phosphate plants, and related industries.
—Idaho State Historical Society

These biplanes belong to Varney Airlines, which began operations in Boise in 1926. Here they are reenacting the first scheduled air mail service with a flight between Pasco, Boise, and Elko. Walter Varney is standing in front of the airplane, Thomas Varney by the car. Varney became the parent of United Airlines.

Detail from the interior of the Egyptian Theatre in Boise. This elegantly decorated structure was built during the 1920s after the opening of King Tut's tomb popularized things Egyptian. —Idaho State Historical Society

The Morrison Center for the Performing Arts makes Boise a renowned cultural stop, with attractions ranging from famous ballets to Broadway plays. Boise's own Little Theater has long produced distinguished plays, and the annual Music Week extravaganza, dating from 1919, has been copied by cities throughout the country. There is a popular outdoor Shakespearean theatre, and the annual Basque celebration, with its colorful dances, is one of Boise's unique attractions.

The city center mixes old buildings with new, and historic walks fan out in all directions. Museums, restaurants, theatres, and galleries rub elbows with the Boise River, which flows through the middle of town. It winds past several city parks, the Boise State University campus, and twenty-one miles of greenbelt, which gives the City of Green a special aura and a unique lifestyle. The national media speak of Boise in glowing terms and declare it one of the most desirable homesites in the country.

Capitol Boulevard

Much of downtown Boise can be seen by driving the length of Capitol Boulevard, from the Spanish-style Union Pacific Depot (now the Morrison-Knudson Building) at the south end to the state Capitol on the north. In between are Boise State University, the Morrison Center (on campus), and Julia Davis Park.

The latter is Boise's oldest park. Here Tom and Julia Davis pioneered the local orchard industry in 1863 by planting a thousand apple trees. They chose a historic spot, for pioneers on the Oregon Trail often made camp nearby. When Julia died, Tom donated these choice riverfront lots to the city, and the park was named in her honor. The Idaho Historical Museum, which re-creates the state's colorful past, is located here, as is the Boise Art Museum, which exhibits both local and national work. The park also boasts an excellent small zoo, and the Discovery Center stands on the northern edge of the park. Visitors get a fresh look at science in hands-on exhibits enabling them to touch, see, hear, and do.

The Capitol stands foursquare at the north end of the boulevard, a study in classical architecture. The exterior is built of sandstone blocks, some as heavy as ten tons, quarried from Table Rock east of town. Beautiful in daytime, the old structure is dramatic at night, when the six-foot golden eagle atop the rotunda glows in a halo of light. The interior is finished in a variety of white marbles, creating a feeling of space and light. The rotunda soars to a height of 208 feet, with circular promenades on each of the four floors.

There is much of interest to see in the statehouse, but perhaps the most unusual thing is the gilded statue of George Washington carved by Charles Leopold Ostner in 1868. He chose for this work a giant ponderosa pine and hauled it by sled to his home in Garden Valley. With a common chopping axe, handsaw, chisel, and gouge he created this lifesize figure of Washington atop his horse. Equally remarkable, most of the work was done at night by the light of a pine torch held by one of his three children. The statue was presented to the Territory of Idaho in an elaborate ceremony on January 8, 1869. The members of the legislature became so excited over the gift that they voted to reward Ostner with $7,500 but later decided the territory was too poor to lay out such a handsome amount and scaled it back to $2,500.

In 1982 a fire roared through the north end of the Capitol. Firemen were able to contain it, and damage was limited primarily to the second floor. Representatives of the Idaho Historical Society helped in an advisory capacity while careful workmen made repairs. Today, the casual observer would never know a disaster had struck here.

Old Boise, Warm Springs Avenue, and the Old Pen

Turn off Capitol Boulevard and head east on Main Street to a picturesque section of town known as Old Boise. Here small shops and sidewalk cafes bring life to charming century-old buildings. Of particular interest in this neighborhood is the Basque Museum, the only such facility in the United States. Boise is home to the largest community of Basques outside Europe, and their heritage is preserved in a former boardinghouse that sheltered immigrants from 1910 through the 1970s.

At one time, this area between Eighth and Sixth streets lay on the fringe of an exotic Chinatown. Nearby was a questionable passage known as Levi's Alley, a stronghold for painted ladies and soiled doves. Historian Nancy Stringfellow says the town's respectable citizens "kept their eyes carefully averted from this blot on the escutcheon." Nevertheless, one memorable day a startling fire riveted attention on this seamy side of the community. Stringfellow writes:

> It was on a Sunday morning . . . and Main Street was filled with families, suitably and soberly attired, on their way to church services. One of the girls tipped over a lamp and a flash fire caught the cheap lumber. Picture the excitement. The fire engine clanging, ladders erected to rescue the

Oinkari Basque dancers add colorful entertainment to many Idaho celebrations. Oinkari means "fast feet," and these performers render a literal translation.

211

fair and frail ones. A busload of people halted in the middle of Main Street gazing in fascination . . . as many of the rescued ones had neglected to snatch even a nightgown.

On down the street, at 210 Main, the old Assay Office stands as a symbol of the wealth of Idaho Territory. Through its doors passed $75 million in gold and silver bullion. Much of it came from Boise Basin, a twelve-mile square centered in Idaho City that produced one of the richest gold discoveries in U.S. history. The stately old building, a National Historic Landmark, is made of local sandstone and has walls two feet thick. It currently houses the administrative offices of the Idaho Historical Society.

Two blocks east of the Assay Office, Main Street becomes Warm Springs Avenue, a prestigious address for more than a hundred years. Today this section, with its distinguished homes, has been designated a historic district on the National Register. In the beginning (about 1892), the attraction here was the warm springs, which made the potbellied parlor stove obsolete. The denizens of the C. W. Moore mansion (1109 Warm Springs Avenue) warmed themselves in the "modern" way, by geothermal heat. It worked very simply. An endless supply of hot water circulated through a set of radiators, and voilà—instant heat. The idea soon caught on. A boom in fashionable houses developed. The old two-wheeled wagon road became Warm Springs Avenue, and Boise made history as the first city in the nation to heat its homes with naturally hot water.

The hot springs that supplied the water were located east of town on the lower slopes of Table Rock. Here a hot mist rose, and the water that bubbled up was hot enough to boil an egg or scald a pig. In 1890 the Boise Water Works began drilling on a steamy piece of ground near the Old Penitentiary and struck two artesian wells that poured out a total of 800,000 gallons of 170-degree water per day. This became the basis of the geothermal system and literally "made" Warm Springs Avenue.

With the blessings of hot water, an electric streetcar soon ran the length of the avenue, past the new Natatorium hot springs pool and the rapidly developing neighborhood. Today the "old Nat" and the streetcar are gone, but residents still warm their homes with heat generated by naturally hot water. Betty Clifford, who lives at the east end of the avenue, speaks enthusiastically about "the system." "We love our hot water," she says. "It is very, very soft and especially wonderful for bathing and laundry. And very inexpensive."

When the great experiment began, some of the skeptics predicted the hot water wells would dry up by the time developers filled the Natatorium pool. However, the water still flows, and the original well house, now restored, may be needed for another one hundred years. The geothermal success on Warm Springs Avenue has expanded to include systems for downtown Boise, making the Idaho statehouse the only capitol building in the country to be heated geothermally.

At the end of Warm Springs Avenue is the Old Penitentiary, a historic site administered by the Idaho State Historical Society. This complex of picturesque buildings dating back to 1870 is one of three territorial penitentiaries in the nation still open to the public. Inmates did much of the early construction—perhaps while dragging leg irons or the "Oregon Boot" (a ball and chain that can be seen in the Old Pen Museum)—using hand-cut stone quarried from the hillside above the prison. Convicts lived here until 1973, when they moved to the new penitentiary south of town.

The gates of these sandstone walls have clanked on thousands of prisoners. One of the more interesting ones, Harry Orchard, spent the bulk of his life here. Orchard came to Idaho in 1898, in time to join the rioters at the Bunker Hill and Sullivan mine near Kellogg (see Kellogg, in North Idaho). He later figured in the conspiracy to assassinate former governor Frank Steunenberg, who had declared martial law in the Coeur d'Alene mines. Orchard was arrested, and the trial was held in Boise during the summer of 1907. Reporters representing some fifty magazines and newspapers from New York to San Francisco descended on the town. Day after day they crowded into the hot little courtroom to report the unfolding drama. Clarence Darrow spoke eloquently for the defense, William Borah for the prosecution. Each emerged from the conflict a national figure.

Harry Orchard was convicted of murder. Others linked to the assassination (such as Big Bill Haywood, an officer in the Western Federation of Miners) went free. Orchard spent the rest of his days at the Old Pen, and apparently it came to feel like home. When offered parole some twenty-five years later, he chose to remain within the sandstone walls.

Another unusual inmate was Lyda Trueblood-Dooley-McHaffie-Lewis-Meyer-Southard-Whitlock-Shaw, otherwise known as Idaho's "Lady Bluebeard." A number of men had a fatal attraction for this diminutive redhead. A pattern developed: marriage, sudden death of the husband, and the collection of life insurance by the widow. Four husbands died mysteriously (as did two or three other persons). Ptomaine poisoning, typhoid fever, or Spanish influenza appeared on the death certificates. However, when suspicious authorities in Twin Falls began a serious investigation, autopsies revealed the victims had all died from lethal doses of arsenic. Lyda declared her innocence but was convicted of second-degree murder anyway. She began serving a life sentence in 1921.

Don Waldhalm, who has written for the Old Pen publication the *Clock*, says Lyda adjusted well to prison life. She became very interested in tending the rose garden and requested steel trellises to support the climbers. Eventually she joined two of these together to make a handy twelve-foot ladder, specially designed by one of her friends in the prison shop. After serving ten years, Lyda sawed her way out of her cell and used the trellises to scale the walls. Once over the top, she rendezvoused with a newly released prisoner who waited for her on the outside. After one more marriage and one more mysterious death (her mother-in-law), she was captured and returned to the penitentiaries for another nine years.

The penitentiary complex also includes the Bishop's House, a Queen Anne mansion dating from 1887 that housed a long line of Episcopalian clergymen. When its original downtown location was marked for a parking lot, the Boise Junior League and Idaho State Historical Society came to the rescue, finding a new location for the venerable structure. Moving day came, and the trees along Warm Springs Avenue were trimmed to allow the mansion to pass down the street; telephone lines came down, and traffic stopped. This fully restored historic landmark now hosts such activities as art shows, seminars, and receptions.

The Greenbelt

Five of Boise's major parks lie along the greenbelt. Paths wind leisurely at the river's edge along manicured parks, stretches of natural terrain, and small, sandy beaches. Cottonwood thickets shelter hummingbirds and bald eagles, beaver, mule deer, and hundreds of other species of wildlife. The Barber Park pool (once a mill pond) toward the east end of the greenbelt provides serene water and habitat for many creatures. This is also the main point of launch for river floaters (rentals available).

Farther downriver sits Municipal Park, adjacent to the Morrison-Knudson Nature Center. These are followed by three parks named for Boise ladies: Julia Davis, Ann Morrison, and Kathryn Albertson. Each one offers special amenities in the heart of town. Several miles downstream lie Veterans Memorial State Park and Eagle Island. This series of parks, linked by the greenbelt path, has been promoted by Boiseans intent on "saving" the river, which was once fouled by the waste of five packing plants. Today the stream is in good shape and provides something of a downtown fishery, although the abundance John Townsend cited in 1834 has certainly diminished. Townsend marveled at the beautiful stream, "clear as crystal, and literally crowded with salmon which are springing from the water almost constantly." The salmon are history, but other fish remain. Throw in a line anywhere and you are likely to catch wild trout.

In *Idaho Wildlife*, Nancy Butler repeats a story concerning Governor Cecil Andrus and a distinguished out-of-town guest. The guest expressed a desire to go fishing, and the governor said, "That's no problem, you can borrow my rod and go down to the river. There's a great hole just below the Broadway bridge."

"You've got to be kidding," the man responded. "You don't mean to tell me you can catch trout right in the middle of town?"

"Just try it," said the governor. His guest did try it and came back with a foot-long rainbow trout.

Boise History

The Boise River, which originates in the Sawtooth Mountains, has always held a fascination for travelers. When John C. Frémont's exploring party stopped here in 1843, he wrote, "[T]he road [Oregon Trail] brought us down upon the bottoms of the river, which is a beautiful rapid stream, with clear mountain water, . . . well wooded with some varieties of timber—among which are handsome cottonwoods. We were delighted this afternoon to make a pleasant camp under fine old trees again."

Before the explorers and fur trappers came, this was the domain of Shoshone Indians, who gathered here to hunt, gather seeds, and fish for salmon. Annual intertribal trade fairs brought delegations of Crows, Umatillas, Nez Perce, and other wide-ranging tribes. They came from all directions via old trails that more or less followed today's US 30 and US 95. The trails converged in this rich valley, where the travelers staked their tepees and proceeded to fish, dance, gamble, and trade their wares. Arrowheads, seashells, carrying baskets, dried buffalo meat, camas, and perhaps even wives changed hands.

The first white men to camp along the Boise River were probably members of Donald Mackenzie's party, a detachment from the overland Astorians. They were followed by Wilson Price Hunt and more Astorians, who straggled in from the desert in the fall of 1811. They had endured a hungry journey from Caldron Linn, where their canoes capsized (see Burley, in Central Idaho). After their desert ordeal, the Astorians must have found the Boise River, with its groves of cottonwoods and willows, especially welcome. According to Washington Irving's *Astoria*, the "poor half-famished wanderers" found an Indian camp here and settled in for the night, making a "sumptuous repast upon fish and a couple of dogs, procured from their Indian neighbors."

The British purchased Astoria during the War of 1812. It passed first to the North West Company and then to the Hudson's Bay Company, whose trappers kept a commanding presence in the Boise Valley until the streams became a "fur desert." When they abandoned this area in 1855, covered wagons had been rolling over the Oregon Trail for about fifteen years. These emigrants also welcomed the river's shade and water, but their destination was Oregon and the green Willamette country. It took the cry of "gold" to set off the stampede that finally brought permanent settlement to the Boise Valley.

In 1862 prospecting parties led by Moses Splawn and George Grimes joined forces to probe the tributaries of the Boise River. They struck pay dirt on Grimes Creek, near Centerville, and news of the strike traveled like lightning. Almost overnight thousands of miners from Florence, Warren's Diggings, Lewiston, and Walla Walla struck out for Boise Basin, where the creeks yielded fabulous gold nuggets "the size of a kernel of corn." Instant cities grew at Placerville, Centerville, Bannock (Idaho City), and Pioneerville. The following year ledges of rich silver ore were discovered at Silver City in the Owyhees, and an army of miners headed in that direction.

The Indians did not take kindly to this invasion. Soon the U.S. Army arrived to protect the miners and the new settlers who were moving in behind them. In 1863 Maj. Pinckney Lugenbeel arrived on the scene and chose a strategic site along the Boise River for a military post. From this location he could keep an eye on both the Owyhee country and the gold camps in Boise Basin.

A few farmers settled along the fertile river bottom to raise vegetables for the soldiers and for the miners scattered throughout the hills. Cy Jacobs freighted in a stock of goods and sold them from a tent as fast as they arrived. Amenities increased at a fast pace. A school, hotel, meat market, blacksmith shop, and dry goods store were soon in place. These were followed by the *Tri-Weekly Statesman* (today's *Idaho Statesman*), which made Boise a leading voice in the territory. B. M. DuRell and C. W. Moore established the First National Bank of Idaho (now West One), and by 1866 a new Episcopal church was ready to begin services. This pioneer chapel is now located on the campus of Boise State University.

The fledgling community grew. Fort Boise gave the town stature (as well as a payroll), and in 1864 Boise City became the capital of Idaho Territory. A year earlier William H. Wallace, the first territorial governor, had designated Lewiston for this honor, but when the second legislature met, it declared for Boise. At that time, most of the population resided in southwestern Idaho in the high-altitude camps of Boise Basin and the Owyhee Mountains. Boise was their supply center.

The new capital city soon became a town of attractive homes, orchards, shaded streets, and flowing water, both hot and cold. Ridenbaugh's irrigation canal (1879) made the city an agricultural center, and Boise acquired "society" as substantial new homes went up on Warm Springs Avenue. But when the Union Pacific Railroad's Oregon Short Line crossed southern Idaho in 1883–84, it bypassed the up-and-coming city, much to the consternation of local residents. Boise lay at river level, some 600 feet below the railroad route, and the steepness of the grade made it difficult for the tracks to reach the town. The railroad stopped out on the desert at Kuna, en route to Nampa, Caldwell, and points west. Later on, a spur line from Nampa provided limited services to Boise, and in 1925 the main line of the Union Pacific came to town. The distinctive Spanish colonial depot made the wait worthwhile, for it is one of Boise's treasures. Morrison-Knudson Company purchased the historic structure in 1990, and today it shines on a hillside of green gardens at the south end of Capitol Boulevard.

Urban development continued as transportation improved, and Boise became the largest metropolitan area in the state. Today it is the center of business, finance, government, and recreational activities that reach across

the intermountain West. It is the largest Oregon Trail city between To-
peka, Kansas, and Portland, Oregon.

Snake River Birds of Prey Natural Area

The state-of-the-art Birds of Prey Visitor Center, six miles south of Boise
on South Cole Road, was finished in the spring of 1994. It is part of a complex where scientists breed and research endangered species. A variety of
falcons, eagles, hawks, owls, and condors from around the world live here.
Some, like the harpy eagle, are very rare. A conservation room features
exhibits on falconry, and a world map documents efforts to save endangered species around the world.

The Snake River Birds of Prey Natural Area, south of Boise, was created
by Congress to provide habitat for the world's greatest concentration of

*Falconer Morley Nelson at Snake River Birds of Prey Natural Area. Nelson has
been influential in arousing concern for birds of prey and in bringing to Boise the
World Center for Birds of Prey.* —Idaho State Historical Society

raptors. It generally follows the river canyon upstream from just below the Swan Falls Dam to Grandview, although additional land adjacent to the canyon is used as a study area. Rare peregrine falcons, eagles, and hawks find nesting sites in the pitted canyon walls. They dine on small mammals such as ground squirrels, rabbits, and mice. Eagles can frequently be seen floating on the thermal winds, and falcons jet from rocky crags to perform their acrobatics. Spring is especially good for viewing, either from the bluffs above the dam or on a guided boat trip.

To access the area, take I-84 west to the Kuna-Meridian exit and follow Idaho 69 to Kuna and the Swan Falls Road. About eight miles south of Kuna, look toward the east for a volcanic butte that rises high above the surrounding sagebrush plain. This is Idaho's "initial point," established in 1867. It is the surveyors' starting place, the prime meridian (for which the town of Meridian is named) by which all land in Idaho is measured.

Historic Swan Falls Dam in the Snake River canyon near Kuna. This includes part of the Birds of Prey Natural Area, which is home to the largest collection of raptors in the world.

Swan Falls Dam

Swan Falls Dam, the first hydroelectric plant built on the Snake River, dates from 1901. It first sent electricity humming through the wires to power equipment at the Trade Dollar Mining and Milling Company at Dewey. Well before 1900 the mining camps in Owyhee County were hurting for timber to stoke the steam-powered stamp mills. Col. William Dewey and his partners in the Trade Dollar (including J. M. Guffey and Andrew Mellon) spent a fortune packing timber from the Boise Mountains. Reasoning that hydroelectric power would be cheaper and more efficient, they hired an engineer and built Swan Falls Dam.

The site in the canyon, which we now know as a primary habitat for raptors, was perfect for a dam. It took twenty-horse teams and hundreds of men with scrapers, shovels, and wheelbarrows to finish the job. Power generated by the turbines lit up the small settlements of Dewey, Silver City, and Murphy, with Boise, Caldwell, and Nampa standing in line. The Idaho-Oregon Power Company later purchased the power plant, and in 1916 it became part of the newly organized Idaho Power.

Originally this section of the canyon was a wintering ground for multitudes of white swans. Native Americans lived here, too, and left their mark at the Wees Bar petroglyphs. Three miles below the dam on the south bank, more than ninety boulders sport curious ancient designs. Interpreted variously as flying birds, stick figures, diamonds, dots, arrows, snakes, or other objects, the configurations have long been a mystery. No Indian villages

Construction workers at Swan Falls Dam in 1901, when most of the work was done with shovels and wheelbarrows. —Idaho Power Company

Tracks of ancient people at Wees Bar petroglyphs, three miles below Swan Falls Dam on the Snake River.

have been unearthed here, but archaeological surveys of the canyon reveal more than seventy-five ancient village sites in a forty-five-mile stretch above and below Swan Falls Dam (see Givens Hot Springs).

Canyon County

Nampa and Caldwell are urban centers for Canyon County, one of the richest agricultural regions in the country. Various crops are grown here, including hops, mints, grapes, sugar beets, and 90 percent of the nation's sweet-corn seed. Fruit is also a traditional crop. One of the choice areas in the county, Sunny Slope, is known for the waves of orchards and vineyards that blanket the rolling hills. In the distance, the Snake River and the Owyhee Mountains offer scenic backdrops. This is Idaho's premier wine country, and visitors enjoy tours and tastings year-round. The orchards take star billing in the fall as roadside stands offer heaps of apples, peaches, pears, and other colorful produce.

Canyon County is interesting not only for its mixed agriculture and scenic beauty but also for its diverse mix of people. Evangelical populations came in the early days of settlement. Idaho historian J. M. Neil calculates some interesting statistics in *Idaho Heritage*. Although the county has less than 10 percent of the state's population, it includes "at least half of Idaho's Nazarenes, Seventh-Day Adventists, Quakers and a number of other evangelical sects." Groups of Brethrens and Mennonites settled here around 1900, and their church communities still thrive.

Greenleaf, one of the smallest towns in the county, was settled by a colony of Quakers in 1904. Today the centerpiece of the little settlement is its school, the Greenleaf Academy. The Seventh-Day Adventist Gem State Academy is a few miles away (near Caldwell), and in Nampa the Northwest Nazarene College continues to flourish along with a close-knit religious community.

Lake Lowell and the Deer Flat National Bird Refuge lie between Nampa and Caldwell toward the south. The lake impounds water for irrigation. It is an early Bureau of Reclamation irrigation project, completed in 1909. Theodore Roosevelt, who was president at the time, designated the area around the lake a National Wildlife Refuge. It has become one of the major wintering places on the Pacific flyway. Thousands of mallards and Canadian geese congregate here and mingle with 190 other species of birds. The headquarters building includes an environmental education center.

I-84, US 30,
Idaho 55 and 45
NAMPA

Nampa is a growing metropolitan center with a diverse economy based on agriculture, business, education, and publishing. The Amalgamated Sugar Company factory in 1905 was one of the first industries to locate here. More recent additions include the Pacific Press Publishing Company (national publishing arm of the Seventh-Day Adventist Church) and the Pintler Winery south of town. Lake Lowell and a number of local parks provide recreation. Much of the town's social and cultural life revolves around Northwest Nazarene College and the Nampa Civic Center.

Northwest Nazarene, a small liberal arts school, is located on a tree-shaded campus south of the business district. In 1916 the three-year-old "Idaho Holiness School" moved to this site and took its present name. Historian Annie Laurie Bird, writing in *My Home Town*, gives credit to enthusiastic citizen Eugene Emerson for bringing the college to town. He prevailed upon the Oregon-Idaho district of the Nazarene Church to found the college, then urged Nazarene families to settle here and help build the community. Their numbers grew, and today this denomination supports seven churches in Nampa and additional ones in the outlying areas.

Nampa began to settle up in 1885 after the Oregon Short Line Railroad crossed southern Idaho. Alexander Duffles filed on the land, and a boom in the sale of town lots soon followed. A few years later the community became the terminus for the Boise, Nampa and Owyhee Railroad (see Murphy). After Colonel Dewey sold the railroad, the new owners extended the line north from Nampa to tap the resources of the Payette River Valley. It reached Emmett in 1902 and later was extended to McCall. With the growth of irrigation projects, farmers continued to move into the area, and Nampa developed its agricultural and industrial base, which continues to expand.

The origin of the name Nampa remains a mystery. An often repeated yarn says the name comes from a renegade Indian called Nampuh (Bigfoot), who supposedly terrorized immigrant trains and white settlers. However, no firm evidence of his existence has come to light. A more credible tradition comes from the late Elizabeth Wilson, a Nez Perce. She said the story of "Mr. Foot" originated when the Shoshones stuffed oversized moccasins and went about making footprints to frighten away the Nez Perce and early white settlers.

The Canyon County Historical Museum, located in the 1902 Oregon Short Line depot in downtown Nampa, places special emphasis on the railroad era. Research materials are available.

Pintler Winery and Sunny Slope Wine Country

Pintler Winery is located on a hilltop amid a great sweep of country that extends across miles of farmland to the scalloped barrier of the Owyhee Mountains. The winery is a welcoming and homey place with premium stock that adds stature to this fledgling Idaho industry. Take Twelfth Avenue South for six miles, turn west at the Pintler sign, and follow the markers for about five miles.

Snake River Stampede

This is one of the top rodeos in the United States, billed as the "Wildest, Fastest Show on Earth." A combination of cowboy celebrities, media stars, and spirited spectators makes this an authentic western celebration. It has been held in one form or another since 1913, when some cowboys staged a "little bucking contest." The full-fledged Snake River Stampede dates from 1937. According to historian Arthur Hart, on July 4 of that year, "President Franklin D. Roosevelt pressed a golden telegraph key in his Hyde Park, N.Y. home to explode the fireworks which inaugurated the first Stampede under the lights in a new arena. It has been going ever since."

Celebration Park

This Canyon County park is reached by way of Melba on Idaho 45, south of Nampa. It borders the Snake River in the Birds of Prey Natural

Cowgirl Bonnie McCarroll followed the national rodeo circuit during the early 1900s. Here she takes a spill from bucking bronc Silver. —Lavina Pence Palmer

Few could match Jack Hensen when it came to riding a bucking horse. He was a local cowboy-rancher who lived in Weiser and participated in valley rodeos circa 1925. —Wilda Hensen

Area and includes beachfront land that was used for centuries as a wintering ground for prehistoric Indians. Picnic tables sit amid huge boulders (dropped here by the Bonneville flood) that provide a gallery of ancient picture writing. In addition to these curious inscriptions, archaeologists have found evidence of many early habitation sites. Although this is something of an "archaeological park," the most visible element is the historic Guffey Railroad Bridge (a remnant of the Boise-Nampa-Owyhee line). It has been rebuilt for foot traffic and leads to hiking/biking trails, boat docks, and wildlife viewing areas.

I-84,
US 20/26 and 30,
Idaho 19
CALDWELL

Caldwell is the hub of a prosperous agribusiness area surrounded by orchards and ranches with the snowcapped Owyhee Mountains in the distance. It is a center of commerce, a county seat, and a college town.

From ancient times, the site of Caldwell lay in the midst of Shoshone territory along the Boise River. Historian Annie Laurie Bird called it Peace Valley because many different tribes met here amicably each summer for a great intertribal fair and carnival featuring trading, dancing, gambling, and socializing.

A surprising mix of trade goods circulated here, including Nez Perce horses, Northern Paiute obsidian arrowheads, Pacific Coast ornamental seashells (brought inland by the Umatilla and Cayuse), Shoshone buffalo hides, and meat from the eastern Snake River Plain. In addition, Cheyenne and Arapaho bands dragged superior cedar tepee poles from Colorado by the hundreds.

In 1813 a group of trappers entered the valley. John Reid, who had previously come overland with Hunt's Astorians, returned with a group of trappers in the service of the North West Company. They built Reid's Fort near the mouth of the Boise River to serve as a base. The Indians, apparently displeased with this invasion, murdered Reid and all his men. Only Marie Dorian, wife of fur trapper Pierre Dorian, and her two small children escaped. Enduring extreme hardship, they crossed the Blue Mountains in the dead of winter to reach friendly tribes on the other side. Their harrowing journey became one of the epic tales of the fur trade.

In later years, the site of Caldwell was on the main route of the Oregon Trail. However, these travelers rolled on toward the Willamette Valley in Oregon. It took the coming of the Union Pacific's Oregon Short Line Railroad to bring permanent settlers. The railroad's public relations man, Robert E. Strahorn, followed the engineers and chose townsites along the right-of-way. He chose this location and named it for Alexander Caldwell, a major stockholder in the townsite company.

Caldwell existed on paper, complete with churches, schools, hotel, depot, parks, and shade trees, while the site was still "as white with alkali as the winter robe of the mountain tops." Sagebrush, greasewood, and cottonwoods stood along the river, but still Carrie Adele Strahorn thought it a "forbidding place to build a home."

She and her husband came by wagon from Boise in the spring of 1882 to drive the first stakes in the townsite. The fledgling community prospered and soon boasted a dozen or so houses and tents, eleven saloons, and a celebrated community pump. Skeptics predicted that no large town would develop here because the land was so "unreclaimed and uninhabitable." The Strahorns stayed on to become leading citizens, helping to build the First Presbyterian Church and the College of Idaho. The success of Caldwell contradicted many prophets. In spite of alkali dust, sage, and coyotes, the city grew. Irrigation transformed a bleak landscape into the rich farmland known today as "the seed heart of America."

Several nationally known businesses have been located here for so long that their names have become synonymous with Caldwell. One of these, the Crookham Seed Company, has produced seed corn here for more than seventy-five years. Its experimental farms grow approximately 185 different varieties of sweet corn, and the company leads the industry in developing award-winning super-sweet varieties. Another, the J. R. Simplot Company, has maintained a commanding presence for the last fifty years. Long before Simplot came on the scene, A. E. Gipson founded Caxton Printers. This family publishing business, dating from 1907, continues in its fourth generation. It is distinguished by excellence in printing books on western Americana.

Caldwell is home to Albertson College, a privately funded liberal arts college with outstanding facilities. These include the Jewett Auditorium, the Rosenthal Gallery of Arts, the Whittenberger Planetarium, and the Orma J. Smith Museum of Natural History. The college was founded in 1891 by the Presbyterian Church and the Reverend William Judson Boone, who served as its president for forty-five years. Originally known as the College of Idaho, it was renamed Albertson in 1890 to honor benefactors J. A. and Kathryn Albertson, loyal alumni and co-founders of a grocery chain that has grown to more than 600 stores.

Albertson is Idaho's oldest institution of higher learning and is well known for its distinguished faculty and bright students. Since 1954 it has produced five Rhodes Scholars. Surprisingly, notes Louie Attebery in *College of Idaho, 1881–1891*, two of the awards came back-to-back, 1967–68 and 1968–69.

Another Caldwell attraction, the Warhawk Air Museum, is located at the Caldwell Municipal Airport and is dedicated to military history. Displays include aircraft from World War II.

Lively Parma draws business from the prosperous farm region to the south near the communities of Wilder and Roswell. It is located on US 95, the north-south ribbon of road that connects Mexico with Canada and runs almost the entire length of Idaho. The highway enters Idaho south of Homedale on the northern fringe of the Owyhee Mountains and continues through a varied terrain of irrigated valleys, rolling uplands, dense forests, and white-water rivers before crossing into Canada at Eastport.

Old Fort Boise Replica

The Old Fort Boise Replica and Museum makes for a historic stop at the east entrance to Parma. The original fort was a British fur trading post located near the confluence of the Boise and Snake rivers. Spring floods long ago swept it away, but this recreation by the Old Fort Boise Historical Society keeps alive its significant story.

Thomas McKay of the Hudson's Bay Company established the post (first called Snake Fort) in 1834. He hoped to lure the Indian trade away from Nathaniel Wyeth at Fort Hall, an American enterprise. For the next twenty-one years, the Union Jack fluttered over Fort Boise to announce the British presence. As the fur trade declined, Fort Boise became an important way station for Americans headed west along the Oregon Trail. Missionaries Marcus and Narcissa Whitman, accompanied by Henry and Eliza Spalding and William H. Gray, brought the first wagon over the trail in the summer of 1836. It broke down before they reached Fort Hall and rolled on to Fort Boise as a two-wheeled cart. After a two-day stay, they left the hospitality of the fort and continued to Fort Vancouver on the Columbia River under the protection of John McLeod and his Hudson's Bay trappers.

Other emigrants followed, and the place gained a reputation as a resting place for tired travelers. The fort became especially noted for hospitality when Francis Payette was in charge from 1836 to 1840. This French Canadian, "a merry, fat old gentlemen," had charming manners and entertained gracefully—even hosting tea parties for distinguished company. Thomas J. Farnham said Payette received his party "with every mark of kindness, gave our horses to the care of his servants and introduced us immediately to the chairs, table and edibles of his apartment." Visitors might well appreciate these "edibles," for the menu was often a lavish wilderness spread that featured fresh salmon, vegetables from the garden, and milk from an emigrant cow that had remained behind. One guest reported feasting on "fowls, Ducks, Bacon, Salmon Sturgeon Buffalow & Elk and our vegitables ware Turnips Cabbag & pickled Beets."

Many notable figures stopped at Fort Boise, including Capt. John Sutter (later of California gold rush fame), explorer John C. Frémont, and fur traders Joe Meek and Doc Newell, who took the first wagon all the way to Oregon. This was a busy place and in some ways a cosmopolitan one. One visitor, quoted by Annie Laurie Bird in *Old Fort Boise*, noted, "The fifteen persons at Fort Boise spoke six different languages besides some dialects."

In 1846 the boundary line with Canada was drawn at the forty-ninth parallel, which definitely placed Fort Boise in U.S. territory. The British stayed on anyway, but the days of the fort were numbered. Boise River floods and the rising tempers of the Indians became increasingly hazardous. In the spring of 1853, high water washed away much of the old fort, and only a halfhearted attempt was made to rebuild it.

The endless stream of emigrants and their covered wagons cut a broad road across the country. With them came thousands of head of livestock, which riddled the rangeland as they moved west. The Indians became angry, and their frustration culminated in the massacre of the Ward party near the present-day town of Middleton in 1854. After U.S. troops punished the guilty ones, not even the British felt safe. They left the tattered remains of Fort Boise and gave the country back to the Indians.

Not much activity occurred at the old Fort Boise site until Jonathan Keeney established a ferry in 1863 to cash in on the rush to the Boise Basin and Owyhee mines. Two years later the Oregon Steamship Navigation Company built the steamboat *Shoshone* here. The company hoped to capture the Snake River trade between Farewell Bend, near the present-day town of Weiser, and the Owyhee Crossing some 100 miles upriver. Considerable fanfare preceded the launching of the boat, and a regular schedule was published for both passengers and freight. However, after a few trips the scheme went awry. Not enough trees grew along the bank to furnish wood for the boilers, and the ship was beached.

In 1870 the steamship company rescheduled the *Shoshone* for duty on the Columbia River, but the boat would have to shoot the rapids of Hells Canyon to get there. Cy Smith, a captain with the company, brought it downstream to Brownlee Ferry at the upper end of the canyon. Here it rested for the winter. In the spring Sebastian Miller, another captain, came to the rescue. He fired up a head of steam and headed downriver. The churning rapids tossed the boat wildly. It lost a few parts here and there as it crashed against the rocks, and pieces of it arrived at Lewiston before the ship did. Captain and crew were frightfully jostled. However, the trip was a qualified success, and after getting repairs the *Shoshone* served on the Columbia River for several years.

The Oregon Short Line Railroad passed the Fort Boise site in 1883. Railroad workers established a tent town named St. Paul, but when the rails continued west the rollicking camp faded away. A few persons stayed to file on the land and built the town of Parma. One of the founders, F. R. Fouch, was interested in classical history and named the town for Parma, Italy.

US 30 and 95
FRUITLAND AND
NEW PLYMOUTH

These small Payette Valley settlements are church and school towns whose business districts cater to a farming community. Today one of the chief crops in the area is sweet corn. Farmers grow great quantities of it under contract with American Fine Foods, headquartered in Payette. Both towns were founded about 1900, missing the early days of bad men, vigilantes, pack trains, and prospectors on the trail.

Fruitland grew when thousands of acres of fruit trees—prunes, apples, cherries, peaches—were planted in the Payette Valley. The trees flourished and provided rich returns to the growers, who regularly took prizes at horticultural shows from St. Louis to Chicago. However, during the Great Depression prices fell, and the end of the orchard boom was at hand. Tons of harvested produce were dumped because shipping costs were greater than the sale price of the fruit. Many farmers pulled their orchards and went into diversified agriculture. A few orchardists hung on, and today a modest number of orchards and packing sheds keep the local industry and the name "Fruitland" alive.

Fruitland's neighbor, New Plymouth, was planned in faraway Chicago. William E. Smythe, chairman of the National Irrigation Congress, wanted to found a colony in the West that would prove some of his agricultural theories. He encouraged a group called the Colonial Club to organize, and the Reverend Edward Everett Hale (a relative of patriot Nathan Hale) gave it his blessing.

The colony purchased land, and the town was laid out according to blueprints in 1897. "Every detail was planned to fit the design of the incorporators," wrote George Yost and Dick d'Easum in *Idaho: The Fruitful Land*. "Each colonist purchased 20 acres of irrigated land and 20-acre shares in the company. The investment entitled him to an acre in the central area set apart for a village, providing he built a house there and lived in it. . . . Farms and orchards were to be within about two miles of the village." The founding of the town seemed a fulfillment of the Reverend Hale's blessing. Quoting from the Book of Kings, he said, "Make the valley full of ditches. Ye shall not see wind, neither shall be seen rain, yet the valley shall be filled with water that ye may drink, both ye and your cattle and beasts."

The quotation was appropriate, for irrigation water from the Payette River was always abundant at New Plymouth: the colonists only had to dig a forty-mile ditch to make it available. The venture was a success and most of the colonists planted orchards, which flourished until the onset of the Great Depression. Today most of their fruit trees have been replaced by fields of corn, mint, and onions, as well as by dairy and cattle farms. W. E.

Smythe went on to help start other farming communities. In 1902 he was influential in establishing the Bureau of Reclamation as part of the Department of the Interior.

US 95, Idaho 52

PAYETTE

Payette is located at the confluence of the Payette and Snake rivers in the midst of rolling hills, apple orchards, and fields of sugar beets, onions, and corn. This pleasant country town boasts a good deal of historic architecture, particularly in its residential section. Families enjoy the big indoor-outdoor swimming pool, shady parks, and easy access to hunting and fishing. Food processing plants, wood products manufacturing, and the county offices provide a steady living for residents.

The Payette County Historical Museum features exhibits on vintage clothing and furniture, as well as a postcard carried on the first airmail flight. Memorabilia from Harmon Killbrew, a local boy who made baseball history and earned a place in the Baseball Hall of Fame, is also on display.

Payette's location at the mouth of the Payette River has a lot to do with the town's long and colorful history. The river flows out of Payette Lake 100 miles to the north and cascades down steep mountain terrain to the Payette Valley. Indians, trappers, lumberjacks, and ranchers all sought the river's bounty at one time or another. Shoshone Indians frequently camped here when game and fish were plentiful. Later, both British and American fur trappers tramped the river bank from mouth to source in search of beaver.

Prospectors came this way during the gold rush, following a trail that took them from the Columbia River across the Blue Mountains to Farewell Bend on the Snake River. From here they followed the Snake to the mouth of the Payette River and then continued upstream to the present site of Horseshoe Bend, where a mountain trail led to the Boise Basin mines. According to contemporary newspaper correspondents, an average day would see ten pack trains (with 50 to 100 animals per train) plodding up the trail, as well as fifteen or twenty freight wagons. Later on, coaches traveled a makeshift road carrying mail and passengers to the mines. With all this traffic, "stopping places" soon developed, and these became nuclei for the first settlements along the river. Payette was one of these.

By 1863 Bluff Station, two miles east of Payette at the mouth of Little Willow Creek, was a major stop. Downriver at Washoe, near the confluence of the Snake and Payette rivers, the Stuart brothers established a ferry and a nefarious roadhouse. The ferry had a long life, but the Payette vigilantes cut their teeth on the Washoe gang. The Stuarts were run out of the country upon pain of death for various misdeeds and felonies.

Placer miners traveling the basin trail eyed the lush cattle range along the river, and many of them decided their future lay in ranching rather than mining. Peter Pence brought a large herd of cattle from Washington state in 1867, and others soon followed, but establishment of a town had to await the coming of the Union Pacific Railroad. Union Pacific agent Robert Strahorn chose the site for a depot, and a railroad camp grew nearby at "Boomerang." Immense booms were built here to catch the railroad ties that floated down the Payette River from the mills. In *All Along the River*, Nellie Ireton Mills wrote that 250,000 ties were cut in the woods of Long Valley (near Cascade) and floated downstream to Boomerang. The town later adopted the name of the river, which honors fur trapper Francois Payette.

Idaho 16 and 52
EMMETT

Emmett is perhaps best known as orchard country, although in the past stock ranching and sawmills have been equally important to the economy. The sandy soil and mild climate at Emmett proved to be just right for peaches, cherries, and apples. In spring the surrounding hillsides are awash with blossoms, which continue to inspire annual pilgrimages by tourists hoping to see the beauty of the trees in full flower. The nearby Black Canyon Dam, with its sizable lake and attractive waterside parks, offers a haven for outdoor enthusiasts.

In the early days, Payette and Emmett were almost sister towns along the Payette River. Payette, at the lower end of the valley, and Emmett, toward the upper end, were connected by a riverside trail that led to the Boise Basin mines. Between them was Falk's Store, for many years the only general store between Boise and Baker City, Oregon. During the 1860s settlers came from miles around to shop here for everything from bacon and beans to red flannel underwear, square nails, and coffin handles.

In 1863 the site of Emmett became a stage station on the trail to the Boise Basin mines. A post office soon followed, and the place was named for Emmett Calahan, the postmaster's son. When the gold rush faded away, settlers turned to more stable occupations such as lumbering and stock ranching.

Shortly after 1900 an Ohio firm organized the Idaho Orchards Company and invited people to invest. Orchards became popular and provided jobs for laborers, who cleared the land, dug ditches, planted trees, and eventually picked the fruit. However, not everyone who planted orchards prospered. Some gave up and went back to Ohio, but others made orcharding a successful business.

Idaho 52 continues from Emmett to Horseshoe Bend, where it joins Idaho 55.

US 95
WEISER

Weiser is located at the lower end of the Snake River Plain, which crosses southern Idaho in a great arc. A few miles downriver from town, the Snake River makes an abrupt turn toward the north and enters the famous Hells Canyon. Closer to town, the Weiser River joins the Snake; the confluence is only a short hike from the city center across the old bridge behind the railroad depot on the far side of Mortimer's Island.

Farming, ranching, food processing, and Washington County government offices keep the economy steady. More and more tourists are finding Weiser, which has become renowned for the National Oldtime Fiddlers' Contest.

The story of humans in the Weiser River Valley goes back a long way. Prior to building a new highway in 1994, the Idaho Department of Transportation called in archaeologists to determine if any significant materials might be disturbed. To the surprise of everyone concerned, workers unearthed 10,000-year-old spear points and other artifacts. These items establish that human habitation began here at an early date, and they are unique in that they come from a seasonal campsite outside the protection of a cave or rock shelter.

The Northern Shoshone Indians, particularly a little band called the Weiser Shoshone, frequented the Weiser Valley before the white men came. They were on hand to befriend the Wilson Price Hunt expedition (see St. Anthony, in Southeast Idaho, and Caldron Linn, in Central Idaho) as it marched past the site of Weiser on November 26, 1811. A host of American and British trappers followed. These included a mix of Indians, Hawaiians, French Canadians, and British in the service of the North West and Hudson's Bay companies. In 1818 Donald Mackenzie led a colorful caravan to this valley that included "55 men, 195 horses, 300 beaver traps, besides a considerable stock of merchandise."

During the gold rush years, the site of Weiser was on the main thoroughfare for miners bound for the Boise Basin. Thousands of prospectors crossed the Snake River at Farewell Bend, ten miles below Weiser. They followed the trappers' route up the Snake, passing the mouth of the Weiser River and pushing on to the Payette, which they followed all the way to the Placerville trail (near Horseshoe Bend). John Hailey soon put stages on the route, and Weiser grew as a major stop.

Around 1900 there were several commercial fisheries between Weiser and Hells Canyon. Most numerous were chinook salmon and steelhead trout, although sturgeon fishermen also did well. These fishermen landed this 820-pound sturgeon near Weiser in 1905. It was actually caught by George Benson, who used a quarter-inch line and a home-made hook. The big fish towed them downriver until the men were able to get a line on his tail and snub him to the boat. Others in the photo are Grover Foster, Jerome Benson, and Bill Harris. —Jack Trueblood, Idaho Department of Fish and Game

Weiser's first permanent settler was Tom Galloway, who came through the valley with a pack train headed for the Boise Basin in 1863. On the way, he spotted a choice oasis along the Weiser River, where the land was rich and flat. He returned the following year as a rancher and town builder. Other settlers followed, and the little burg grew. It captured the seat of the new Washington County in 1879, and by the time the Oregon Short Line Railroad came through in 1883, Weiser was a fairly well-established frontier town. Three saloons and a brewery flourished alongside general stores that furnished everything from beans to saddlery to fine cashmeres. The town also possessed a blacksmith shop, a "flouring mill," and two drugstores advertising "pure, fresh drugs." As a safety measure, all vials or envelopes containing morphine were wrapped in scarlet paper.

The name of both the town and the river comes from Peter Weiser, who was a member of the Lewis and Clark expedition. Following their journey of discovery, Weiser's name was given to a tributary stream on the upper Snake River near the Henrys Fork. This geographic label appeared on the map later published by Captain Clark and probably would have been permanent if not for the daring overland journey of young trailblazer Robert Stuart. He carried messages from Wilson Price Hunt at Fort Astoria to John Jacob Astor in New York. At Farewell Bend, he forded the Snake River and continued to its confluence with a stream he did not recognize. Stuart had apparently heard about a river named for Peter Weiser and assumed that this was it. The notation in his journal (*On the Oregon Trail: A Journey of Discovery*) for August 15, 1812 says he reached "Wisers" River, "a stream 60 yards wide, well stocked with small wood and Beaver." Stuart's choice prevailed, and Weiser it has been ever since.

Intermountain Cultural Center and Museum

This historical museum housed in the main classroom building of the pioneering Intermountain Institute features exhibits that tell the story of the Weiser area.

The Intermountain Institute was the dream of E. A. Paddock, a minister and educator who came to town in 1892. Seven years later he launched the institute, formed a corporation, and acquired 340 acres for an economic base (later increased to 2,400 acres by "homesteading teachers"). Paddock announced that his school "offered an education and a trade for every boy and girl willing to work for them." The school was nondenominational, but Bible classes were part of the required curriculum, and Paddock outlawed smoking, drinking, and profanity.

"How Sweet It Is." Nationally known bulldogger Yakima Canute at the Weiser Roundup, circa 1916. He later went to Hollywood and performed in several movies as a stand-in for Tom Mix. —Lavina Pence Palmer

The institute became a beehive of industry inside and out. Students attended classes and worked five hours a day grubbing sage, milking cows, cooking, and gardening. The presence of a strong vocational program alongside a traditional academic curriculum marked the school as very progressive. It aimed at the modern educator's goal of "educating the whole person."

Idealistic young teachers from prestigious institutions signed on to teach. Cornell, Yale, Oberlin, Mount Holyoke, and Bryn Mawr all were represented. The school grew in stature, and the rich and famous offered financial support. Benefactors included George Eastman, "the Kodak man"; Andrew Carnegie, who funded a library (and was ever after sweetened up with honey from the institute farm); the Kimball Piano Company, which sent eleven pianos; and Kellogg's of Battle Creek, Michigan, which sent cases of shredded wheat biscuits. Dozens of wealthy easterners contributed money to help build the campus.

Many institute alumni distinguished themselves in one way or another, but James Stevens is perhaps the most widely known. At the urging of H. L. Mencken, he created wonderful stories about that mythical giant of the

The late Jim Stevens, who attended the Intermountain Institute at Weiser and later became famous for his stories of Paul Bunyan and Babe the Blue Ox.
—Special Collections, University of Washington

woods, Paul Bunyan, and his blue ox Babe. He also wrote hundreds of articles for eminent magazines. Stevens enrolled at the institute as an eighth grader, "as raw and unruly as a cayuse colt." He admitted to finding his first taste of real "culture" here, although he described himself and his companions as "a profane, cigarette smoking, tobacco chewing, cursing, raring-tearing rip-snorting bunch." It was on these very points that he ran aground. Mr. Paddock expelled him from school before he finished the ninth grade. The good minister might have been pleased to know that Stevens went on to lead an admirable life and achieve distinction in his career, never forgetting the inspiration he received at this unusual school.

The "Old Tute" might have lasted forever had it not become a victim of the Great Depression. Farm prices plunged, former benefactors could no longer contribute, and the institute failed to open in the fall of 1933. Two vocational schools and Weiser High School eventually used the campus on a temporary basis. In 1977 Hooker Hall, the main classroom building, became the Intermountain Cultural Center and Museum, an outgrowth of the Washington County Museum and the Fiddlers' Hall of Fame. Private individuals bought the remaining buildings on campus. Chunks of farm ground were sold over a period of years, and the proceeds were donated to private schools. Institute alumni hold an annual August reunion on campus.

Safeway supermarket at Weiser, circa 1935. —Intermountain Cultural Center and Museum

The McCune family out for a ride in their St. Louis Motorworks Horseless Carriage, 1904. This was the first car in Weiser and among the first to be licensed in Idaho. —Intermountain Cultural Center and Museum

Walter Johnson Memorial Park

Weiser has several parks, but this one is distinguished by a baseball diamond named in honor of hall of famer Walter Johnson. Johnson came to Weiser when baseball was young and played for the local team. After pitching eighty-five innings without allowing a run, the "cyclone pitcher" began to attract attention. A scout for the Washington Senators came to town in 1907 and offered Johnson a contract. He declined until the scout guaranteed him enough money for a return ticket to Weiser. As it turned out, Johnson didn't need this bit of insurance. He pitched twenty-one seasons for the Senators and led them to victory in the 1924 World Series.

They called him "The Big Train"—and when he opened the throttle, look out. During his years in the big leagues, the "Weiser Wonder" set career records for strikeouts (3,508) and shutouts (110) and once pitched 56 consecutive scoreless innings, a record that was not broken for fifty-five years.

In 1936 Johnson became a charter member of the Baseball Hall of Fame at Cooperstown, New York, along with Ty Cobb, Babe Ruth, Christy Mathewson, and Honus Wagner.

National Oldtime Fiddlers' Contest

Each year during the third week in June, Weiser resonates with hoedowns and sweet fiddle music. Dozens of musicians who could "fiddle the

Walter Johnson, charter member of the Baseball Hall of Fame, when he pitched for the Weiser Kids in 1906–7. —National Baseball Library, Cooperstown, NY

bugs off a sweet potato vine" line up to compete for the title of Grand National Champion. The town doubles in size as friends, fans, banjo pickers, guitarists, and judges drift into town. They begin arriving the week before the contest, squeeze into a good campsite, and settle down to do some serious fiddling—or listening, as the case may be.

Weiser has always been a fiddling town. This was the music of the pioneers, and many were the schoolhouse dances where feet flew to the beat of "Turkey in the Straw" and "Over the Hills to Charley." In 1914 Weiserites staged their first fiddling contest, but in the years that followed, enthusiasm for the instrument declined as newer forms of entertainment nudged aside the fiddle and the bow.

In 1953 Weiser picked up fiddling again, holding a small local contest during the intermission of a square dance festival. From this small beginning the competition multiplied in size, growing to regional and then na-

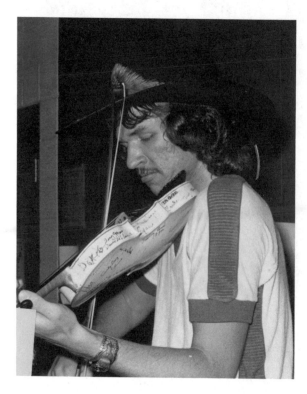

Mark O'Connor during his days as a contestant at the National Oldtime Fiddlers' Contest in Weiser. Now he's fiddling everywhere, from Nashville to the Boston Pops. His white fiddle, with its many signatures, is now featured at the Fiddlers' Hall of Fame at Nashville.

tional proportions. Today the Weiser contest is most often compared with the Grand Masters of Nashville. The same fiddlers take top money in both places.

US 95
MIDVALE

This tiny village in the midst of farm and ranch country is distinguished by an enviable community spirit. Its library and swimming pool were built with hard-earned funds collected from bake sales and community dinners, and on the Fourth of July the community puts on the best down-home entertainment for miles around—the Midvale tractor pull.

At the beginning of the twentieth century, settlers raised grain and livestock on the surrounding hills. However, life here goes far back into antiquity. South of town, on the slopes of Midvale Hill, archaeologists have found evidence of a rock quarry that was used perhaps as far back as 4,500 years ago. This is part of the Midvale Complex, where prehistoric people left remnants of knives, scrapers, choppers, pestles, and milling stones. These suggest a camping, hunting, fishing, and seed-gathering lifestyle.

Cambridge is the gateway to Hells Canyon and a popular stop en route to the boating, fishing, and sight-seeing activities at Brownlee, Oxbow, and Hells Canyon reservoirs.

Cambridge replaced an older settlement called Salubria, which developed east of town in the luxuriant Salubria Valley. The first white people to come through were stragglers from the Tim Goodale wagon train (see Camas Prairie, in Central Idaho), which was traveling from Fort Hall to the Florence mines. Some of them returned to settle here in 1868. Highlights of pioneer life included long hog drives. Each fall farmers bunched their pigs and herded hundreds of them to markets as far away as Boise, Idaho City, and Silver City. Local children looked forward to periodic visits from Chris the peddler, who carried little necessities used by every household. He drove a one-horse hack fitted up like a miniature store, a moving mercantile that offered a treasure in trinkets, lace, calico, and thread. In return, says Elsie Marti in *Salute to Pioneers*, he accepted produce such as eggs and vegetables, fresh butter, and chickens.

The Pacific and Idaho Northern Railroad, "borne on the wings of steam and steel," reached this area on January 1, 1900. Replaying a familiar story, the railroad bypassed Salubria for a location about one mile away on the opposite side of the Weiser River. Resigned to their fate, Salubrians picked up and moved. An engineer on the railroad named the new town for Cambridge, Massachusetts. No trace of Salubria remains today.

The small Cambridge Museum is housed in the oldest building in town. Specialties here are local history, geology, and Native American culture.

Hells Canyon

At Cambridge turn west on Idaho 71 for the sixty-five-mile drive to Brownlee, Oxbow, and Hells Canyon dams. Idaho Power maintains excellent parks and campsites at each location. Hells Canyon National Recreation Area lies below the last dam.

Brownlee Dam is in the old mining district of Heath. A few ghosts may still be lurking here, especially at the old Cavanaugh cabin, which sits high on a hill overlooking the reservoir. Tom Cavanaugh's blood still stains the attic floor, and the story of his murder continues to circulate in Brownlee country. The late Hugh Beggs, Brownlee pioneer, related this version.

Cavanaugh, a Yale man and civil engineer, came west to settle on Brownlee Creek, perhaps because some cousins by the name of Ruth were already there. When a rash of horse stealing broke out one fall, the cattlemen's association hired Cavanaugh to investigate quietly. All the evidence pointed to cousin Dan Ruth and his partner Jim Elliott (who was married to Dan's sister Rose). Dan and Jim soon learned that cousin Tom was looking into their illicit horse business and drew straws to determine who would shoot him. Dan got the short stick. On a wintry night, he saddled his horse and rode up the mountain trail to Cavanaugh's cabin. The two men visited a while, and when Cavanaugh turned to push a log into the stove, Dan took aim and fired. Then he faced the problem of what to do with a hot body on a cold night. His answer? Shove it through the hole in the attic, of course. There Tom lay, stretched out in his own house, frozen stiff until the spring thaw.

People began to wonder why they hadn't seen Tom Cavanaugh lately, and the cattlemen's association posted a $1,000 reward to learn of his whereabouts. In the meantime, down on Brownlee Creek, Dan Ruth was busy trimming brush. When it was time to burn the pile, he hauled the corpse down the mountain on Tom's horse, intending to cremate the evidence. Then he heard of the reward. Why not "find" the body and claim the $1,000?

Nobody was fooled, and Dan Ruth was charged with murder. The trial was held in Weiser, and on December 6, 1917, Ruth received a life sentence (of which he served only a small part). Jim Elliot's hair turned snow white, and poor Rose went mad. Those who speculate on matters of this kind now say that Dan probably didn't do the killing but took the rap for Elliott.

The Brownlee district is named for John Brownlee, who operated a ferry here at the old Nez Perce Indian crossing from 1862 to 1864. Ferry service resumed in 1875, long after Brownlee had left the country, and it continued until 1920. Hugh Beggs remembered a later ferry and told a Prohibition tale as well.

Blackie and Whitey Houston worked a still up some forbidden canyon, where they kept 1,000 gallons of "juice" in hogshead barrels. To get the stuff to market, they floated the barrels down Cave Creek to the Snake River and across to Oregon by ferry. On a certain trip, they filled the ferry with barrels and still had one to spare. They lashed the extra to the underside, below the water, and promptly forgot about it. There it rode for years. Before the Brownlee Dam was built, Beggs and some of his friends went to search the old ferry, soon to be dismantled. They found the barrel still swinging underneath. "Best whiskey I ever drank," said Beggs.

A bridge at Brownlee Dam crosses into Oregon, and at Copperfield Park on Oxbow Reservoir another bridge crosses back into Idaho. From here it is twenty-three miles to Hells Canyon Dam. The country becomes increasingly rugged along this stretch as Hells Canyon begins to manifest itself. The Wallowa Mountains form the canyon wall on the Oregon side. On the Idaho side, the Seven Devils thrust upward to a staggering 7,900 feet above the river to form the deepest gorge in North America. (The highest point on the rim of the Grand Canyon is 5,630 feet above the Colorado River.)

In this awesome country sheer walls, sharp ridges, and solid rock faces can change in a moment from black and gray to soft shades of jade, pink,

Oxbow Dam and Reservoir located between Brownlee and Hells Canyon dams on the lower Snake River.

and buff. Shadows continually shift across the landscape, shaping a thousand contours. This awesome canyon world seldom wears the same mood for long.

Humans have used the canyon for thousands of years. Indians, homesteaders, miners, and dam builders all have left their mark. Both the Nez Perce and Shoshones developed a canyon culture, and life here stretches back beyond their tribal memory. Archaeologists have identified many ancient village sites that hold secrets of early humans.

Several fur trappers attempted to use Hells Canyon as a shortcut between Farewell Bend and the Columbia River, but only "Perpetual Motion" Mackenzie succeeded in making the trip. In 1819 he maneuvered a bateau up the Snake River from the site of Lewiston to Farewell Bend, but after hiking and pulling the boat through rapids most of the way he decided this was not a practical route.

Many were the plans for a highway or railroad through the canyon. A survey was begun by Union Pacific builders as early as 1883. They discovered just how steep the perpendicular walls were. In many places, points

241

The Snake River is diverted through a tunnel while Hells Canyon Dam is under construction. —Idaho Power Company

could not be reached to station the instruments, and the calculations had to be done by triangulation. One boatload of surveyors wrecked below the Oxbow rapids (now the site of Oxbow Dam). Two men drowned, and the project was abandoned. Strangely enough, two steamboats shot through the whitewater of Hells Canyon, and all aboard lived to tell about it. The *Shoshone* journeyed downstream in the spring of 1870 (see Fort Boise), and the *Norma* took the perilous run in 1895, "hurled from side to side like a feather in a blast."

A man named Albert Kleinschmidt owned copper mines high above the canyon near Cuprum, on the fringe of the Seven Devils Mountains. He developed a cliffhanger of a road called the Kleinschmidt Grade, over which he expected to haul ore from his mines down to the Snake River. Here it would be transferred to the steamboat *Norma*, then hauled upstream to the Union Pacific Railroad at Huntington, Oregon, and shipped east for pro-

Steamboating in Hells Canyon. This boat, similar to the Norma *in size and power, traveled only the lower sections of the canyon, well below the worst of the rapids.*

cessing. Kleinschmidt soon discovered that boating on the Snake was no ordinary sport. The venture failed, but the Kleinschmidt Grade served the backcountry well for nearly a century.

Sportsmen and adventurers still drive the Kleinschmidt. The road begins opposite Hells Canyon Campground and leads to the ghost town of Cuprum, ten miles uphill. It continues on to Kinney Point, which overlooks Hells Canyon. The grade itself is six miles long, a single track with turnouts. The faint of heart will want to travel *up* the Kleinschmidt only and return via the Hornet Creek road to Council on Highway 95. The downhill traffic on the grade takes the outside edge—and the dropoff can be considerable.

Between Oxbow Dam and Hells Canyon one can look across the river to see a curious stand of weathered cabins amidst a jumble of old trees. This is the remnant of Homestead, a copper mining community that boomed about 1900. Copperfield, a sister camp, has vanished under the waters of Oxbow Reservoir.

Homesteaders, sheepmen, and miners have had a long history in this vertical environment, but today nearly all of the Snake River Canyon and the adjoining mountains are part of the 652,488-acre Hells Canyon National Recreation Area (see Riggins, in North Idaho). The main launch for downriver rafting is immediately below Hells Canyon Dam.

US 95
COUNCIL

Council, a small town located on the fringe of pine-clad mountains, is a center for lumberjacks and ranchers and the seat of Adams County.

Settlers first came here in 1878, when the George Mosers chose a homesite near a junction of trails heading west toward the Seven Devils and north to Salmon Meadows. They built a lodge here as a way station for travelers. Over time, a town grew up around it. The settlement was named Council because generations of Indians once met to parley beneath a grove of ponderosa pines that grew along the Weiser River northwest of town.

During the copper rush to the Seven Devils Mountains, Council became an outfitting point for the mines. Early in the 1900s, it profited from the

Fourth of July celebration at Council, circa 1900. —Idaho State Historical Society

244

rush to Mesa Orchards, seven miles south of town. Today a small highway
sign points to Mesa. Old buildings can still be seen in the folds of the hills,
remnants of a bustling little village that was once the heart of the largest
single apple orchard in the United States. Here, on a high grassy prairie,
some 1,500 acres of apple trees were planted. The town had all the trappings of orcharding, including packing sheds, a cannery, and, seasonally, a
tent town of fruit pickers. Perhaps most impressive were the eight miles of
thirty-six-inch redwood irrigation pipe that brought water to the fields and
a massive four-mile long tramway that marched across the hills, carrying
boxes of apples to the Pacific & Idaho Northern (P&IN) Railroad siding.

This giant operation began to sag when the price of apples dropped during the Great Depression. In the following years, intermittent freezes took

At the photographer's studio in Council. —Idaho State Historical Society

245

the crop, and the dream disintegrated. Now the rolling prairie has reverted to grassland, and Mesa is being recast as a small residential community. A few newcomers have established homesites, and the Catholic sisters of Marymount are building The Hermitage, a permanent retreat open to the public.

Cuprum

Cuprum, more than thirty miles northwest of Council via the unpaved Hornet Creek and Forest Service roads, has teetered on the verge of becoming a ghost town for years. Today no mines are operating, and the community is mostly abandoned. A picturesque mountain hideaway on the fringe of the once famous Seven Devils Mining District, it forms a major part of the east wall of Hells Canyon. The old town lies near the access to the Black Lake–Six Lakes Basin at the southern end of the Devils. A hiking trail from Emerald Lake leads to the heart of the Seven Devils on the Boise Trail.

Cuprum is Latin for "copper," which is found in turquoise-colored ore that has all the shadings of a peacock's tail. Appropriately, the richest and most enduring mine in the area was called the Peacock. Copper-bearing ore was first discovered here in 1862, and among the early owners were Montana luminaries Granville Stuart and Samuel Hauser, the future territorial governor. The inaccessible terrain slowed development, and nothing much happened until 1887, when Albert Kleinschmidt (also from Montana) arrived. He immediately began spending huge sums of money for equipment, smelting facilities, and roads. He constructed the Kleinschmidt Grade between his mines and the Snake River, where he planned to transfer the ore to the steamship *Norma* (see Hells Canyon). The plan failed, but all the activity generated a copper rush. Mining men gravitated here like bees to nectar, and many declared Cuprum would become another Butte. A post office was established, and the town quickly became a meeting place for prospectors. Sensational publicity touted the mines as the largest and richest copper deposits in the world, and hordes of miners came to prove it, climbing the ravines, staking claims, and gathering in ephemeral camps.

By the summer of 1899, a crew of thirty men at the Blue Jacket mine kept a stream of high-sided freight wagons on the road hauling the turquoise-colored ore to the railroad at Weiser. Across Smith Mountain in the Black Lake Basin, Ed and Sim Ford were finishing a fifty-ton cyanide mill and hoisting works for their Idaho Gold Coin Mining Company. The camps of Helena and Landore, near the fabled Peacock, were booming. Lack of transportation to the outside world seemed the only obstacle in this exciting district. Then the Pacific and Idaho Northern Railroad, an offshoot of the Union Pacific, entered the picture with plans to build a line connecting the Seven Devils mines with the transcontinental railroad at Weiser. Prosperity seemed assured.

The P&IN reached Council in 1901. But the investors, who were also mine owners, became bogged down in mining litigation, and this interesting route into the Devils failed to materialize. The tracks were never laid. By 1904 the best of the boom was over, although the Peacock and Blue Jacket mines worked sporadically until the 1960s.

Mining excitement in this unexplored wilderness inspired a rush of another color: green. A hardy breed of botanists braved the terrain to identify and describe the abundant plant life here. One of the first to come was Marcus E. Jones. He received a double assignment from the Union Pacific—to work openly as a botanist and covertly as a scout for coal deposits, presumably to stoke the boilers on the proposed railroad. The area turned up more plants than it did coal, and a long line of botanists followed Jones. The area is a fascinating one, as the Hells Canyon climate and altitude sustain plants in life zones ranging from desert to alpine.

Richard T. Bingham, a contemporary plant collector, has spent many years studying the Hells Canyon–Seven Devils flora and has uncovered a large body of botanical history and literature relating to more than forty individual plant collectors. His annotated checklist hints at the diversity here, listing 722 plant taxa in 293 genera and 71 families.

US 95, Idaho 55
NEW MEADOWS

The town of New Meadows lies in a grand valley rimmed by mountains and cut by the waters of the Little Salmon River. In earlier times the valley was known as Salmon Meadows. Both Nez Perce and Shoshone gathered here to fish when the stream was choked with salmon. During the gold rush years, the trail from Lewiston to Boise Basin cut across the meadows, then turned east toward Goose Creek, Payette Lakes, and the Payette River trail.

Settlers began coming into the valley in the 1880s. Among them were Charlie and Caroline Campbell, who with their family built the 20,000-acre Circle C Ranch. For many years this was the largest cattle operation in the state. Charlie died in 1932, but the resourceful Caroline continued the business. In 1937 the Campbells shipped 4,500 head of Herefords, filling 108 railroad cars. At the time, notes Grace Jordan in *Idaho Reader*, this was the largest single shipment in the history of the Union Pacific.

The Pacific and Idaho Northern Railroad reached the site of New Meadows in 1911. Col. Edgar Heigho, president and general manager of the railroad, envisioned a planned community. He drew up a design that provided for an elegant railroad depot on the west end of town facing the palatial Hotel Heigho on the east end. Both of these structures became a reality, but the rest of the town grew helter-skelter. Today the hotel is called the

A southwest Idaho cattle drive.

Heartland Inn and, along with the old depot, it remains a prominent local landmark.

Packer John State Park

Approximately three miles east of New Meadows is the restored cabin of Packer John Welsh. He carried in mail and supplies from Lewiston to the Boise Basin when it was still a primeval wilderness. The cabin served as a storage place for supplies and a shelter on stormy nights. In his *Reminiscences*, W. A. Goulder described the structure as "a small, rude log pen roofed with shakes." Nevertheless, Idaho Republicans met here in 1863 for their first territorial convention, giving the place a mantle of importance. Goulder noted that the delegates arrived on horseback, leading their pack animals. In addition to conducting the work of the convention, they cooked their own meals and selected "sleeping apartments under the trees which proved sufficient in number to accommodate all the distinguished guests there assembled." This first meeting was so successful that a year later the Democrats reined in to hold their territorial convention.

Today Welsh's cabin is called Packer John State Park, the smallest one in Idaho. There are no services.

Zims Plunge

Zims Plunge, five miles north of New Meadows, is one of the enduring delights of the valley. Generations of Nez Perce Indians came here to take mud baths and soak their arthritic bones in the hot mineral waters. When white settlers arrived, they took their turn at the spa. Improvements came slowly, and today Zims is a year-round family resort.

Idaho 95 proceeds north across the Meadows Valley, then winds through a rocky canyon along the Little Salmon River and plunges all the way to Riggins. There the highway meets the main Salmon River, and the Mountain Time Zone gives way to the Pacific Time Zone.

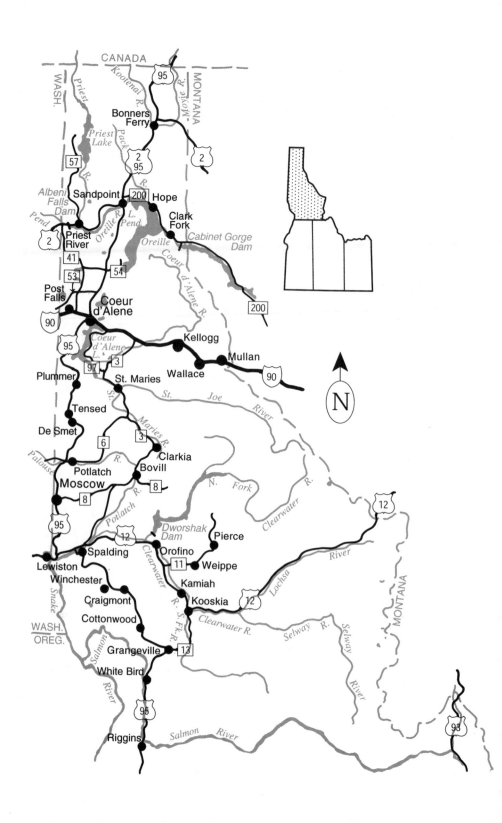

～ PART 4 ～

North Idaho

L oosely defined, north Idaho runs between the Salmon River and the
  Canadian border. It is a region of dense forests, glacial lakes, tumultuous rivers, and a relatively mild Pacific climate—a land where ancient cedars and hemlocks grow amid luxuriant ferns, where Palouse country farmland and massive stands of white pine punctuate the landscape.

Loggers, miners, and farmers shaped the course of history here. When
lumber ruled the economy, swift-flowing rivers delivered millions of logs to
mills at Coeur d'Alene, St. Maries, Priest River, and Lewiston. Steamboats
plied the larger lakes, bringing passengers and supplies to outlying settlements. For a while Lake Coeur d'Alene was called "Little Erie of the West."

Silver Valley mines in the Coeur d'Alene Mountains yielded fabulous
riches for almost a century. Giant corporations developed mines with extensive underground tunnels, and the region drew national attention just
before the turn of the century when the Western Federation of Miners
clashed head-on with the Association of Mine Owners.

Timber and mining made the economy hum, but recreation always played
a part, too. Early in this century people flocked to north Idaho for steamboat excursions, huckleberry camp-outs, and a bevy of outdoor experiences.

Nez Perce Country

US 95
RIGGINS

Riggins, set in a deep canyon at the confluence of the Salmon and Little
Salmon rivers, is a gateway to recreation on the Salmon River and the Seven
Devils Mountains. Jet boaters, hikers, fishermen, and campers flock to this
popular getaway.

251

Roadside travel, when a lot of time could be spent waiting for horses to come to the rescue.
—Idaho Department of Transportation

The town stretches out beside the Salmon River on a bank long used as a camping site by the Nez Perce Indians. If an early story can be believed, the land was not very valuable. In 1891 Mike Deasy, owner of the future townsite, traded it off for two ponies and a watch. Dick Riggins, who later became postmaster, settled here in 1900 and helped establish the settlement that bears his name.

Salmon River Jet Boat

The Salmon River is rich in pioneer lore. Upriver adventures to the Shepp Ranch, the old Polly Bemis place, or Buckskin Billy's are well within reach of a one-day jet boat trip.

Polly Bemis, the Chinese slave girl turned Salmon River pioneer, was a legend in her own time and has been made even more famous by a movie that recounts her life, *Thousand Pieces of Gold*. She became celebrated for the prize trout she pulled from the stream and for the produce she grew at the river's edge—strawberries, watermelons, plums, pears, and vegetables of all kinds. These she readily shared. And if Shepp and Klinkhammer, her neighbors across the river, had poor luck fishing, Polly would chide, "You catch none? You no good. You fella come over Sunday. I cook a big one I catch today."

Journalist Cissie Patterson rode downriver with Bill Guleke in 1921, and they stopped at the Bemis place. Patterson was fascinated with Polly and widely circulated her story. She described her subject as not much over four feet tall, "neat as a pin, wrinkled as a walnut, and at sixty-nine full of dash and charm." Polly related to Patterson something of her origins, "darting her wise old eyes about to see if the others were listening: 'My folluks in Hong Kong had no grub. Day sellee me . . . slave girl. Old woman she shmuggle me into Portland. I cost $2,500. Don't look it now, hmmm! Old Chinee-man he took me along to Warrens in a pack train.'" (See Warren, in Southwest Idaho.)

After their marriage in 1884, Polly and Charlie Bemis moved to this homesite along the Salmon River. Bemis died in 1922, and Shepp and Klinkhammer looked after the aging Polly. In return, she deeded them her ranch. Polly's cabin has been restored and is now part of the Salmon River Resort. It stands across the river from the Shepp place, which has become a guest ranch.

The late Buckskin Billy's stronghold is four miles upriver from Mackay Bar, another wilderness lodge. Buckskin Billy (Sylvan Ambrose Hart), "the last of the mountain men," settled here during the Great Depression and stayed for more than forty years. This eccentric hermit, a graduate of the

Polly Bemis at her cabin on the Salmon River.

Buckskin Billy at home on the Salmon River. —Idaho State Historical Society

University of Oklahoma, became a fixture on the river. When whitewater rafting became popular, floaters delighted in pulling ashore at his place. He was a showman, an entertainer, and a rugged individualist. Surprisingly hospitable, he enjoyed showing off his camp, with its odd mix of tools—beautiful rifles, knives, copper pots, and unique furniture, all crafted with his talented hands. Several of these items are now in the St. Gertrude Museum at Cottonwood. Best of all was Billy himself, best described by Leo Snider in a letter to *High Country*:

> He was a quixotic little pear-shaped man with a lofty harmonious laugh. His buckskin pants did not have the snug fit and fringe that Hollywood has made us believe was characteristic of wilderness dress. The stiff leather pants stood open at the fly and his long johns showed underneath. He wore a 'helmet' fashioned from bearskin and sported a beard that grew from under his chin. . . . He was very soiled. But he only looked faintly silly because he was so peacefully and perfectly dignified. . . . It wasn't just that Buckskin survived in a remote location that made him interesting . . . it was that he survived so well and with such elan.

Riding the bouncing Salmon River is a thrill in any season, but early spring and late fall bring special bonuses: elk and deer range along the shoreline, and the steelhead run is on.

Buckskin Billy's fortress on the Salmon River, which was built for defense when he believed the Forest Service would try to evict him. The ongoing fuss made him famous.

Heavens Gate and the Seven Devils

The Heavens Gate Scenic Viewpoint is part of the Seven Devils Mountains and the Hells Canyon National Recreation Area. For some forty miles the Seven Devils Range, with an average height of 5,500 feet, forms the eastern wall of the Snake River. The Devils themselves sweep upward from the river to an altitude of 9,300 feet. These majestic peaks, with their hidden valleys and streams, form a prime recreational area with some thirty alpine lakes and numerous hiking trails that penetrate the heart of the wilderness.

Powerful forces involving plate tectonics have been at work here. Geologist Tracy Valier, who has spent a lifetime studying the Seven Devils area, concludes that the mountains originated as a volcanic island chain near the equator. Over the centuries an accretion of sea animals, plants, and tropical coral reefs formed in warm ocean water. These metamorphosed into limestone, and some 200 million years ago the whole land mass migrated northward on the Pacific Plate. This plate slid under the Continental Plate, and the islands came ashore only a few miles from Riggins.

But this was only the beginning of the formation of Hells Canyon and the Seven Devils Mountains; still to come were the Columbia River basalts. About 13 million years ago, this molten rock flowed across the landscape to a depth of 2,000 feet in places. Next came the Snake River, which began cutting its tortuous path perhaps 2 million years ago. Then the Bonneville flood gouged the river channel all the way from Red Rock Pass (see Preston, in Central Idaho) to the Columbia River. Glaciers scoured out the tops of the Devils and created the many alpine lakes that now dot the wilderness.

The Heavens Gate lookout sits on a rocky point that presents an unparalleled vista of the Seven Devils, with the Hells Canyon country to the west and the Salmon River Mountains to the east. On a clear day the view includes parts of Washington, Oregon, Idaho, and Montana. Native Ace Barton says, "From Heaven's Gate you can almost see into tomorrow." One mile south of Riggins, turn west at the Hells Canyon/Seven Devils Scenic Area marker. It is nineteen miles on a good gravel road to Windy Saddle Camp and Seven Devils Lake, two miles farther to Heaven's Gate.

At one time the Seven Devils harbored a promising gold-silver-copper mining district, with several camps scattered throughout the area. The main "thoroughfare" was a branch of the Boise Trail that ran from New Meadows to Windy Saddle camp and south to the mines at Black Lake, connecting with Lick Creek and the town of Council. (The original trail came from Lewiston through New Meadows to McCall and along the Payette River to the Boise Basin mines.) Old Town and Rankin Mill, off the Boise Trail on Rapid River, are reminders of the laborious but largely misspent activity that occurred here at the turn of the century. A dozen decaying cabins mark the site of Old Town, silent now except for the splash of the river. At nearby Rankin Mill, scraps of equipment, rusting iron pipes, and collapsed buildings are all that remain of a failed $50,000 ore processing mill. The more successful mines were located around Cuprum on the southern fringe of the Devils. Here the copper mines lasted off and on for fifty years. (See Council, in Southwest Idaho.)

US 95
WHITE BIRD

North of Riggins the highway parallels each twist and turn of the Salmon River—calmed here to a smooth flow, at least by comparison to the roiling rapids of the upriver wilderness. Here the stream has eroded a magnificent canyon of rocky escarpments interspersed with sandbars and green oases.

Gold miners found their way into this country in 1861, and a fabulous camp grew across the mountains at Florence, about fourteen miles due east of Lucille. For a year or so it saw a lot of action, although today all traces of the old town have vanished. Thousands of miners flocked in, along with the usual hangers-on. Two members of Henry Plummer's old gang, Billy Mayfield and Cherokee Bob, came to town with a woman named Red-Headed Cynthia; they kept things lively until Bob cashed in while defending her honor in a gunfight. Plummer himself showed up briefly, but perhaps the best diversion for the miners was furnished by Joaquin Miller, who later achieved fame as the "Poet of the Sierras." He rode the mail route between Walla Walla, Washington and Florence, bringing letters from home and news of the outside world. Neither sleet, nor snow, nor bandits on the trail stopped the romantic Joaquin. When the snow was too deep for horses, he walked the 200 miles, carrying the mail pack on his back.

Near the picturesque village of White Bird, the Salmon River veers west to join the Snake. U.S. 95 continues north up historic White Bird Hill. Those who want to go adventuring might try the side road to Pittsburg Landing, the only vehicle access on the Idaho side to Hells Canyon below Hells Canyon Dam (although it can be reached by jet boat from Lewiston). The seventeen-mile drive from White Bird over a steep, single-lane gravel road is not advisable for RVs because of one downward plunge with a 19 percent grade.

Pittsburg Landing, a bench area located at the widest point in Hells Canyon, covers 1,000 acres of meadowland. It is a favorite stopping point for floaters and jet boaters. The fascinating boulders strewn about the bar were dropped by the rampaging waters of the Bonneville flood about 15,000 years

The historic White Bird Hill highway, a great engineering feat but a white-knuckle ride. Actually, it was a great improvement over its predecessor. Today it is part of the White Bird Battlefield Auto Tour.

ago. Many of them are decorated with petroglyphs incised by people who probably arrived about 8,000 years ago. Recent excavations at Pittsburg Landing, supervised by Kenneth Reid of Washington State University, have revealed the site of an ancient Indian village. Pit houses, burial sites, and some 10,000 bone artifacts, stone tools, and arrow points have been unearthed. According to the late Earl Swanson, a distinguished Idaho anthropologist, the Hells Canyon area contained numerous villages and is rich with clues of ancestors to the Nez Perce.

The town of White Bird and White Bird Hill (both named for a Nez Perce chief) figured in the opening shots of the Nez Perce War. In May 1877 the army ordered the "nontreaty" Nez Perce, including Chief Joseph's band from the Wallowa country in Oregon, onto a reservation at Lapwai. En route, some of the young braves attacked white settlers. One of the shooting sprees that precipitated the war occurred at Samuel Benedict's store in White Bird. Several young warriors wanted to avenge the unprovoked killings of Indians by whites and to give Benedict his comeuppance for Indian baiting. Benedict never fostered much goodwill among the Nez Perce. In *Hear Me My Chiefs*, L. V. McWhorter quotes a man from Chief Looking Glass's band as saying, "Maybe a poor woman with only a little money want buy pound of coffee, thirty cents; or maybe two bits worth of sugar. Buy only one of these and hand him fifty cent or maybe one dollar. She never get any change back. That store man all time keep all the money."

After shooting Benedict, the raiding party seized his supply of whiskey and drank enough spirits to fire a three-day spree of carnage. The killings, numbering eighteen, were mostly reprisals for years of plunder and murder by miners and settlers.

When news of the uprising reached Gen. O. O. Howard at Fort Lapwai, he immediately sent troops to White Bird under the command of Captain David Perry, advising him, "You must not get whipped." Perry intended to surprise the Indians, but they watched his movements as several bands converged on White Bird, a traditional gathering place. Most of the Indians did not want war. Joseph, White Bird, and lesser chiefs were hopeful that General Howard would not punish all the people for the rash acts of a few young men. Six Nez Perce warriors approached Howard's advance troops as peace envoys, carrying a white flag. However, Arthur Chapman, a civilian volunteer, raised his rifle and shot twice. This brought a return shot from the Indians, who picked off the bugler. Losing him thoroughly confused the troops. Their battle plan was communicated via the bugle, and the captain could not now direct them. The troops panicked, and the day was lost.

A historic marker points out the battle terrain at an interpretive overlook about halfway up White Bird Hill. This is part of the Nez Perce National Historic Park, whose twenty-four developed sites are scattered throughout the Clearwater River country and beyond. A personal version of the battle, quoted by L. V. McWhorter, comes from Weyahwah Tsitskan (known to the whites as John Miller), who was an eyewitness. He said:

It was a truly startling scene. Unlike the trained white soldier, who is guided by the bugle call, the Indian goes into battle on his own mind's guidance. . . .

All the warriors, whoever gets ready, mount their horses and go. In this charge against the soldiers' right flank, Wahlitits, Sarpsis Illppilp and Tipyahiahnah Kpskaps were the first to start in the charge, all of them wearing full length blanket coats [bright red in color]. These coats were to show their contempt, their fun-making of the soldiers, to draw their rifle shots, of which they were not afraid.

Other warriors follow them singly, and many hanging on the side of their horses, shielded thus from the soldier's sight. There is fast shooting and wild yelling and whooping as the horsemen stream by, an occasional horse shot down.

It is a bad mix-up for the soldiers. They do not stand before that sweeping charge and rifle fire of the Indians. Their horses go wild, throwing the riders. Many of their saddles turned when the horses whirled, all badly scared of the noisy guns. Soldiers who can, remount, and many without guns dash away in retreat. It was a wild deadly racing with the warriors pressing hard to head them off.

After the battle one-third of Howard's ninety-nine troopers lay dead, whereas the Nez Perce, whose participating warriors numbered about seventy (many of them without guns), had only three slightly wounded. One soldier of fortune who carried battle scars from afar was Lt. William Parnell, an Irishman who had fought with the British in the Crimean War. He was one of the few who had survived the legendary Charge of the Six Hundred at Balaclava, later immortalized by Alfred Lord Tennyson in "Charge of the Light Brigade." Parnell lived to fight another day after the skirmish at White Bird, too. Incidentally, the proportion of losses at Balaclava was almost identical to those at White Bird.

Near the top of White Bird Hill, follow the signs to the sixteen-mile White Bird Battlefield Auto Tour. The undisturbed terrain remains a place of grassy knolls and rocky ravines, much as it was in 1877. Equally striking is the road itself, part of old US 95. For decades this twisting miracle of engineering made a harrowing connection between north and south Idaho. The view is spectacular and gives the traveler a fair overview of the Nez Perce ancestral lands. To the south lies the Salmon River; on the west the Snake River, Hells Canyon, and the Seven Devils Mountains; and beyond these the misty Wallowa Mountains of Oregon, the traditional home of Chief Joseph's band. To the north lies the Clearwater River country, the heart of the former Nez Perce lands.

Just beyond White Bird Summit a panorama of Grangeville and Camas Prairie comes into view, a high plateau marked off in a patchwork of wheat fields and alfalfa. A sea of blue camas once grew here and furnished a major food staple for the Nez Perce. The prairie is part of the Clearwater drainage, separated from the Salmon River drainage by White Bird Hill. This vast area stretches in a wide band from the Bitterroot Mountains in the east to the Snake River on the west.

The Nez Perce lived throughout this region, a place of great variety in climate and terrain, ranging from the depths of Hells Canyon to the 10,000-foot heights of the Bitterroot Mountains. A country of rolling hills and sweeping prairies laced with a network of snow-fed streams, it was an ideal habitat for both man and beast. The land supported great numbers of deer, elk, antelope, and waterfowl. The streams teemed with fish, and berries of all kinds ripened on the higher slopes. The prairies were a carpet of cous and camas, the hillsides lush with grasses that kept the Indians' horses sleek.

There was plenty of room here for all the Nez Perce, who numbered about 4,500 at the time Lewis and Clark came through. They lived in some 125 permanent villages but traveled seasonally to hunt or gather roots and berries. Tribal historian Yellow Wolf hinted at their contentment in a conversation with Virgil McWhorter: "We were raising horses and cattle—fast horses and many cattle. We had fine lodges, good clothes, plenty to eat, enough of everything. We were living well. Then General Howard and Indian Agent Montieth came to bother us."

Elizabeth Wilson displaying the fruits of a camas dig. — Idaho State Historical Society

The town of Grangeville sits on the southern edge of the big Camas Prairie, whose ripening fields of wheat and barley make it one of Idaho's richest agricultural regions. Here some 80,000 acres produce millions of bushels of grain annually. Timber, cattle, and recreation add diversity to the economy. Grangeville is a major access point to roads skirting the Selway-Bitterroot Wilderness, the Gospel Hump Wilderness, and the Salmon River Breaks Primitive Area (north of the Salmon River). It is also the county seat of Idaho County, the largest in the state. Four of the federally designated wilderness areas in the state lie within the county's boundaries: Frank Church–River of No Return, Selway-Bitterroot, Gospel Hump, and Hells Canyon. It also claims six Wild and Scenic Rivers. The Nez Perce National Forest office, an excellent source for maps and backcountry information, is in Grangeville.

Longtime resident Eleanor Wagner declares that Grangeville is the all-American town, with a wonderful sense of community. The highlight of the summer is Border Days, when the town celebrates with a rodeo, parade, and barbecue. "It is homecoming for anyone who has ever lived here," she says.

Appropriately, Grangeville traces its beginnings to a group of farmers who in 1874 organized the first grange in Idaho. Led by Henry Hart Spalding (son of Lapwai missionary Henry Harmon Spalding), the group wanted to locate in the old settlement of Mount Idaho, but the key landowner there opposed the interlopers. They moved across the hills to a new site, where they built the grange hall and a flour and grist mill. The settlement grew in spite of Indian scares and the Nez Perce War and was still around twenty years later to become an outfitting center for the Buffalo Hump mines.

The first residents in this area were the Nez Perce Indians, who gathered each summer to participate in a great camas festival. Villages of tepees clustered about the fringes of a shimmering sea of blue camas. Children played, dogs barked, men raced their horses, and women dug camas, no doubt trading the latest news as they worked. This was a social time among friends and relatives, who perhaps hadn't seen each other since the last camas dig. The women dug the bulbs with narrow horn scoops, heaping them in piles. They cleaned each bulb by peeling away the outer layers, then placing them against heated stones in grass-lined earthen pits. A cover of clean grass went over the top, followed by a layer of earth. Finally, they built a fire on top of the pits to keep them hot. After two or three days the bulbs cooked to a soft, sweet paste. The Nez Perce could eat this on the spot or, more likely, sun-dry it and store it for winter use. The camas provided a wealth of staple food to see them through the cold season and was an important item of trade.

Ray Holes Saddle Company

Ray Holes saddles are famous among cowboys and saddle collectors. This Main Street landmark has been turning out custom saddles since 1934. Today Gerald Holes, a second-generation craftsman, designs the saddles and tools the leather with freehand patterns that make each piece unique.

Bicentennial and Country Memories Museums

Interpretive exhibits at the Bicentennial Museum depict the early mining era and include a large display of Nez Perce items—native dresses, tools, and corn-husk bags. The privately owned Country Memories Museum, half a mile west of Grangeville, sits on an 800-acre working ranch. It is a "find" for 1930s buffs, as it presents well-exhibited memorabilia from the Great Depression.

Tolo Lake Archaeological Site

Tolo Lake was an ancient gathering place for the Nez Perce people. It lay close to the center of their tribal lands, on the fringe of Camas Prairie at the bottom of White Bird Hill, and they converged here in times of crisis. Over the years the lake basin has partially filled in with windblown soil. In the fall of 1994 the Idaho Department of Fish and Game attempted to deepen the lake, and in the process of bulldozing the site, workers uncovered a field of ancient mammoth fossils. Officials of the Idaho Historical Society were called in, and state archaeologist Robert Yohey determined that these rare bones belonged to the *mammuthus* species, the largest known mammoth in North America. It stood fourteen feet tall at the shoulders, weighed an estimated five to six tons, and disappeared about 10,500 years ago. No cultural artifacts have been found with these fossils.

Development of the site for educational and recreational purposes is ongoing.

Idaho 14
ELK CITY

An excellent side trip can be made from Grangeville to Elk City and on to the Red River country. Take Idaho 13 north of Grangeville until it joins Idaho 14, which follows the South Fork of the Clearwater all the way to Elk City, approximately sixty miles away. The road passes through wooded country interspersed with rolling meadows and sparkling streams.

Elk City still carries an aura of the Old West and remains a lively center for backcountry fishermen, hunters, and general sightseers. It is located on a section of the old Nez Perce Trail, once used by Indians to get to the buffalo country of western Montana. Elk can still be seen in the area, but residents no longer have to shoot off strings of firecrackers to scare them out of the meadows and away from the livestock.

A Forest Service road has been constructed over this part of the trail, also known as the Magruder Corridor. It is a popular route for those who want to want to reach Darby, Montana, via a wilderness route. The trail was named to honor Lloyd Magruder, who was murdered forty-three miles east of Elk City in the fall of 1863. He was returning to Lewiston from Virginia City, Montana (then actually in Idaho Territory), with about $30,000 in cash and gold dust, his earnings from a load of supplies he wrangled to Virginia City aboard a sixty-mule pack train. Outlaws got away with the treasure, but lawmen caught up with them in San Francisco. The murderers ultimately were executed (see Lewiston).

Soon after the discovery of gold at Pierce City, the first strike in present-day Idaho, a group set out to explore the South Fork of the Clearwater River. They struck it rich at Elk City in the summer of 1861, making it the second gold camp in Idaho. By fall a town had been laid out, with several stores and perhaps 1,000 inhabitants. But the following spring miners stampeded over the hill to Florence, draining away most of the Elk City population.

The creekside mines at Elk City presented a special problem: In the spring, melting snows brought roaring high water; after the runoff, the water was too low. The hillside claims were always dry. Consequently, during the winter of 1862–1863 the 200 or 300 miners who remained in Elk City bent their backs and dug ditches to carry water to the claims. Six of these cooperative conduits measured three to nine miles in length, and the giant of them all stretched out for seventeen miles.

Several hundred Chinese miners drifted into town about 1870 to work the less attractive claims, and some of them stayed for twenty years. One of the favorite local stories involves a shipment of opium that came to the Chinese community in 1893 (opium smoking was a legal activity until 1904). Jack Anderson carried the mail from Mount Idaho to Elk City, a distance of sixty miles, over the old Nez Perce Trail. In winter he walked and carried the mail sack on his back because the snow was too deep for horses. On one trip, as he trudged along, mile after mile, one of his shoulders became sore from rubbing against a hard lump inside the sack. That night, when he made camp, he decided to fix the problem. He laid the locked mailbag on the ground, picked up a piece of heavy wood, and pounded it until the hard spot became smooth. In due time he arrived at the Elk City post office and opened the sack—but little mail was distributed. The hard lump he had flattened was a tin of opium, and the sticky stuff had oozed out and cemented all the letters and papers together.

A mining revival occurred about 1885. Large companies started taking out ore-bearing quartz with hydraulic equipment and began dredging operations on the old placer mines. This work continued until well into the twentieth century, making Elk City one of the longer-lasting placer districts in north Idaho.

Law and order may be somewhat tighter today than in earlier years. In *My Yesterdays in Elk City*, town historian Gertrude Maxwell, an ex-schoolteacher and colorful outfitter who for many years wrangled dudes into the wilderness, tells about the time a deputy sheriff came in from Grangeville to investigate a murder. He looked the situation over and decided, "The guy couldn't have shot himself the way the powder burns were . . . but he was a son-of-a-bitch and needed killing anyway." That ended the investigation, as most of the townsfolk agreed with him.

Red River and Dixie

A trip to Elk City can be extended to include Red River Hot Springs, fourteen miles away, or the old mining town of Dixie, thirty-two miles distant. Follow the Red River Road to the ranger station, where it divides. The north fork continues to Red River, the south fork to Dixie.

Red River Hot Springs sits in a luxuriant streamside meadow rimmed by the Bitterroot Mountains. This resort, a spot favored by families, offers a geothermal pool, cabins, camping, and a fast food bar. In the early days Irad and Emma Meinert owned the hot springs. Gertrude Maxwell relates an afternoon scene that took place on the lodge porch one Sunday. Irad was

Red River Hot Springs near Elk City.

sitting in his wicker rocker, visiting with a group that had gathered around, when a young smart aleck approached. Attempting to be witty, he asked Irad if the pool ever froze over. "Irad cast a calculating eye in the young man's direction," writes Maxwell, "and without so much as a grin answered, 'Oh yes, many times. Why just here last winter it froze over and Emma was skating; broke through and scalded her foot.'"

Dixie makes for a good stop at the end of a scenic backcountry drive. It is a colorful little place with a restaurant, overnight accommodations, and a couple of 1930s gas pumps where the Confederate flag waves aloft. One can almost hear the banjos strumming "Dixie." It seems that the two adventurers who discovered gold here in 1862 were Southern sympathizers and named their camp accordingly. Dixie is mostly a summer place, but the pace is beginning to change, as snowmobilers roar over the mountain to enliven the winter scene.

US 95
COTTONWOOD

At first glance Cottonwood seems like an ordinary farming community tucked among rolling hills on the fringe of Camas Prairie. But a surprise is in store for anyone who takes the time to find St. Gertrude's Convent and Museum. Shortly after 1900, a group of Benedictine sisters decided to settle here, and their cluster of hilltop buildings is both charming and instructive. The sisters supervised the construction of a stunning Romanesque chapel, which rises above the prairie like a medieval church, a gem of locally quarried blue porphyry with classic twin towers and a rose window.

In 1931 the sisters added St. Gertrude's Museum, which for many years was in the care of the late distinguished historian Sister Alfreda Elsensohn. The collection here is eclectic, with exhibits ranging from Ming dynasty ceramics to exquisitely crafted Swiss needlework. Significant local memorabilia include rare items pertaining to two of Idaho's most colorful characters—Polly Nathoy Bemis, who came to Warren's Diggings as a Chinese slave girl in the 1870s, and Buckskin Billy (Sylvan Ambrose Hart), "last of the mountain men," who lived in the primitive area along the Salmon River. Polly's gold scales and certificate of marriage to Charlie Bemis are here. Among Buckskin Billy's items are several of his famous handmade and beautifully decorated guns and knives.

Cottonwood was first settled in 1862 as a way station on the route from Lewiston to the mines. At Cottonwood pack trains could take the trail either to Elk City on the Clearwater or to Florence and Warren in the Salmon River drainage. Later on, stockmen came with herds of cattle that grew fat on the luxuriant bunchgrass that covered the hills. Settlers followed with plows, seeds, and permanent homes, forcing the Indians to retreat.

Cottonwood became involved early in the Nez Perce War. After the Battle of White Bird, several settlers were killed, and a detachment of cavalry was stationed here for guard duty. Two civilian volunteers sent on a reconnaissance mission were attacked, and ten cavalrymen under Lt. Sevier Rains were wiped out in a rescue attempt. Following this disaster a group of seventeen volunteers lost two men while holding off an overwhelming force of Indians. However, after the summer of 1877 the skirmishes moved on down the Clearwater River, and in Cottonwood life returned to normal.

US 95, Idaho 62
CRAIGMONT

This town is a successful marriage of two rival communities, Ilo and Vollmer. They faced each other across the Camas Prairie Railroad track but finally decided to quit feuding and join forces. They chose a neutral name that honors a doughty pioneer, William Craig, who came west as a fur trapper with Robert Newell in 1829. When the trapping days were finished, he married the daughter of Chief James and settled down among the Nez Perce. Craig drew the boundaries for the Indian lands agreed to in the Treaty of 1855 and during the parley served as an interpreter for Isaac Stevens, governor of Washington Territory. He received a land claim of 640 acres under the 1850 Oregon Donation Land Law, making him the first permanent settler in the future Idaho. One of his descendants, Bert Robie, became prominent in Boise as a partner of Alexander Rossi in a major sawmill. Robie Creek is named for him.

US 95
WINCHESTER

There is no mistaking Winchester. A replica of the famous rifle hangs suspended above Main Street to let visitors know they have arrived. The town lies about one mile off US 95 and provides the access to Winchester State Park.

In the process of logging, the Craig Mountain Company built a dam across Lapwai Creek to create a mill pond, and this became Winchester Lake. The mill is gone now, but beautiful old pine trees and Douglas firs still surround the lake. Ponderosa Point, shaded by 400-year-old trees, is the showcase of this 418-acre park. Families come to picnic and hike the mile-long nature trail, and guideposts spell out the history, geology, and environmental relationships of this forested area. Boating facilities are available for summer recreation; winter pastimes include skating and cross-country skiing.

Spalding is headquarters for the Nez Perce National Historic Park, which comprises twenty-four widely scattered sites, each one having special significance for the Nez Perce people. They range from small roadside stops to the White Bird Battlefield that covers more than 1,000 acres. Several of the sites are off the reservation, and a complete tour is about a 400-mile trip. Maps are available at park headquarters. Current plans include the development of fourteen additional locations. The Visitor Center Museum showcases Nez Perce history. Nearby lie the sites of Lapwai Mission, Spalding Park, and the Mission Cemetery.

In the museum, priceless artifacts and interpretive displays define Nez Perce culture. The exhibits are a rare treat and include examples of exquisite Nez Perce workmanship—buckskin, corn husk bags, and decorative items for horses. Many unique objects for daily use are also on display. The Reverend Henry Harmon Spalding began this collection when he first came to Lapwai in 1836. Since then much of it has traveled a circuitous route—from Lapwai to a private party in Ohio, to Oberlin College, to the Ohio Historical Society, and back to Lapwai, where it was on loan to the National Park Service until December 1995, when it was finally returned to Ohio.

Nez Perce corn husk bags, originally twined from native bear grass and hemp.

For generations this area has belonged to the Nez Perce. Lewis and Clark saw their lodges here in 1805, and it was here that Henry Harmon Spalding began his Christian mission in the summer of 1836. Many Idaho "firsts" occurred here, beginning with the arrival of a printing press from Hawaii—a gift from missionaries stationed there. Spalding was euphoric about receiving the press. He soon turned out a set of laws he devised for the tribe, a twenty-page book comprising a Nez Perce alphabet and grammar, and four books of the New Testament in the Nez Perce language. Spalding also built Idaho's first sawmill, first gristmill, and first school, where his wife, Eliza, taught the Indian women to read and write. They were devoted to her and admired her gentle ways, which contrasted sharply with those of the stern Henry.

Spalding was a severe man who demanded strict obedience and often used the whip to make a point. According to historian Virgil McWhorter in *Hear Me, My Chiefs*, Spalding once seized Chief Blue Cloak for a minor infraction of the rules at the evening prayer meeting and administered fifty lashes—and confiscated the chief's horse to boot. The good missionary once had three children whipped for stealing corn, and on another occasion one of his colleagues, Asa Smith, recorded: "[A]fter we arrived here Mr. Spalding caused a woman to be whipped 70 lashes. He had married her to Williams the Blacksmith who abused her. She ran away but was brought back and whipped. After she had been punished the people were determined to whip Williams and it was with great difficulty that Mr. Spalding could prevent it. He deserved it probably more than the woman and the Indians knew it." As McWhorter exclaimed, "Seventy Gospel lashes for a heathen wife!"

The most profound result of the missionary work was the separating of the Nez Perce people into two factions, Christian and non-Christian—or, as Spalding put it, "the Christian party" and the "heathens." The converts enjoyed an elevated status, with life centered around school, church, the orchards, and cultivation of the land. Certainly they pioneered Idaho agriculture. As early as 1837, the farmers at Lapwai cultivated fifteen acres of peas, potatoes, and other garden vegetables along with a nursery of apple trees. The unconverted continued a lifestyle of hunting, root digging, moving about with their horses on the ancestral lands, and, in religion, paying reverence to Mother Earth.

In 1863 federal Indian commissioners held a famous parley at Lapwai to discuss a new treaty with the Nez Perce that would drastically shrink their 1855 reservation. This agreement would turn the Indian lands along the Clearwater and Salmon rivers—where Pierce, Oro Fino, and Florence were already flourishing gold camps—over to the United States. Many of the Indians refused to surrender their territory and left the meeting. In their absence, Chief Lawyer and several others signed the document. This action split the tribe into "treaty" and "nontreaty" factions.

As the gold camps proliferated, many Indians became involved in the economy of the mines, supplying food and labor and taking on the miners' culture. Historian Francis Haines says, "They ate the miners' food, donned the white man's shirts and pants, drank their liquor, and began to swear, talk and think like the prospectors. Within a few months, as the Nez Perce adopted the white man's traits, the gold rush accomplished what fur traders, missionaries, soldiers, and agents had failed to do in decades"—that is, break down their culture and traditional way of life.

During the Nez Perce War of 1877, the bands that were fighting—or more accurately, retreating in search of refuge across the Lolo Trail—were the nontreaty bands. These included the people of Chief Joseph, Looking Glass, White Bird, and Red Owl, all of whom are well known in history. After suffering defeat in the Bear Paw Mountains in Montana, only a few people from these bands returned to Lapwai after years of exile. Today the Nez Perce own 86,500 acres of land (less than 13 percent of the land promised by the 1863 treaty) and are active in several business enterprises. It is a matter of pride that Nez Perce National Historic Park celebrates their culture.

US 12 and 95
LEWISTON

Water is Lewiston's reason for being. The town grew at the confluence of the Snake and Clearwater rivers, and this propitious location channeled its development into shipping, timber-related industries, and tourism. Al-

Camas Prairie Railroad carries freight between Grangeville and Lewiston, crossing many historic wooden trestles that level the terrain. —Barry Kough, *Lewiston Tribune*

though located 420 miles from the Pacific Ocean, Lewiston has become Idaho's port city and a link to world markets. A series of dams and locks on the lower Snake and Columbia rivers create a navigable waterway. Each year barges haul tons of wheat, peas, and lentils downriver, bringing in items such as petroleum, fertilizers, and heavy equipment on their return.

The giant Potlatch Corporation, since 1926 a *Fortune* 500 company, has figured prominently in Lewiston's prosperity. Today the company operates Idaho's largest wood processing plant here. Lewiston offers many amenities. The City Department of Parks and Recreation maintains fifteen parks with picnic areas, swimming pools, playgrounds, tennis courts, and lots of shade for summer refuge. At only 741 feet above sea level, Lewiston is the lowest spot in Idaho and often the warmest both in summer and winter.

The site of Lewiston has long been historically significant. Lewis and Clark reached this area via canoe in October 1805 as they came downriver from Canoe Camp, near present-day Orofino. They camped near the future Spalding and traded with the Indians for fish and dogs, prompting Captain Clark to remark in his journal, "[A]ll the Party have greatly the advantage of me, in as much as they all relish the flesh of dogs, Several of which we purchased of the natives for to add to our Store of fish and roots &c."

As the party continued downriver, they observed fishing camps and lodges spaced along the banks, peopled by Indians "who continue all day on the

Today barges instead of steamboats dock at Lewiston. —Port of Lewiston

Unloading wheat at the Port of Lewiston.

bank to view us." The captains, in turn, viewed them. Clark described the Nez Perce

> as stout likely men, handsom women, and verry dressey in their way, the dress of the men are a white Buffalow robe or Elk Skin dressed with Beeds which are generally white, Sea Shells—ie the Mother of Pirl hung to their hair . . . some few wore a shirt of dressed skins and long legins, & Mockersons Painted . . . The women dress in a Shirt of Ibex Skins which reach quite down to their anckles . . . their Shirts are ornemented with quilled Brass, small peces of Brass Cut into different forms, Beeds, Shells and curios bones &c.

Near the confluence of the Clearwater with the Snake, Clark noted "an open Plain on either Side . . . the water of the South fork [Snake] is greenish blue, and the north [Clearwater] as clear as cristal."

In 1812 Donald Mackenzie of Astor's Pacific Fur Company established a short-lived fur trading post on the Clearwater about five miles above this confluence. His clerk, Alfred Seton, observed the Indians all along the river and thought they seemed "numerous & powerful & very independent." He also saw them as "quiet and peaceable folks who devoted themselves to the rearing of numerous herds of horses."

Their peace and quiet was shattered as the gold rush got under way. News of gold on Orofino Creek reached Walla Walla and the West Coast during the winter of 1860. By the spring of 1861, a stampede for the diggings was on. Both men and supplies came by steamboat up the Columbia River from The Dalles. About the time cannons were booming at Fort Sumter, the steamboat *Colonel Wright* reached the site of Lewiston, bulging with miners and their accoutrements. On this first trip the *Colonel Wright* took on the uncharted waters of the Clearwater and steamed upriver as far

Steamboat Lewiston *in home port.* —Luna House Museum

as Ashaka (near Orofino) to deposit the prospectors closer to the Pierce City mines. However, the boat very nearly capsized in the swirling stream, and succeeding cargoes were landed at the junction of the Clearwater and the Snake.

Within two weeks of the first steamboat landing, a thriving business was carried on here, with pack trains leaving daily for the mines. Soon a metropolis of tents, a "ragtown," was strung out along the banks of the Clearwater and onto the adjacent hills. No permanent buildings were allowed because the whole settlement was an illegal trespass on Nez Perce lands.

The city of tents grew with feverish speed, and when a more or less legal townsite was laid out a few months later, it took the name Lewiston to honor Meriwether Lewis. Within a year the settlement was a full-fledged city, and when Idaho Territory was formed in 1863 (out of Washington Territory), Lewiston became the capital city. The legislators arrived via horseback, followed by pack animals loaded with blankets and camp gear. They found a city in ferment. Brawling outside the legislative "hall" was not uncommon, particularly between Union men and the "Sesesh" (Southerners favoring secession), for by 1863 the Civil War was in full stride. When A. S. Gould started the *Golden Age*, Idaho's first newspaper (August 2, 1862), he raised the Stars and Stripes over his office, and the Sesesh promptly fired twenty-one shots into it.

Among the miners who found their way to this new El Dorado were a substantial number of Chinese. Their Chinatown grew along C and D streets, where merchants dealt in rice, soy sauce, firecrackers, and herbs. Although scorned as heathen "Celestials" in the early years, they eventually earned a place for themselves in the social fabric of the town. Their celebrations became standard Lewiston events, their joss house a source of curiosity and respect. Here, in a world of lanterns, incense, and brass gongs, dwelt the gods who gave direction to their lives. The Chinese were meek and hardworking, and they caused no disturbances.

Plenty of others did that. Horse thieves, highway robbers, and questionable characters were on the loose both in and out of Lewiston. However, the town was fairly safe, especially when compared with isolated trails on which robbery and murder were common. Lloyd Magruder was perhaps

Historic Buick Eye Mao Joss House in Lewiston. Quon Lee and Owen Eng are behind the altar. —Idaho State Historical Society

the most famous victim—at least, he became the most famous thanks to his friend Hill Beachy's dedication in pursuing his killers.

One August morning in 1863, Magruder, a well-respected packer, loaded up his sixty mules and headed for Virginia City, Montana (then in Idaho Territory). Four wranglers went along to help with the mules, and after a day or two they met three "travelers." The trio and Magruder's caravan rode along together for mutual support. At Virginia City, Magruder disposed of his goods in exchange for about $30,000 in gold dust. When he was ready to head back toward Lewiston, the "travelers," who had gained Magruder's confidence, signed on for the return trip. But all three—Christopher Lower, James P. Romain, and David Renton (alias Doc Howard)—were questionable characters, up to no good. Also joining the group was William Page, a harmless, tobacco-chewing, yarn-spinning mountaineer who apparently entertained them all.

On the trail some forty miles from Elk City, at a beautiful wooded spot along the Nez Perce Trail, the bad men decided to make their move. Magruder sat at the campfire one night visiting with Lower, who suddenly left to bring in more wood, careful to take his axe along. When he returned to the campfire, Lower slipped behind Magruder and drove the axe into his head. Renton and Romain dispatched the four wranglers and dumped all the bodies over a precipice. Even the sixty mules were shot. They spared Page, the old storyteller, and frightened him into silence.

When Magruder failed to return to Lewiston, Hill Beachy suspected his friend had met with foul play. A day or two later he saw four suspicious characters leave town on the Walla Walla stage, each one with a cantina on his lap—a small metal and leather case often used for carrying gold.

Following a hunch, Beachy checked the livery stables and discovered some of the pack string animals and gear the suspects had brought to Lewiston. He was able to identify one mule, a saddle, and a shotgun as the property of Lloyd Magruder. Beachy immediately received a deputy sheriff appointment from Sheriff James Fisk as well as a warrant for the arrest of the four characters and the proper interstate requisitions for their return to Idaho. Then he set off with Tomas Farrell to dog the trail of the alleged road agents. At Portland they gave the lawmen the slip by booking passage to San Francisco on the steamer *Sierra Nevada*. Beachy and Farrell then set out for California traveling overland, and at Yreka wired the San Francisco police to be on the lookout for the fugitives.

A few days later, Beachy claimed the prisoners and escorted them back to Lewiston in chains. "We'll fix you for this," Renton told him. But they never had a chance. During the ensuing trial, the villains couldn't get past the heavy guard, and Page, who told such good yarns, spilled the whole story. Judge Samuel Parks slapped death sentences on the three desperados. A gallows was erected southeast of town in what is now Vollmer Park, and a well-attended hanging it was. Most of Lewiston gathered around, and many Indians from Lapwai came as well. Legend has it that when all three were in place, Lower said, "Launch the boat, she's nothing but a mud skow anyway." The trap was sprung, and three bodies dropped, signifying the triumph of frontier law at Lewiston. This was the first trial in an Idaho court (January 1864), and these were the first legal executions in Idaho. (Those who had died earlier by the rope had been lynched.) In the spring, Beachy and some of his friends returned to the spot where Magruder was murdered. They found the bodies of the men and mules, which verified the testimony of William Page.

When the second legislature met in 1864, most of the mining activity and population had shifted to the southern part of the territory. Several new counties were formed, and their delegates wanted the capital at Boise. The Boise faction mustered enough votes to pass a bill that changed the capital city from Lewiston to Boise. The Lewiston delegates were furious and pulled out all the legal stops to enjoin the south from moving the territorial seal and archives. Caleb Lyon, the newly appointed governor, dallied about town for a while, not knowing how to proceed. Fearing he might even land in jail, he journeyed downriver to Portland to await the arrival of the new territorial secretary, Clinton deWitt Smith. Lyon passed the buck to Smith, who took fast action. Upon arriving at Lewiston, Smith secured a detachment of cavalry from Fort Lapwai. The soldiers rode into Lewiston and quickly spirited away the territorial seal and archives. Both Smith and the cavalry were loudly condemned in Lewiston, but the climate changed as they rode into Boise with the prize on April 14, 1865. The capital stayed put this time, but the political fracas left scars. It created a rift between north and south Idaho that took decades to heal.

Lewiston settled down to mature on the strength of agricultural trade, Lewis-Clark State College, and the business associated with being the seat of Nez Perce County. When the timber industry came to Idaho, Lewiston became a lumberjack town and the center of a growing forest products industry.

In 1906 Potlatch Lumber Company built a mill at Potlatch, and Lewiston indirectly profited as lumber camps mushroomed along the Clearwater River. But the big boost came twenty years later, when the Clearwater Lumber Company (later part of the Potlatch Corporation) erected a mammoth mill along the river east of town. In 1949 and 1950 the corporation added a pulp and paper mill, where presto logs were invented and first manufactured.

For years Lewiston was the terminus of giant log drives on the Clearwater. Even with the advent of modern equipment, the Clearwater could still move the maximum number of logs in the minimum time and at the least expense. The romance and pure gutsiness of the spring drive is over, but historians have preserved the picture. Cecil Dryden tells the story in *Clearwater of Idaho*:

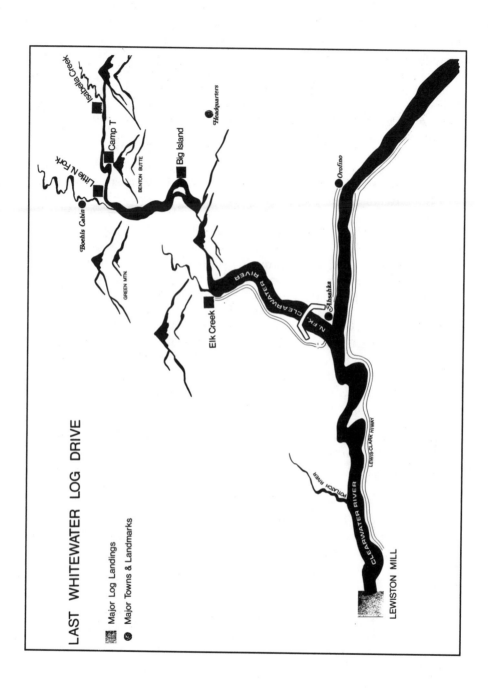

LAST WHITEWATER LOG DRIVE

Major Log Landings
Major Towns & Landmarks

Isabella Creek

Camp T

Little N. Fork

Boehls Cabin

Headquarters

Big Island

BENTON BUTTE

GREEN MTN.

Elk Creek

CLEARWATER RIVER

N. FK. CLEARWATER RIVER

Ahsahka

Orofino

LEWIS-CLARK HIWAY

POTLATCH RIVER

CLEARWATER RIVER

LEWISTON MILL

River "pigs" guiding a logjam down the Clearwater River. —Ross Hall

Repairing the caulked boots, the river driver's best friend and greatest assurance against accidents.
—Potlatch Corporation

The drive starts from the North Fork about ninety miles upstream from Lewiston. . . . In cleared areas along the banks sawlogs have been ricked up in mile-long stacks, awaiting the pulling of the key log which catapults some 50,000,000 board feet into the wild waters with a rumble and a splash. They are then off on their tumultuous race to the millpond at Lewiston.

The second act in the log-drive drama begins when the peavey crew of some thirty-odd experienced rivermen known as the "jacks" or "pigs" walks onto the watery stage to finish the job: that is, follow the logs downriver, retrieving the strays, picking jams apart—in short seeing that approximately ninety-nine per cent of the herd is safely corralled in the millpond of the Lewiston plant.

The drive might have lasted one to ten weeks, and during this time the lumberjacks lived in wanigans. These contrivances were made up of a cookhouse and two bunkhouses lashed together and floated on rubber rafts. The log drives ended in 1971, when Dworshak Dam blocked the river.

The wanigan, a combination cookshack and bunkhouse that traveled with the crews as they drove logs down the Clearwater River from the forest to the millpond at Lewiston.
—Potlatch Corporation

Logs in the millpond at Lewiston. —Potlatch Corporation

Luna House Museum

This excellent historical museum is stocked with artifacts that tell the story of Indians, pioneers, and steamboating. Many people come to view the large photo archives. Others study the fascinating Chief Joseph portrait by Dan Piel of the fine arts faculty at Washington State University.

The museum takes its name from the original Luna House, the leading hotel during the stirring days of the 1860s, when Hill Beachy was the proprietor and the territorial legislature was in town.

Lewis-Clark State College

Lewis-Clark State College dates from 1893. It has a well-rounded four-year curriculum and is especially known for its Confluence Press and the many writers it helps to develop. The school is located on a tranquil, tree-shaded campus close to the center of town.

Dogwood Festival

This April and May fling has developed into an extended affair of music and the arts, garden tours, wine fairs, and sporting competitions. People

279

come from far and near to participate. Information is available from the Lewis-Clark State College Artists Series office.

Hells Gate State Park

Lewiston is the northern gateway to Hells Canyon, and excursions begin here. A number of jet boat options are available for upriver travel to Hells Canyon. This favorite riverside park, two miles from town, has sandy beaches, a marina, playgrounds, bicycle paths, and bird watching. Stop at the park headquarters for current information.

Lewiston Hill

At one time, this hill was an almost insurmountable barrier between Lewiston and points north. Negotiating the 2,000-foot drop between the upper prairie and the valley below was a hazardous undertaking. However, Lewiston took steps to conquer the hill, hoping to draw neighbors from Moscow into town to trade. The city hired John Silcott to build a road wide enough to accommodate "a wagon and eight yoke of cattle."

With horses, scrapers, and plows, Silcott finished his masterpiece in 1874, and it served the area well for the next forty-three years. As for comfort, that is another matter. In *Lewiston Country*, historian Margaret Day Allen records the plight of two Salvation Army officers who took a midnight stage down the plunging profile in 1895: "[T]alk about the alps, and the bottomless pit, that wonderful Lewiston Hill was a fright. Down we went at breakneck speed for 1,200 feet in the middle of the night turning first to the left and then to the right around the edge of that high point until five miles were behind us. The stage driver yelled blood and fire at the ferry man to get him to take us across to Lewiston, sleeping peacefully in the forks of the Clearwater and Snake rivers."

Times changed, the rivers were bridged, and the new automobile age required an improved road. Surveying began in 1915. All of Lewiston marveled at the big Caterpillar steam shovel that trembled with energy, "still digging, still climbing, still creeping out of the valley over its own triumphant trail along . . . this great wall of nature." When finished, the road was declared a marvelous example of engineering, a "spiral highway" with thrilling curves and hairpins turns—quite a chug for the Model Ts, whose engines were often seen boiling at the water hole halfway to the top.

Fifty years later, another new highway was in the offing, one that could carry the flow of modern traffic at freeway speed. Finished in 1977, this newest Lewiston Hill accommodates cars that can skim from bottom to top in eight minutes. Highways change and viewpoints are altered, but on a clear day the view from the top is still a compelling one. Immediately below the 2,000-foot bluff lies the city of Lewiston, its shimmering rivers winding through the valley.

Clearwater Canyon Scenic Byway

US 12, the Lewis and Clark Highway, follows the wild and scenic Lochsa River along the northern edge of the Selway-Bitterroot Wilderness from Kooskia to the Montana border. This route approximates the Lolo Trail of Lewis and Clark, which is a National Historic Landmark. The original trail follows the ridges above the road, a four-wheel-drive adventure. The paved highway winds through the canyon at river level. Long before the doughty explorers came this way, this ancient Nez Perce route linked the Clearwater homeland with the buffalo hunting grounds on the northern plains. The Indians called it Khusahna Ishkit, "the buffalo trail." The entire distance between Kooskia and Lolo Pass is 101 miles, but traveling any portion of this highway is rewarding for the rich historical associations and the sparkling Lochsa River.

The route includes the mountain outpost of Lowell, situated where the Selway and Lochsa rivers meet to form the Clearwater, seventeen miles from Kooskia. This is a good stop for basic services. Scenery and recreation lure families and fishermen, who come from afar to experience this untouched wilderness.

Although US 12 follows the Lochsa River, the Selway River Recreation Area can be reached from Lowell. Take the Selway River road, Forest Road 223, and stop at the historic Fenn Ranger Station four miles upriver for camping and recreation information. Twelve miles beyond that is Selway Falls, a fifty-foot cataract that splashes down the Selway. Relatively few people know this pristine river because it does not serve as a highway corridor.

From Lowell, US 12 continues on to Lolo through the picturesque Lochsa River canyon. This stream is as pure and undisturbed as any in the country. White-water rapids are interspersed with smooth, glassy stretches where every stone on the pebbled bottom shines through the transparent water. On almost any spring day, river rafters can be seen bouncing along the rollicking current. Also keep an eye out for black bear, elk, and deer.

A point of interest along the highway is the Lochsa Historical Ranger Station. This backcountry outpost, built in the 1920s, was accessible only by trail until 1956, when the Lewis and Clark Highway reached it. The station is staffed by retired Forest Service employees and is open daily from Memorial Day to Labor Day.

Among the delights of the Lochsa-Selway country are the unexpected plants that grow here—leftovers from ancient times, when the Cascade Range was of low altitude and rainy coastal weather systems reached the Bitterroot drainage. When the Cascades rose, they cut off most of this rainfall, and only a few warm, moist pockets were left to support these disjunct species. Red cedar, Sitka spruce, alder, western larch, hemlock, and Pacific dogwood grow along the rivers with a lush understory of sword fern, Pacific yew, and other species more common to the Rocky Mountains.

Toward the Montana end of US 12 stands the Bernard de Voto Cedar Grove, named in honor of the western writer who edited the Lewis and Clark journals. De Voto loved this particular spot, whose magnificent, ancient trees make for an unmatched cathedral setting. At the riverside, a bronze plaque preserves the memory of de Voto, a conservationist and historian of the West.

Ten campgrounds and two picnic areas are located along the highway, and numerous trailheads provide hiking access into the wilderness area. The Clearwater National Forest visitor center on the eastern end of the highway provides Lolo Trail interpretive history. Travel on to Montana or return downstream on US 12 to complete the Clearwater Canyon Scenic Byway.

US 12, Idaho 13
KOOSKIA

The quiet little town of Kooskia lies north of Grangeville at the junction of US 12 and Idaho 13, where the South Fork of the Clearwater meets the Middle Fork. During the last week in July the pace quickens for the annual Kooskia Days, featuring such events as an old-time fiddlers' jamboree, raft races, a horse show, and a parade. The Clearwater National Forest office here provides good historical and recreational information.

The town dates from 1895, when the Nez Perce lands were opened for settlement and several persons applied for patents at the townsite. The place grew as a trading center, and with the arrival of the Northern Pacific Railroad in 1899 it enjoyed a genuine boom. Originally known as Stuart (for a prominent Nez Perce Indian), the town was christened Kooskia ("clear water") when it was incorporated in 1901.

In earlier days, Chief Looking Glass lived here with his band of Nez Perce in a village located a short distance above town along the Clearwater River. This regular home was well within the boundaries of the reservation created in 1863. Here they raised potatoes, corn, beans, squash, melons, and cucumbers—"everything we wanted," said tribesman Peopeo Tholekt. A herd of milk cows and many horses (600 to 700 head) also contributed to the good life here.

Looking Glass and his people did not participate in the Battle of White Bird Hill and expected to wait out the conflict in their camp along the Clearwater. They made an honest stand for peace, yet Gen. O. O. Howard sent two companies of cavalry against them with orders to arrest Looking Glass and all other Indians camped with him. They were to be given over to the settlers at Mount Idaho for "safekeeping." During a white-flag parley with the soldiers, a trigger-happy volunteer sent a shot into the village, wounding Red Heart. The troops then opened fire, and the Indians scattered for their lives. Several died in the attack, although most came out of hiding unscathed. Their village, however, lay in ruins. Tepees were burned, caches of food were destroyed, and possessions prized by the tribe for generations were stolen. Eyewitness Peopeo Tholekt told historian L. V. McWhorter, "Much had been carried away and many objects destroyed or badly damaged. Brass buckets [kettles] always carefully kept by the women lay battered, smashed and pierced by bayonet thrusts. Growing gardens trampled and destroyed. Nearly all our horses taken and every hoof of cattle driven away."

Looking Glass and his band escaped arrest but were infuriated by the wanton assault on their village. They threw in their lot with the Indians who fought at White Bird. When the Nez Perce gathered in council on Weippe Prairie, Looking Glass assumed a leading role.

US 12
KAMIAH

The modern town of Kamiah sits on the west bank of the Clearwater River and has long been a Nez Perce village site. Today the tribe maintains the Wa-a-Yas, a community center, and sponsors two annual celebrations: Lincoln's Birthday Festival in February and Chief Looking Glass Days in

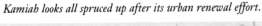
Kamiah looks all spruced up after its urban renewal effort.

August. The latter includes a powwow and Indian dancing. The public is invited. Another popular event hosted annually by the chamber of commerce for more than thirty years is the Labor Day Saturday barbecue. A hospitable spread is provided free to all comers.

Heart of the Monster

East Kamiah, about two miles south of town, is one of the sites in the Nez Perce National Historic Park. This broad area along the Clearwater is rich in Indian lore. Here lies the Heart of the Monster, a volcanic outcropping that plays a central role in the creation myth of the Nez Perce people.

The myth says that in the misty dawn of time, before men lived, animals had the characteristics of humans. Coyote, who could perform wondrous deeds, was the cleverest of them all. He contrived to slay the fearsome Kamiah monster and scatter his body parts to the four winds. These became the Indian tribes of today. Coyote sprinkled the land along the Clearwater with the monster's blood, and from it sprang the most noble tribe of all—the Ne-Mee-Poo or "The People," the Nez Perce. The Heart of the Monster site has an interpretive shelter and a picnic facility.

Floaters on the Clearwater River between Kamiah and Orofino.

284

Also of interest at East Kamiah is the 1874 Presbyterian church. It was built by the government for the Indians and led by Henry Harmon Spalding during his second stint among the Nez Perce, shortly before his demise. After his death, Kate and Sue McBeth ministered to the Indians here.

During the spring of 1806, Lewis and Clark camped near Kamiah for several weeks while waiting for the mountain snows to melt so they could continue their return trip east. They lived on the most friendly terms with their Indian neighbors and came to believe these were "the finest Indians, the most intelligent and manly." Many of them crowded into the camp for medical treatment or to view York, Clark's black cook, who was a great curiosity. The travelers were equally fascinated by the local "long house," a structure that measured 150 feet in length and contained a row of twenty-four campfires straight down the middle. Here the women, in their long, buckskin-fringed dresses, pounded cous roots, creating a din that sounded like a "nail factory."

Lewis collected many botanical specimens during the trip. At Kamiah he found an elegant wildflower and named it *Clarkia pulchella* for his co-captain, William Clark. He also gathered the first cascara known to white men in the Kamiah Valley and returned east with a portion of the bark.

According to Sister Alfreda Elsensohn in *Pioneer Days in Idaho County*, the name Kamiah is related to a species of dogbane (*Apocynum cannabinum*), which the Indians used to make ropes and fishing lines. Lewis recorded the site of their camp as "Kamiarp," apparently taken from the Indian word "kamia," which described the litter that remained after the kamo or dogbane had been crafted into rope.

Idaho 11
WEIPPE

At Greer, turn off US 12 and take Idaho 11 for a spectacular drive to Weippe and Pierce. The highway is excellent, though winding and steep. Sweeping vistas of prairies, mountains, and flowered meadows lifted high above the Clearwater Valley make for a fresh and exhilarating experience. Add to this a whisper of history that blows on the breeze.

At Weippe Prairie, Lewis and Clark first met the Nez Perce, who were camped here on a camas dig. Seventy-three years later, the area still figured prominently in the lives of the native people. After fighting Gen. O. O. Howard to a draw on the South Fork of the Clearwater during the 1877 war, the Nez Perce gathered here for the famous Weippe council to determine whether to fight, retreat, or attempt to return to their respective villages. Chief Looking Glass harangued the conference with a fiery appeal to proceed to Montana. "Listen to me, my chiefs!" he said, "The Crows are

The late Agnes Moses digging camas on Weippe Prairie using a crutch-handled digging stig. The prairie is now a national historic landmark.

the same as my brothers! If you go there with me you will be safe!" His argument carried the day. Chief Joseph and others dissented, but democracy won. The next morning, the camp packed up and began the historic trip across the Bitterroots via the Lolo Trail. Historian McWhorter expressed the dissenter's viewpoint: "Misfortune of misfortunes! Chief Looking Glass was now in supreme command."

The retreating tribe hoped General Howard might give up, might not send his cavalry after them over the long, tedious trail. One can visualize the long cavalcade of mounted horsemen stretching out from Weippe as the Nez Perce began their epic retreat, their trail of tears. The exodus included 250 warriors, more than 400 women and children, and roughly 2,000 horses—half a nation riding off to their destiny. After their thousand-mile retreat and bitter battles with the pursuing cavalry, only a few would return to the homeland. The route they took has been designated the Nez Perce National Historic Trail.

Idaho 11
PIERCE

The Idaho gold rush began at this mountain village in the midst of the Clearwater National Forest. It still retains some of the flavor of its gold camp days, although recreation is in the limelight now.

The best stop in town is the historic courthouse, built in 1862. This small brown frame building preserves the look of the frontier. Tiny barred windows identify the room used as a jail. Inside, interpretive panels tell the story of old Pierce City and the Oro Fino Mining District. The structure, Idaho's oldest government building, is administered by the Idaho Historical Society.

A bateau of the type that followed the log drives down the Clearwater River sits next to the town library, and a privately owned timber museum is close by. Also of significance is the site of the Chinese cemetery, a remnant of the days when these pigtailed prospectors added their exotic touch to the settlement. Pierce holds two popular annual events, a winter carnival in February that features snow sports and a three-day summer festival called "1860 Days" that celebrates the town's rowdy past.

Thousands of miners stampeded across Weippe Prairie after E. D. Pierce and his party struck gold on Orofino Creek in the fall of 1860. In the *Pierce Chronicle*, the lucky fortune hunter said, "We found gold in every place in the stream . . . in the flats and banks and generally diffused from the surface to the bed rock. I never saw a party of men so much excited. They made the hills and mountains ring for joy." In December the Pierce City townsite was marked off, and the motley crew devised mining laws. During a trip to Walla Walla for supplies, word of the new El Dorado spread quickly, and hopeful prospectors hit the trail for the new diggings.

During the spring of 1861, some 2,000 gold seekers swarmed across the mountains to the new Pierce City. Already, "half a dozen gambling mills were in full swing." The streets were a din of mules braying, hammers pounding, pack trains arriving, and pedestrians stirring, all to the tune of fiddles emanating from the several saloons and gambling halls. It was an exciting time, but not everybody struck it rich. Some moved down the creek a couple of miles to establish a second camp, called Oro Fino. Others fanned out across the mountains, prospecting as they went. Colors were soon raised in fabulous camps along the Clearwater and Salmon rivers, and places such as Elk City, Florence, and Warren joined Pierce City and Oro Fino in turning the course of Idaho history toward permanent settlement.

The mining season in all these high-altitude camps was fairly short—from June to October, maybe shorter, depending on the length of the winter and the supply of water in the streams. In the fall, most of the miners left for the low country, but a few hardy souls always remained in the snowbound mountain camps. William A. Goulder stayed in Oro Fino during the

Modern Pierce still retains the flavor of its historic look. —Idaho State Historical Society

winter of 1861–1862, when the whole country lay under a thick mantle of snow. The unoccupied prospectors spent the long evenings in various ways, Goulder wrote in *Reminiscences*. One group developed "some of the finest chess players ever met with on the continent," and the dozen gamblers in town sat at the poker table day and night.

Goulder himself went in for reading. He tells about a man named Harris who kept a small newsstand, and among the treasures on his shelves was a nearly complete set of Sir Walter Scott's novels.

> My comrades in the cabin agreed to buy and pay for the books if I would agree to read them aloud evenings while they rested in their bunks and did the listening. To this I very willingly agreed, with the condition that they should keep duly awake and attentive. When all was arranged and ready, I would begin to read, throwing into my voice all the mellifluous tones and soporific effects that I could muster. Very soon they would be both sound asleep and snoring. . . . Then I would cease reading aloud and enjoy for an hour or two a season of intense delight and profitable reading. . . . I thus read for the first time all of Scott's stories, except "The Fair Maid of Perth" whose delicate constitution and refined superstructure had thus far kept her away from the rude scenes of a wild mining camp.

The entrance of miners into the Clearwater and Salmon placers clearly violated the Nez Perce Treaty of 1855. However, this was of small consequence to the trespassers. B. F. Kendall, superintendent of Indian affairs in Washington Territory (of which Idaho was then a part), said that "to attempt to restrain miners would be, to my mind, like attempting to restrain the whirlwind." A new treaty was wrenched from the Indians in 1863 to legalize the miners' presence. The agreement reduced the reservation to one-sixth its original size and laid the foundation for the Nez Perce War of 1877.

The Chinese Hanging

Two miles south of Pierce and a quarter of a mile off Idaho 11, markers point to the site where five Chinese residents were hanged in 1885 for the murder of D. M. Fraser. At this time, Pierce was a predominantly Chinese settlement, with Oriental prospectors reworking the placers abandoned by white miners. Only a handful of whites remained. One of them was Fraser, a leading storekeeper whose chief competitor was a Chinese merchant named Lee Kee Nam.

On the morning of September 10, 1885, Frank Carle discovered the still-warm body of Fraser "in a horrible state of mutilation." Circumstantial evidence pointed to the Chinese community. A special messenger left immediately to alert officials in Lewiston, and a group of vigilantes formed in great excitement and set out to avenge the murder.

Five Chinese men were arrested after an overnight "set up" in jail, and something of a trial began. No confessions were forthcoming, so the authorities decided to loosen some tongues by means of a mock hanging. In 1959 Kenneth Owens wrote in *Idaho Yesterdays*:

> They placed a noose around Lee Kee Nam's neck, hoisted him into the air and dropped him, unconscious. Then the vigilantes brought Lee's partner to view the apparently dead merchant. Threatened with the same fate the terrified partner babbled that the "dead" man was indeed responsible. But when Nam came around he blamed the partner, so vigilantes decided they were both guilty. For good measure, they also charged "a hard-featured barber . . . a gambler . . . and a parasite of one of the Chinese prostitutes in camp."

Having concluded their "trial," the vigilantes turned the accused over to the local deputy sheriff, who was to haul them off to the county seat at Murray some 250 miles away (see Silver Valley) to await formal trial. Nine deputies were sworn in as guards, and the prisoners were loaded into a wagon and jostled out of town. About two miles down the road, masked men disarmed the deputies and took custody of the unfortunate five. Soon each one was "hanging by the neck on a pole lashed to two pine trees, stone dead."

The unseemly affair might have passed for a typical western lynching, but racial tensions were rampant throughout the Northwest. The hangings soon became an international incident. An alarmed Chinese consul in San Francisco alerted his minister in Washington D. C., who lobbied the secretary of state for an investigation. Governor E. A. Stevenson visited Pierce City to collect information. Only "trustworthy" Chinese were permitted to give evidence. After delving into the facts, Governor Stevenson was inclined to believe the vigilantes were justified in their actions, and he issued a statement not calculated to soothe international relations with China. He said in part, "Many devilish acts have been perpetrated by the Chinese, and their low, filthy habits, their highbinder piratical societies, have disgusted our people."

Headquarters

The site of Headquarters is twelve miles north of Pierce on Idaho 11. After the Camas Prairie Railroad came through in 1927, this community grew as a jumping-off point for fifteen Potlatch logging camps. For fifty-five years, trains creaked in and out of Headquarters with flatbeds piled high with logs. Now it is a ghost town, but the hamlet once boasted shops, a cookhouse, and bunkhouses where men gathered around wood stoves in the wintertime to spin Paul Bunyan yarns and spit tobacco juice. Conveniences were few. Richard Guth and Stan Cohen provide a personal peek at daily living among the lumberjacks in *A Pictorial History of the U.S. Forest Service, Northern Region*:

> Most of the lumberjacks wore woolen two-piece underwear winter and summer. Usually they came in sweaty and often wet and hung their wet sweaty clothes and socks around the heating stove to dry. The smell was indescribable. Talk about air pollution and smog! This was something, with tobacco smoke, and 50 men drying their clothes and socks, and all the other odors of hard working men who seldom took a bath or changed their clothes for weeks and sometimes months at a time for the simple reason that there were no facilities for bathing or laundering. . . . There was one redeeming feature of the old-time logging camps; they had good cooks, served good food, and plenty of it.

In later years Headquarters became a modern company town with families, a library, a school, a grocery, a post office, and the only swimming pool for miles around. Now the train is gone, along with the logging trucks, the lumberjacks, and the endless crops of trees.

Travelers can proceed to Orofino from the junction at Hollywood Camp six miles south of Headquarters on an improved county road or return to US 12.

290

Orofino is the busiest town on the Clearwater. Prosperous logging and recreation industries have long thrived here alongside an active farming and ranching community. The Clearwater National Forest headquarters is immediately west of town along US 12 and makes an excellent stop for maps, brochures, and information on regional history and travel.

A double celebration is held here annually: The Clearwater County Fair and Lumberjack Days follow one another nonstop during the third week in September. Parades, sawing, birling, axe throwing, and any number of other timber- and agriculture-related events make this pair of festivals worth attending. Another worthy stop, the Clearwater County Historical Museum, tells the story of Orofino and its mining, timber, and agricultural background.

Orofino grew from hopeful beginnings in 1895 when former Nez Perce lands were opened for settlement. It is located at the mouth of Orofino Creek and named for the historic gold camp (spelled Oro Fino) once located near the headwaters of the same creek. So the alpha and omega of this little stream is "Orofino."

Konkolville

This picturesque settlement three miles east of Orofino is the site of the family-owned Konkolville Lumber Company. In addition to the mill, facilities here include a motel, a restaurant, and a unique cedar overpass across the highway. This structure, designed by Andrew Konkol, rests on a base made of cedar logs nine feet in diameter and more than 1,000 years old. At the restaurant, diners can overhear old-timers using logging terms such as "crooked elbow" (an occupational hazard enjoyed by thirsty loggers hitting town after a long dry spell), "stows his grub with a number 9 scoop" ("he's a big eater"), and "folded up his face" ("he quit talking").

Canoe Camp Site

This Lewis and Clark site sits a few miles west of Orofino on US 12 at the junction of the main Clearwater and the North Fork. The explorers arrived here on September 26, 1805, on their way to the Pacific and camped near Twisted Hair's village until October 10. Members of his band drew a map showing them how to reach the ocean by way of the Clearwater, Snake, and Columbia rivers. With Nez Perce instruction, the men began "burning out the holler of our canoes."

The work proceeded even though many of the men were ill, probably from eating too much dried salmon and too many camas roots. Fresh meat, their usual staple, was scarce. Clark said, "[O]ur hunters with every diligence Could kill nothing," but the Indians brought fish and roots into camp and took away an assortment of articles. On one occasion Clark mentioned giving "a small Pice of Tobacco to the Indians, 3 broachs & 2 rings with my Handkerchief divided between the five of them." During this time Captain Lewis was ill and "scarcely able to ride on a jentle horse." Though unwell himself, Clark kept busy dispensing "rushes Pills . . Tarter emetic & etc" to the indisposed.

Within two weeks the travelers had recovered fairly well, and the five canoes were ready to launch. Chief Twisted Hair agreed to care for their thirty-eight horses, and on October 10 the explorers pushed off on the last part of their westward journey.

Dworshak Dam and Fish Hatchery

The dam, located approximately six miles from town on Idaho 7, spans the North Fork of the Clearwater River. The reservoir backing up from this monolith winds for fifty-three miles along the base of forested slopes in the Clearwater National Forest and offers prime recreational opportunities. The highest straight-axis dam in the western world, Dworshak provides enough power to light a city of 100,000. Construction of the dam began in 1959 and foreshadowed the end of the Clearwater log drives from Orofino to Lewiston. An excellent visitor center sits atop the structure.

The 14,000-acre Dworshak State Park lies on the west side of the dam and can be reached via a twenty-five-mile scenic drive from Orofino. Not all of the road is paved, and parts of it are steep and winding. Dworshak Fish Hatchery, four miles west of Orofino on Idaho 7, is the largest producer of steelhead in the world. A self-guided tour of the rearing ponds makes it easy to view the life cycle of this seagoing trout. The dam, park, and hatchery are named for Henry Dworshak, former logger and U.S. senator from Idaho.

Lenore Site

For hundreds of years the Clearwater River has been important to the Nez Perce people, and many sites along its banks are associated with their heritage. One of these, Lenore, is located on US 12 sixteen miles downriver from the Dworshak Dam turnoff. A small park here makes for a restful stop and provides an opportunity to sit at the streamside and ruminate on one's place in the natural world. Here the Nez Perce and their predecessors have lived continuously for some 10,000 years.

Palouse Country

Moscow is a bustling university town and the hub of an enormous agricultural industry. Surrounded by the Palouse hills with their rolling seas of wheat, peas, and lentils, the city mixes country charm with city sophistication. Visitors can drift into the Farmers' Market at Friendship Square on Saturdays or take in any amount of dance, drama, music, and visual arts in this "Heart of the Arts" town. The streetscape is interesting, too, with its many historic buildings dressed up in patterned brickwork, arched windows, ornamental stone, and generous curlicues.

The Palouse country surrounding the town of Moscow is distinguished by rare soil deposits called "loess." This rich, deep soil is believed to date from Pleistocene times, when dust-laden winds blew across an ancient lake bed in central Washington and dropped their load. Soil piled up to depths of 10 to 200 feet as the winds sculpted the graceful, rolling hills of the Palouse. This unique geology covers some 4,000 square miles. The soils are deepest in the area around Moscow, Pullman, and Colfax, thinning toward the mountains on the north and east and toward the scablands to the west.

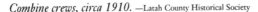

Combine crews, circa 1910. —Latah County Historical Society

Modern combines at work in Palouse country.

Excellent soil and a mild climate made this area ideal for agriculture. When the first settlers arrived, the hills were covered with teeming stands of bunchgrass interspersed with meadows of blue camas—an ideal spot for cattle. But when the pioneers discovered the richness of the prairie soil, they plowed the grasses under to make way for wheat. Early in the twentieth century, the Palouse region became famous for its grain harvests. Huge threshing machines pulled by thirty-two-horse teams and managed by crews of twenty men rolled over the hills, cutting wheat and spitting chaff. Today one man can manage a combine while sitting in an enclosed cab, perhaps with air conditioning and two-way radio communication. In big fields half a dozen giant combines may converge to get the job done quickly. They move in tandem along the contours of the hills, up and down and around, cutting the grain in wide, curving swaths, as if the whole procedure were choreographed.

For decades wheat has been grown here in rotation with peas and barley. Ninety-seven percent of the nation's seed peas and split peas are grown in these hills, along with 40 percent of the lentils. High-yield soft wheat is the favored grain. It is always in demand for specialty items such as noodles, pasta, and pastries. Alternative crops include rapeseed, mustard, sunflowers, and alfalfa.

Before white settlers came, the Nez Perce Indians came here each summer to set up their tepee villages and dig for camas. They called the area Tatkimmah, meaning "the place of the young or spotted deer." However, this tender name blew away on the prairie winds when the homesteaders arrived with their herds of livestock. Their pigs soon became addicted to

The Palouse is barn country. This classic is near Troy.

rooting out the delicate camas bulbs, so the settlers dubbed their community "Hog Heaven."

Later settlers called it Paradise Valley, which no doubt described the fresh-flowered meadows and fragrant pines. However, one more name-change was to come. When local resident S. M. Neff completed the application for a post office, he wrote "Moscow" on the dotted line. The name honored two towns Neff had previously lived in: Moscow, Pennsylvania, and Moscow, Iowa. Richard Beck, a Latah County historian, began to wonder: How many Moscows are there? He found twenty-one of them scattered from Maine to Tennessee to Idaho. The pronunciation is "MAHS-ko," not "MAHS-cow." Either way, as Beck says, "It beats Hog Heaven."

Moscow grew slowly on its agricultural base and might have remained a country village on the order of Genesee or Princeton if not for some powerful community boosters who understood politics and skillfully finessed a state university and a county seat for the hometown. William J. McConnell, Moscow's "Prince of Merchants," was a staunch pioneer. He had previously struck it rich growing green onions and peddling them to the Placerville miners during the Boise Basin gold rush. He also organized the Payette vigilantes. McConnell was a force to be reckoned with, and he desperately wanted to free Moscow from the economic clutches of Lewiston. Most of all he coveted the county seat of Nez Perce County, even though it was already established at Lewiston.

McConnell and his friend Willis Sweet, another astute Moscow politician, plotted strategy with Fred T. Dubois, Idaho's territorial delegate to Congress. Dubois agreed to push through Congress a bill to divide Nez Perce County. The northern half would be called Latah, and Moscow would be named the county seat. Lewiston protested, but the legislation came off without a hitch. Latah County became the only county in the nation to be established by the U.S. Congress, May 14, 1888.

Having helped birth the fledgling county, Willis Sweet stayed around to guide it. When the territorial legislature met in Boise, he attended as the delegate from Latah. His chief mission was to shepherd a bill that would create a University of Idaho and place it at Moscow.

The hottest political issue in 1889 was whether Idaho Territory should apply for statehood, and Sweet used this debate as a lever. North Idaho boosters generally favored annexation with eastern Washington over joining in statehood with southern Idaho and the Boise bunch, who had so rudely stolen the territorial capital. However, Sweet and John Brigham, a delegate from Genesee, saw a chance to make a horse trade. They agreed to deliver northern Idaho votes for statehood in the upcoming general election if the southern Idaho faction in the territorial legislature would vote to place the university at Moscow. Brigham introduced the university bill during the eleventh hour of the last territorial legislature, and Governor Stevenson signed it on January 30, 1889. The northern faction voted for statehood, and Idaho entered the Union on July 4, 1890.

Moscow seemed to nourish men who could think big and turn the vision into reality. One of these was Frank Robinson, who huckstered his special brand of mail-order religion during the 1930s and 1940s. He called it "Psychiana," a mix of psychology and the power of positive thinking that caught on quickly during the years of the Great Depression. In *Psychiana*, Keith Peterson sums up Robinson's vision this way: "You can be whoever you make up your mind to be. You need not be sick. You need not be poor. You need not be unsuccessful." This message of hope and self-help seems commonplace today but was strong stuff in 1930.

Robinson spread his message with evangelistic fervor. At any given time his fascinating ads appeared in 180 magazines and 140 newspapers across the country, and the word went out over the airwaves from 60 radio stations. Millions of people scraped up $20 to enroll in Robinson's correspondence course, which outlined how to capture "God Power." This was a growth industry and the largest mail-order religion in the world. Robinson became the major private employer in Moscow. More than 60,000 pieces of mail went out of his office daily, and thousands of checks came in.

Robinson prospered with Psychiana for twenty years, and thousands of people credited him with enhancing their health, happiness, and prosperity. Today the University of Idaho is the repository for a voluminous collection of Psychiana records.

Camas Winery and Life Force Honey

This Main Street winery is housed in an antique building that has led many lives. The staff here makes fourteen kinds of wine, including a specialty called Hog Heaven Red that recalls the settlement's first name.

Camas also makes an unusual honey wine known as "mead" for Life Force Honey, another Main Street enterprise. Their Life Force Mead has been toasted from London to Tokyo. The habit of quaffing mead has delighted folks from the beginning of time and long ago entered the realm of romance—it is the origin of the word "honeymoon."

University of Idaho

Like Moscow itself, the University of Idaho is set among the Palouse hills. Of interest here is the administration building. Its Gothic tower peeps out among leafy trees and offers both architectural and natural interest. A special grove of trees decorates the grounds, and it can be both instructive and entertaining. Each tree has been planted to honor a particular person; each bears a marker naming the special person and identifying the species of tree.

Landmark clock tower at the administration building. —University of Idaho campus

The mining and metallurgy department features geology displays on the second- and third-floor hallways. Exhibits include old tools, mining artifacts, and fabulous gemstones from Idaho. Sports fans enjoy the Kibbie Dome sports complex and covered stadium, with its 150-foot-high wooden arches. When Kibbie was completed in 1975, it was selected as the Outstanding Civil Engineering Achievement of the year, which puts it in good company. The St. Lawrence Seaway, the Gateway Arch in St. Louis, and other unique projects have been so honored in other years.

The student union, with its adjacent bookstore, offers fascinating shopping for Idaho books and miscellany. Pick up a map here for a self-guided tour of the campus.

McConnell Mansion Historic House Museum

The mansion was the family home of William J. McConnell, one of Moscow's chief boosters and Idaho's third governor (1893–1895). Mary McConnell, who later married Senator William E. Borah, spent her girlhood here. The house is a Victorian charmer with period furnishing.

A substantial library and photo collection is located in the Centennial Annex across the street from the mansion. This is the heart of the Latah County Historical Society, which manages the museum and interprets local history. Lifestyles ranging from 1887 to 1987 are examined in the ongoing educational process here.

Appaloosa Horse Club Museum

This national club, located two miles west of town on Idaho 8, exists to promote the Nez Perce Appaloosa, a horse that had all but vanished by 1938, when the club was formed.

The Nez Perce were skilled horsemen. They practiced selective breeding and had many fine animals among their herds, but the distinctive Appaloosa seems to have been a favorite. After the Nez Perce were defeated during their 1,350-mile retreat toward Canada, Generals Miles and Howard and the U.S. Cavalry confiscated their herds. They sold what they could and slaughtered the rest. On the new reservation, no horses were permitted. Officials believed the Nez Perce would forget their native culture more easily without fast horses, racing, pleasure rides, and the trappings of the old semi-nomadic life.

In 1938 George Hatley of Moscow, along with other local horsemen, decided to rescue the Appaloosa from oblivion. A few still lived in the canyonlands along the Snake and Clearwater rivers, and these became foundation stock from which to regenerate the breed. Today it numbers over a quarter of a million horses. Each year the Appaloosa Horse Club sponsors two major shows, the National Appaloosa Show and the World Championship Halter and Performance Show. Each is held in a different section of

Riders and their spotted ponies on the annual Chief Joseph Trail Ride.
—Appaloosa Horse Club

the country from year to year. Other activities include pari-mutuel racing in sixteen states and the annual Chief Joseph Trail Ride in the Palouse country.

The resurgence of the Appaloosa is not only an equine success story but also a significant historical event, for these distinctively spotted horses go far back in time. Fifty thousand years ago, Cro-Magnons drew pictures of them on cave walls at Lascaux, France. The horses appear repeatedly in the decorative arts of the Persians and on Grecian pottery of the first century.

Very likely the Appaloosas were brought to Mexico by the conquistadors and from there migrated north until they reached the Shoshones and the Nez Perce. "Buffalo Bill" Cody had a showman's eye for drama and included several of these uniquely dappled broncs in his traveling Wild West Show, and the cowboy artist Charlie Russell sometimes added the hallmark spotted rump to an Indian pony. Nobody can certify the origin of the name Appaloosa, but it seems likely that as settlers took up the Indian lands along the Palouse River they described the horse as "a Palouse." The expression became combined into Apalouse or Apalousie until Appaloosa evolved.

One of the fascinations of these animals is their coloration. No two are alike. Their spots are said to be as different as human fingerprints, yet unmistakably "Appaloosa." Edith Stanger, who breeds horses at Idaho Falls,

Well-bred Appaloosa foal at the Appaloosa Horse Club near Moscow.

says in *Conversations*, "Appaloosa breeders never die in the spring because they are waiting to see how much color they get in the colt crop."

Appropriately, the Nez Perce Appaloosa has been named Idaho's state horse.

Mary Minerva McCroskey State Park

Twenty-six miles north of Moscow on US 95, a sign signals the turnoff to the park. The main attraction is the twenty-five-mile-long Skyline Drive, which winds along the crest of four mountains to emerge at Farmington, Washington. The park is undeveloped and provides a near-wilderness experience. Elk, deer, bear, coyotes, and most other inhabitants of the northern woods live here.

At 5,292 acres, this is the largest state park in Idaho. Virgil McCroskey donated it to the state of Idaho in honor of his mother and all pioneer women.

Idler's Rest Nature Preserve

This Nature Conservancy preserve lies six miles northeast of Moscow on the Idler's Rest Road. It contains a 100-year-old stand of western red cedars as well as patches of ponderosa pine, Douglas fir, and grand fir. Short trails meander through the trees. The preserve is administered by the College of Forestry, Wildlife and Range Sciences at the University of Idaho.

US 95, Idaho 6
POTLATCH

The small town of Potlatch, across the Palouse hills eighteen miles north of Moscow, takes its name from the Potlatch River. "Potlatch," a term used by the coastal Indians, was originally translated as "giving." Today it is used to describe any festive gathering.

In appearance the town is fairly typical of other small communities across Idaho, but it began as a company town. All the town's residents worked at the Potlatch Lumber Company mill, shopped at the company store, bowed their heads in the company church, imbibed "culture" at the company opera house, and educated their children at the company school. To get out of town, they even rode the company rails. However, nobody drank at the company bar, for the town was "dry."

Today the Potlatch Lumber Company is gone, and Potlatch is a self-governing village. Most of the residents commute to jobs in outlying communities. Some of the old spirit still remains, for the Potlatch Lumber Company built well. In 1986 the Idaho Historic Preservation Office placed forty-four buildings on the National Register of Historic Places.

The town began in 1906, when a new lumber mill at Potlatch joined the growing Weyerhauser syndicate, which already had an interest in mills at Sandpoint, Coeur d'Alene, and Boise. The Weyerhauser family owned more than a million acres of forest land, and some of these riches stood along the upper reaches of the Palouse and Potlatch rivers. Both Moscow and Palouse (a small town across the state line in Washington) wanted the proposed mill. In *Company Town*, historian Keith Peterson recounts a meeting in Moscow at which the company directors discussed their options. General manager William Deary came in wet and dripping from a trek through the woods, took off his shoes and socks by the stove, and prepared to dry out until he heard someone say, "Moscow." He rose to his bare feet and made for the conference table, on which a map was spread out. Sputtering in his heavy Irish brogue, he declared, "Gintlemen, Moscow doesn't have enough water to be baptizin' a bastard. The mill will be here," and his forefinger gouged the future site of Potlatch along the Palouse River.

When the first log buzzed through the saws in 1906, company officials touted their new creation as the largest white pine sawmill in the world. And it called for the best company town on the West Coast, if not in the world. C. Ferris White, a Spokane architect, was hired to design homes, commercial buildings, churches, and schools. In less than two years' time the town came to life. Homes in a variety of sizes stairstepped up and down the hillsides. Generally, the higher up the hill one lived, the more amenities one enjoyed. However, everyone mingled on the downtown streets and shopped in the company stores, the chief one being The Merc, which sold groceries and dry goods. Nobody owed his or her soul to the company store. On the contrary, prices were so reasonable that people came from miles around to snap up the bargains on sale days.

In addition to building the mill and the town, the company constructed a railroad that linked up with transcontinental lines and gave Potlatch products access to far-flung markets. Named the Washington, Idaho & Montana Railroad, it began at Palouse, Washington (where it connected with the Northern Pacific & Spokane), and ended forty-nine miles later at Bovill, where it connected with the Milwaukee road to St. Maries, Chicago, and the Midwest. The Montana extension was never built. Now owned by the Burlington Northern, it continues to haul freight on a regular basis.

The railroad also opened up formerly isolated sections of land for settlement. A series of towns whose names have long stimulated curiosity grew along the tracks. Three of these towns—Harvard, Deary, and Bovill—developed into modest communities. Modern residents move in for the scenic beauty of the surrounding countryside, but originally the towns were mere whistle-stops where lumberjacks caught rides to and from the logging camps.

Harvard apparently received its name as a fitting response to the pioneer town of Princeton, which was settled by ranchers long before the Potlatch era. As young college men surveyed the right-of-way and supervised railroad construction, Cornell, Vassar, Stanford, and Yale joined Harvard and Princeton on the route. This distinguished nomenclature attracted national attention. It appeared in Ripley's "Believe It or Not," and a 1946 issue of the *New Yorker* listed the famous stops under the headline, "Dept of Higher Education (Choo Choo Division)."

From Potlatch, return to US 95 and head north to Coeur d'Alene, or continue on Idaho 6 and the White Pine Scenic Byway to St. Maries.

St. Maries/St. Joe River Country

East of Moscow on Idaho 8 is a green and rolling country with intermit-tent patches of wheat and stands of pine. Beyond the old lumber settlement of Troy, about ten miles from Moscow, the mountains rise higher and the wheat fields blend into hillside pastures dotted with horses and cattle. Twenty-four miles out of town the highway passes through the old railroad town of Deary. Not much is left of the brisk little station on the Washing-ton, Idaho & Montana Railroad. In 1907 William Deary, Potlatch Lumber Company general manager, located the townsite and sold off the lots. When lumber and rail activity began to dwindle, so did the town.

Bovill, ten miles beyond Deary, also has lapsed into a quiet spot among the green mountains. Potlatch Corporation, the mainstay for many years, has shut down its logging operation, but the town remains interesting for its unique beginning. The founder was Hugh Bovill, youngest son of Sir William Bovill. English primogeniture laws left him with no prospect of inheritance, so he set off for America seeking adventure. In Nebraska he met Charlotte Robinson, the girl of his dreams. She also was an English immigrant of considerable stature. Her father was a canon in Yorkminster and a direct descendant of King Edward III. These two shirt-tail blue bloods teamed up and eventually landed in this Idaho valley, where they purchased the Warren Meadows ranch in 1901. They stocked the place with cattle and horses, built a home, and developed a fishing and hunting lodge with a store and a post office. The spread became popular not only with sports-men but also with land speculators, timber cruisers, tourists, and friends.

In a few years, logging in the white pine country intruded on Bovill's paradise. Potlatch Lumber Company eyed the location as a possible rail-road terminus for its Washington, Idaho & Montana Railroad. Bovill sold them a site in 1907. Three years later the Chicago, Milwaukee, St. Paul & Pacific was completed to Bovill, and the traditional golden spike ceremony connecting the two railroads was held on May 30, 1910. Many dignitaries from east and west stepped off one train or the other, including William E. Borah, Idaho's new senator. The occasion was festive and providentially marked by a bright flare from above, as Halley's Comet seared the sky that night.

Between the loggers and the railroad construction crews, Bovill grew into a brawling settlement. Saloons, bawdy houses, and wild, wild, "wimmin" transformed the wilderness ambience. In a few years peace and quiet would return, but the Bovills couldn't wait. They packed up their memories of friends and fishing and moved to Coeur d'Alene.

Elk River gamblers. —Idaho State Historical Society

Elk River

Twenty miles east of Bovill on Idaho 8 is Elk River. This one-time lumber town grew when a Potlatch mill was built here in 1911. Today this tiny village set in the midst of the Clearwater National Forest is a gathering place for campers, hikers, and fishermen. One of the sights here is a champion western red cedar, 3,000 years old and eighteen feet in diameter, ten miles north of town. Also of interest is the roaring Elk River Falls, reached from a trailhead three miles south of town. It is a half-hour hike to the falls, where Elk Creek drops 300 feet in three separate cascades. These can be reached from a system of loop trails.

Return to Bovill or go adventuring on a good gravel road from Elk River to Dworshak Dam and Orofino.

Idaho 3
CLARKIA

This mountain settlement has a population of sixty-two, but for a spot that one could easily miss in a blink it holds a good deal of fascination.

Clarkia has depended on timber-related jobs since the turn of the century, and decks of logs piled in the meadow are evidence that logging still lives. Local merchant Chuck Skilling, better known as "Clear-Cut" (he's bald), points out how techniques have changed: "In years past, logging boomed with the crosscut saw and horse being the primary tools of trade. With progress, crosscut saws [misery whips] were replaced by chainsaws [mechanical beavers], and horses were replaced by cats and skidders."

As logging diminishes, Clarkia depends more on tourists and the elk hunters who flock to the mountains in the fall. Fishing for cutthroat and rainbow trout in nearby creeks is also popular, and in midsummer people swarm the hillsides on huckleberry safaris. Skilling says you can spot them by their "purple fingers and tongues." Wintertime brings snowmobilers, who converge on Clarkia to ride miles of groomed trails or take a spin around the Fossil Bowl track. And herein lies a tale.

Several years ago, when Francis Kienbaum was constructing a snowmobile track, he bulldozed the side of a hill, and strange leaves and fossil clay fell from the bank. He called in Dr. Charles Smiley from the University of Idaho to assess the find. Smiley and his group of diggers uncovered approximately 120 different species of forest plants—including magnolias, bald cypress, dawn redwood, and laurel—that grew here 15 million years ago, when the climate was considerably warmer than it is now. Clarkia was sitting on a rare, world-class fossil deposit.

Eons ago, during Miocene times, lava oozed out of cracks in the earth's crust, flowed across the land, and formed the Columbia lava plateau. One of these flows dammed the St. Maries River, forming a lake. After 200 to 1,000 years, the lake began to fill with sediments. As this occurred, the water grew stagnant and low in oxygen. Consequently, everything that fell into the lake sank to the bottom and remained there in a nearly perfect state of preservation (no oxygen, no bacteria, no decomposition). According to Dr. Smiley, a most remarkable thing about these plant fossils is that both cellular and chemical properties remain intact. A few of the leaves still hold their colors of green, red, or tan and furnish some of the world's oldest known DNA.

Although this is a great scientific discovery, the fossils are poor specimens for hobby collecting because they disintegrate rapidly in fresh air. One of the ancient fish uncovered here was a twenty-eight-inch trout, but by the time the damp clay lost its moisture, the fish shrank some three inches—a fish story in reverse!

Hobo Cedar Grove

The main feature of the Hobo Cedar Grove Botanical Area is its magnificent stand of giant red cedars. It lies near the Grandmother Mountain roadless area on the headwaters of Marble Creek. The area, with twenty-seven miles of National Recreation System trails, is part of the ongoing Marble Creek Centennial Project, which encompasses thirty miles of backcountry between Clarkia and Avery on the St. Joe River. An interpretive center with logging memorabilia will be located on the St. Joe (see St. Maries).

Inquire at the Forest Service office half a mile north of town for trail information and for directions to the Cedar Grove.

Emerald Creek Garnet Mines

Five miles north of Clarkia on Idaho 3, a directional sign points the way to the Emerald Creek Garnet Mines. Just off the highway, mounds of dredged-up earth mark the site of the commercial mine, which is said to be the world's largest producer of industrial garnets. The garnet "dust" is used in sandblasting, steel cutting, and aluminum polishing, in the manufacture of filters for water purification, and in dozens of other applications almost nobody thinks about.

Recreational diggers may want to stay overnight at Garnet Creek campground, four miles from Idaho 3 (overnight accommodations are available at St. Maries, thirty miles away). The parking lot for the garnet area is two miles farther on. Hike half a mile to the Forest Service office and purchase a permit ($5.00), each one good for five pounds of garnets. The "panning" process is quite a wallow in the mud; the deeper one digs, the more the water tends to puddle. A change of clothing is advisable, maybe some hip boots, and certainly a screen to wash the gravel. Additional information is available from the St. Maries Ranger District.

The rare aspect of these garnets emerges in the polishing, as a four- or six-rayed star often materializes from the depth of the stone. In the rough they are an interesting twelve-sided (dodecahedron) shape. The star garnet occurs in only two known locations in the world, at Emerald Creek and in India. Appropriately, it has been named the Idaho state stone. From the Garnet Mines it is approximately ten miles to the junction of Idaho 3 and Idaho 6, the White Pine Scenic Byway to St. Maries.

Mining for garnets near Clarkia.

306

This is a town of two rivers, the St. Maries and the St. Joe. The unusual beauty of these streams makes this a popular recreation and sight-seeing area. St. Maries is a pleasant town with easy access to tennis courts, a city park, a swimming pool, picnic facilities, and a boat launch. Mullan Trail Park makes a cool stop beneath old-growth timber.

For more than 100 years, St. Maries has been a lumberjack town, with Potlatch Corporation still going strong. Visitors are welcome to tour their mill. Newer on the economic scene is Al Bruner's wild rice business. He ships this unlikely crop to gourmet shops and restaurants around the world. The innovative venture traces its beginning to waterfowl hunters, who scattered Wisconsin wild rice on the wetlands around nearby Benewah Lake to attract geese and ducks. The grain grew so profusely that it eventually clogged the open water. The Idaho Department of Parks and Recreation decided to harvest the stuff so it wouldn't reseed. It opened the job up to bids, and St. Maries Wild Rice was born.

Since 1986, Al Bruner has been at the helm and has expanded his wild rice acreage from state land to private leased tracts. As a former wildlife manager, Bruner is in a unique position to mix ecology with business, to the benefit of both. "We never drain the meadows," he says. "All our rice is grown in standing water and our harvesters leave plenty of crop residues for wildlife. . . . No pesticides are used."

The quality of St. Maries wild rice has made it a blue-ribbon winner in both national and international competitions, and the market continues to expand. In the meantime, ducks and geese who come to feed during the spring and fall migrations number in the tens of thousands.

The town of St. Maries received its name from missionaries. The first settlers arrived when a few curious pioneers made their way up the St. Joe River not long after Coeur d'Alene was established. One of these was Joe Fisher, who took one look at the vast stands of timber covering the mountainsides and decided to stay. He built a sawmill at the mouth of the St. Maries River, and a town soon gathered around it. Other settlers came to stake out the wild hay meadows that filled the valley of the St. Joe. Fortunately, the cavalry mules at Fort Sherman constituted a ready market, so the "bonanza hay farmers" had merely to cut their crop and ship it across the lake by steamer.

Logs traveled across Lake Coeur d'Alene just as easily as hay and provided an even greater bonanza. The St. Maries River flowed through the largest single stand of white pine in the world, timber just waiting to be plucked. Prodigious amounts of pine and cedar and fir also grew along the St. Joe River. It was enough to quicken the beat of any lumberman's heart.

The rivers provided an additional bonus, as no expensive mills would need to be built in the backcountry. Whole logs could be floated down any number of streams to the main rivers and on to Lake Coeur d'Alene. Every year for forty years, beginning about 1910, the Weyerhauser combine (later Potlatch Corporation) and smaller outfits poured millions of board feet downstream to mills at St. Maries, Harrison, Coeur d'Alene, and a dozen lesser spots.

St. Maries soon became a hectic waterfront town as lumber barons, timber cruisers, fortune hunters, and laborers flocked here as if to a gold rush. Compared with other boomtowns, St. Maries was apparently a fairly peaceable place. However, many lumberjacks died with their boots on, not from gunfire but from staggering out of the saloons and falling in the river. There were plenty of watering holes, along with poker, roulette, and many memorable characters.

Among the well-remembered personalities were the O'Gara sisters, who operated two or three restaurants and a boarding house. They were Irish girls from County Cork who spoke with a soft brogue, "dark haired Anna and Margaret and red-haired Mary." Historian Ruby Hult writes in *Steam-*

St. Maries waterfront, early 1900s. —Museum of North Idaho

boats in the Timber that they amassed a small fortune parting lumberjacks from their money, not as prostitutes but as clever businesswomen. A large percentage of their profits came from bootlegging.

Prohibition had not yet arrived, but restrictive state and federal statutes made alcohol scarce. Stories are legion about how the girls hid their whiskey from nosy revenue officers. One time Margaret poured the spirits into a sterile chamber pot for a successful masquerade; another time it went into a tea kettle. Once, when she was warned the place would be raided, "she brought the small whiskey keg into the kitchen and spread her voluminous skirts around it. There she stood adamant while officers searched the quarters. She later said that since the officers were gentlemen and did not try to pinch her leg the ruse worked."

St. Joe River Drive

A trip to St. Maries would not be complete without a drive up the shadowy St. Joe River, whose quiet waters still mirror the willows and cottonwoods that line its banks. Take Forest Road 50 half a mile north of St. Maries. Follow the river along its corridor of bottomland, which resembles a flat green trough winding between the mountains. Several campgrounds are interspersed along the highway, including the Shadowy St. Joe, eleven miles from St. Maries. This idyllic spot on the river's edge offers boat launch facilities as well as camping, picnicking, and good family tubing.

About eleven miles upriver from St. Maries lies the site of the old waterfront town of Ferrell, which later consolidated with St. Joe. During the timber craze at the turn of the century, life here could be fairly lively. However, the pace quickened considerably during the building of the Chicago, Milwaukee, St. Paul and Pacific Railroad in 1907. The tracks crossed the Bitterroot Mountains at St. Paul Pass (above Avery) and came straight down the St. Joe Valley to St. Maries and on to Bovill (where they connected with the Washington, Idaho & Montana line to make a transcontinental connection with the Great Northern at Palouse, Washington).

All groceries and other supplies came by water from Coeur d'Alene. In *Steamboats in the Timber*, Ruby Hult wrote:

> The boats brought everything. If you lived in the St. Joe valley and wanted a needle or a stovepipe, a hat or tent, a button or a baby carriage, it came up from Coeur d'Alene by boat. . . . Daily the boats brought tons and tons of groceries. They brought barrels and barrels of beer and cases of whiskey. The old boat Fleetwood was made into a special liquor-hauling barge with an iced hold capable of carrying a whole carload of beer and whisky, and this floating liquor store was towed upriver behind a bigger boat.

All this activity made St. Joe–Ferrell a busy place. According to one old-timer, it was "downright vulgar." The town hummed continuously as the nineteen saloons never closed. Whiskey flowed faster than the St. Joe, and gamblers could choose between faro, craps, blackjack, or roulette. One of the favorite spots was Baby Face Andy's, where as much as $10,000 could be stacked on the table. Hult wrote of one episode in which a man named McFee, a construction worker for the railroad, placed a $2,000 bet. As the cards came up, the dealer wanted some advice from the boss. "Taking his knife and pinning the high card to the table, he went upstairs and wakened Baby Face to ask if he should call McFee or let him go and take him for more later. Baby Face said, 'Call him.' McFee got 'took,' the dealer raking in the four-thousand-dollar pot."

After the railroad tracks passed on down the valley, St. Joe–Ferrell settled back to lumberjack status. However, the frantic boom in logging slowed considerably after the terrible 1910 fire, in which the St. Joe Valley "had its guts burned out."

Thirty-two miles from St. Maries, at the point where Marble Creek enters the St. Joe, work has begun on the Marble Creek Centennial Project. White pines have been logged continuously from this fabled drainage for almost 100 years, and relics litter the countryside. The Forest Service has identified 130 historic sites that hold steam donkeys, chutes, flumes, logging camps, splash dams, and other significant remnants. The project will include an interpretive center, hiking trails, and expanded campgrounds.

Forty-six miles from St. Maries, the settlement of Avery—once a transportation center for the Chicago, Milwaukee, St. Paul & Pacific Railroad—

Truckloads of mules head for a fire where they will pack men and supplies in to the fire lines, circa 1930. —U.S. Forest Service

310

has quite faded away. During the 1910 fire, panic prevailed here as terrified families caught evacuation trains to Spokane or Missoula. Firefighters set backfires that saved the town, and the Avery Ranger Station became the firefighting headquarters for the entire St. Joe River area.

Stories are legion about the days of logging and fire fighting on the St. Joe. Bert Russell compiled authentic tales directly from the participants in *Hardships and Happy Times*. One of these old-timers, Ed Hanson, cooked on the fire lines in 1931 and earned a reputation as a doughnut cook for 200-man crews. Hanson said,

> I was cookin' the doughnuts and biscuits. Old Baldy Fropes he cooked the bacon and ham and somebody was the coffee cook.
>
> We had to have a cook for each article. We had them Kimmel stoves about 4 ft. long and 3 ft. wide and no bottom except the ground. Paul Resor fired while I cooked doughnuts on top of the stove. It kept him busy poking wood in all them stoves. I mixed dough in a big container, then slopped flour on the board and put a wad of dough on it and slipped more flour on top and patted it out. Then I rolled it with a candle using both hands. Then I cut the doughnuts square and shoved my thumb through the middle to make a hole and slipped 'em into the fry grease.

A flunky fished the doughnuts out with a willow stick. Mountains of them passed for gourmet pastries when the hungry fire crews came.

Modern firefighting techniques put fires out quickly.
—National Interagency Fire Center at Boise

Above Avery, the St. Joe is designated a Wild and Scenic River. Here white water churns between descending stretches of falls and rapids. The historic Red Ives Ranger Station (and the end of the road) lies thirty-nine miles farther upriver. Several Forest Service campgrounds are spaced along the way, and at Red Ives trailheads fan out into the upper St. Joe backcountry.

Return to St. Maries to make a connection with US 95 via Idaho 5 or with I-90 via Idaho 3.

Coeur d'Alene Country

US 95
DE SMET, TENSED, AND PLUMMER

These towns are all located on the Coeur d'Alene Indian Reservation, each one significant to the tribe. The tribal school is located at De Smet, named after the Catholic missionary who in 1842 authorized the establishment of their first mission, on the St. Joe River.

The nearby community of Tensed was originally called De Smet, but when the residents applied for a post office the name was denied because the post office at the mission had already been so designated. They turned the name around and reapplied with the name "Temsed," but because of a postal error it came out "Tensed."

Plummer is in the heart of the reservation and close to the tribal headquarters, which functions as a small county government. The new headquarters is dedicated to the late Joseph Garry, a great-grandson of the renowned chief for whom the city of Spokane is named. Garry was the first Indian to hold a seat in the Idaho legislature and was a leader of the Northwest tribes. He was president of the National Congress of American Indians from 1953 to 1959.

I-90, US 95
COEUR D'ALENE

Coeur d'Alene sits dramatically at the north end of Coeur d'Alene Lake. As the hub of a burgeoning tourist industry, the place sizzles with energy, yet the atmosphere remains small-town and picturesque. The Coeur d'Alene

Lodge gives the lakeside retreat a world-class convention center, nearby North Idaho College sets the pace for things educational and cultural, and a thriving artists' colony keeps the many downtown galleries well stocked. Out on the fringes, Coeur d'Alene takes on a city look with freeway bridges (although some of these show a spectacular view of mountains and water) and miles of malls.

This modern resort town little resembles the village that developed from Fort Sherman in the late 1870s. Gen. William T. Sherman of Civil War fame arrived here via the Mullan Road in 1877 while on an inspection tour of northwest forts. Charmed by the beauty of the lake, he recommended on his return to Washington, D. C., that a military post be constructed here to keep the Indians at bay. Congress speedily set aside 1,000 acres for Fort Sherman, originally called Coeur d'Alene, most of which now belongs either to the city or to North Idaho College.

The fort was barely completed in 1878 when the government authorized construction of the first steamboat on the lake. Capt. C. P. Sorensen and several craftsmen came from Portland to take charge of the enterprise, and the steamer was launched in 1880. It was christened the *Amelia Wheaton* after the daughter of General Wheaton, then post commander. Its main job was to haul hay from around the lake to Fort Sherman to feed the cavalry mules. Sorensen stayed on as first captain and during these forays gave names to the various bays and inlets. He also made the first steamship run up the Coeur d'Alene and St. Joe Rivers, both of which empty into the lake.

The quiet lakeside settlement suddenly became a hive of activity when A. J. Prichard and his partner Bill Keeler discovered gold on the North Fork of the Coeur d'Alene River in 1883. After several years of prospecting they had finally struck it rich, and one August afternoon they went to Spokane to celebrate. In *Silver Strike*, eyewitness William T. Stoll writes that a crowd had gathered around the pair by the time they reached the first saloon. Prichard was a quiet sort, but Keeler dramatized their find. He poured a pile of dust from his pouch into the palm of his hand and roared, "The hills up thar air lousy with it. . . . Pard here and me—we panned this out in ten days. Whar? Why Prichard Creek of course!"

This news sent a motley horde 1,000 strong to the new diggings in a rush. Their outfits included "pack saddles and burros, sheet iron stoves, tents, shovels, picks, grub and that first necessity to human peace and comfort—whiskey." Once arrived in Coeur d'Alene, the prospectors bought passage on the *Amelia Wheaton*, which took them to the Old Mission Landing at the head of navigation on the Coeur d'Alene River. From here they packed their gear, on foot or horseback, over the Jackass Trail to the new El Dorado. The haphazard towns of Eagle City and Murray grew like magic in the wilderness.

In the midst of all this excitement, Coeur d'Alene boomed with hotels, restaurants, sawmills, wharfs, new steamboats, and an oversupply of saloons.

Ruby Hult wrote in *Steamboats in the Timber*: "Just outside the fort grounds was the old Dividend Saloon, where soldiers and miners drank and gambled together and sometimes shot at each other . . . most notorious of all, Fatty Carroll's dance hall, harboring about forty dizzy damsels and women of the underworld. There were from various estimates fifteen to twenty other saloons."

The steamships *General Sherman* and *Coeur d'Alene* soon joined the *Amelia Wheaton* on the lake. And a profitable business it was, with each trip across the lake netting $1,000 or more. Miners plunked down $10 apiece for standing room only, and freight was proportionately high.

Before the gold boom dimmed, the fabled Bunker Hill and Sullivan silver/lead deposit was discovered at Kellogg. This led to a frenzy of new strikes, and towns with names like Wallace, Burke, Wardner, and Mullan grew on the mountaintops and up the canyons. Lake Coeur d'Alene became a highway to the mines, bringing supplies in and ore out. In 1886 the Northern Pacific Railroad Company entered the picture, building a narrow-gauge track from the mines down to the landing at Cataldo and adding a fleet of steamers to carry the ore across the lake to Coeur d'Alene. Here a main line connected with Spokane and national markets.

As Coeur d'Alene was riding the tide of mining prosperity, yet another boom was on the horizon. This one brought the timber barons who had "logged hell out of Minnesota and Wisconsin" and were looking westward.

Around Lake Coeur d'Alene and along the tributaries of its river network (the St. Joe, St. Maries, and Coeur d'Alene) stood 15 billion feet of salable timber—white pine, yellow pine, fir, and tamarack. The St. Maries Valley alone accounted for the largest single stand of white pine in the world. Big money moved in with operators such as the Weyerhausers (forerunner of the Potlatch Corporation), and the lake became a "magnificent mill-pond." The town buzzed with the sound of sawmills and brisk trade at the new banks, hotels, stores, and docks.

Logging and mining continued to fuel the Coeur d'Alene economy for decades. Though diminished today, they still widen the economic base. The emphasis now is on tourism, a rebirth of an early-twentieth-century phenomenon. At that time, the arrival of holiday trains was a regular summertime occurrence. They came from Spokane and other Inland Empire towns—Tekoa, Latah, Moscow, Colfax, Wallace, Kellogg, St. Maries, and Harrison. On Sundays Coeur d'Alene often swelled by 900 or 1,000 people. One Fourth of July, nearly 2,500 visitors swarmed off the train, ready to sign on for steamboat excursions. The Electric Line train carried 7,000 persons between Spokane and Coeur d'Alene on July 4, 1905, and the crowds continued to multiply. A summer regatta held in 1936 brought 35,000 people.

Weekday trips were popular, too. Travelers often crossed the lake and steamed up the St. Joe or Coeur d'Alene. Both streams were crystal clear with cottonwoods and silver beeches on both banks arching overhead.

Coeur d'Alene City Beach, circa 1940. The Ferris wheel is about where Coeur d'Alene Lodge is now. —Museum of North Idaho

Coeur d'Alene City Beach with Coeur d'Alene Lodge in the background.

Steamers could travel up the Coeur d'Alene as far as the Old Mission Landing, where they turned around at Big Eddy. Here galley cooks threw out kitchen scraps, creating a mecca for fish. They gathered by the thousands to feed in the transparent waters—a constant source of amazement to boat passengers.

Some steamers carried as many as a 1,000 people. With the addition of dining, dancing, and moonlight cruises, the excursion business became quite a profitable affair. During the week, boats carried freight and crews of lumberjacks traveling in and out of logging country. J. C. White, who controlled the Red Collar Line of some fifty steamers, is reported to have netted $250,000 in one summer.

The lake has lost little of its charm, and the beaches and waterfront parks are major centers of activity. City Beach and Park at Independence Point, directly west of the unmistakable Coeur d'Alene Resort, is popular for swimming, picnicking, cruises, and boat rentals. A three-quarter-mile floating boardwalk encircles the resort marina, inviting visitors to take a fresh-air, over-the-water hike. Any morning or evening groups of strollers, hikers, singles, and families walk over the twelve-foot-wide boards for the unique constitutional.

Sanders Beach, McEuen Park, and Tubbs Hill constitute another waterfront complex. Tubbs Hill, part of the city park system, offers a scenic 135-acre urban wilderness. The trailhead for a two-mile nature hike takes off from McEuen Park, located directly east of the Coeur d'Alene Resort. Turn off Sherman at Third Street and drive toward the lake.

Museum of North Idaho

This excellent facility, handily located between City Park and the college, interprets local history, particularly the influence of the mining and timber industries and the steamboat era. Also here is the stump of the famous Mullan Tree, the last surviving route marker from the Mullan Road. As the road building crew chopped its way across the Idaho panhandle toward Montana in 1861, they celebrated Independence Day at Fourth of July Pass, eight miles east of town, and blazed the date into this giant white pine: "MR July 4, 1861." On that day, Capt. John Mullan added to the festive occasion by handing out extra rations of "molasses, ham, whiskey, flour and pickles." Before the day was finished the men were whooping it up, and the Indians reported to the priests at Cataldo that the road builders had gone completely "kultus." A historical sign at the top of the pass marks the spot. The Mullan Road passed in front of this museum site.

North Idaho College

Much of the campus once belonged to Fort Sherman. The original powder house is now a museum, with displays of artifacts and information relating to the old fort. The Fine Arts Auditorium offers entertainment by the

Coeur d'Alene Summer Theatre. For almost three decades this organization has presented award-winning musicals during July and August.

I-90, Idaho 41 and 53
POST FALLS

This picturesque, fast-growing town on the Spokane River (the outlet for Lake Coeur d'Alene) attracts many travelers. The Coeur d'Alene Indians lived on this stretch of the Spokane in a village called Q'emiln. Seltice was their chief. Frederick Post arrived in 1871 and negotiated with the chief to buy land at the falls. A rock wall at Treaty Rock Park in downtown Post Falls records the purchase agreement. Post built grist and lumber mills, and the town developed around the mills, although the section adjacent to the falls was later sold to Washington Water Power for a hydroelectric dam site.

The timber industry is still important here, and the area is widely known for the fields of Kentucky bluegrass that blanket the Rathdrum prairie north and west of town. Most of the grass is harvested for seed and reaches national and international markets.

Coeur d'Alene Scenic Byway

For this twenty-eight-mile tour, follow I-90 to the east end of the lake and exit on Idaho 97. The drive is full of variety and charm as the road winds above quiet bays through forests of pine, cedar, and hemlock. Inlets lap peacefully between wooded hills, hinting at the elongated shape of the lake and the many twists and turns down its long green trough. Dammed by moraines of the Continental Ice Sheet more than 10,000 years ago, it is approximately 25 miles long (with an actual shoreline of about 125 miles) and 1 to 3 miles wide.

Early in the drive travelers get a lovely glimpse of Beauty Bay, "that noble sheet of water" described by Capt. John Mullan in the mid-1800s. Beyond Beauty Bay, the Mineral Ridge day area offers a three-mile hike on good trails that lead to breathtaking views. Farther along is Squaw Bay Resort, a picturesque stop with marina, campsites, and food. After another twenty miles through the woods, the historic town of Harrison emerges through the trees. Harrison sits on a tranquil bay and has a lakeside city park and marina. The paddle wheeler *Harrison* takes passengers on charter trips up the Coeur d'Alene and St. Joe rivers. From the park, a walk down one of the oldest streets in town leads to One-Shot Charlie's Saloon, a tangible bit of Harrison's past that still lives.

In its heyday the town, named for President Benjamin Harrison, was a rough-and-tumble place. Half a dozen sawmills and cedar shake mills, a dozen saloons, and a red-light district kept the place lively. It had the good fortune to be located along the lakeshore at the mouth of the Coeur d'Alene River, so it became a main port for steamers. Upriver traffic to the Old Mission Landing kept a steady supply of freight and loggers passing through town.

Beyond Harrison, toward the south end of the lake, the road overlooks the former site of the St. Joseph Indian Mission, near the mouth of the St. Joe River. Father Nicholas Point arrived here in 1843 and with the Indians built a simple church. He placed it under the "powerful protection of the Sacred Heart," and it became the forerunner of today's Old Mission at Cataldo. The site they chose was already a historic campground with an ancient spring that had long been a watering hole for Indians and their ponies as well as for elk and deer. Game of all sorts was plentiful here, and thousands of fish darted about in the sparkling St. Joe. Father Point dubbed it the "River of Gold and Green." Here he labored among his "dear neophytes," sharing their experiences and observing their customs at a time when Indian life was undiluted by white men's ways. Out of these years came his unique illustrated journal, *Wilderness Kingdom*. Discovered more than 100 years later in the archives of the College of Saint-Marie at Montreal, it was published in 1967.

Although Point introduced the Indians to the "mysteries of plowing and planting," they spent much of their time moving about, gathering roots and

Indian huckleberry camp, circa 1930.

berries, and hunting at favorite spots. During the winter hunt—occurring when they were most hungry—they often bagged 300 deer, but the take could be much greater. Father Point recalled a time during the Feast of the Purification when the village was camped below some hills where a canyon opened onto the plain:

> On this day, just as it was becoming light, the man in charge of the camp guard looked toward the mountains and saw black bands descending onto the plain from all sides. There were deer, and more deer, and more deer. "My brothers," he cried, "put on your snowshoes and take your arrows." In a few minutes all the hunters had reached the deer and, laying their rifles and bows and arrows aside, they dispatched the deer by taking hold of their antlers and twisting their necks.

When the hunt was over the men brought to Father Point a pile of little sticks equal to the number of deer killed. The count came to 600! This was good medicine and caused one of the most skeptical among them to remark, "Ah! Now, we see very well that the prayers of the Blackrobes are more powerful than ours."

The Coeur d'Alene country abounded in game, and Point observed that "perhaps nowhere does so small an area contain such a variety." He went on to mention deer, elk, mountain lion, "carajou," white sheep, big horn, goat, wolf, fox, wildcat, mink, marten, beaver, bear, wolverine, and half a dozen smaller species.

In 1846 the spring runoff raised the level of the St. Joe River to flood stage and inundated the mission grounds. Father Point then selected the hilltop location at Cataldo for the new church.

Seven miles from Harrison, Idaho 97 joins Idaho 3. This highway follows the northern end of the White Pine Scenic Byway, which meets I-90 at the end of a twenty-two-mile drive. Much of the drive follows the path of the Coeur d'Alene River and its several small, adjacent lakes.

I-90
OLD MISSION STATE PARK

Old Mission State Park, five miles from the junction of Idaho 3 and I-90, makes a natural conclusion to the scenic byway. Perched on a hill overlooking the Coeur d'Alene River, the old church has all the earmarks of a romantic-genre painting. Here is Idaho's oldest building, a structure of great charm and dignity, built in the classical style in the midst of a primeval wilderness.

Today the venerable church and its scenic hilltop make up the Old Mission State Park. The church has been named a National Historic Landmark. Several annual events connect the present with the past. Three of

Historic church at Old Mission State Park dates from 1853.

particular interest are the Historic Skills Fair, held on the second Sunday of each July; the annual pilgrimage of the Coeur d'Alene Indians, held each August 15 to celebrate the Feast of the Assumption; and the Mountain Man Rendezvous, held on the third weekend of August.

The old St. Joseph Mission relocated here in 1846, about the time Father Point applied for a transfer to French Canada. A temporary chapel was built to serve immediate needs, and Father Joseph Joset was placed in charge. Father Anthony Ravalli came from St. Mary's Mission in Montana in 1850 and may have brought the church blueprints in his pocket. Nobody knows for sure when construction began, but Ravalli was certainly the chief architect and building supervisor. He had been recruited in Italy by Father Pierre Jean De Smet, head of Jesuit missionary activity in the Northwest. Ravalli was a Renaissance man who came steeped in classical education, with training as an architect, sculptor, mechanic, craftsman, and physician as well as a priest. In his own time he was most revered as a gifted doctor—it was said his bedside manner alone could effect a cure. With the Old Mission as tangible evidence, we remember him today as an architect and craftsman.

Ravalli set forth a daring design for the church. The building was to be ninety feet long by forty feet wide and twenty-five feet from the floor to the ceiling. These massive dimensions required gigantic timbers that were squared and mortised together, then locked with wooden pegs driven into auger holes. The largest timbers were used to support the arch and vault over the altar. Two massive piers, each squared from a single tree, measure three feet by three feet by twenty-five feet tall.

The crew consisted of about 320 Indians who resided at the mission, Brother V. Magri ("a maltese joiner"), and Father Ravalli. Father Joset describes the beginnings of this remarkable building in *Father Ravalli's Missions*:

> Large quantity of heavy timbers were to be hewn, 24 post over 25 feet long, squared 2½ by 2½ feet, some 3 by 3. Sills, joists, wall plates, rafters, all in proportion; 20,000 feet of boards to be manufactured at the saw-pit, to be dressed by hand, 50 thousand shingles; stones for the foundation to be dug from the mountains, 30,000 cubic feet; then the whole to be brought to place, on the top of the hill; the stones ½ mile, timbers some more than a mile; large quantity of clay to serve as mortar and filling between the posts.

It was no small task to raise all the supporting posts and ponderous timbers for the frame with ropes and pulleys. Once construction began the place was like a beehive. Men, women, and children made mortises, shaped columns, carried water, and mixed clay while the priests kept an eye on everything. The project must have been an overwhelming one, yet the Indians labored enthusiastically and were proud of their work.

Contemporary Coeur d'Aleneans still speak of this achievement. Margaret Stensgar of De Smet learned the story of the church from her grandmother, Hapshineh, who went to the mountain and carried on her back rocks for the foundation. Stensgar wrote in *Idaho Indians, Tribal Histories*:

> Our people did all the work themselves. They had no idea you could build anything so big. . . . At first they didn't have boards for the walls. Brother had them drill holes in the sides of the huge upright timbers. Then they put poles through, where the walls were supposed to be. They cut tall grass from the fields, and braided it solid between the poles. Other Indians hauled clay and mud up from the river, and plastered it thick over the braided grass. That's all the walls they had for a few years.

The slurry of grass and clay made a well-insulated adobe finish that was encased with framing in 1859, six years after the Indians completed their work. Among the finishing touches to the church were Father Ravalli's sculptures, the decorated ceiling panels, and the charming altar he painted to simulate marble.

When finished, the church looked out over an uncharted wilderness—but not for long. Congress wanted to connect Fort Benton on the upper Missouri with Fort Walla Walla on the Columbia via a military road that could move men and supplies quickly in case of Indian problems. Lt. John Mullan, a young engineer and adventurer, was commissioned for the task. Between 1859 and 1862 his 100-man crew constructed the 624-mile wagon road.

The road was little better than a trail through the wilderness, and Congress soon lost interest in it because of the trauma of the Civil War. However, it did serve as a route of travel for gold prospectors and the settlers following them. The completion of the Mullan Road also marked a division in time separating the Indian way of life from that of the miners and lumberjacks. Today I-90 follows the route of Mullan Road across north Idaho.

Ironically, the Indians who built the Old Mission and farmed the surrounding valleys found themselves crowded out by white settlers. As land allotments changed, their church stood outside reservation boundaries. In 1878 the Jesuit priests and the Coeur d'Alene chiefs chose a new location at De Smet, where they built a mission and school. The Coeur d'Alene family groups that had always lived around Cataldo moved to the new site, where their descendants still live.

I-90
SILVER VALLEY

Silver Valley is the name given to the old Coeur d'Alene Mining District. It stretches out along I-90 for some forty miles along the Osborne Fault, from Pinehurst to Mullan. The ninety mines located here have turned out record amounts of silver, lead, and zinc for more than a century. According to the Idaho Geological Survey, Silver Valley holds the world record for silver production. The Sunshine mine alone has lived up to its name by producing more than 350 million ounces of silver, a record that puts the riches of Nevada's Comstock Lode to shame.

Today most of the mines are closed. Companies cannot balance escalating expenses against rock-bottom prices for metals. However, some, like the Coeur d'Alene Mines Corporation, continue to do exploration work and to acquire new properties.

I-90, Forest Road 9
MURRAY

Leave I-90 at exit 43 to reach Forest Road 9. The first notable spot is the popular Enaville resort and family restaurant, known locally as the Snake Pit. This historic building dates from around 1890, when it was a jumping-off place for miners and loggers headed for the backcountry.

The thirty-mile drive to Murray follows the placid Coeur d'Alene River. The road meanders along the base of wooded hills, past little farms and patches of wildflowers that, as Shakespeare said, "do paint the meadows with delight." Stands of cottonwoods line the stream, filling the air with their fragrance. In the background, the pine-clad Coeur d'Alene Mountains frame the picture-perfect scene.

Twenty-three miles from Enaville the settlement of Prichard comes into view. Look closely or you'll miss it. The name for the town and the nearby stream honors Andrew Jackson Prichard, who came to the Coeur d'Alenes from Walla Walla via the Mullan Road. He was seeking a timber contract but found gold instead. By 1883 the news was out and the stampede was on. Five thousand gold-hungry prospectors and hangers-on found their way up the Coeur d'Alene River and onto Prichard Creek, where they settled in the boisterous camps of Prichard, Murray, and Eagle City.

All of them have faded away except Murray. Mounds of gravel six to ten feet high line the river like a stone dike thrown up by careless workmen. A Yukon Gold Company dredging operation left these piles between 1918 and 1925, long after the boomtown luster had faded. The company turned up gravel twenty-five feet deep to extract the gold.

Murray, a remnant of the Old West, sits at the base of a mountain, its one street lined with a few old buildings that retain the flavor of the past. In

There is life in old Murray, although it is not the booming place it was when Wyatt Earp lived nearby. The Sprag Pole Inn building, at the heart of town, dates from the 1880s.

its glory days this was the seat of Shoshone County (succeeding Pierce and later giving way to Wallace) and the destination of an unfortunate group of Chinese who were lynched before they arrived (see Pierce).

Today Murray is inhabited by prospectors, loggers, and retirees. Two businesses remain open, the Sprag Pole Restaurant and Museum and the Bedroom Goldmine Bar. Shirley Corder, who owns the Sprag Pole with her husband, Don, says, "There used to be a dozen saloons on this side of the street. And they all got rich. Now this is the only one." The Sprag Pole occupies one of the town's original buildings, erected in 1884. Its name reflects the Silver Valley heritage, a sprag pole being an upright timber placed to shore up a mine tunnel. A tattered poker machine sign still lingers on one wall—"for recreation only," it says. The machine went out in a surprise FBI raid in 1992. The adjoining museum is a treasure trove of 100-year-old memorabilia, including the grave marker for soiled dove Maggie Hall, better known as Molly B'Damn.

The story of the Bedroom Goldmine Bar is more or less told in its name. One day in 1969, Chris Christopherson (not the singer) felt an intuitive urge and decided to sink a shaft in the cabin floor. He panned out pay dirt for a tidy profit and uncovered a nine-ounce nugget to boot.

Among the historic personages that frequented Murray were Molly B'Damn and Wyatt Earp. In 1884 the dapper Earp actually lived in Eagle, two miles from Murray. He joined the business community, opening a tent saloon of some proportions—fifty feet in diameter and twenty-five feet high. He was also the deputy sheriff, although frequently in trouble himself. He kept busy fending off claim-jumping suits but settled them in court rather than by gunfire. He actually located several claims but seems to have left town broke and possibly in a hurry. The county commissioners took title to his tent saloon and other property for failing to pay taxes amounting to $8.57.

Molly B'Damn, a shady lady who won the hearts of the miners, is remembered annually at the Molly B'Damn Days, a mountain soiree scheduled in August.

Murray is twenty miles from Wallace over the Dobson Pass road. However, it is high and winding, and some travelers prefer to return via the Coeur d'Alene River route.

I-90
KELLOGG

The Bunker Hill smelter stacks are still Kellogg landmarks along I-90, but today the alpine tower of a new Ski Haus identifies the flavor of the town. Searching for a way to keep their city alive, local citizens decided to capitalize on their mountain backdrop and with enviable community spirit

Silver Mountain Ski Haus, near the top of the mountain where the view takes in Washington, Montana, and British Columbia.

created a world-class ski resort. Freeway travelers keep the place humming in the summertime too, flocking in to inspect the Ski Haus, dally in the gift shops or restaurant, and board the lift for a ride to the top. At 3.1 miles, this is the world's longest gondola ride. It climbs 3,400 vertical feet and provides breathtaking views of Silver Valley. From the top, the vista stretches across waves of mountains that reach Montana on the west and British Columbia on the north. Self-guided nature trails, mountain bike paths (bikes may be carried up in the gondola car), the Mountain Haus Restaurant, and mountaintop amphitheatre provide abundant mountaintop recreation.

City-owned and city-managed, this summer and winter project bodes well for Kellogg's future. The heart of town is a good stop, too. Spruced up with an alpine ambience, it offers boutique shopping, city park amenities, and an American Youth Hostel affiliate.

Kellogg traces its beginnings to 1885, when Noah Kellogg, disappointed with the gold placers around Murray, packed up his gear and wandered over to the South Fork of the Coeur d'Alene River. He woke up one morning to find his mule had slipped the tether and disappeared. But the donkey brayed loudly, and Kellogg set off up the mountainside, guided by the "hee-haw." It was a hot day and the mountain was steep. He sat down on a ledge to rest, lit his pipe, and picked up a loose rock that had crumbled from the

Silver Mountain ski lift, close to downtown Kellogg.

ledge. It was almost pure galena. A few blows with his pick revealed a deep, wide vein of this silver-lead ore. Eventually it would become one of the most fabulous mines in the world.

After locating the vein, Kellogg took on new partners and repudiated the men who had grubstaked him and supplied the mule. The grubstakers said it was the braying of their mule that led Kellogg to the rich lode and sued for their share. In the litigation that followed, half a dozen claimants participated. When Simeon Reed of Portland bought the claim for $600,000, the money was distributed according to the several ownerships. The mine was named the Bunker Hill and Sullivan, and the adjoining town was named for Noah Kellogg.

Reed (of Reed College in Portland, Oregon) financed the original development of the mine. Eventually 150 miles of tunnels and shafts would be built, as well as a zinc plant and a smelter to process silver. For years this mining and metallurgical complex was the lifeblood of the valley. Gulf Resources and Chemical Plant purchased the Bunker Hill holdings in 1968, but in 1981 it closed the whole operation with a loss of 2,100 jobs. At this time the facility was providing 20 percent of the nation's lead and zinc and 25 percent of its silver. The silver mine reopened in 1988 and operated for four additional years. By the time the last closure came in 1992, Kellogg had moved on to a new way of life.

Big Creek Sunshine Memorial

Four miles east of town, this monument commemorates ninety-one miners who died in 1972 when flames broke out at the Sunshine mine. Bulkhead timbers covered with a fire-retardant foam smoldered in the blaze, creating a deadly carbon monoxide gas that invaded the maze of tunnels. One hundred eight miners scrambled to safety. Some of the victims were found, Pompeii-like, still seated at their lunches. Miraculously, two men survived in a remote area and were rescued seven days later.

The local mining museum, housed in a turn-of-the-century mansion sitting on a hillside above town, is hard to miss. Exhibits here relate the story of Bunker Hill and mining in the Silver Valley.

I-90
WALLACE

Wallace is ten miles from Kellogg and, to the casual observer, something of a "twin." In fact, outsiders often run "WallaceandKellogg" together as one word. However, the two towns are sometime rivals and historically have had different orientations. Kellogg was traditionally the workers' abode, virtually a company town (Bunker Hill), whereas Wallace became the financial center, pulling in mine owners and managers. This well-to-do population built stylish homes and substantial downtown buildings, many of which remain intact. Consequently, the whole town has been placed on the National Register of Historic Places. Gables and turrets, decorative glass, and cast-iron cornices can be seen in a variety of architectural styles—Victorian, neo-Classical, Queen Anne, Art Deco, and various unidentified curlicues. The chamber of commerce provides a walking-tour brochure.

One notable edifice, the chateau-style Northern Pacific Railroad Depot, dates from 1902. The materials used in its construction lend a romantic touch. The first floor is finished with buff-colored Chinese bricks. Wallace historians Patricia Hart and Ivar Nelson say the bricks were brought to the West Coast in the 1890s, "carried as ballast on sailing ships chartered by the Northern Pacific to bring tea to the United States." The second story is half-timbered and stuccoed with an aggregate made from mine tailings, with perhaps a few glints of silver here and there. Today the depot, owned by the city, houses a railroad museum and has been restored to mint condition.

Colonel W. R. Wallace settled here in 1884, staked out the Oreonogo-Hecla mine, and platted the townsite a mile away. He was not really a colonel, but the title gave him distinction among his well-known cousins—Lew Wallace, author of *Ben Hur*, and William H. Wallace, Idaho's first territorial governor.

*This elegant Northern Pacific Railroad station in Wallace looks more like a
Queen Anne mansion than a depot. Now owned by the City of Wallace, it has
been restored and is functioning as a museum.*

Wallace chose a good location because his town was to occupy the center
of a fabled mining district. It was positioned to grow into a brisk county
seat, a mine-owners' town reported to sprout millionaires, and a Wild West
outpost replete with gambling, prostitution, and saloons. Even during Prohibition, "vice" flourished with the acquiescence of leading citizens. Down
at city hall, liquor licenses became soft drink permits. The Feds raided speak-
easies from time to time and often rounded up substantial citizens, but rarely
did anyone receive a conviction. Beulah Preston remembered that some
forty persons were arrested in a 1929 raid. Of those indicted, only the sheriff and county assessor went to prison, serving short terms. While the assessor was gone his wife filled the office, and when the sheriff returned to
town, he stepped into the postmaster's job.

The latest raid occurred in the winter of 1992, when FBI agents unex-
pectedly appeared in every bar in Wallace (and throughout Shoshone
County) to gather up illicit poker machines that had been operating for
years. Again, about forty persons were arrested for a brief time. The sheriff

faced charges of public corruption but was acquitted, and the hometown celebrated his innocence.

The Silver Valley is fairly isolated and likes to play out its frontier mining town heritage. In *Paradox Politics*, Randy Stapilus quoted former governor Robert Smylie as saying: "It was part of the old mining syndrome. . . . Shoshone County was an independent judicial district with its own judge. And if you try to do anything up there law enforcement-wise from the state level . . . you'd get enjoined by the local judge. Then you'd have to go to the Supreme Court [of Idaho] to get it undone." The valley was so remote that the easiest policy was to ignore the goings-on.

The history of Wallace has included many dramatic episodes, some dealing with fire and flood and vice, others with mining wars. These battles touched every other Silver Valley town, too. Especially vulnerable were Wardner, at the head of a canyon near Kellogg, and Gem and Burke, near Wallace. Two major altercations occurred that shook the foundations of Silver Valley, one in 1892, the other in 1899. Hart and Nelson retell the incidents superbly in *Mining Town*.

Almost as soon as miners started blasting and drilling underground, they began to organize labor unions. The work was dangerous, wet, and dirty, and the miners wanted better pay and safer working conditions. But if labor

Hand mining in the Hercules Tunnel at Burke, 1905. The man in the white shirt is apparently dressed for the photo.
—Bernard Stockbridge Collection, University of Idaho

Burke, about 1890. The Northern Pacific track ran through the center of town.

could organize, so could management. The two groups polarized into contending camps that eyed each other across the barricades before touching off a rumble that sounded far beyond the valley.

The miners won the first round. After a strike in the summer of 1891, they gained a $3.50-per-day wage for every miner who went underground. The following spring, the mine owners shut down the mines while negotiating with the Northern Pacific for lower shipping rates. Six months later, when a settlement was reached, they wanted to send the miners back to work at the old pay scale. Miners refused to work and spent their time scaring off the "scabs" who arrived daily to work the mines. The mine owners tried injunctions and various other schemes to gain the upper hand. They finally hit upon a winning ploy by hiring Charles Siringo, a Pinkerton detective, to spy on the union. Posing as a miner named Leon Allison, Siringo appeared to successfully catch the union spirit. He glad-handed the boys at the Gem local and became its secretary. From this position he passed union secrets on to the mine owners.

Labor in the mines was divided between union and nonunion men. The Gem mine near Burke was virtually barricaded to keep out union men, and both sides went armed to the teeth. In this trigger-happy atmosphere, the union discovered "Allison" was an undercover agent working for the mine owners. One of his friends, an Irishman named Johnny Murphy, gave him a warning. William T. Stoll repeats the conversation in *Silver Strike*.

"Thayre's a spicial meetin' to-night , Allison," he [Murphy] said. . . .

Murphy's blue eyes narrowed: he spat a great gob of tobacco juice and shrugged his broad shoulders reflectively. "Allison," he advised, "Oi'm yer friend-ye know that; Oi wouldn't go, not if Oi was yez" . . . .

"Fact is, Johnny," Siringo explained, "I'm secretary, I've got to go. You don't think I'm a quitter, do you?"

"No, not a-tal a-tal; but if ye ask me, Allison, Oi'm sayin' tis better if ye was'nt secretary" . . . .

The report's got aboot thot thayre's a Pinkerton man wurikin' in the union; sacrits is lakin' out where sacrits should niver lake out. . . . They been watchin' yez Allison. Skip out while the skippin's good."

Siringo ignored the advice and joined the crowd at the Gem union meeting, where he read the minutes that night. He managed to save his skin despite the accusations of One-Eyed Dallas and the grumblings of nearly 1,000 men. But the meeting was a catalyst for violence. A few days later, the union forces sent a load of dynamite into the Frisco mill. Several men were killed, and the four-story structure collapsed into a heap of lumber and fragments of iron. Nonunion miners at the Gem surrendered under a white flag, management left hurriedly for Spokane, and Siringo took to the hills. Soon the union held every mine, mill, powder house, store, and railroad in the district.

Siringo knew the miners would try to settle with him next, so he returned to his rooming house in Gem to make a Hollywood-style escape. He had previously sawed an escape hatch in his ground-floor room and camouflaged it with a rug. Now he pulled the covering aside and dropped down to the damp earth beneath the house. From here he wriggled his way under a high boardwalk to hear the search party walk on the boards above him and curse the "dirty traitor." The miners stormed the rooming house, but by the time they discovered his avenue of escape (his landlady had thoughtfully replaced the rug over the hole in the floor) it was too late. Siringo had inched his way under the boardwalk to the open foundation of a saloon, where he found an exit to the outside and disappeared. Siringo lived to engage in future escapades, including a chase after Butch Cassidy and the Wild Bunch.

Meanwhile, a message went out from the Silver Valley: "HELL BROKE LOOSE TEN THIS MORNING. FRISCO MILL DYNAMITED. TWO OUR MEN KILLED. MINERS HOLDING EVERY MINE AND MILL IN DISTRICT. ANARCHY REIGNING." Radical union leaders such as George A. Pettibone and One-Eyed Dallas were in control and railing against the "Coeur d'Alene Octopus," otherwise known as the Association of Mine Owners.

Union euphoria dissolved when Governor Norman B. Willey (once a placer miner at Warren's Diggings) declared martial law. Federal troops occupied every town in the district and made wholesale arrests. Some 600

Miners in the bull pen following the 1892 riots when military law came to the Coeur d'Alene mines. —Idaho State Historical Society

miners were rounded up and herded into "bull pens" hastily thrown up at Wallace and at Wardner near the Bunker Hill mine.

The military occupation lasted for five months. Trials were held, but most of the union men either were acquitted by local juries or had their convictions overturned on appeal. A few served a short time in jail, but within a year all were free.

Union officer George Pettibone and some colleagues served a few weeks in the Ada County jail at Boise. Far from being cowed, however, they decided to organize a stronger union. After serving their time, they went directly from Boise to Butte, Montana, where they met with other delegates to form the powerful Western Federation of Miners (WFM). Here was a union to be reckoned with. By 1899 the new organization had successfully established itself in all the Coeur d'Alene mines except the Bunker Hill and Sullivan, which was a constant irritation.

One spring day in April 1899 they decided to unionize the Bunker Hill. A large delegation of miners called on manager Frederick Burbidge. Seeing the size of the crowd, Burbidge agreed to pay union wages but would not permit Bunker Hill workers to become union members. This attitude caused more mass meetings, and a few days later an army of miners moved on the Bunker Hill. They commandeered a train, loaded it with 3,000 pounds of dynamite from the Frisco powder house, and traveled down the Burke canyon to Wallace and then to Kellogg, Wardner Junction, and the Bunker

Hill mine. Some 800 miners rode the train, some sitting on the roofs, others riding the coal cars as if they were on a holiday jaunt.

When word reached the mine that the "dynamite express" was headed their way, the management and nonunion workers headed for the hills. When they arrived, the miners chose their target—the new Bunker Hill and Sullivan lead and silver concentrator. This mill was the pride of the company and one of the most advanced in the world. The fuse was lit, and in an astonishing display of fireworks the mill was blown to smithereens.

When news of the violence reached Boise on April 29, 1899, Governor Frank Steunenberg declared martial law in the Coeur d'Alenes. He appealed to President McKinley for troops. Just about every miner in the district was arrested and incarcerated in the newly constructed bull pens. Fourteen men were brought to trial, but the most devastating development for the union was a new technique—the permit system. This initiative, which amounted to official blacklisting, was put in place by the mine owners' association and the governor's personal representative. Under the new rules no miner could work without a permit, but to obtain one he had to certify he was not a member of the WFM and had never participated in any dynamiting. Then he still had to be cleared by a state agent. With the U.S. Army standing by,

The new Bunker Hill and Sullivan silver concentrator after the "dynamite express" hit it on April 29, 1899. —Idaho State Historical Society

the Western Federation of Miners could not resist the system. This measure broke the power of the union but could not exorcise years of accumulated bitterness.

Six years later some of the union men decided to avenge the "persecution" of labor by eliminating former Governor Frank Steunenberg, now retired to his home in Caldwell. Consequently, the ex-governor walked home one snowy evening in 1905, unlatched his front gate, and triggered a homemade bomb. He fell, mortally wounded.

The bomber, Harry Orchard, did not leave town fast enough. He had made the lethal device in his room at the Saratoga Hotel, and police quickly apprehended him. He confessed to the murder, insisting he was a secret agent for the Western Federation of Miners and had been instructed by its officers to blow up Steunenberg.

Subsequently, union officials Charles Moyer, William D. Haywood, and George Pettibone were indicted for conspiracy to assassinate Steunenberg. A spectacular trial, know chiefly as the Haywood Trial, ensued. The eyes of the world focused on Boise as miners, celebrities, reporters, and gadflies came to town. An impressive array of lawyers graced the courtroom, including Clarence Darrow for the defense and William Borah for the prosecution. The murder was billed the "crime of the century," as the landmark trial spoke to the universal struggle between capital and labor. Overall, the case generated bad publicity for both mine owners and the Western Federation of Miners.

Darrow and Borah emerged from the trial as national figures. Officials of the Western Federation of Miners were acquitted, but Harry Orchard received a life sentence, which he served at the state penitentiary in Boise. Here he repented of his sins and grew roses. After his acquittal, Haywood and the more radical membership helped organize the Industrial Workers of the World (IWW), which in the Coeur d'Alenes became more active in the timber industry than in the mines.

Throughout its history, Wallace has attracted more than its share of drama. The town was rebuilt after an 1890 fire, and memories of the mining wars were still fresh when a devastating flood roared through town. Perhaps the town's worst calamity was the 1910 fire, which cut a wide swath of terror and destruction. Wallace was in the path of the spectacular "Big Burn" of 1910. Strong winds fanned the blaze as the fire approached, and residents watched the orange glow advance on the town. Finally, with flames licking the outskirts, the mayor rang the evacuation bell. Panic-stricken women and screaming children scrambled aboard trains headed for Spokane and Missoula, leaving able-bodied men behind to help fight the fire. Approximately 100 buildings—one-third of the town—burned. (In the rebuilding process a wide variety of architectural styles emerged, many of which can still be seen on the popular downtown walking tour.)

Edward Pulaski became a hero during the 1910 fire that swept north Idaho.
—U. S. Forest Service

While Wallace residents were working to save their town, Forest Service crews were still on the fire lines, struggling to survive in the midst of heat, smoke, and explosions of flame. One crew of forty-two men under ranger Edward Pulaski made a miraculous escape. He led them to the shelter of the War Eagle mine tunnel three miles from Wallace. However, burning trees toppled and slid down the bank in front of the tunnel, sucking out oxygen until the men were gasping for breath. Some of them panicked and would have run from the mine to certain death had not Pulaski held them at gunpoint. He demanded they lay face down on the damp tunnel floor, where they could breathe in the last bit of oxygen. Several hours later, when the fire had moved on, the unconscious men began to stir. All but five of them survived. The episode made Pulaski famous as a cool head under pressure. Today a well-used firefighting tool, a combination axe and hoe, is named for him. In 1984 the Forest Service dedicated a Pulaski memorial one mile south of Wallace.

335

Wallace District Mining Museum

An extensive mineral collection, mine-related displays, photo exhibits, and an excellent historical video make this educational stop worthwhile. The story of Wyatt Earp at Eagle City and Murray is also featured.

Sierra Silver Mine Tour

For this step back into history, visitors don hard hats and become miners for a couple of hours. The tour descends into the mysterious underground world of shafts and tunnels, where exhibits show machinery working in all facets of hard-rock mining.

I-90
MULLAN

This small town seven miles east of Wallace near the Montana border was a way station on the Mullan Road and later grew as a townsite when silver was discovered here in 1884. Two historic mines are nearby, the Lucky Friday and the Morning. In 1905 the Morning was purchased by John D. Rockefeller, who supposedly paid for it with $3.2 million in gold coins.

The Panhandle

US 95, Idaho 54
LAKE PEND OREILLE AND FARRAGUT STATE PARK

Farragut State Park on the southern tip of Lake Pend Oreille is twenty-five miles from Coeur d'Alene. Its 4,000 acres of lakeside meadows, pine forests, sandy beaches, and campgrounds on the shore of Idaho's largest lake provide a memorable outdoor experience. A visitor center and museum displays fascinating exhibits that spell out the park's unique history as the World War II Farragut Naval Station. Named for Adm. David Farragut, it was at that time the nation's second-largest naval station. Life here was officially documented by the late Ross Hall, a nationally acclaimed Sandpoint photographer, and many of his rare photographs are on display. His pictures show activities at the station from start to finish, from dress parades to galley cooks up to their elbows in pie dough.

Hollywood star Lana Turner selling war bonds at Farragut during World War II. —Ross Hall

At first glance, the Idaho mountains seem an unlikely place for a naval base. But the inland location made it safe from invasion, and the lake's massive size and depth (1,150 feet deep) made it suitable for submarine research and training. Twenty-two thousand workers spent six months building the base. A few German prisoners of war did the landscaping, and one local resident says they liked it so well here that some of them went over the hill at repatriation time and became permanent residents.

When the "boots" started coming, this was the largest city in Idaho. Six self-contained training units housed 5,000 men apiece, and each camp had its own mess hall, dispensary, recreation, ship's store, and training ground. Here the recruits went through a daily routine of running through abandon-ship drills, working with ordnance and gunnery, swabbing decks, stowing gear, and standing watch. Altogether, nearly 300,000 sailors received their basic training at Farragut.

Lana Turner swung through north Idaho on a bond selling tour during World War II. She is a native of Wallace.
—Ross Hall

The station was decommissioned after the war, although submarine research still continues. After a series of ownership changes, the site was recast as a state park in 1965. Because of its large size it has hosted gatherings, such as national and international Boy Scout jamborees and Girl Scout roundups. However, the most appreciated event may be the annual Farragut Naval Training Station reunion, when veterans come to reminisce.

The park is located adjacent to Bayview, a pioneer town on the lakeshore that grew on the strength of timber, fishing, and lime quarrying. Remnants of the old lime kilns can still be seen here. At one time Bayview was on the express route between Walla Walla, Washington, and Wildhorse, British Columbia.

US 2 and 95, Idaho 200
SANDPOINT

This small town on the north shore of Lake Pend Oreille possesses an abundance of natural beauty. US 95 makes a dramatic entrance into town, crossing a two-mile bridge that spans the lake. As the town comes into focus, sprawled along the shore with a grand mountain backdrop, you know this has to be a special place.

The first settlers who came to Sandpoint in the 1880s found plenty of wood for homes and land for farming, but growth was slow until the arrival of the Northern Pacific and Great Northern railroads. They linked Sandpoint with the outside world and soon attracted timber interests. The Humbird Lumber Company (a Weyerhauser subsidiary) came to town in 1901, and prosperity was assured. White pine, yellow pine, fir, and tamarack were all important sources of lumber. Sandpoint was especially identified with cedar, becoming the largest shipper of cedar telegraph, telephone, and electric light poles in the Northwest.

Because of its prized setting, the mantle of "resort" settled on this timber and railroad town early in its history. Summer homes and lodges developed around the lake's 110-mile shoreline, and smaller communities such as Hope and Bayview grew at key locations. However, then as now, Sandpoint was the leading commercial center around the lake.

Today Sandpoint is bustling with energy and is fast becoming known as a summer and winter recreational retreat. One of its endearing features is a broad sweep of beach at the downtown City Beach Park, where families picnic, children play, and boats come and go. Nearby, the unique Cedar Street Bridge and its arcade of boutiques and art galleries hint at the surge of new growth. A thriving artists' colony, theatrical events, and a strong musical climate add to the lively cultural milieu.

Sandpoint on Lake Pend Oreille. Note the famous two-mile bridge on the right. —Dann Hall

"This is the end of the line, buddy." Many jobless men hooked a ride to anywhere in railroad boxcars during the Great Depression. —Bonner County Museum

A grassroots effort sparked construction of the attractive new Bonner County Museum building, located at lakeside in the city park. Exhibits include a walk-through history display emphasizing the Kootenai Indians, lumbering, and railroads. Of special interest are rare, mural-sized photographs from the Ross Hall collection that vibrate with the spirit of log drives, lumberjacks, and railroads.

One of the hottest events in town (and in the Northwest) is the annual Festival at Sandpoint. This August musical extravaganza features a series of lakeside concerts under the stars, everything from Bach to jazz wafts on the mountain air. With distinguished teachers and conductors, students, and the Spokane Symphony Orchestra, this event rivals the famous Berkshire Music Festival at Tanglewood.

Schweitzer Mountain Resort

Head north out of Sandpoint and follow the signs to Schweitzer Mountain Road. It is eleven miles to the resort, where an eyeful of powerful scenery awaits. Lake Pend Oreille spreads across the valley floor, with forested slopes and meadowlands defining its shoreline. Looking down from the mountain, it seems as if all of creation lies below.

Schweitzer is a resort for all seasons. Winter skiing and sleighing give way to summer hiking and biking. In August, it's music, music, music as the Festival at Sandpoint moves into teaching mode. Talented students hone their skills here, and just about any evening visitors can casually take in a starlight concert featuring anything from classical to rock.

Idaho 200
HOPE AND CLARK FORK

Take US 95 north of Sandpoint and turn right onto Idaho 200 a mile beyond the chamber of commerce visitor center. It is approximately twenty-five miles to Hope, twelve more to Clark Fork, and an additional ten to the Montana border. This beautiful excursion along the north shore of Lake Pend Oreille offers recreation, pioneer history, and a peek far back into geologic time.

North Idaho was once covered by continental glaciers that moved south out of Canada along the Purcell Trench. They gouged out many of north Idaho's lake basins, retreating and coming back many times. They deposited an ever higher wall of glacial ice at the mouth of the Clark Fork River a few miles upstream from Hope. Eventually the accumulation of ice, rocks, and soil dammed the river and formed ancient Lake Missoula. This huge body of water spread east into Montana, covering some 3,000 square miles and reaching a depth of 2,000 feet near Clark Fork.

When the water level in the lake reached the top of the ice dam about 18,000 years ago, it spilled over in a horrendous flood. Geologist Terry Maley says the maximum rate of flow is calculated to have reached 386 million cubic feet per second, which represents about ten times the combined flow of all the rivers of the world. The waters rushed down the Clark Fork Valley and on to Spokane, scouring out the scablands and coulees of eastern Washington as they went. The glacial basin of Lake Pend Oreille filled during this monumental flood.

The village of Hope clings to a hillside overlooking Lake Pend Oreille. If it ever hoped for a million-dollar view, that wish has been fulfilled. However, neither expectation, desire, nor anticipation suggested its name. It came from a local veterinarian, one Dr. Hope, who cared for the work horses during construction of the Northern Pacific Railroad.

Hope grew on a mixed economy of timber and mining. When the Northern Pacific Railroad came through in 1882, Hope became a division point. Chinese laborers worked on the construction gangs, and many stayed on after the railroad was finished. They made jobs for themselves, doing everything from gardening to tailoring uniforms for railroad conductors. Their Chinatown grew at the east end of Hope, where things such as tea, lichee nuts, and "dried ducks hanging from the ceiling" provided a constant source of fascination.

Hope native Paul Croy recalled one Chinese migrant named Ah Sing, who periodically came up the street selling vegetables. The diminutive fellow carried his wares in bamboo baskets attached to each end of a wooden yoke slung across his shoulders. He sold radishes, lettuce, onions, and vegetables in season. Croy says, "He must've gotten up at daybreak to get ready. . . . The vegetables were always washed clean and bunched together with grass. He would call out to my mother, 'Edna, Edna, want something?' She always bought from him."

For many years the arrival of the circus train was a big event. It stopped here only long enough for the cooks to feed the circus crew and for the animals to have a dip in the lake. Marie Heath recalled this eagerly awaited diversion in *History of Bonner County*: "Standing on the first bench above the tracks, all watched the animal keepers lead the elephants to the water a few feet away, where the big animals enjoyed a bath, spraying the cold water over themselves. Imagine seeing rhinoceros and bears, chained, of course, in Lake Pend Oreille!"

Three miles east of Hope a monument marks the approximate site of Kullyspell House, a trading post built by David Thompson in 1809. Thompson made friends with a small tribe of Kalispel Indians, whose permanent village was at the mouth of the Clark Fork River. The location seemed ideal for a wilderness post, but it proved to be too far off the main trails. It was abandoned two years later in favor of Spokane House. Kullyspell was the white man's first habitation in the Pacific Northwest.

Thompson had followed Alexander Mackenzie and Simon Fraser in exploring the Fraser River country and the upper Columbia in Canada, but he was the first to travel this far south. He was a fur trader of rare ability whose primary interest was in geography and mapmaking. Idaho historian Dr. Merle Wells calls him one of the great geographers of all time. Thompson traveled some 50,000 miles by canoe, on horseback, and on foot—and surveyed half a continent in the process. Pioneers, railroads, and highways later followed the routes of travel he established. He also initiated the Idaho fur trade, which was dominated by his North West Company and its successor, the Hudson's Bay Company.

Most of the leaders in the Montreal-based North West Company were Scots, but Thompson was a Welshman. In *History of Idaho*, Merrill Beal and Merle Wells note, "His figure was short and compact, and his black hair was worn long all around, and cut square, as if by one stroke of the shears, just above the eyebrows." Thompson was a religious man and a zealous foe of demon rum. When his superiors demanded that he set out from their Lake Superior post with a good supply of liquor for the Indian trade, he handled the matter in an ingenious way. He dutifully loaded the canoes with two kegs of spirits, but when the party reached the mountains and changed to horses, Thompson said, "I placed the two kegs of alcohol on a vicious horse; and by noon the kegs were empty, and in pieces, the Horse rubbing his load against the Rocks to get rid of it." That settled the mix of firewater and Indians on Thompson's watch.

The sleepy town of Clark Fork, named for Capt. William Clark, lies on the Clark Fork River delta. Of special interest here is the state fish hatchery, which raises a variety of trout, including the giant kamloops rainbow.

The community grew after 1892, when the Northern Pacific Railroad constructed a siding here. The settlement furnished railroad ties and other building materials from the dense stands of timber that surrounded it. Later Clark Fork became a mining center, with silver and lead mines that produced into the 1950s. The geology here resembles that found in the Coeur d'Alene mining district in that the metals follow a fault line—in this case the Hope Fault, which parallels highway 200 along the lake and extends for 100 miles into Montana.

A mile or so beyond Clark Fork the discerning eye can identify rocks scraped and polished by the glaciers of the continental ice sheet. The Cabinet Mountains to the east also make an interesting subject for speculation. A mix of exposed granite and Belt Series rocks more than 800 million years old, they were formed from ancient sea sediments eons before they were warped, folded, and thrust up. Scientists have found fossilized stromatolites, an ancient algae and perhaps the first life form among these rocks. Here one can almost touch the dawn of time.

US 2, Idaho 57
PRIEST RIVER AND PRIEST LAKE

From Sandpoint, follow US 2 along the Priest River for twenty-nine miles to the town of the same name. Priest Lake is an additional twenty-two miles away on Idaho 57.

The town, the lake, and the stream itself have always had close ties. Their common name comes from the Indian word *kaniksu*, generally translated as "black robe," which refers to the Catholic priests who came among them. Economically they were linked by the lumber industry, as giant log drives floated out of Priest Lake and down the river to sawmills in town. Today the common bond is recreation.

The twenty-five mile long Priest Lake lies in the shadow of the Selkirk Mountains, surrounded by dense cedar and shemlock forests and miles of sandy beaches. There are several small resorts around the shoreline, but

little development has taken place. The lake retains much of its pristine beauty and wilderness atmosphere. The main lake is connected to a small upper lake by a two-mile neck of water, the delight of canoeists.

For a glimpse of Priest Lake's past, look for the museum sign on the west shore road (Idaho 57) between Hills Resort and the Luby Bay campground. The Priest Lake Museum is housed in a 1935 cabin, handcrafted by men in the Civilian Conservation Corps (CCC). Exhibits depict early logging, trapping, settlement, CCC camps, and Forest Service memorabilia. The staff at the museum can give directions to Hanna Flats Nature Trail, which winds through a twenty-two-acre virgin cedar grove nearby. This area has been protected for more than forty years and holds a rich variety of native trees, shrubs, and flowers.

Priest Lake State Park offers three widely scattered units for camping. One of these, Lionhead, lies in a cathedral-like setting of old-growth timber at Nell Shipman Point, named for a talented silent screen actress who put Priest Lake on the map in the 1920s. Nell established a movie camp here in 1921 with her Shipman Production Company, which filmed cliffhanger movies in a glorious outdoor setting. Nell often worked as producer, director, and actress. It was no easy life. The filmmakers hauled materials and supplies in by boat and dogsled, built their cabins (including the now famous Lionhead Lodge), chopped their wood, poached game, read by lamplight, and generally led a rugged life.

Nell Shipman, pioneer filmmaker whose location was Priest Lake. —Idaho State Historical Society

Although popular in their time, these pioneer movies fell into obscurity. Boise State University professor Tom Trusky rediscovered a few of them in the early 1980s when he made a crusade of tracking down Shipman films. Historic Idaho movies such as *Grub Stake*, *Trail of the North Wind*, and *A Bear, A Boy, and A Dog* now receive acclaim at prestigious film festivals and museums around the world.

US 2 and 95
BONNERS FERRY

Bonners Ferry is located in the beautiful Kootenai River Valley, enclosed by the Selkirk Mountains to the west and the Purcells on the east. Both the mountains and the valley were affected by the ancient continental glaciers. Most of these mountains were covered by glacial ice, which scraped their tops off and ground away the rough edges, leaving them relatively low and roundly contoured. The deep valley soil comes from silt deposited by the retreating glaciers.

The smell of sawdust scents the air here, as trees cover almost 90 percent of Boundary County. Logging and lumber still provide a payroll, and most homes and businesses post signs proclaiming their alliance with the timber industry. Agriculture is also important and wonderfully diversified, with Christmas tree farms, nurseries, hops, and potatoes, as well as the traditional hay, grain, and livestock.

The Kootenai River Valley was originally home to a small group of Kootenai Indians, who led a peaceful existence here as hunters and gatherers. During the first 100 years of settlement they had no designated reservation. In 1974 they declared war on the United States and received title to an eighteen-acre village homesite three miles east of town. The Kootenai Sturgeon Hatchery, located here, is involved in an experimental program to restore this historic species to the Kootenai River. In earlier years these giant fish left Kootenai Lake in British Columbia and swam upriver to Bonners and beyond to spawn on the gravel bars. The tribe runs the hatchery in cooperation with the Idaho Department of Fish and Game.

Few white men found this valley until the 1863 gold rush to British Columbia. David Thompson, fur trader and explorer; Father Pierre Jean De Smet, visiting missionary; and the boundary commission that came to set the U.S.-Canadian border in 1858 were about the only ones. However, the picture changed with the discovery of gold in Canada. Thousands of men took to the Wildhorse Trail in the stampede for the mines. Where the trail crossed the Kootenai River, Edwin Bonner built a ferry and cashed in on the gold fever. Each foot passenger paid 50 cents and each loaded pack animal cost $1.50. Camels apparently crossed for the same price as horses or mules, although they must have raised quite a stir. They were part of a failed western experiment promoted by the American Camel Company of San Francisco.

Later, passengers and freight traveled by steamship up the Kootenai between Bonners Ferry and the British Columbia mines, creating a nostalgic bit of history that ended when the Great Northern Railroad arrived in 1892.

The Boundary County Museum on Main Street in Bonners Ferry features historical photographs and artifacts depicting early-day life in the county, including the culture of the Kootenai Indians.

Selected Bibliography

Books

Allen, Harold. *Father Favilli's Missions*. Chicago: School of the Art Institute, 1972.

Allen, Margaret Day. *Lewiston Country*. Lewiston: Nez Perce County Historical Society, 1990.

Arrington, Leonard J. *History of Idaho*. Vol. 1. Moscow: University of Idaho Press, 1994.

Attebery, Louie W. *The College of Idaho, 1891–1991*. Caldwell: Caxton Printers, 1991.

Bailey, Robert G. *River of No Return*. Lewiston: R. G. Bailey Printing, 1947.

Beal, Merrill D. *"I Will Fight No More Forever."* Seattle: University of Washington Press, 1963.

Beal, Merrill D. and Merle W. Wells. *History of Idaho*. Vol. 1. New York: Lewis Publishing, 1959.

Bird, Annie Laurie. *Old Fort Boise*. Parma: Old Fort Boise Historical Society, 1971.

____. *Boise, the Peace Valley*. Caldwell: Caxton Printers, 1934.

____. *My Hometown*. Caldwell: Caxton Printers, 1968.

Blanchet, A.M.A. *Journal of a Catholic Bishop on the Oregon Trail*. Translated by Edward J. Kowrack. Fairfield, Wash.: Ye Galleon Press, 1978.

Boone, Lalia. *Idaho Place Names*. Moscow: University of Idaho Press, 1988.

Borg, Hendrickson. *Clearwater Country*. Kooskia, Idaho: Mountain Meadow Press, 1989.

Brooks, Charles E. *The Henrys Fork*. New York: Lyons & Burford, 1986.

Chamberlain, V. E., et al. *Guidebook to the Geology of Northern and Western Idaho and Surrounding Area*. Moscow: University of Idaho Press, 1989.

Crowder, David. *Tales of Eastern Idaho*. Idaho Falls: KID Broadcasting, 1981.

d'Easum, Dick. *Sawtooth Tales*. Caldwell: Caxton Printers, 1977.

Dryden, Cecil. *Clearwater of Idaho*. New York: Carlton Press, 1972.

Elsensohn, Sister M. Alfreda. *Idaho Chinese Lore*. Cottonwood: Idaho Corporation of Benedictine Sisters, 1970.

_____. *Pioneer Days in Idaho County*. 2 vols. Caldwell: Caxton Printers, 1951.

Etulain, Richard W., and Bert W. Marley, eds. *The Idaho Heritage: A Collection of Historical Essays*. Pocatello: Idaho State University Press, 1974.

Federal Writers' Project. *Idaho: A Guide in Word and Picture*. Caldwell: Caxton Printers, 1937.

Fulton, Arabella. *Tales of the Trail*. Montreal: Payette Radio Limited, 1965.

Gibbs, Rafe. *Beckoning the Bold*. Moscow: University of Idaho Press, 1976.

Gittins, H. Leigh. *Idaho's Gold Road*. Moscow: University of Idaho Press, 1976.

Goulder, William Armstead. *Reminiscences*. Reprint. Moscow: University of Idaho Press, 1989.

Greenwood, Annie Pike. *We Sagebrush Folks*. New York: D. Appleton-Century, 1934.

Grover, David H. *Debaters and Dynamiters*. Corvallis: Oregon State University Press, 1964.

_____. *Diamondfield Jack*. Reno: University of Nevada Press, 1968.

Guth, Richard, and Stan B. Cohen. *A Pictorial History of the U.S. Forest Service, Northern Region 1891–1945*. Missoula: Pictorial Histories Publishing, 1991.

Haines, Aubrey L. *Historic Sites Along the Oregon Trail*. St. Louis: Patrice Press, 1981.

Haines, Francis D., ed. *The Snake Country Expedition of 1830–31: John Work's Field Journal*. Norman: University of Oklahoma Press, 1971.

Haines, Francis. *Appaloosa: The Spotted Horse in Art and History*. Austin: University of Texas Press, 1963.

_____. *Nez Perces: Tribesmen of the Columbia Plateau*. New York: G. P. Putnam's Sons, 1970.

Hamilton, Ladd. *This Bloody Deed*. Pullman: Washington State University Press, 1994.

Hart, Patricia and Ivar Nelson. *Mining Town*. Seattle: University of Washington Press, 1984.

History Publication Committee, eds. *Twin Falls County*. Twin Falls: Standard Printing, 1962.

Helmers, Cheryl. *Warren Times*. Wolfe City, Texas: Henington Publishing, 1988.

Hult, Ruby. *Steamboats in the Timber*. Caldwell: Caxton Printers, 1952.

Huntley, James. *Ferry Boats in Idaho*. Caldwell: Caxton Printers, 1979.

Hutchinson, Daniel J., and Larry R. Jones, eds. *Emigrant Trails of Southern Idaho*. Boise: Bureau of Land Management and Idaho Historical Society, 1993.

Idaho Transportation Department. *Idaho's Highway History, 1863–1975*. Boise: Idaho Transportation Department, 1985.

Irving, Washington. *Astoria*. Clatsop Edition. Portland: Binfords & Mort, 1967.

_____. *The Adventures of Captain Bonneville*. Klickitat Edition. Portland: Binfords & Mort, n.d.

Jackson, W. Turrentine. *Wells Fargo and Co. in Idaho Territory*. Boise: Idaho State Historical Society, 1984.

Jordan, Grace Edgington, ed. *Idaho Reader*. Boise: Syms-York, 1963.

Just, Rick. *Idaho Snapshots*. Meridian: Radio Idaho, 1990.

Kingsbury, Lawrence A. *Cleadon Slope Garden*. McCall: Cultural Resource Management Program, Payette National Forest, 1990.

Madsen, Brigham D. *Northern Shoshoni*. Caldwell: Caxton Printers, 1980.

_____. *The Lemhi: Sacajawea's People*. Caldwell: Caxton Printers, 1979.

_____. *Chief Pocatello*. Salt Lake City: University of Utah Press, 1986.

Maley, Terry. *Exploring Idaho Geology*. Boise: Mineral Land Publications, 1987.

Malone, Michael. C. *Ben Ross and the New Deal in Idaho*. Seattle: University of Washington Press, 1970.

Marti, Elsie. *Salute to Pioneers of Washington and Adams Counties*. Council, Idaho: Council Printing & Publishing, 1984.

McWhorter, L. V. *Hear Me, My Chiefs*. Reprint. Caldwell: Caxton Printers, 1983.

_____. *Yellow Wolf, His Own Story*. Reprint. Caldwell: Caxton Printers, 1983.

Meatte, Daniel S. *Prehistory of the Western Snake River Basin*. Pocatello: Idaho Museum of Natural History, 1990.

Mills, Nellie Ireton. *All Along the River*. Montreal: Payette Radio, 1963.

Miller, John B. *The Trees Grew Tall*. N.p., n.d.

McConnell, William J., and Howard R. Driggs. *Frontier Law*. New York: World Book, 1924.

Morgan, Dale L. *Jedediah Smith and the Opening of the West*. Lincoln: University of Nebraska Press, 1953.

Moulton, Gary E., ed. *Journals of the Lewis and Clark Expedition, July 28–November 1, 1805*. Lincoln: University of Nebraska Press, 1988.

National Park Service. *Nez Perce Country, A Handbook for Nez Perce National Historical Park*. Washington, D.C.: U. S. Department of the Interior, 1983.

Native American Committee. *Idaho Indians*. Boise: Idaho Centennial Commission, n.d.

Oatness, Lillian W. *A Great Good Country*. Moscow: Latah County Historical Society, 1983.

Oberg, Pearl. *Between These Mountains*. New York: Exposition Press, 1970.

O'Reilly, Betty. *The Magic of McCall*. Boise: Lithocraft, 1989.

Palmer, Tim. *The Snake River: Window to the West*. Washington, D.C.: Island Press, 1991.

Parke, Adelia Routson. *Memoirs of an Old Timer*. Weiser, Idaho: Signal-American Printers, 1955.

Peterson, Keith C. *Company Town*. Pullman: Washington State University Press, 1987.

_____. *Psychiana*. Moscow: Latah County Historical Society, 1991.

Plew, Mark G. *Archaeology of Southern Idaho*. Boise: Hemingway Western Studies, 1986.

Point, Father Nicholas. *Wilderness Kingdom*. New York: Holt, Rinehart and Winston, 1967.

Reed, Mary, and Keith C. Peterson. *Harriman*. Boise: Idaho Department of Parks and Recreation, 1991.

Reid, Agnes Just. *Letters of Long Ago*. Caldwell: Caxton Printers, 1936.

Reitzes, Lisa B. *Paris, A Look at Idaho Architecture*. Boise: Idaho State Historical Society, 1981.

Russell, Bert, ed. *Hardships and Happy Times*. Harrison, Idaho: Lacon Publishers, 1978.

_____. *Swiftwater People*. Harrison, Idaho: Lacon Publishers, 1979.

Russell, Osborne. *Journal of a Trapper*. Reprint. Lincoln: University of Nebraska Press, 1965.

Smucker, Samuel M., ed. *The Life of Col. John Charles Frémont, and His Narrative of Explorations and Adventures in Kansas, Nebraska, Oregon and California.* New York: Miller, Orton and Mulligan, 1856.

Spaulding, Kenneth A., ed. *On the Oregon Trail: Robert Stuart's Journey of Discovery.* Norman: University of Oklahoma Press, 1953.

Stacey, Susan, ed. *Conversations.* Boise: Idaho Educational Public Broadcasting Foundation, 1990.

Stapilus, Randy. *Paradox Politics.* Boise: Ridenbaugh Press, 1988.

Stoll, William T. *Silver Strike.* Reprint. Moscow: University of Idaho Press, 1991.

Strahorn, Carrie Adell. *Fifteen Thousand Miles by Stage.* 2 vols. Reprint. Lincoln: University of Nebraska Press, 1988.

Sunder, John E. *Bill Sublette, Mountain Man.* Norman: University of Oklahoma Press, 1959.

Taylor, Dorice. *Sun Valley.* New Haven: Eastern Press, 1980.

Thalman, Ray R. *Hard Work and Guts.* N.p., n.d.

Thompson, Bonnie. *Folklore in Bear Lake Valley.* Salt Lake City: Granite Publishing, 1972.

Tuttle, Bishop Daniel Sylvester. *Reminiscences of a Missionary Bishop.* New York: Thomas Whittaker, 1906.

Victor, Frances Fuller. *The River of the West.* Reprint. Oakland: Brooks-Sterling, 1974.

Walgamott, Charles Shirley. *Six Decades Back.* Reprint. Moscow: University of Idaho Press, 1990.

Wells, Merle W. *Gold Camps and Silver Cities.* Reprint. Boise: Idaho State Historical Society, 1974.

Wilde, J. Patrick. *Treasured Tidbits of Time.* Providence, Utah: Keith W. Watkins & Sons Printers, 1977.

Williams, Gary J., and Ronald W. Stark, eds. *The Pierce Chronicle.* Moscow: Idaho Research Foundation, n.d.

Wyeth John B., and John Kirk Townsend. *The Overland Journeys of John B. Wyeth and John Kirk Townsend.* Reprint. Fairfield, Wash.: Ye Galleon Press, 1970.

Yarber, Esther. *Stanley-Sawtooth Country.* Salt Lake City: Publishers Press, 1976.

Yost, George and Dick d'Easum. *Idaho, the Fruitful Land.* Boise: Syms-York, 1980.

Periodicals

Latah Legacy. Semiannual journal of the Latah County Historical Society.

Patchwork. Annual publication of Salmon High School's Patchwork Class. Lemhi County.

Snake River Echoes. Quarterly publication of the Upper Snake River Valley Historical Society.

Idaho Yesterdays. Quarterly publication of the Idaho State Historical Society.

Idaho Heritage. Commercial publication no longer in print.

Tebiwa. Miscellaneous papers of the Idaho State Museum of Natural History.

Letters

Harry Gordon letters, copies from Esther Binning to Author, 1968.

Index

Deer Flat National Bird Refuge, 221
DeLamar, Joseph, 183
DeLamar Silver Mine, 183
Dempsey, Jack, 62
Dewey, William, 178, 183, 204–5, 219
Dixie, 264–65
Dog Derby, 44
Donnelly, 198
Dorian, Marie, 224
Driggs, 54–55
Dubois, Fred, 30, 296
Dubois, 15, 36
Duck Valley Indian Reservation, 172, 174
Dwight, George, 189
Dworshak Dam, 292

Eagle Rock, 16, 34
Earp, Wyatt, 324
Elk City, 262–63, 274
Elk River, 304
Elliott, Jim, 239–40
Elmore County Museum, 171
Elsensohn, Sister Alfreda, 265
Emmett, 222, 230
Experimental Breeder Reactor (EBR–1), 35

Fairfield, 164–66
Falk's Store, 230
Farewell Bend, 183, 231, 233, 241
Farnham, Thomas, 226
Farnsworth, Philo T., 38
Farragut Naval Station, 336–38
Farragut State Park, 336
Featherville, 171
Fire of 1910, 310–11, 334
Fisher, Vardis, 39, 119, 206
Florence, 256
Ford, Ed and Sim, 246
Fort Boise (military post), 216
Fort Boise (trading post), 26, 226–27
Fort Hall, 23, 26, 27, 166, 226
Fort Hall Indian Reservation, 16, 27, 28
Fort Sherman, 313
Fossil Bowl, 305
Frank Church–River of No Return Wilderness, 1, 139, 198, 206, 261
Franklin, 82

Fraser, D. M., 289
Frémont, John C., 70, 170, 215

Galloway, Tom, 231
Garden Valley, 193
Garnet Mines, 330
Garry, Joseph, 312
Gilmore, 151
Gilmore and Pittsburg Railroad, 149–51
Gipson, A. E., 225
Givens Hot Springs 183–84
Glenn, Gus P., 170
Glenns Ferry, 169–70
Godin, Antoin, 57
Gold Road, 14, 15
Golden Age, 272
Goodale, Tim, 156, 239
Goodale's Cutoff, 156, 171
Gooding, 167
Gordon, Harry, 51, 53
Goulder, William A., 287–88
Grandjean, Emil, 192
Grandjean, 191
Grandview, 177, 218
Grangeville, 259, 261
Grangeville Bicentennial Museum, 262
Gray, William H., 226
Grays Lake, 69
Grangeville, 259, 261
Great Rift, 33, 160
Greenleaf, 221
Greenwood, Annie, 109

Hagerman, 22
Hagerman Horse, 22
Hagerman Fossil Beds National Monument, 117
Hagerman Valley, 116
Hagerman Valley Historical Museum 117–18
Hailey, 121
Hansen, George, 21
Hanson, Ed, 311
Harriman, Averill, 46, 123–24
Harriman, Roland, 46
Harrison, 317
Hart, Sylvan Ambrose. *See* Buckskin Billy
Hatch, Lorenzo, 83

Lemhi Pass, 4, 139, 148
Lemhi River, 139, 149
Lemhi Valley, 148–49
Lenore Site, 292
Lewis, Meriwether, 139
Lewis and Clark, 4, 5, 6, 139–40, 270, 285, 291–92
Lewis-Clark College, 275, 279
Lewiston, 241, 269–72, 275
Lewiston hill, 280
Limbert, Bob, 129, 162
Little Lost River, 148, 153–55
Little Salmon River, 247
Llama Ranch. *See* High Llama Ranch
Lochsa Historical Ranger Station, 281
Lolo Pass, 5
Lolo Trail, 140, 281
Long Valley Museum, 198
Lowman, 191
Lugenbeel, Pinckney, 216
Luna House Museum, 279
Lyon, Caleb, 275

Mackay, 158
Mackenzie, Donald, 75–76, 154–56, 172, 215, 231, 271
Magic Valley, 91
Magruder, Lloyd, 273–74
Magruder Corridor, 263
Malad City, 18
Malad Gorge State Park, 113
Malad River, 18, 113
Marble Creek Centennial Project, 305, 310
Market Lake, 36
Marsing, 184
Mary Minerva McCroskey State Park, 300
Marymount Hermitage, 246
Massacre Rocks State Park, 87
Maxwell, Gertrude, 264
McCall, 193, 198–200, 222
McConnell Mansion Museum, 298
McConnell, William J., 193, 295
McKay, Thomas, 25, 26, 226
Meek, Joe, 62
Mesa Falls, 44
Mesa Orchards, 245
Midvale, 238
Miller, Joaquin, 256

Milner Dam, 101
Milwaukee Road. *See* Chicago, Milwaukee, St. Paul & Pacific Railroad
Minidoka Dam, 92–93
Minnie Miller Springs, 117
Montana Trail, 13, 14
Montpelier, 64, 70–72
More, J. Marion, 190
Mores Creek, 186
Morrison-Knudson Nature Center, 214
Moscow, 293–95
Moser, George, 244
Mount Borah, 159
Mountain Home, 170–71
Mountain Home Air Force Base, 170
Mud Lake, 36
Mullan, 336
Mullan, John, 316, 322
Mullan Road, 313, 316, 322
Murphy, 178
Murray, 322–25
Museum of North Idaho, 316

Nampa, 216, 220, 221–24
National Oldtime Fiddlers' Contest, 236
New Meadows, 247
New Plymouth, 228
Nez Perce Indians, 4, 5, 50, 140, 241, 247, 259–60, 261, 268–69, 272, 282, 292, 294
Nez Perce National Historic Park, 38, 258–59, 267, 269, 284
Nez Perce Trail, 262, 274, 286
Nez Perce War, 258, 266, 269, 289
Nicola, 153
Northern Pacific Railroad, 282, 314, 327, 330, 339, 343
Northern Paiute Indians, 4
North Fork, 143
North Idaho College, 313, 316
Northwest Nazarene College, 221
Nuttall, Thomas, 26

Oakley, 94
Old Mission Landing, 314, 316, 318
Old Mission State Park, 319
Old Penitentiary Museum, 213–14

Oneida Pioneer Museum, 18
Opal Mines, 38
Orchard, Harry, 213, 334
Oregon Short Line Railroad, 19, 72, 120, 170, 216, 222, 224, 227, 232
Oregon Steamship Navigation Co., 227
Oregon Trail, 5, 64, 70, 85, 88, 92–93, 101, 177, 184, 215, 216, 224
Oro Fino Creek, 271, 287
Orofino, 291
Ostner, Charles L., 210
overland Astorians, 42–43, 101
Owl Cave, 33
Owyhee Avalanche, 181
Owyhee Country, 171–74
Owyhee County Historical Complex and Museum, 178
Oxbow Reservoir, 240–43

Pacific & Idaho Northern Railroad, 239, 246, 247
Packer John State Park, 249
Paddock, E. A., 233
Pahsimeroi Valley, 148, 153
Palouse, 293–94
Paris, 74, 77–78
Parke, Adelia Routson, 201, 206–7
Parma, 226–27
Parnell, William, 259
Patterson, Eleanor Madill "Cissie," 142, 253
Payette, 229–30
Payette County Historical Museum, 229
Payette, Francois, 226
Payette Lakes, 198, 229
Payette River, 193, 228–31
Payette River Scenic Byway, 193
Payette Vigilantes, 229
Pence, Peter, 230
Perrine, I. B., 103
Perris, Frederick T., 77
Perry, David, 258
Phosphate. *See* Western Phosphate Field
Picabo, 163
Pierce, E. D., 287
Pierce City, 263, 285, 287
Pine, 171

Pintler Winery, 222
Pioneer Historic Byway, 70, 82
Pioneer Museum, 67
Pioneer Relic Hall, 83
Pioneerville, 186, 216
Placerville, 190, 193, 216
Pocatello, 18, 19, 21
Pocatello Land Sale, 20
Point, Father Nicholas, 318–19
Ponderosa Pine Scenic Byway, 185
Ponderosa State Park, 200
Porter Park, 39
Portneuf Canyon, 14
Portneuf River, 60, 61, 84
Post Falls, 317
Potato museum. *See* Idaho World Potato Exposition
Potlatch, 301–2
Potlatch Corporation, 270, 307
Potlatch Lumber Company, 270, 275, 303
Pound, Ezra, 121
prehistoric animals, 22, 33, 172–74, 262
prehistoric peoples, 22, 148, 172–174, 184, 206, 219, 224, 231, 238, 258
Preston, 83
Priest Lake, 343–44
Priest Lake Museum, 344
Priest Lake State Park, 344
Priest River, 343
Pritchard, A. J., 313, 323
Pulaski, Edward, 335

Ravilli, Father Anthony, 320–21
Red River Hot Springs, 264
Red Rock Pass, 84–85
Redfish Lakes, 129
Reed, Simeon, 326
Reid, Agnes Just, 17
Reid, John, 224
Rexburg, 39
Rich, Charles C., 64, 76–78, 80
Rich, Joseph C., 80
Ricks College, 42
Rigby, 38
Riggins, 251, 255
Robinson, Frank, 296
Rock Creek Station, 107
Roosevelt, 205, 206

Swanson, Earl, 148, 258
Sweet, Willis, 296

Taylor, Glen, 22
Taylor, Matt, 16, 17, 33
Teater, Archie, 119
Teeter, Charles, 189
Teton Dam Flood Museum, 39
Teton River, 39, 55
Teton Valley, 54, 56
Teton Valley Rendezvous, 57
Tetonia, 54, 59
Tevanitagon, Pierre, 55
Thalman, Ray, 158–59
Thompson, David, 342, 346
Thousand Springs Valley, 115–16
Three Island State Park, 170
Thunder Mountain Mines, 204–5
Tolo Lake, 262
Townsend, John, 23, 25, 26, 166, 214
Trusky, Tom, 345
Turner, Lana, 338
Tuttle, Bishop Daniel S., 188
Twin Falls County Historical Museum, 105

U.S. Sheep Experiment Station, 36
Union Pacific Railroad, 19–20, 124, 170, 171, 199, 216, 224, 230, 242, 247
University of Idaho, 296, 297–98
Utah & Northern Railroad, 13, 15, 16, 17, 19, 34, 151

Valier, Tracy, 255
Victor, 54, 58
Vienna, 127

Walgamott, Charlie, 102, 106

Wallace, 327–36
Wallace District Mining Museum, 336
Wallace, W. R. 327–28
Walters Ferry, 183
Ward Massacre, 227
Warhawk Air Museum, 225
Warm Lake, 196
Warm Springs Avenue, 210–13, 216
Warren, 201, 202
Washington, Idaho & Montana Railroad, 302, 309
Washington Territory, 6
Wees Bar petroglyphs, 219–20
Weippe Prairie, 5, 285
Weiser, 231–37
Weiser, Peter, 232
Welsh, John, 248–49
Western Federation of Miners, 332–34
Western Phosphate Field, 65–67
Weston Winery, 185
Weyerhauser Syndicate, 301, 308, 339
White Bird, 257
White Bird Battle Auto Tour, 259
White Bird Hill, 257–58
Whitman, Marcus and Narcissa, 5, 226
Wilkins, Kitty, 175
Willey, Norman B., 331
Winchester State Park, 266
Wyeth, Nathaniel, 23, 57, 165

Yankee Fork Creek, 131
Yearian, Emma, 149
Yellow Pine, 204
Yellow Wolf, 50, 260
Yellowstone National Park, 53
York, Lem, 182
Young, Brigham, 64, 72, 76–77, 148

Zims Hot Springs, 249